Cultural Constructions of Identity

Cultural Constructions of Identity

Meta-Ethnography and Theory

EDITED BY

LUIS URRIETA, JR.

AND

GEORGE W. NOBLIT

OXFORD
UNIVERSITY PRESS

Oxford University Press is a department of the University of Oxford. It furthers
the University's objective of excellence in research, scholarship, and education
by publishing worldwide. Oxford is a registered trade mark of Oxford University
Press in the UK and certain other countries.

Published in the United States of America by Oxford University Press
198 Madison Avenue, New York, NY 10016, United States of America.

Library of Congress Cataloging-in-Publication Data
Names: Urrieta, Luis, editor. | Noblit, George W., editor.
Title: Cultural constructions of identity : meta-ethnography and theory /
edited by Luis Urrieta, Jr. and George W. Noblit.
Description: Oxford ; New York : Oxford University Press, [2018] |
Includes bibliographical references and index.
Identifiers: LCCN 2017048283 (print) | LCCN 2017056188 (ebook) |
ISBN 9780190676094 (updf) | ISBN 9780190676100 (epub) | ISBN 9780190676087 (pbk.)
Subjects: LCSH: Ethnicity. | Ethnology. | Ethnopsychology. | Identity (Psychology)
Classification: LCC GN495.6 (ebook) | LCC GN495.6 .C825 2018 (print) | DDC 305.8—dc23
LC record available at https://lccn.loc.gov/2017048283

CONTENTS

This book began in a conversation between Luis and George. The conversation (somewhat muddled by the passage of time) began as a bemoaning of how people were not hearing what qualitative research had to say. This lament is familiar to all of us who do this work. The refrain goes: People do not value qualitative research, people do not value research, people are not listening to anything but their own interests, and so on. Luis and George had had this conversation before and will have it again after this book—for the issues involved will not be resolved by what we do on our side but rather requires others to do something as well. Clearly, though, qualitative researchers want to be heard and have taken great pains to make our work more accessible to nonresearchers. We have experimented with language and writing forms, with representation, with multimedia, and so on. We will, and should, continue with such endeavors, but it is unlikely to turn the tide and make us trusted voices in the contested terrain of our world. But in this case, our discussion turned to meta-ethnography, the qualitative synthesis approach George and Dwight Hare had developed some 25 years before. And while Luis and George had, and have, no illusions that meta-ethnography would be a magic bullet in helping others hear what qualitative researchers have to say, we did, and do, think it is a tool that could play some role in this.

Dwight Hare had recently passed, suddenly and all too young, and in part as homage to him we decided to return to meta-ethnography. I say "return" because George, while serving as an advisor to several qualitative synthesis projects but having written little on it, had been busy doing qualitative research for those 25 years and because Luis had been reading and thinking about the approach but was also taken up with doing qualitative research and especially thinking about the role of theory. We began, like intellectuals do, by catching up with the literature— much of it in nursing and health. But we are not patient intellectuals, and thus we soon began to work our intellectual networks for folks who would return to meta-ethnography with us to see how it looked and what it could accomplish *now*. We were expansive when we started and wanted to address everything from theory to policy and practice. But we realized that policy and practice were intellectual arenas themselves that needed much thought, and the qualitative synthesis work in nursing and health was pointing to these issues. Further, in thinking about all this, we also had to think about theory anew. This was clearly too much for one project. Our partners who were willing to join us were also deeply interested in identity theory, Luis's specialty, and shared our interest in critical perspectives. Thus we chose to start with examining the relation of a critical meta-ethnography and theory and using identity theory as our case in point.

Our colleagues went to work, and work it was, as synthesis is not all revelation. Rather it takes a dogged determination to search out all that can be found, to create decision rules about what to keep and what to set aside, to refine and reconceptualize what one is in fact addressing and what one is not, to read deeply and repeatedly, and then try to figure out what all the studies say as a group, and ultimately what one as a researcher thinks they say about the area of focus and about identity theory. Work, work, work. For all of us, though, all this work was worth it. This book does speak well about the relation of synthesis and theory and about where each may benefit from more thought.

There is of course more to do, and more things to come. That is part of the never-ending nature of intellectual work. We hope it starts readers thinking about their next step in making qualitative research more part of everyday discourse than it is today—and to get on with doing it.

ACKNOWLEDGMENTS

Editing a book is not as easy as I thought! It is tedious, intellectual work, and it requires a great deal of time, diligence, and the ability to coordinate well with others. For that reason I want to thank the people and institutions that most supported me in completing this project. To start I could not have completed this book without the collaboration of my mentor, friend, and co-editor, George Noblit. Thank you, George, for allowing me the honor of working with you in editing this volume. I would also like to thank Juan Portillo and Beth Hatt for providing valuable feedback on multiple drafts of the introductory and final chapters of this book and for allowing me to think out loud as I tried to sort through the theoretical contributions of this work. Special thanks to all of the contributors of this volume; this book would not exist without your generous and valuable intellectual and empirical contributions! The bulk of the writing and editing of this book was completed while I was the Anne Ray Fellow and resident scholar (2016–2017) at the School of Advanced Research in Santa Fe, New Mexico. I am indebted also to my home institution, the University of Texas at Austin and to my department chair, Cinthia Salinas, for allowing me the time to work on this book, and to the generosity afforded to me by the Adams family through the Suzanne B. and John L. Adams Endowed Professorship in Education. *¡Gracias!* to my beloved family, Rosa, my partner, and children Luis, Erandi, Miguel, and Uriel for your unending kindness, loving patience, and unconditional support.

Luis Urrieta, Jr.

Collaboration is a two-way street. Luis has taught so much over the years, and this project was no exception. I thank him, and all the chapter authors, for being willing to work, think, and learn together. Like Luis, there are many people who made this book possible. My wife, Mary, and my adult children, Chloe, Clayton, and Ben, provide the love, support, and laughter I so need. My colleagues at UNC-CH in the cultural studies and teacher education doctoral programs, and my students, past and current, have taught me that academics is all about relationships. This book is testimony to the power of all these relationships. I, like Luis, have been supported by gifts from others as well. The Joseph R. Neikirk Distinguished Professorship of Sociology of Education provided the funds, time, and travel that were needed for me to do this book. I thank the Neikirk family for their many years of support.

George W. Noblit

CONTRIBUTORS

Silvia C. Bettez
Department of Educational Leadership
and Cultural Foundations
University of North Carolina at
Greensboro

Orisanmi Burton
Criminal Justice Program
University of the District of Columbia

Aurora Chang
Teaching and Learning Program
Loyola University of Chicago

Cherese Childers-McKee
Honors College
University of North Carolina at
Charlotte

Timothy Conder
School of Education
University of North Carolina at
Chapel Hill

Kathleen E. Edwards
Department of Educational Leadership
and Cultural Foundations
University of North Carolina at
Greensboro

Tommy Ender
School of Education
Loyola University Maryland

Beth Hatt
Department of Educational
Administration and Foundations
Illinois State University

Elena King
Department of English
Communication and Media Studies
Greensboro College

Lan Quach Kolano
Department of Middle, Secondary,
and K-12 Education
University of North Carolina at
Charlotte

Alison LaGarry
School of Education
University of North Carolina at
Chapel Hill

Leslie Locklear
Department of Educational Leadership
and Cultural Foundations
University of North Carolina at
Greensboro

Karla Martin
Community Services Division
Director
The Poarch Band of Creek Indians

George W. Noblit
Cultural Studies and Literacies
    Program
University of North Carolina at
    Chapel Hill

Hillary Parkhouse
Department of Teaching and Learning
Virginia Commonwealth University

Summer Melody Pennell
Department of English and Linguistics
Truman State University

Charles Price
Department of Anthropology
University of North Carolina at
    Chapel Hill

Esmeralda Rodríguez
Cultural Studies and Literacies
    Program
University of North Carolina at
    Chapel Hill

Luis Urrieta, Jr.
Department of Curriculum and
    Instruction
University of Texas at Austin

Luis Urrieta, Jr., PhD, is the inaugural Suzanne B. and John L. Adams Endowed Professor of Education, Department of Curriculum and Instruction, College of Education, University of Texas at Austin. He is an interdisciplinary scholar who specializes in the study of identity, agency, social movements related to education, and learning in family and community contexts. He is specifically interested in Latinx and Indigenous cultures, Indigenous migrations, Indigenous knowledge systems, and oral and narrative methodologies.

George W. Noblit, PhD, is a Joseph R. Neikirk Distinguished Professor of Sociology of Education, School of Education, University of North Carolina–Chapel Hill. He is a sociologist of education who specializes in the study of educational equity using qualitative research methods. He has won awards for his qualitative research and is widely known for having created (with Dwight Hare) the most popular approach to qualitative research synthesis, meta-ethnography, and for collaborating in creating postcritical ethnography.

Cultural Constructions of Identity

Cultural Identity Theory and Education

What We Have Learned About Selves and Others

LUIS URRIETA, JR. ■

This book, like most, is the result of curiosity, uneasiness, and a lot of work. It began as a conversation between George Noblit and me during a visit to North Carolina in 2012. Meaning no disrespect, I asked George why his meta-ethnography method for qualitative synthesis had been taken up mostly in public health and other fields and not as much in education, the field for which meta-ethnography was intended. Because of my research background, I was especially interested in the relationship between meta-ethnography and theory and the role of theory in meta-ethnographic synthesis, especially since a lot of syntheses focus on aggregate findings and utility-oriented "best practices," but not necessarily in theory-generating endeavors.

This conversation led to a meeting convened by George in a hotel lobby during the annual meetings of the American Educational Research Association in San Francisco in 2013, in which we called upon colleagues and friends studying identity-related issues and who were also familiar with, or interested in, meta-ethnography. From this meeting we committed interest in writing papers for future panel presentations at professional organizations. We have since continued to engage in this project as a collective, ultimately culminating in this edited volume.

The purpose of this edited book is to explore the effort to have qualitative and ethnographic studies speak to theory by way of meta-ethnography. Meta-ethnography, first developed by Noblit and Hare in 1988 and currently the most popular form of qualitative synthesis, uses a translation theory of interpretation so that the unique aspects of studies are preserved to the highest degree possible while also revealing the analogies between studies (Doyle, 2003). The studies presented in this book use different identity analytic frames to study race and ethnicity at the intersection of gender, age, class, and sexuality; thus this collection addresses identity work broadly. Our main goal is to focus on what these studies reveal about the relationship between identity and identification theory and meta-ethnographic synthesis.

Although we value scholarly enterprises around theory as academics, we agree with Charles Lemert's (2016) broad and perhaps more democratic definition of theory:

> Social theory is a basic survival skill. This may surprise those who believe it to be a special activity of experts of a certain kind. True, there are professional social theorists, usually academics. But this does not exclude my belief that social theory is something done necessarily, and often well, by people with no particular professional credential. When it is done well, by whomever, it can be a source of uncommon pleasure. (p. 1)

Lemert broadens for us, and for this book, the usually limited, exclusive, and exclusionary perspectives of theory often held hostage by academics. Lemert highlights that all people theorize as a survival skill, including individuals with no particular professional credential.

Lemert's (2016) definition of theory is important because one of the goals of interpretivist, critical, and postmodern ethnographic work (at least it should be!) is to understand the *emic* perspective of their participants and the ways in which they theorize their social and cultural worlds. Lemert continues: "Social theory is the normal accomplishment of socially adept human creatures figuring out what other creatures of the same sort are doing with, to, or around them" (p. 2). By way of this assertion that "social theory is a normal accomplishment of socially adept human beings," Lemert debunks a great myth of the academy—that theory has a particular form and that only a select few are smart enough to know such a form.

Building from Lemert's (2016) theory premise, one of the goals of this book is to explore the relation of meta-ethnographic synthesis to social and cultural theory, something that George and I agree has not been fully explored. The set of meta-ethnographic syntheses of qualitative studies in this book are the vehicle to speak across individual studies to more broadly comprehend cultural identity theory. Democratizing our perspective of theory through Lemert, together with meta-ethnography, facilitated for our chapter contributors a broader, more accessible, and interdisciplinary theorizing process with and through the synthesis.

The book begins with two introductory chapters; one focuses on cultural identity theory and a second concentrates on the qualitative research synthesis approach of meta-ethnography. In this first introductory chapter, we selectively present an overview of the study of identity as an epistemology, or how the idea of "identity" shifted and evolved over time. This review is not meant as a comprehensive overview of identity. Other significant volumes have already devoted time and attention to that effort. We will, however, explain how, with the help of scholars before us, we arrived at our working definition of identity for this book.

Who influenced whom, and who changed or shifted the train of thought? Why do we need self or group identities? What is at stake when membership is denied? What do we mean when we say that the study of identity is embodied? Questions like these guide this chapter. We argue throughout that there is a lot at stake in the study of identity, and what is at stake changes depending on the time period and locations of that embodiment.

In particular, the chapter highlights two aspects of cultural identity as a concept: first, the power that cultural identity has for identity politics, followed by the political dimensions of cultural identity used by oppressed and minoritized groups in social movements and activism, especially those related to education. In addition to giving attention to race and ethnicity, the chapter builds on the analysis of cultural politics by attending to the nuances and complexities of intersectionality by addressing the importance of intersectionality in understanding the cultural construction of identities. Cultural identity is understood as both open to strategic essentialism around race and ethnicity (Spivak, 2012), as well as thoroughly exposed to the fluid, dynamic, contested, complex, and malleable deconstructions of these concepts (Hall, 1996).

Returning to Lemert's perspective on theory, the chapter concludes by addressing how and why meta-ethnography cannot be understood as empirical results alone and why theory in meta-ethnography must be seen as interpretive and inductive, an *explanatory synthesis*.

OUR WORKING DEFINITION OF IDENTITY

In this section, we introduce the way we conceptualize our working definition of identity and briefly the major concepts that we draw from. We were guided by the following questions: What is identity and why study it? Does it have to do with roles in society, or with imagined, intrinsic characteristics of people? What are the stakes (power) in studying identity?

Our understanding of identity is interdisciplinary and premised broadly on cultural and sociological theory with interpretive and critical paradigmatic orientation. In part we ground ourselves in the cultural and the social because we were trained in these theories, but we also see the value of a nuanced, critical interdisciplinary analysis situated at the crossroads between anthropology, sociology, cultural, ethnic, and feminist studies. We adhere to interpretive and critical paradigms because we recognize that our positionalities influence our analytic frames, while our work is oriented toward social justice.

Identity is a complex concept that we define broadly as self-understandings, especially those with strong emotional resonances, and often marked with socially constructed raced, gendered, classed, and sexual identity "labels"—such as "smart boy," "pretty girl," or "at-risk student" (Holland, Lachicotte, Skinner, & Cain, 1998; Urrieta, 2009). We base our definition of identity on two assumptions: (a) the study of identity is the study of subject formation. The study of who counts as belonging to a category, a concept of the self, or a group. Identity is always a process of becoming with multiple consciousness depending on social location. The stakes that membership carries are also important; thus our second assumption: (b) identity is about power. Power is at the root of who "counts" as belonging to an identity, as well as who is able to self-define, self-identify, and deny to others their identity.

The term *identity* was initially used as a descriptive naming of how one was positioned by others and/or positioned oneself; however, it has evolved to engage more nuanced explorations of subject formation over life experience. *Identity now is defined as a self-concept, or self-perception, that is both existential and categorical, both individual and sociocultural, and that shifts and develops over time.* Individually identity is tied to a person's *identifications* or senses of and activity around belonging. *Identification is therefore the work of belonging that occurs as a person identifies characteristics that help him, her, or they determine what constitutes or does not constitute "membership" in a particular identity, group, or collective.* Collective identity is about how those notions of self- and other- "groupings" are formed inside and outside of the individual and impact the formation of social categories of belonging (Hall, 1996). The "work" aspect of identity involves the activities around the "auto-naming," or "self-authorship" (Holland et al., 1998) that evolves from how and when individuals come to construct their personhood and by extension their groupings around the particular salient identities in their lives. Personhood is a concept for understanding the status of "being" a person, and being recognized as such by others, especially as a mature, functioning social actor in a culture and society.

Identity and why we study identities is rooted in power. Power as a concept is fundamental in the study of identity because power, while dynamic, is systematically distributed in society, most often unevenly, with some sectors of society exerting it as a form of domination over others (de Lissovoy, 2016). Economic power, for example, is tied to the control of materiality such as resources, to production and accumulation, and in enterprise to monopolies and consumption. Both material economic power and social and symbolic power such as status (prestige) and their distribution play important parts as sources of identification in the labels, or positionings of identities (Giddens, 1991). Through the distribution of power, some identities, like "illegal alien" or "special education student," are imposed on groupings of people, while others, like "genius" and "gifted," are reserved for a select few; thus the stakes in studying identity and how power is distributed through identities are high. We next proceed to trace the ways in which Western thought has evolved and the preoccupation with (and understanding of) identity with it.

HISTORICAL IDEAS ABOUT SELF AND OTHER

The study of identity and the preoccupation to define the self dates back a long time. Historically, an existential sense of an individual self has often been attributed in philosophy to Descartes' famous (1644) *cogito ergo sum*, "I think; therefore,

I am," situating identity firmly, at least in the academy, as a Western concept. Heir to Greco-Roman philosophy and Medieval Christian and early modern Protestant theology, European man's ability to self-identify verified his individual existence and gave him power over the natural world (we are purposefully using male pronouns). Rooted in Judeo-Christian theology, *naming* was critical to the formation of power over that which was to be controlled (Bourdieu, 1991). In Protestantism, the individual self, alone in faith to believe in his own salvation and guided by a devotion to work, paved the way to modern individualism in the capitalist state (Weber, 1905). The stakes in studying identity (self) were indeed high for this early "self" because it was used as proof of European man's thinking ability by divine will that allowed for the assertion of his self-existence in the external world. The unequal distribution of power that resulted from this early study of Euro-Western man's recognition of (him)-self was that women and people of color were denied a full humanity. This denial of a full humanity persists to the present day.

Later, the scientific revolution, Age of Reason, and Enlightenment (starting in the 17th century and through the early 19th century) all further contributed to the development of intellectualism, reductionism, and empiricism and away from the absolutisms of theology and clericalism. Euro-Western man was encouraged to follow his intellect, rationality, and the application of reason and no longer that of divine revelation. For rationalists, such as Descartes, Spinoza, and Liebnitz, championing liberalist ideals around protecting and enhancing individual freedoms to promote equity aligned with the need for emerging governments to protect individuals' liberty. Generally, they believed that the government would protect individuals' rights, including freedom of thought and speech. On the other hand, empiricists, such as Locke, Hume, Mills, and Smith, while also placing primacy on individual political, ethical, and economic rights and freedoms, did so based on an ideology of a minimalist state with utilitarian self-interest that also privileged the development of free-market principles. Setting themselves apart from these two camps, Kant (comprehensive philosophy), Hegel (self-consciousness), and Marx (historical materialism, alienation, collective consciousness) each within their analyses and manner set out to situate the self as an individual within a collective in a historically produced socially unequal and structured material reality. For Marx especially, power inequities formed on the basis of base (economy) and superstructure (social and cultural institutions), resulting in the formation of classes, domination, and alienation. Through liberating philosophies of a collective class consciousness and class antagonisms (conflict between the bourgeoisie vs. proletariat), social revolutions would lead to a greater collective good for Marx.

While power played a prominent role in Marx's (Marx & Engels, 1848/1998) materialist perspective on class consciousness, Weber (1905/1958) focused not only on class stratification but also on status and power. To Weber, class identity was economically determined, but status was not necessarily so. Education, prestige, religion, popularity, and political power could bestow status on individuals without economic power. Class and status, therefore, formed an individual's power, or life chances for Weber, who viewed capitalism as rational, efficient, and merit-based, although also disenchanting when taken to the extremes. Societal power is also tied to economic strength but reaches further into social, political, juridical, and cultural (official language, history, school curricula, etc.) spheres of power. Bourdieu (1977) referred to these manifestations of power as forms of "capital" that people are born into as habitus and that shape their dispositions. The forms of capital (economic, social, cultural, etc.) in turn transform into each other in fields of power that perpetuate generational societal inequities. For all of these thinkers there was a greater collective good, which was of course largely focused on Euro-Western men and their collective good as full citizens of their respective countries—these were the stakes for the study of identity in their time periods.

Modern Subject Formation and Identity

After following a chronology of how Western thought has broadly danced around the notion of a self, we now explain what set in motion the way we study identity now. Binary dichotomous thinking, tied to both material and symbolic power (Marx, Weber, Bourdieu) was largely at the root of modernist subject "I" formation. We cannot emphasize enough here the relationship between identity and power because there is a lot at stake when it comes to identity and who can have membership or count as a particular identity. Power relations determine and distribute identities and who has access to certain "types" of identifications or not. In the modernist "I" binary, one is what the other is not. The Euro-Western "I" (individual and collective) was constructed as a dominant subject in a world of others through the construction of categorical hierarchies of power. Through colonial enterprises nature was to be dominated and exploited, and Others (people of color), in the collective sense, were to be conquered, "developed," or "civilized." While subjectification, as in subject "self" formation, also implies a submission, as in subjects to a higher power, objectification implies a "thingification" that was often used to control land and nature and to dehumanize Others into submission and domination. The study of the self in relation to others has since driven various currents of scholarly inquiry.

The study of identity has been specifically associated with the question: Does identity start inside an individual's consciousness, or is it a result of the limitations imposed by society? Scholarly inquiry in the foundations of psychology skirting around this question started at the end of the 19th century with William James's (1890) *Principles of Psychology* and Emile Durkheim's (1897/1951) *Suicide*. These early classics engaged the relationship between the self and the emerging societies of their time. Society was the basis of self-consciousness and personal identity for James, and society was a source of individual moral guidance for Durkheim.

At the turn of the century, Sigmund Freud's (1900) *The Interpretation of Dreams* further engaged the relationship between the individual and society in psychoanalysis by laying out the id, ego, and superego as the components of human personality. Each of these ids, egos, and superegos (either conscious or unconscious), while within the individual, were subject to the moral demands, stimuli, and threats of the social world. Other prominent scholars whose works have influenced our understanding of the relationship between personhood and society from this period are Charles Horton Cooley, Georg Simmel, and W. E. B. Dubois. Horton Cooley's (1902) "looking glass self" explored how individual's interior self came to see itself as others see it. Simmel (1903) studied the interdependence of individuality with society. In *The Souls of Black Folk*, DuBois (1903) theorized the identity and selfhood of African Americans as a process of double consciousness through which the social lenses of both White and Black society had to process self-understandings for African Americans.

For G. H. Mead (1913, 1925), the self was formed as an interior dialogue between the I-Me, a concept he generated. The Me developed from the social (exterior) world, while the I was the (internal) response of the individual to the exterior society's influence. Mead's theory of the social-genesis of the self, and later the theory of symbolic interactionism, have led to sophisticated analyses of identity in relation to broader social and cultural constructions, such as of nationalities, ethnicity, race, gender, religion, class, particular professions, political affiliations, as well as specific micro-localities and broadly across physical, social, and cultural geographies (Camaroff & Camaroff, 2009). A now well-studied example is that of nationalism (and subsequently of the conception of citizenship), which according to Benedict Anderson (1983) arose through the formation of "imagined communities," helping (or coercing) people to see themselves invested in norming practices that generate a national "collective" sense of membership. These thinkers and their works collectively teach us that individual selves (and identities) are not autonomous but interdependent with and emergent from their social worlds.

The ongoing study of the relationship between the individual and society was tested during the Second World War, opening up spaces for critical critiques not only of populism, fascism, and propaganda but also of liberalist and empiricist political ideologies. Drawing from Marxism and Freudian psychoanalysis, the Frankfurt School of critical theory was formed during the 1930s and further developed after the horrors of Nazism and other atrocities of the Second World War. Critical theory was strongly influenced by Antonio Gramsci's concept of cultural hegemony and ideology, which explained how state elites use cultural institutions to maintain power over their citizens. Critical theory as an analytic was situated in historical, sociopolitical contexts of reflective assessment and critique, which sought to reduce the entrapment of reductive systems of dominance or dependence. Critical theorists (i.e., Horkheimer, Adorno, Marcuse, Benjamin, Fromm) teased through the merits and faults of existing frameworks that did not adequately address the liberation and oppression of individuals within and of society.

Critical theory became particularly appealing to liberation struggles in the decades that followed throughout the world. For people of color and other marginalized groups, critical theory opened up *another* theoretical and practical space for critique against the structures of domination in society. We highlight the word "another" because we are well aware that critical theory was not the only theoretical and practical space for critique for people of color. Africana scholars, for example, attribute a wider and more diverse contribution to critical theory by

African American intellectuals such as DuBois and Carter G. Woodson (Asante, 1991; Rabaka, 2010). In terms of influencing research paradigms, "critical" has come to mean change, not just interpretation or description. Critical theory also had *an* influence in subsequent postcolonial, poststructuralist, and postmodern thought. In contemporary use, for example, drawing from the current "critical turn" in critical ethnic studies and critical Indigenous studies (Moreton-Robinson, 2016; Simpson & Smith, 2014), the term *critical* denotes an alignment with particular intellectual and political projects. Highlighting the critical signals an analytic that is part of a reflective conversation to break open the entrapments of Western reductive binaries. Breaking open these entrapments of dominance/dependence or oppression/agency is particularly salient to our understanding of identity and agency in this book because it allows us to think about identity as an ongoing process with multiple consciousness and about agency as dynamic and creative, not just reactive and reductive.

Breaking entrapments became apparent in Erik Erikson's work on identity development in the 1950s, where he challenges taken-for-granted notions of identity as studied by Freud in order to answer questions of the time, bringing us one step closer to how we study identity now. Erik Erikson's work on identity development is perhaps the most well-known regarding modern identity studies generally and is also one of the most popular in education. Erikson's work on identity emerged in response to a context of postwar prosperity, White suburban development, and growing concern over adolescence and youth development in the United States. Erikson's (1950) *Childhood and Society* outlines a psychoanalytic theory with eight stages through which all people ideally go through from birth to adulthood. In *Childhood and Society* Erikson posits the notion of an "identity crisis," a concept that resonated widely at that time and a typical invocation even today. Following Erikson, James Marcia's (1966) contribution to developmental psychology regarding identity is that individual cognition and collective behavior both form psychosocial self-development, which he elaborated in identity status theory.

Identity studies based on Erikson and Marcia's work focus on ego identity development and effective psychosocial functioning rather than on cultural influences in identity construction and self-making (Bernal, Knight, Ocampo, Garza, & Cota, 1993). Such theories have been formulated using models that suggest a linear development of identity "scales" often based on stage-like phases that indicate a progression. These psychological models have also influenced the development of ethnic and/or racial identity development theories (Pizarro & Vera, 2001). For example, Phinney's (1989, 1990, 1993) three-stage model of ethnic minority identity development often cited as the basis for understanding Latina/o identity development is also based on (some would say restrictive) psychological premises that conflate ethnic identity development with racial identity (Pizarro & Vera, 2001). Most of these theories of identity development emphasize their strong connection with psychology, are based on survey questionnaire data and studies mostly of men, usually US college students, and largely ignore the dynamic, fluid, and flexible nature of cultural production and individual self-making.

These psychology-based theories, however, have been particularly salient to the study of Nigrescence theory and Black racial identity theory (BRIT), which we recognize as influential and important for the study of African American racial identity development. William Cross's (1971) Nigrescence theory and its 1991 revision (Cross, 1991) have made a lasting contribution to Black racial identity theories (BRITs). BRITs are based on heuristic models that outline progressive scales ranging from negative self-perceptions of blackness through to achieve a positive and humanist Black racial identity. Nigrescence and BRITs have been particularly empowering for African Americans and are an excellent example of why we argue that the stakes in studying identity are high. They are high because these theories have offered a form of psychological response to the damage inflicted on African Americans by US racism. Janet Helms' (1990) contributions to this theory in that regard are noteworthy because she posits that all people, including Whites, have racial identities and that in their most advanced stages, Whites would stand against racism. Racial identity theories in this vein thus directly challenge racism in society, and it is no coincidence that they emerged in the 1970s, a time of political struggles against social inequalities and civil rights activism. One of the influences of Cross's work has been the subsequent development of the Cross Racial Identity Scale, which researchers have used to continue their studies of US Black racial identity (Cokley, 2002) and of African immigrants' incorporation in to US racial identity schemas (DeWalt, 2011). In regard to youth, Beverly Tatum's (1997) acclaimed book *Why Are All the Black Kids Sitting Together in the Cafeteria?* also draws from Cross's racial identity theory to highlight the relevance and importance of a positive racial identity, especially for youth of color. Tatum argues that educational achievement, mental health, and psychosocial well-being depend on healthy racial identities.

Social and Cultural Perspectives on Identity

Undoubtedly, we value and support the positive impact and social justice political struggles of BRITS, but we step away from psychology-based perspectives on identity for social and cultural ones because we believe these to be most conducive to studying identity in more intimate and multifaceted ways. The analytic frames of anthropology (Holland et al., 1998), sociology (Apple, 1996), feminist studies (Butler, 1990), cultural studies (Hall, 1996), and literature (Moya, 2002) have moved us into more progressive thought about identity in nuanced and complex ways. For example, identity was initially conceived as "roles" in the social psychology of selfhood (Smith, 1988), but the idea of "roles" was later critiqued as static, formal, and ritualistic. Davies and Harré (1990, p. 26) in response proposed a positioning theory, in which the concept of "position" functions as a central organizing concept to analyze how people "do" being a person (personhood) through linguistic discourses by offering two forms of positioning. The first is reflexive positioning, which is self-positioning, and the second is interactive, or the positioning of others. Positioning generally involves race, gender, and class positioning; thus positioning is embedded in power, which plays prominently in the relationship between individuals and society, making the stakes in studying identity higher, especially for those imposed with positionings that limit and negatively impact their lived experiences.

Positionings are more broadly understood today as those socially and culturally constructed labels or identities offered to, or imposed on, people. Whether that be of a "loud Black girl," "quiet Asian boy," (Lei, 2003), or the criminalization of males of color as early as elementary school (Lewis, 2003). Holland et al. (1998) state that positioning limits people to varying degrees of accepting, rejecting, or negotiating identities. Stuart Hall's (1996) cultural studies' contribution to identity studies joins identity to identification in a suture: identification being identity's ongoing abstract and evident process of articulation, its continuous classifying act. We, therefore, highlight the significant influence that role theory, positioning theory, and identification have had on identity studies, especially those that today more explicitly address race and ethnicity, such as critical race theory (CRT), Latino critical race theory (LatCrit) and other Crits, and their intersectionality with gender, class, sexual orientation, ability, age, immigration, accent, and other categories (Solórzano & Delgado Bernal, 2001).

Feminists' Contributions to Identity

Feminists' contributions to identity include a challenge to the notion that the political is not personal, and feminists of color especially challenged the idea that emotions and personal experience are not valid ways of knowing. Nancy Hartstock, Sandra Harding, and Donna Haraway contributed "standpoint theories" as a concept; however, standpoint theories affirming women's experiential knowledge as feminist epistemologies in and of themselves are their contribution. Feminists of color especially contributed to our understanding of identities as the standpoint products of gendered, classed, and sexual differences that are inherently intersectional regarding race and ethnicity. Grounded in CRT and black feminism, intersectionality is an analytical and heuristic tool introduced by Kimberlé Crenshaw in 1989. Crenshaw's intersectional framework problematized the marginalization of Black women within institutionalized power relations (e.g., law and policy) and highlighted how discourses of resistance (e.g., antiracism and feminism) could challenge women's marginalization. As stated by Crenshaw (1995), "the fact that women of color are situated within at least two subordinate groups that frequently pursue conflicting political agendas . . . is a dimension of intersectional disempowerment which men of color and white women seldom confront" (p. 360). Patricia Hill Collins' (1990) Black feminist thought is another example of standpoint theory in which for Black women "standpoints" are achieved through lived experience and collective political struggle. Identities, for Hill Collins, are constructed as historically contextual "locations" that are also fluid, multiple, dynamic, and intersectional.

Chicana feminists such as Norma Alarcón, Ana Castillo, Beatriz Pesquera, Chela Sandoval, Denise Segura, and Emma Perez (amongst others) also contributed theory from their unique embodiment of gendered, racialized, classed, and sexuality, political standpoints. Chicana lesbian theorist Gloria Anzaldúa (1987) stands out among Chicana feminists because her concepts of the borderlands and mestiza consciousness offer insight into the unique experiences of US Latinas. Borderlands, according to Anzaldúa, symbolize an *invisible* border within the self that opens up the space of hybridity and contradiction in being Latina, living between cultures. Through the concept of *nepantla* (in-betweenness), she challenges the history of colonization of the mind, as well as argues for consciousness development as a result of border crossing within the intersectional spaces of identities (Keating, 2006; Pacheco, 2014). Intersectional scholarship has since facilitated a necessary shift from viewing difference and categories of difference from a one-identity axis approach to one of multiple and intersecting categories (Grant & Zwier, 2014). The locations of identity embodiment for feminists of color are thus explicitly tied to political struggles; surfacing to the top in their work are the political dimensions and high stakes involved in the study of identity.

Recent Developments in Identity

Studies of identity associated with politics, activism, and social movements also became increasingly coupled with analyses of will, resistance, or agency (Melucci, 1988, 1990). The incorporation of agency ranged from binaries around structure (oppression) and resistance to more proactive stances on behalf of the individual and/or collective action (Della Porta & Diani, 2006). While some scholars downplayed agency in the face of social constraints and binding structures, others offered more liberating (perhaps to some unrealistic) visions of humans' agentic capabilities via the identity–agency dialectic.

One particular ground-breaking work of the late 1990s, and especially important to our understanding of identity, is Holland et al.'s (1998) sociocultural practice theory of identity and self. This theory brought together various established (sometimes opposing) schools of thought that included culturalists, constructivists, universalists, and particularly the work of Soviet scholars Vygotsky (psychologist) and Bakhtin (philosopher and literary critic). Holland et al. suggest that cultural production and heuristic development are necessary processes for identity analyses because they move us away (but not completely) from cultural determinism and situational totalitarianism to make (some) way for the importance of improvisation and innovation. Employing Bakhtin's concept of addressivity to engage "dialogism" (Holquist, 1990), or the ability of people to entertain multiple internal simultaneous dialogues, Holland et al. describe the space of authoring as complex and potentially contradictory. Holland et al. state that the world must be answered and that authorship is not a choice; however, the form of the answer is not predetermined. In figured (cultural) worlds people are offered positions that they accept, reject, or negotiate; they must make choices and respond to these forms of addressivity. Attention is focused on identities forming in process or activity, primarily organized activity in and around figured worlds. Identity is always a process of "figuring" or becoming, while more enduring aspects of self (history-in-person) remain important to ongoing and future identity constructions. Because improvisation can be either spontaneous or self-guided, it can effect and affect permanent changes in future responses. Critical "moments" during the interaction process are therefore important for Holland et al. to recognize agency in practice (Bourdieu, 1977), thus privileging individual and collective agency.

Although interest in identity studies has drifted since the late 1990s due to a perceived exhaustion of the concept, identity continues to be attractive as an area of study. In the new millennium, paradigms to investigate identity continue to range from post-positivist perspectives of a knowable external reality and a centered core self to postmodern contestations to truths and singular or lasting selves. For example, postpositivist realist literary theorist Paula Moya (2002) asserts that people of color possess "epistemic privilege" due to their experiences with the realities of oppression, or "truer" perspectives of an external social reality than people who are blinded by their categorical (race, gender, class, and sexuality) privileges. The stakes in Moya's argument is clearly an attempt at inverting power by claiming for people of color a more valid and objective perspective of (T)truth. At the other extreme, Brian Ott (2003) argues from a postmodern perspective that "mediated images," such as those of Bart, Homer, and Lisa Simpson in the TV hit *The Simpsons*, model identities for people that sort into an "identity pastiche" (p. 71), often based, like the characters, on unreal, not lasting, or multiple assemblages to sort from. Vast frameworks thus continue to generate a broad range of claims about the study of identity and self, but they are always situated within time and space with particular stakes involved.

Most recently a trend for important comprehensive books, edited volumes, and handbooks has been devoted to identity. Amongst these is Anthony Elliott's (2016) *Identity Troubles*, with a strong review of the sociological literature on identity. In it, Elliott extends identity theory into an exploration of posthumanist and transhumanist discourses of identity. Another important book is Victor Seidler's (2010) *Embodying Identities: Culture, Differences and Social Theory*, which also reviews the sociological literature on identity. This book lends itself to the existential exploration of self by readers engaging the question, "Who am I?" Other comprehensive volumes that address identity are the *Handbook of Identity Theory and Research* (Schwartz, Luyckx, & Vignoles, 2011), as well as *The SAGE Handbook of Identities* (Wetherell & Mohanty, 2010). With two volumes and 40 chapters, the *Handbook of Identity Theory and Research* is certainly comprehensive, covering a wide variety of foci in identity theory from a range of disciplines and interdisciplinary perspectives. This book brings together varied and often unfamiliar theories of identity development ranging from traditional psychology to sociology and puts them in conversation with each other. Similarly, *The SAGE Handbook of Identities* is a volume of more than 26 chapters that focus on social and cultural theories of identity. This volume offers a much more critical review of the identity literature, including from ethnic studies and postcolonialist perspectives. These volumes are all monumental and admirable projects; however, their mega-accomplishments also tend to be to their detriment because they often do not lend themselves to practical classroom teaching.

To not replicate the remarkable accomplishments of mega-volumes, we locate identity within social and cultural theory and particularly within a historical sociopolitical context in relation to people of color. This means that the stakes involved for people of color in the study of identity are the product not only of the Western trajectory of identity studies we just reviewed but also of the particular political locations of embodiment of these identities that we situate in the work of scholars of color. Namely, when people of color and women come into this identity landscape, what lessons can we learn from their social locations?

IDENTITY AND PEOPLE OF COLOR

We are particularly interested in identity as a powerful, political concept and organizing principle for people of color. We center on race and ethnicity because these have played a foundational role in power relations and domination. Racial and ethnic identity have also been important in the struggle for equity and justice for people of color in response to structured forms of institutionalized oppression (in the United States and larger global perspective). Even today, race and ethnicity continue to be important and relevant to the study of identity. Highly racialized, anti-Black, anti-immigrant, anti-refugee, pro-conservative, White supremacist political climates have recently openly prevailed in the United States and other western countries. We define White supremacy as the official and unofficial institutions (including racism, schooling, the law, etc.), principles, morals, norms, history, and overall culture that privilege Whites in society (Urrieta, 2009). White supremacy is not just endemic to the United States, but through colonialism, imperialism, and now global capitalism (i.e., through media, consumer products, labor exploitation, etc.), it is also part of the "racial contract" in most of the world (Mills, 1997).

Colonization, imperialism, and global capitalism have justified the oppression and exploitation of people of color through the positioning of some races and ethnicities as inferior to others. The Euro-West dehumanized and thingified everything non-European, including the people (Idigenous, Black, Aborigine, etc.), through the glorification of all things western. Dehumanization justified chattel slavery and other forms of physical possession and exploitation of subaltern bodies, while lands and resources were seized and extracted through the governing structures of settler colonialisms (Calderón, 2014) and other forms of colonial dispossession (Cusicanqui, 2012). Skutnabb-Kangas (2000) states that glorification in the colonial process involved the promotion of the colonizer's society and culture as superior and included the appropriation of Indigenous cultures. Colonization was rationalized by the Euro-West as benevolent and missionary, and it was suggested that the Natives should be thankful, for, without European uplift, uncivilized savagery would have persisted (Smith, 1999).

Identity-related social movements and collective action have always, however, been important to the collective senses of self for people of color. Negative conceptions of Indigenous societies were always challenged in ongoing postcolonial struggles, and collective senses of self were especially important in the face of colonial, imperial, and global corporate invasion of the world by Europe and the United States. Identity was central to liberation, postcolonial, and to resistance movements from Africa, to India, and Asia (Loomba, 1998), as well as in the United States for people of color (DuBois, 1903; Urrieta, 2009). Identity has thus been a powerful claim in the struggle to decenter, decolonize, and dislodge from the power of whiteness and White supremacy for people of color's cultural, social, and political thought and survival. After the Second World War, these struggles resulted in full on Third World national liberation movements, based on high-stakes collective identity constructions of nationhood in opposition to the invading colonial powers.

Frantz Fanon's (1963, 1967) challenges to European colonialism through his scholarly work in *The Wretched of the Earth* and *Black Skins, White Masks* is an excellent example of decentering and dislodging from the power of whiteness. Fanon's sophisticated and enlightening analyses examine the psychosocial effects of colonialism on people of color, especially concerning senses of self. According to Fanon (1967), colonialism takes on more than a physical form of oppression and becomes complexly internalized in psychosocial ways, creating unresolved feelings of inferiority in the colonized. Fanon (1963) states, "colonialism forces the people it dominates to ask themselves the question constantly. 'In reality, who am I?'" (p. 250). Fanon's implicit attention to identity in the experience of colonization is foundational to postcolonialism and contributed significantly also to critical and Marxist analyses of colonialism. Edward Said's (1978) *Orientalism* is also a most noteworthy response to the cultural representations (identity constructions) that were the basis for Western scholars' patronizing and dehumanizing depictions of the "East" (Asia, North Africa, and the Middle East) as Orientalism. According to Grossberg (1996), Foucault's (1978) analysis of discourse, knowledge, and institutional power became an aperture for Said's autochthonous critique and rejection of the construction of "Otherness" in the "East." Orientalism, according to Said, which resulted from European Enlightenment thinking, justified colonialism by constructing the East as inferior, mysterious, exotic, and ultimately antithetical to the West. These are exemplary of how the Euro-West constructed itself as superior with its opposites as deficient in an us/them binary. For Fanon, Said, and others such a Memmi, Bhabha, and Spivak, the contestation or challenge to the collective racialization (positioning) of the Other supported simultaneously identity-building discourses and ideologies that disrupted the objectification of who they call the "subaltern" (see Guha & Spivak, 1988), while igniting and fueling collective resistances to domination. In either response, whether the Euro-West's claim to superiority or people of color's liberation struggles, collective identities were essential and high-stakes elements to sustain struggles and resistance.

Similar to Third World national liberation movements in Africa, the Middle East, and Asia, the social and civil rights movements of the 1960s in the United States had important mutual influences and impact. Memmi, Fanon, Spivak, Hall, and Said were widely read in the United States, as were DuBois, Frederick Douglas, Marcus Garvey, Ana Julia Cooper, and civil rights leaders like Martin Luther King Jr. and Malcolm X abroad. However, the 1960s and 1970s activism around civil rights in the United States usually revolved around community-based, grassroots organizations that often focused on racial or ethnic (mostly male) empowerment and pursued the self-determination of segregated, often Black and Latino, communities (Acuña, 2000). These included cultural nationalist movements like the Black power movement, the Chicano movement, the American Indian movement, and the lesser known Asian American movements (Pulido, 2006). Internal colonialism was often used as a theoretical analysis to help situate the identity-based struggles of the different racial and ethnic movements in the United States (Barrera, 1997).

In the United States, identity was also a powerful concept for people of color, especially after the social movements of the 1960s. Identity, however, was quickly politicized in part because some White elites recognized it as a collective threat to White supremacy because it undercut their calls for people of color and immigrants to assimilate. Both the power of the identity concept for people of color and immigrants and the resulting politicization led to the term being theorized in various academic disciplines, which led in part to the creation of ethnic studies. These theories and ethnic studies noted the power of identity for oppressed and minoritized groups, especially for youth of color and communities organizing around race and ethnicity (Muñoz, 1989). These studies of race and ethnicity also later highlighted that identity, particularly in its intersectional forms, was less fixed and stable and more contested, complex, and changeable (Butler, 1990).

Social movements have changed since the 1960s, and, according to Castells (2006), for new social movements of the 1980s and beyond, place and locality remain important sites for contestation and resistance. In this new economic context of neoliberal restructuring, resistance to the privatization of public services like welfare, health care, and education have become prominent. While community empowerment and access to civil and political rights were the motivations in the 1960s and 1970s, today's movements demand from the state the basic public necessities of a democratic society. For example, public education has been under assault since the 1990s through conservative accountability movements focused on high-stakes testing (which are very profitable for testing and curriculum development companies), austerity measures, and the incorporation of business-like practices in schooling, especially in high minority areas. Through "crisis" propaganda, top-down decision-making, and market-oriented reforms (Sturges, 2015), entire cities like New Orleans (a predominantly Black city) have lost their public school systems to charter schools and other public/private enterprises. Community struggles, primarily by people of color to keep their local public schools open, are being waged throughout the United States.

Social movements, in this new market globalism (Steger, 2009), provide different means for studying identities, including for example Chicana/o activist identities (Urrieta, 2009). Today's Chicano/a/x identities, while they are continuities of 1960s movements, are also presently different because more intersectional analyses that incorporate racial, feminist, and sexuality frameworks allow us more sophisticated understandings of the social and cultural contexts of identity (Urrieta & Villenas, 2013). With the shift to neoliberalism, new social movement theorists emphasize culture, and not necessarily class consciousness in the traditional Marxist sense, as the site for struggle (Harvey, 1989). Movements are now understood as transformations of changing, adaptable, and multiple discourses, especially of culture and identity, in new contexts (Calhoun, 1994; Melucci, 1989) that revolve around particular communities embracing cultural and identity politics (Calhoun, 1997). We see an example of this in relation to the recent reactionary racial justice movements (i.e. #BlackLivesMatter) to the murder of Black men by police officers in various cities throughout the United States.

Martin Alcoff and Mohanty (2006) associate "identity politics" with activists and with social movements that invoke the concept of identity in their struggles for social justice and also with identity-based scholarly programs (such as ethnic, women's, gender and sexuality studies) that emerged from the struggles of the 1960s. Often invoking essentialisms to foment strong collective senses of belonging (Spivak, 2012) and entitlement to rights and reparations under humanist discourses, identity and identity politics have once again become high stakes to collective action in the new millennium. Identity politics, however, has been a double-edged sword of sorts for identity-based movements due to the strong critiques charged against them from multiple sides of the political spectrum for decades. Critics of identity politics claim that these movements have an "agenda" and dub them "special interest groups." They tend to point out that identity-related social movements can be antagonistic and divisive. Identity-based political movements today, however, are an empowering practice for both on-the-ground action such as in marches and protests and an analytic for theoretical and political organizing.

From this brief overview it is clear that identity and identity-based movements have been particularly powerful for minoritized communities and people of color. In terms of race and ethnicity and the objectification of the Other, colonialist and later imperialist self-formations established a world system of White male supremacy that positioned the Euro-West and subsequently settler colonial states (like the United States, Canada, Australia, New Zealand, etc.) as superior and as the arbiters of world power, including through current corporate globalisms (Steger, 2009). Identity has, however, been used to foment and support individual and collective senses of self that assert liberating struggles and resistance for people of color, as evidenced in Third World national liberation movements and US civil rights movements. Through generational cohorts (Whittier, 1995), these identity-based and identity politics movements persist to the present day, albeit in modified forms. Although some scholars claim that identity is a useless and outdated analytic (Brubaker & Cooper, 2000), we counter that identity, especially around race and ethnicity and its inseparable intersections with gender, sexuality, and class, as evidenced by the 2016 US presidential election, still are crudely important and needed identity concepts to think through and to work from, both in theoretical and practical ways.

CULTURE, IDENTITY, AND IDENTIFICATION

From our review of identity, including the relevant historical concepts and its importance to people of color, we now put forth our expanded understandings of culture, identity, and identification in this book. From a social and cultural standpoint, identity and self are concepts that are not only constituted by the labels that people place on themselves and others. Identity is also very much about how people come to understand themselves, how they come to "see" who they are, through the social and cultural "worlds" that they participate in and how they relate to others within and outside of these worlds. Identity, self, personhood, subjectivity, and by extension will and human agency are all related Western and modernist concepts, closely tied to individualism (Elliott, 2016; Wojciehowski, 1995). Identity and self are also rooted in conflict between the development of rationalist and empiricist thought and created out of relational difference (Lemert, 2012). Identity, although focused first on the individual as conceptual and emotional self-understandings, is, however, never outside of the external "reality" of social, cultural, political, economic, and philosophical forces. Wenger (1999) argues that these individual and social forces should be thought of as mutually constituted and not as dichotomous and that identity itself serves as a pivot between the two; we agree. The external forces are structural, both physical and symbolic, and discursive and ideological (Gee, 2000). In that sense, identity is both abstract and evident, both a concept and an embodied lived reality.

Identity is always said to be relational, contrastive, and even oppositional because *one is what the other is not*. The relational aspect of identity is therefore not autonomous of an exterior other according to Western views of the self. Sarup (1996) states, "it is always within representation that we recognize ourselves . . . identity is always related to what one is not—the Other. . . . identity is only conceivable in and through difference . . . That one is not what the Other is, is critical in defining who one is" (p. 47). Similarly, Holland et al. (1998), incorporating the concept of dialogism, or the capacity for people to have internal, often contradictory dialogues that allow for self-authorship, define identity as: "People tell others who they are, but even more important, they tell themselves and then they try to act as though they are who they say they are (p. 3). According to Holland et al., identities are always internal and external processes and mostly unfinished products in constant flux. Similarly, Moran (2011) writes that identities are dialogic processes, never singular and a confluence of different influences and historical trajectories. Because identity is always exteriorly shaped, it is also collective and therefore also dependent upon relationships between the individual and social and cultural Others. These associations always require "work" and are not always stable; in fact, more often than not, we believe that identity work is a contradictory struggle, and yet identity remains "a powerful organizing presence in social life" (Leve, 2011, p. 513).

Identification is closely tied to identity, and we believe it is a fundamental component to its understanding. Following Stuart Hall (1992), and for this book, we define identification as processual, ongoing acts of classifying that often arrive, even if temporarily, at articulations of identities. Identification is, therefore, a *process* of identity construction that "reflects not only the process by which we take on subject positions as identities, but also our own role in this process" (LeCourt, 2004, p. 38). According to Hall, the meeting point, or "suture," between discourse and self where people decide to invest in and take up certain subject positions becomes part of identity construction. Holland et al. (1998), rather than invoking a suture, refer to this process of investment in an identity as a codevelopment and recast identification as "the formation of a concept of self as an actor" by privileging activity (p. 120), where aspects of oneself, including one's feelings and thoughts, are self-understood and self-organized through access, investment, and participation in a cultural world. This means that the "rules" of the cultural world are taken up as one's own through "self-authorship" in self-guided self-formation. Introducing a feminist perspective, for Butler (1990), identification is an incomplete process because it is conceived in fantasy and does not fully meet the body and the gendered practices ascribed to it. Identification for Butler is an idealization, in which power forms identities through a subjection of the self to an exclusionary matrix. Subjectification is premised on a constitutive outside (what one is not) because subject formation is idealized through repetition of normativity. Identity then becomes performative and subjected to power for Butler because identity, although sedimented through repetition, is always unfinished and is subject to challenge. We might also add that for Wenger (1999), identification is also about "doing" a relational, experiential, subjective, and collective "negotiation." This aspect of identification could be compared to Holland et al.'s notion of a "thickening" of identity.

Identification, whether a suture, codevelopment, or idealization, is for us a classifying, negotiated act of "doing" that enables identities to "thicken." Identification is abstract and bounded by social and cultural discourses and ideologies that influence cognitive processes of dialogic self-formation (Holquist, 1990), while also engaged in the daily, experiential acts of "doing" life. Identities, guided by social and cultural factors, are the historically produced labels that position individuals and groups within landscapes of sociopolitical action, making us/them recognizable personae (Holland et al., 1998). Conceived through personally experienced, relational, contextual, and temporal realities, identities are always also mutually constituted by their socially and culturally "evident" exteriorities through the identification process.

Further, we argue that culture remains important as an organizing principle to understand human individual and collective behavior in relation to identification and identity's social and culturally evident exteriorities. We recognize that culture is a problematic and contested concept, especially after the sharp critiques of anthropology that emerged in the 1970s (Borofsky, Barth, Shweder, Rodseth, & Stolzenberg, 2001; González, 1999). However, we also agree that culture is still useful as an organizing analytic, especially when addressing issues related to identity and identification because we do not view culture, or cultures, as static or essentialized collectives or as sets of characteristics assigned to groups. We especially do not subscribe to the idea of inherent or biological traits as being essentialized to a particular "culture." Rather, we view cultures as complex, dynamic, and multifaceted, historically produced repertoires of practices for participation that endure or change for communities over time (Gutiérrez & Rogoff, 2003), which are embedded within intra- and inter-diverse, sociopolitical landscapes of power. Identification is therefore also guided by the daily "doing" that emerges from the discourses and the ideologies that guide the repertoires of practices of social and cultural everyday life.

We explicitly define cultural identities as self and collective understandings of belonging, or memberships to particular groups that share a common difference and/or shared practices to other identifiable groups or groupings. These differences and practices may be physical, social, cultural, political, and/or imagined (Anderson, 1983). Cultural identities are therefore learned ways of knowing (epistemologies) and being in the world (ontologies)—learned repertoires of practices for participating in collective, cultural communities with different degrees of involvement and competence that develop and change over time (Urrieta, 2013). For example, as a child learns the shared repertoires of practices for engaging others in a community where she is recognized and valued (or not), she becomes more active in participating in those social and cultural practices with increasing expertise while gradually joining in forming part of the larger social and cultural webs of that community. Rogoff (2016) and others would refer to this as learning by observing and pitching in. Eventually, this child will develop not only physically but also as an identifiable, "knowable" person, subjectively organized around particular ways of knowing, being, and doing that are culturally and socially appropriate and recognizable to others. She might even become specialized, gain status, and be highly regarded (or despised) within and outside of her community. Lave and Wenger (1991) refer to this as situated learning in communities of practice. Holland et al. (1998) call their activity-dependent cultural worlds, "figured worlds," where people "figure" identities in relation to others.

Holland et al.'s (1998) figured worlds, in particular, are a significant contribution to understanding the cultural contexts of the production of identities. In figured worlds, people "figure" who they are through the activities and in relation to the social types that populate these worlds. Figured worlds are processes or traditions of apprehension giving people shape and form as their lives intersect with them. Importantly, figured worlds are recreated by work, often contentious work with others; thus drawing from Leontiev, Holland and colleagues focus on the importance of activity, not just in a restricted number of figured worlds but across landscapes of action. Thus we place emphasis on activity or practice and intra- and inter-diversity within and across cultural worlds in the development of selves and others.

Generally, figured worlds have also been a valuable conceptual tool for understanding the cultural construction of identity in educational contexts, especially learner identities and the complexity around what "learner" means in different contexts (Boaler & Greeno, 2000; Jurow, 2005; Luttrell, & Parker, 2001; Tonso, 2006; Wortham, 2005); teacher identities (Sloan, 2006); and race, class, and gender identities (Leander, 2002; Wortham, 2004), despite the critique that agency is overprivileged in this sociocultural theory of identity and self. The syntheses in this book, although geared to speak to the cultural construction of identity broadly, most explicitly address sociocultural studies of identity and self (Holland et al., 1998; Holland & Lave, 2001, 2009; Saxe, 2003). Studying identity within education we agree is particularly useful. Identities within schools are constructed in relation to a powerful institution in society. Given the amount of time most people will spend within schools, and the number of multiple figured worlds that intersect with, and within them, schools are an important site for the formation of selves. Most of the chapters in this volume indeed focus on identity and education and highlight the vast proliferation of sociocultural studies of identity in the field (Bartlett, 2007; Hatt, 2007; Rubin, 2007; Urrieta, 2007, 2009; Vågen, 2011).

To conclude, cultural identities as cultural productions are therefore dynamic, fluid, participatory, always in process, and, like learning, continuous and never fully accomplished. Because cultural practices are themselves dynamic and depend on individual and collective participation (as in communities of practice, or figured worlds), cultural boundaries, while sometimes seemingly formidable and impenetrable, are also malleable and never fully totalized (Anzaldua, 1987). Bhabha (1996) writes, "cultures are never unitary in themselves, nor simply dualistic in relation of Self to Other" (p. 207). Ethnic hybridity, for example, is therefore the emergent set of beliefs and values shared by a group of individuals in response to these cultural, social, economic, or political interactions. Even though most persistent, and often hegemonic, collectivist distinctions may be around broad identity markers such as nationality, race, ethnicity, gender, or social class and their intersections, local particularities such as language inflection, clothing styles, physical expressiveness, and/or selective musical genres may also become sources of cultural investment and distinction. Through our invocation of culture, we cast a wide net over what we mean by social and cultural identities and the role that culture as a "thick description," as dense texture of the accounts of social life, plays as an organizing principle in understanding identification and identity processes (Geertz, 1973), especially in education.

IDENTITY AND EDUCATION

In this section, we look briefly at identity in education, especially at sociocultural studies of education. We address how notions of identity have shifted historically to new, more current understandings, theorizing identity as an internal process of oneself to how the internal concepts of self are shaped by and interact with the external messages about self, especially in schools. Because discourses of race and ethnicity are highly politicized, scholarship on education and identity has been dominated by race and ethnicity (Carter & Goodwin, 1994). The consistent focus on race includes the historical de jure and current de facto segregation of African Americans, Latinxs, and other ethnic groups in US schools (Donato & Hanson, 2012).

Theoretically, the field of education writ large has been heavily influenced by cognitive and developmental psychology and what have come to be known as the learning sciences, often defining learning and development on Euro-White American standards (Urrieta, 2015). Learning and intelligence were initially conceived as an individual function, connected to personal characteristics and biological factors, and only minimally influenced by social and cultural interaction. Psychometrics, including intelligence testing like IQ, dominated the field from its institutionalization to the detriment of people of color (Valencia, 1997). Richard Valencia demonstrated how through discourses of pseudo-scientific measurement, psychological deficit views of minority children were justified by using often inappropriate culturally biased psychometric instruments such as intelligence and standardized tests. These deficit discourses became racialized positionings and constructions of Latina/o, African American, and other minority children as "at risk" (Brown, 2016), less smart (Hatt, 2012), or possessing little intellectual, conceptual knowledge in their family and cultural communities (Foley, 1997). Scholars (McDermott & Verenne, 1995; Pizarro, 2005; Yosso, 2005) have since argued that students of color continue to be negatively affected when educators and school administrators continue to adhere to deficit views of their cultures and families by delegitimizing their "smartness" (Hatt, 2007) or cultural "giftedness" (Carrillo, 2013) by continuing to base definitions of intelligence on White middle-class social, cultural, and moral standards. McDermott and Verenne contend that persistent beliefs in minority genetic deficits as well as in cultural and social deficits are a barrier to academic "success," and educators are in effect "disabling" students through an ethnocentric cultural myopia.

Returning to Holland et al. (1998), we observe that in figured (cultural) worlds, people encounter narratives borne out of historical significance (ranging from oppressive to liberating) that distribute power, rank, and prestige at both the individual and collective level. In the United States, for example, a collective whitestream majoritarian narrative, laden with issues of power, racism, and discrimination, is that African Americans, especially African American males, are prone to criminality (Brown & Donner, 2011). African American boys thus enter the educational system already positioned as potential criminals by, often, White, middle-class, female teachers—the majority of the US (80%) teaching force (Ladson-Billings, 2011). For example, in Amanda Lewis' (2003) ethnography, Rodney, an elementary school African American child, when asked what he wanted to do when he grew up stated that he wanted to go to college but first he had to go to prison. When questioned by his White teacher, Rodney added, "All Black men go to prison" (p. 54). The criminalizing positioning of African Americans, especially males, in whitestream society can have a powerful impact in self-making (Urrieta, Martin, & Robinson, 2011).

Hegemonic discourses and dominant ideologies, such as that of African American boys as criminals; of Latinas as docile, quiet, or hypersexual (Mariscal, Velásquez, Agüero, & Urrieta, 2017); of Black girls as loud (Lei, 2003); and of Asians as smart (Ngo, 2010), and the disrespect of Native peoples through sports mascots (Ramírez, 2006), are often created and actively enforced to support normative structures in schools. These "governing" discourses and ideologies are usually historically produced and maintained through economic and sociopolitical processes, including through institutions like governments, the heteronormative patriarchal family, churches, prisons, and schools that support these dominant narratives (Goffman, 1961). Goffman would call some of these institutions, like clinics and schools, "total institutions" that hold people "captive" in them. In that sense, some scholars have referred to schooling as a total institution, especially for people of color, where "subtractive schooling" promotes rapid assimilation by stigmatizing subaltern cultures and languages and by disciplining bodies (Valenzuela, 1999). Deficit perceptions in subtractive schooling portray Other(ed) students as lacking and deficient and from families that do not value education or simply are not expected to do well in schools (Urrieta & Quach, 2000). These normative structures of schooling usually reproduce hierarchical systems with vast social and economic inequities that privilege some over others (Bourdieu & Passeron, 1990), including by "culture," often used as a proxy for race and ethnicity, but also by gender, class, and sexual orientation. In schools, official curricula are created and taught to explain away these inequities as normal and fair, such as through the myth of meritocracy (Lewis, 2003). Drawing from Foucault (1979), we pay attention to how the governmentality of these normative institutional structures in schools are internalized as "technologies of the self."

In education, however, African American and Latina/o scholarship far before the 1960s by W. E. B. DuBois, Carter G. Woodson, Anna Julia Cooper, and Alain Leroy Locke (Grant, Brown, & Brown, 2016) and George Sánchez raised demands for including the knowledge and experiences of people of color in school curricula. After the 1960s, the multicultural education movement was also an outcome of the civil rights movements. Multicultural education, although transitioned through many phases, remains a call for inclusiveness and the critical analysis of race, class, gender, sexuality, religion, and other issues central to its development (Banks, 2003; Gay, 1994; Grant & Gomez, 1996). The rise in critical education researchers of color in the 1990s such as James Anderson, James Banks, Antonia Darder, Lourdes Diaz Soto, Concha Delgado Gaitán, Daniel Solórzano, Norma González, Henry Trueba, Kris Gutiérrez, Carol Lee, Luis Moll, and Guadalupe Valdés (to name a few) and thereafter have consistently challenged and debunked the racialized and deficiency positionings of minoritized students and families.

Culturally relevant (responsive, congruent, etc.) pedagogy (Ladson-Billings, 1994) is also a social justice pedagogy that emerged from struggles around race and ethnicity in education. Culturally relevant pedagogy (CRP) challenges deficit views of students of color, their families, and communities by exhorting teachers to develop cultural competency to better meet the needs of the growing majority of students of color in public schools. Recall that the majority (80%) of teachers usually come from very segregated communities and tend to be White, middle-class, female, and monolingual and often have had little exposure to people of different racial, class, and linguistic backgrounds. For that reason, identity issues are central to CRP's theoretical underpinnings and to practice; teachers must develop sociocultural understandings of themselves as "cultural beings" in relation to others (especially of different racial and class backgrounds). Caring, high expectations, and valuing students' prior knowledge are essential in this asset-based approach to teaching. Culturally relevant teaching assists students of color in developing positive racial and ethnic identities and a critical sociopolitical consciousness to critique and challenge historical and contemporary inequities. Prominent CRP scholars include Geneva Gay, Jackie Jordan Irvine, Carl Grant, Gloria Ladson-Billings, Tyrone Howard, William Tate, and others.

Moll, Amanti, Niff, and González (1992) and González, Moll, and Amanti (2005) have also successfully rearticulated Latina/o/x immigrant family labor histories and home knowledge into a "funds of knowledge" framework that effectively challenged the deficiency approach to Latina/o/x education. Funds of knowledge reposition Latina/o/x immigrant children and their families as resource and knowledge "rich," encouraging educators to explore and use that knowledge in significant ways in their classrooms. Yosso (2005), building on ethnic studies, funds of knowledge, and CRT, also challenged the racist assumptions embedded in deficit perspectives by positing a community cultural wealth paradigm. Yosso (2005) exhorts educators to value the aspirational, linguistic, familial, social, navigational, and resistant capital Chicana/o/x students possess as forms of cultural wealth, repositioning Chicana/o/x communities as "wealthy" as opposed to culturally impoverished. Similarly, other scholars such as Chapman and Bhopal (2013) have used CRT in empowering ways to challenge perceived deficits in their communities, such as of parenting, and positing in response the ways that African American mothers advocate for their children in education.

Identity, especially racial and ethnic identity, has been a central issue in education both in detriment and in defense of people of color. Scholarship, politics, and policy in education and schooling have overwhelmingly been about race, access (gained or denied), and equity. Current trends in education indicate that race and its correlation with socioeconomic access to schools and quality of education are not going away, especially since de facto segregation continues to be a pressing problem in our society.

IDENTITY WORK AND META-ETHNOGRAPHY

The paradigmatic turn of the latter half of the past century enabled a phenomenal growth in research studies in the new millennium that explore the multiple, fluid, and changing complexities of culture and identity in education (Bartlett, 2007; Garcia, 2012; Ngo, 2010; Norton, 2000; Urrieta, 2007). The nuanced, contradictory, and process-oriented nature of identity and identification has meant that these studies of identity in education are largely, and appropriately, qualitative and ethnographic. Qualitative work allows the researcher to explore more intimate conceptualizations of and experiential knowledge of identity with participants and communities. However, because qualitative studies are marked by their focus on the particular (Noblit, 1999), it has been difficult to discern what they contribute to identity *theory* collectively.

Ethnographic work, in general, seeks to provide a nuanced and generative understanding of an issue within a larger social, cultural, historical, and political context. Ethnographic findings not only help us understand this context better in terms of these context backdrops but provide us with "insider" knowledges and knowings with theoretical explanations about "human creatures figuring out what other creatures of the same sort [and not of the same sort] are doing with, to, or around them" (Lemert, 2016, p. 2) and various other important implications. As a result, qualitative research is a perfect fit for studying identity as it incorporates a close observation of practice and the meanings people ascribe to those practices themselves. Unfortunately, it is becoming increasingly difficult to do ethnographic work given the encroaching (and often choking) neoliberal, market-based coercive politics and constraints around what counts as scientifically based research in education. This includes the ever-increasing rapid turnover of scholarly work, the high pace of knowledge production, and the increased value of shorter and shorter articles instead of longer manuscripts or books.

To contextualize why people want to produce findings, "evidence-based" approaches are driving this disposability of knowledge process in neoliberalism. The fast-paced production of scholarship, the notion of "datedness" in research that is more than a few years old (expiration date), the decontextualization and ahistoricism of findings, and research as extractivist practice (no commitment to people or communities) are partially to blame for the focus on aggregate findings and utility-oriented "best practices." Research of this sort is not theory of practice, it is theory of power, which is driven to speak to policy in reductive sound bites and bullet points. Impact is about power as opposed to understanding, and the rules of action are different than the rules of knowledge; how knowledge is generated does not fit how knowledge is constructed.

Qualitative and ethnographic methods are thus essential to the study of identity, and in this book we use the case studies to engage how ethnographic and qualitative studies can be useful through synthesis for speaking to theory. Our book therefore comes to life by becoming a "synthesis" itself for understanding how qualitative studies or "practice" can speak directly to theory. The most amazing of ethnographic and qualitative studies are those that transform the researcher's perspectives and worldviews (which are theory!) in the process. Positionality and reflexivity are important because they help the researcher understand his, her, their identity and how it influences the entire research process, including for meta-ethnographic analysis.

Meta-ethnography is not a meta-analysis, as in quantitative research, which seeks the accumulation of findings to produce a more complete version of Truth (capital T). Meta-ethnography is a comparative textual analysis of ethnographic and/or qualitative studies that seek the recovery of these complex larger social, cultural, historical, political, and theoretical contexts and their comparison across studies. Meta-ethnographers seek a "comparative understanding" rather than an aggregate understanding of cross-context interpretations and synthesis. In this process *interpretation* refers to comparative translation, while *synthesis* refers to translation of interpretations with the understanding that ethnography cannot be understood as empirical results alone. Focusing upon empirical results alone would not help us understand the contributions of ethnographic studies beyond a descriptive or theoretical level.

So what can meta-ethnography teach us about theory? Theory in meta-ethnography is seen as interpretive and inductive, an *explanatory synthesis*. Theory is understood as translations rather than generalizations across ethnographic studies selected around particular themes or topics but situated within larger nuanced contexts. The cross-study focus helps us to see "something more than what we were seeing" in a single study, or the "omissions" not addressed by the researchers. A cross-study focus pushes against the limits of normative knowledge production. Normative knowledge production includes the politics of selecting what is included in a study's findings (and what is not), researcher reflexivity, and the inherent biases and power relations of the peer review process.

Drawing from the emic perspectives and knowledges within ethnographic works and Lemert's less elitist definition of theory we might also highlight the potential contributions of meta-ethnography to theorizing from experience, theorizing from the flesh, theorizing from the mind-body-spirit in studies that use these frameworks (CRT, Chicana feminism, etc.). In that sense meta-ethnographies can contribute to alternative theories (interpretations of interpretations) of social, cultural, historical, and political exploration. This includes exploring the "something more" that is often missing—especially taking knowledge synthesis seriously in literature reviews and in teaching our students to take literature reviews seriously—but also using meta-ethnography for social and cultural theory synthesis, to inform policy studies, and to inform policy in a more nuanced and complicated way. Finally, meta-ethnographies can potentially contribute to practice and pedagogy by remaining open to different approaches and interpretations and through the intent to encourage a dialogue that informs theory and theorizing, not just what we know.

CONCLUSION

In this chapter we explored briefly the development of the concept of identity, its importance to people of color (and intersections with other aspects of identity), and its relevance to education. We also put forth our working definition of identity, identification, and culture and argued that the stakes remain high in studying identity. Identities for us are social and cultural self-understandings, individual and collective, internal and external. Identities have high emotional resonance and are embodied in people's daily lives. Through identification we all engage daily in the "work" of being certain identities by the time and effort we invest in managing how we see ourselves to be and how we want others to see us. Finally, identities are also about power, and the implications are strong for who can identify in certain ways and who can be excluded from those identifications.

To summarize, we organize identity broadly into three intersecting aspects: (a) self-making, (b) subjectivity, and (c) self-management. As self-making, identity is about how we come to make sense of who we are in relation to our own self, in relation to others, and in relation to our social and cultural worlds. As subjectivity, identity is an inner and outer process both cognitive and performative that helps us to "recognize" to whom and where we belong. Subjectivity is shaped as a life-long process of formation and becoming, never complete, that informs our inclinations, orientations, and dispositions. These in turn are shaped by the distribution of power in our lives—literally the structures that open and shut doors of possibility, creating and ending our futures for us on a daily basis. As self-management, identity is about our internal struggle to keep and organize our identities in ways that make sense to us (see Lachicotte, 2002), including our multiple consciousness within and across social and cultural worlds. Self-management is about orchestration and ordering of our self to ourselves and to others (Holland et al., 1998). Identity is therefore not just an epistemology, but it is also embodied (lived) as ontology.

REFERENCES

Acuña, R. (2000). *Occupied America: A history of Chicanos.* New York: Longman Press.

Anderson, B. (1983). *Imagined communities: Reflections on the rise and fall of nationalism.* London: Verso.

Anzaldúa, G. (1987). *Borderlands/La Frontera: The new mestiza* (4th ed.). San Francisco: Aunt Lute Books.

Apple, M. W. (1996). Power, meaning and identity: Critical sociology of education in the United States. *British Journal of Sociology of Education, 17*(2), 125–144.

Asante, M. K. (1991). The Afrocentric idea in education. *Journal of Negro Education, 60*(2), 170–180.

Banks, J. (2003). Multicultural education: Historical development, dimensions, and practice. In J. Banks & C. A. M. Banks (Eds.), *Handbook of research in multicultural education* (2nd ed., pp. 3–24). San Francisco: Jossey-Bass.

Barrera, M. (1997). A theory of racial inequality. In A. Darder, R. Torres, & H. Gutiérrez (Eds.), *Latinos and education* (pp. 3–44). New York. Routledge.

Bartlett, L. (2007). To seem and to feel: Situated identities and literacy practices. *Teachers College Record, 109*(1), 51–69

Bernal, M., Knight, G., Ocampo, K., Garza, C. & Cota, M. (1993). Development of Mexican American identity. In M. Bernal & G. Knight (Eds.), *Ethnic identity: Formation and transmission among Hispanics and other minorities* (pp. 31–46). Albany: State University of New York Press.

Bhabha, H. K. (1996). Cultural diversity and cultural differences. In B. Ashcroft, G. Griffiths, & H. Tiffin (Eds.), *The post-colonial studies reader* (pp. 206–209). London: Routledge.

Boaler, J., & Greeno, J. G. (2000). Identity, agency, and knowing in mathematics worlds. In J. Boaler (Ed.), *Multiple perspectives on mathematics teaching and learning* (pp. 171–200). Westport, CT: Ablex.

Borofsky, R., Barth, F., Shweder, R., Rodseth, L., & Stolzenberg, N. M. (2001). A conversation about culture. *American Anthropologist, 103*(2), 432–446.

Bourdieu, P. (1977). *Outline of a theory of practice.* New York: Cambridge University Press.

Bourdieu, P. (1991). The peculiar history of scientific reason. *Sociological Forum, 6*(1), 3–26.

Bourdieu, P., & Passeron, J. C. (1990). *Reproduction in education, society, and culture* (Vol. 4). Thousand Oaks, CA: SAGE.

Brown, A., & Donner, J. K. (2011). Toward a new narrative on black males, education, and public policy. *Race Ethnicity and Education, 14*(1), 17–32.

Brown, K. (2016). *After the "at-risk" label: Reorienting educational policy and practice.* New York: Teachers College Press.

Brubaker, R., & Cooper, F. (2000). Beyond "identity." *Theory and Society, 29*(1), 1–47.

Butler, J. (1990). *Gender trouble: Feminism and the subversion of identity.* London: Routledge.

Calderón, D. (2014). Uncovering settler grammars in curriculum. *Educational Studies, 50*(4), 313–338.

Calhoun, C. (1994). *Social theory and the politics of identity,* Malden, MA: Blackwell.

Calhoun, C. (1997). Nationalism and the public sphere. In J. Weintraub & K. Kumar (Eds.), *Public and private in thought and practice* (pp. 75–102). Chicago: University of Chicago Press.

Carrillo, J. (2013). I always knew I was gifted: Latino males and the meztiz@ theory of intelligences (MTI). *Berkeley Review of Education, 4*(1), 69–95.

Carter, R. T., & Goodwin, A. L. (1994). Racial identity and education. *Review of Research in Education, 20,* 291–336.

Castells, M. (2006). *The power of identity, Vol. II* (2nd ed.). Malden, MA: Blackwell.

Chapman, T., & Bhopal, K. (2013). Countering common-sense understandings of "good parenting": Women of color advocating for their children. *Race Ethnicity and Education, 16*(4), 562–586.

Cokley, K. O. (2002). Testing Cross's revised racial identity model: An examination of the relationship between racial identity and internalized racism. *Journal of Counseling Psychology, 49*(4), 476–483.

Collins, P. H. (1990). *Black feminist thought.* Boston: Unwin Hyman.

Comaroff, J., & Comaroff, J. (2009). *Ethnicity Inc.* Chicago: University of Chicago Press.

Crenshaw, K. (1989). Demarginalizing the intersection of race and sex: A Black feminist critique of antidiscrimination doctrine. *University of Chicago Legal Forum, 1989,* 139–168.

Crenshaw, K. (1995). Mapping the margins: Intersectionality, identity politics, and violence against women of color. In K. Crenshaw, N. Gotanda, G. Peller, & K. Thomas (Eds.), *Critical race theory: The key writings that formed the movement* (pp. 357–383). New York: The New Press.

Cross, W. E. Jr. (1971). The Negro-to-Black conversion experience. *Black World, 20*(9), 13–27.

Cross, W. E. Jr. (1991). *Shades of black: Diversity of African-American identity.* Philadelphia: Temple University Press.

Cusicanqui, S. R. (2012). Ch'ixinakax utxiwa: A reflection on the practices and discourses of decolonization. *South Atlantic Quarterly, 111*(1), 95–109.

Davies, B., & Harré, R. (1990). Positioning: The discursive production of selves. *Journal for the Theory of Social Behaviour, 20*(1), 43–63.

de Lissovoy, N. (2016). *Education and emancipation in the neoliberal era: Being, teaching, and power.* New York: Springer.

Della Porta, D., & Diani, M. (2006). *Social movements: An introduction.* Malden, MA: Blackwell.

DeWalt, P. S. (2011). In search of an authentic African American and/or Black identity: Perspectives of first generation US-born Africans attending a predominantly White institution. *Journal of Black Studies, 42*(3), 479–503.

Donato, R., & Hanson, J. (2012). Legally white, socially "Mexican": The politics of de jure and de facto school segregation in the American Southwest. *Harvard Educational Review, 82*(2), 202–225.

Doyle, L. H. (2003). Synthesis through meta-ethnography: Paradoxes, enhancements, and possibilities. *Qualitative Research, 3*(3), 321–344.

DuBois, W. E. B. (1903). *The souls of Black folk.* New York: Bantam Classic.

Durkheim, E. (1951). *Suicide: A study in psychology.* New York: The Free Press. (Original work published 1897)

Elliott, A. (2016). *Identity troubles: An introduction.* London: Routledge.

Erikson, E. (1950). *Childhood and society.* New York: W. W. Norton.

Fanon, F. (1963). *The wretched of the earth.* New York: Grove Press.

Fanon, F. (1967). *Black skin, white masks.* New York: Grove Press.

Foley, D. (1997). Deficit thinking models based on culture: The anthropological protest. In R. Valencia (Ed.), *The evolution of deficit thinking: Educational thought and practice* (pp. 113–131). Washington, DC: Falmer Press.

Foucault, M. (1978). *The history of sexuality,* Vol. I: *An introduction.* New York: Pantheon.

Foucault, M. (1979). On governmentality. *Ideology and Consciousness, 6,* 5–21.

Freud, S. (1900). *The interpretation of dreams.* London: Hogarth.

García, L. (2012). *Respect yourself, protect yourself: Latina girls and sexual identity.* New York: New York University Press.

Gay, G. (1994). Coming of age ethnically: Teaching young adolescents of color. *Theory into Practice, 33*(3), 149–155.

Gee, J. P. (2000–2001). Identity as an analytic lens for research in education. *Review of Research in Education, 25,* 99–125.

Geertz, C. (1973). *The interpretation of cultures: Selected essays.* New York: Basic Books.

Giddens, A. (1991). *Modernity and self-identity: Self and society in the Late Modern Age.* Cambridge, UK: Polity Press.

Grant, C., & Gomez, M. L. (1996). *Making schooling multicultural: Campus and classroom.* New York: Simon & Schuster.

Goffman, E. (1961). *Asylums: Essays of the social situation of mental patients and other inmates.* Garden City, NJ: Anchor Books.

González, N. (1999). What will we do when culture does not exist anymore? *Anthropology & Education Quarterly, 30*(4), 431–435.

González, N., Moll, L., & Amanti, C. (2005). *Funds of knowledge: Theorizing practices in households, communities, and classrooms.* Mahwah, NJ: Lawrence Erlbaum Associates.

Grant, C. A., & Zwier, E. (Eds.). (2014). *Intersectionality and urban education: Identities, policies, spaces & power* (Urban Education Studies Series). Charlotte, NC: Information Age.

Grant, C., Brown, K., & Brown, A. (2016). *Black intellectual thought in education: The missing traditions of Anna Julia Cooper, Carter G. Woodson, and Alain LeRoy Locke.* New York: Routledge.

Grossberg, L. (1996). Identity and cultural studies: Is that all there is? In S. Hall & P. du Gay (Eds.), *Questions of cultural identity* (Vol. 126, pp. 87–107). Thousand Oaks, CA: SAGE.

Guha, R., & Spivak, G. C. (1988). *Selected subaltern studies.* New York: Oxford University Press.

Gutiérrez, K., & Rogoff, B. (2003). Cultural ways of learning: Individual traits or repertoires of practice. *Educational Researcher, 32*(5), 19–25.

Hall, S. (1992). Race, culture, and communications: Looking backward and forward at cultural studies. *Rethinking Marxism, 5*(1), 10–18.

Hall, S. (1996). Introduction: Who needs identity? In S. Hall & P. du Gay (Eds.), *Questions of cultural identity* (Vol. 126, pp. 1–17). London: SAGE.

Harvey, D. (1989). *The condition of postmodernity: An enquiry into the origins of social change.* Malden, MA: Blackwell.

Hatt, B. (2007). Street smarts vs. street smarts: The figured world of smartness in the lives of marginalized urban youth. *The Urban Review, 39*(2), 145–166.

Hatt, B. (2012). Smartness as a cultural practice in schools. *American Educational Research Journal, 49*(3), 438–460.

Helms, J. (1990). *Black and White racial identity: Theory, research, and practice.* New York: Greenwood Press.

Holland, D. C., & Lave, J. (2001). *History-in-person: Enduring struggles, contentious practice, intimate identities.* Santa Fe, NM: School of American Research.

Holland, D. C., & Lave, J. (2009). Social practice theory and the historical production of persons. *Actio: An International Journal of Human Activity Theory, 2,* 1–15.

Holland, D., Lachicotte, W. Jr., Skinner, D., & Cain, C. (1998). *Identity and agency in cultural worlds,* Cambridge, MA: Harvard University Press.

Holquist, M. (1990). *Dialogism: Bakhtin and his world.* New York: Routledge.

Horton Cooley, C. (1902). *Human nature and the social order.* New York: Scribner's.

James, W. (1890). *The principles of psychology.* New York: Henry Holt.

Jurow, A. S. (2005). Shifting engagements in figured worlds: Middle school mathematics students' participation in an architectural design project. *Journal of the Learning Sciences, 14*(1), 35–67.

Keating, A. (2006). From the borderlands and new mestizas to nepatlas and nepantleras: Anzaldúan theories for social change. *Journal of Sociology of Self-Knowledge, 4*(3), 5–16.

Lachicotte, W. (2002). Intimate powers, public selves: Bakhtin's space of authoring. In J. Mageo (Ed.), *Power and the self* (pp. 48–66). Cambridge, UK: Cambridge University Press.

Ladson-Billings, G. (1994). *The dreamkeepers: Successful teachers of African American children.* San Francisco: Jossey Bass.

Ladson-Billings, G. (2011). Boyz to men? Teaching to restore Black boys' childhood. *Race Ethnicity and Education, 14*(1), 7–15.

Lave, J., & Wenger, E. (1991). *Situated learning: Legitimate peripheral participation.* Cambridge, UK: Cambridge University Press.

Leander, K. M. (2002). Locating Latanya: The situated production of identity artifacts in classroom interaction. *Research in the Teaching of English, 37,* 198–250.

LeCourt, D. (2004). *Identity matters: Schooling and the student body in academic discourse.* Albany: State University of New York Press.

Lei, J. L. (2003). (Un)Necessary toughness? Those "loud Black girls" and those "quiet Asian boys." *Anthropology and Education Quarterly, 34*(2), 158–181.

Lemert, C. (2012). A history of identity: The riddle at the heart of the mystery of life. In A. Elliot (Ed.), *Routledge handbook of identity studies* (pp. 3–29). New York: Routledge.

Lemert, C. (2016). *Social theory: The multicultural, global, and classic readings* (6th ed.). Boulder, CO: Westview Press.

Leve, L. (2011). Identity. *Current Anthropology, 52*(4), 513–535.

Lewis, A. (2003). *Race in the schoolyard: Negotiating the color line in classrooms and community.* New Brunswick, NJ: Rutgers University Press.

Loomba, A. (1998). *Colonialism/postcolonialism.* London. Routledge.

Luttrell, W., & Parker, C. (2001). High school students' literacy practices and identities, and the figured world of school. *Journal of Research in Reading, 24*(3), 235–247.

Mariscal, K., Velásquez, Y., Agüero, A., & Urrieta, L. (2017). Latina urban education: At the crossroads of intersectional violence. In W. Pink & G. Noblit (Eds.), *Second international handbook of urban education* (pp. 875–886). New York: Springer International.

McDermott, R., & Verenne, H. (1995). Culture as disability. *Anthropology and Education Quarterly, 26*(3), 324–348.

Marcia, J. E. (1966). Development and validation of ego-identity status. *Journal of Personality and Social Psychology, 3*(5), 551–558.

Marx, K., & Engels, F. (1998). *Communist manifesto.* London: Verso. (Original work published 1848)

Mead, G. H. (1913). The social self. *Journal of Philosophy, 10,* 374–380.

Mead, G. H. (1925). The genesis of the self and social control. *International Journal of Ethics, 35,* 251–277.

Melucci, A. (1988). Getting involved: Identity and mobilization in social movements. *International Social Movements Research, 1,* 329–348.

Melucci, A. (1989). New perspectives on social movements: An interview with Alberto Melucci. In J. Keane & P. Mier (Eds.), *Nomads of the present: Social movements and individual needs in contemporary society* (pp. 180–232). Philadelphia: Temple University Press.

Melucci, A. (1990). The voice of the roots: Ethno-national mobilizations in a global world. *European Journal of Social Science Research, 3*(3), 351–363.

Mills, C. W. (1997). *The racial contract.* Ithaca, NY: Cornell University Press.

Moll, L., Amanti, C., Niff, D., & González, N. (1992). Funds of knowledge for teaching: Using a qualitative approach to connect homes and classrooms. *Theory into Practice, 31*(2), 132–141.

Moran, A. (2011). Indigenous identities: From colonialism to post- colonialism. In A. Elliot (Ed.), *Handbook of identity studies* (pp. 347–363). London: Taylor & Francis.

Martin Alcoff, L., & Mohanty, S. (2006). Reconsidering identity politics: An introduction. In L. Martin Alcoff, M. Hames-Garcia, S. Mohanty, & P. Moya (Eds.), *Identity politics reconsidered* (pp. 1–9). New York: Palgrave.

Moreton-Robinson, A. (2016). *Critical indigenous studies: Engagements in first world locations*. Tucson: University of Arizona Press.

Moya, P. (2002). *Learning from experience: Minority identities, multicultural struggles*. Berkeley: University of California Press.

Muñoz, C. Jr. (1989). *Youth, identity, and power: The Chicano movement*. New York: Verso.

Ngo, B. (2010). *Unresolved identities: Discourse, ambivalence, and urban immigrant students*. Albany: State University of New York Press.

Noblit, G. (1999). *Particularities: Collected Essays on ethnography and education*. New York: Peter Lang.

Noblit, G., & Hare, D. (1988). *Meta-ethnography: Synthesizing qualitative studies*. Thousand Oaks, CA: SAGE.

Norton, B. (2000). *Identity and language learning: Gender, ethnicity, and educational change*. London: Longman.

Ott, B. (2003). "I'm Bart Simpson, who the hell are you?": A study in postmodern identity (re)construction. *Journal of Popular Culture, 37*(1), 56–82.

Pacheco, M. (2014). Nepantleras in the new Latino diaspora: The intersectional experiences of bi/multilingual youth. In C. A. Grant & E. Zwier (Eds.), *Intersectionality and urban education: Identities, policies, spaces & power* (pp. 97–123). (Urban Education Studies Series): Charlotte, NC: Information Age.

Phinney, J. (1989). Stages of ethnic identity development in minority group adolescents. *Journal of Early Adolescence, 9*, 34–49.

Phinney, J. (1990). Ethnic identity in adolescents and adults: Review of the research. *Psychological Bulletin, 108*(3), 499–514.

Phinney, J. (1993). A three stage model of ethnic identity development in adolescence. In M. E. Bernal & G. P. Knight (Eds.), *Ethnic identity: Formation and transmission among Hispanics and other minorities* (pp. 61–79). Albany: State University of New York Press.

Pizarro, M. (2005). *Chicanas and Chicanos in school: Racial profiling, identity battles, and empowerment*. Austin: University of Texas Press.

Pizarro, M., & Vera, E. M. (2001). Chicana/o ethnic identity research: Lessons for researchers and counselors. *The Counseling Psychologist, 29*(1), 91–117.

Pulido, L. (2006). *Black, brown, yellow and left: Radical activism in Los Angeles*. Berkeley: University of California Press.

Rabaka, R. (2010). *Africana critical theory: Reconstructing the Black radical tradition, from W. E. B. Du Bois and C. L. R. James to Franz Fanon and Amilcar Cabral*. Lanham, MD: Lexington Books.

Ramírez, R. (2006). *Native hubs: Culture, community, and belonging in Silicon Valley and beyond*. Durham, NC: Duke University Press.

Rogoff, B. (2016). Culture and participation: A paradigm shift. *Current Opinion in Psychology, 8*, 182–189.

Rubin, B. C. (2007). Learner identity amid figured worlds: Constructing (in)competence at an urban high school. *The Urban Review, 39*(2), 217–249.

Said, E. W. (1978). *Orientalism* (1st ed.). New York: Pantheon Books.

Sarup, M. (1996). *Identity, culture, and the postmodern world*. Athens: University of Georgia Press.

Saxe, G. B. (2003). Ethnic and academic identities: A cultural practice perspective on emerging tensions and their management in the lives of minority students. *Educational Researcher, 32*(5), 14–18.

Schwartz, S., Luyckx, K., & Vignoles, V. (2011). *Handbook of identity theory and research*. New York: Springer.

Seidler, V. (2010). *Embodying identities: Culture, differences, and social theory*. Bristol, UK: Policy Press.

Simmel, G. (1903). *The metropolis and mental life*. Dresden, Germany: Petermann.

Simpson, A., & Smith, A. (2014). *Theorizing native studies*. Durham, NC: Duke University Press.

Skutnabb-Kangas, T. (2000). *Linguistic genocide in education—or worldwide diversity?* Mahwah, NJ: Lawrence Erlbaum Associates.

Sloan, K. (2006). Teacher identity and agency in school worlds: Beyond the all-good/all-bad discourse on accountability-explicit curriculum policies. *Curriculum Inquiry, 36*(2), 119–152.

Smith, L. T. (1999). *Decolonizing methodologies: Research and indigenous peoples*. London: Zed Books.

Smith, P. (1988). *Discerning the subject*. Minneapolis: University of Minnesota Press.

Solórzano, D. G., & Delgado Bernal, D. (2001). Examining transformational resistance through a critical race and LatCrit theory framework: Chicana and Chicano students in an urban context. *Urban Education, 36*(3), 308–342.

Spivak, G. C. (2012). *Outside the teaching machine*. London: Routledge.

Steger, M. (2009). *Globalisms: The great ideological divide of the twenty-first century*. Lanham, MD: Rowman & Littlefield.

Sturges, K. (2015). *Neoliberalizing educational reform*. Rotterdam: Sense Publishers.

Tatum, B. D. (1997). *Why are all the Black kids sitting together in the cafeteria?* New York: Basic Books.

Tonso, K. L. (2006). Student engineers and engineer identity: Campus engineer identities as figured worlds. *Cultural Studies of Science Education, 1*, 273–307.

Urrieta, L. Jr. (2007). Identity production in figured worlds: How some Mexican Americans become Chicana/o activist educators. *The Urban Review, 39*(2), 117–144.

Urrieta, L. Jr. (2009). *Working from within: Chicana and Chicano activist educators in whitestream schools*. Tucson: University of Arizona Press.

Urrieta, L. Jr. (2013). Familia and comunidad-based saberes: Learning in an indigenous heritage community. *Anthropology & Education Quarterly, 44*(3), 320–335.

Urrieta, L. Jr. (2015). Learning by observing and pitching-in and the connections to indigenous knowledge systems. *Advances in Child Development and Behavior, 49*, 357–379.

Urrieta, L. Jr., Martin, K., & Robinson, C. (2011). "I am in school!": African American male youth in a prison/college hybrid figured world. *The Urban Review, 43*(4), 491–506.

Urrieta, L. Jr., & Quach, L. (2000). My language speaks of me: Transmutational identities and L2 acquisition. *The High School Journal, 84*(1), 26–35.

Urrieta, L. Jr., & Villenas, S. (2013). The legacy of Derrick Bell and Latina/o education: A critical race testimonio. *Race Ethnicity and Education, 16*(4), 514–535.

Vågen, A. (2011). Towards a sociocultural perspective on identity formation in education. *Mind, Culture, and Activity, 18*(1), 43–57.

Valencia, R. (Ed.). (1997). *The evolution of deficit thinking: Educational thought and practice*. Washington, DC: Falmer Press.

Valenzuela, A. (1999). *Subtractive schooling: U.S.-Mexican youth and the politics of caring*. Albany: State University of New York Press.

Weber, M. (1958). *The Protestant Ethic and the Spirit of Capitalism*. New York: Scribner's. (Original work published 1905)

Wenger, E. (1999). *Communities of practice: Learning, meaning, and identity*. New York: Cambridge University Press.

Wetherell, M., & Mohanty, C. T. (2010). *The SAGE handbook of identities*. Thousand Oaks, CA: SAGE.

Whittier, N. (1995). *Feminist generations: The persistence of the radical women's movement*. Philadelphia: Temple University Press.

Wojciehowski, D. (1995). *Old masters, new subjects: Early modern and poststructuralist theories of will*. Stanford, CA: Stanford University Press.

Wortham, S. (2004). From good student to outcast: The emergence of a classroom identity. *Ethos, 32*(2), 164–187.

Wortham, S. (2005). *Learning identity: The joint emergence of social identification and academic learning*. New York: Cambridge University Press.

Yosso, T. (2005). Whose culture has capital?: A critical race theory discussion of community cultural wealth. *Race Ethnicity and Education, 8*(1), 69–91.

2

Meta-Ethnography

Adaptation and Return

GEORGE W. NOBLIT ■

INTRODUCTION

Our original work on meta-ethnography is now almost 30 years old. There was little response when it was published. Harry Wolcott, the educational anthropologist now deceased, complained at an American Educational Research Association meeting in 1989 not about the concept but that nonanthropologists were making a claim to the term *ethnography*. But that was about it. Today, meta-ethnography is well established in health research and now is being picked up in education. A special issue of *Ethnography and Education* on meta-ethnography in education was published in 2017 (Kakos & Fritzsche, 2017), and Elsie Rockwell and Kathryn Anderson-Levitt edited a book also in 2017 for the American Educational Research Association comparing education ethnographies across borders that pushes new ways of thinking about speaking across ethnographies. This book started before these efforts but clearly has been energized by them.

This book came about because Luis Urrieta mentioned to me that he felt this tool had been left aside and from his perspective needed to be reintroduced to education. Luis, though, unlike many of whom I worked with on qualitative synthesis projects as a consultant over the years (e.g., the team led by Campbell and Britten; [cf. Britten et al., 2002], Margarete Sandelowski's group, and with a project with the Education Development Center), was primarily concerned about social theory. I had bemoaned the focus on empirical findings and on a naïve utilitarianism that puts a focus on what practices should result from knowing what studies said (Thorne, Jensen, Kearney, Noblit, & Sandelowski, 2004). But Luis was asking: What is the relationship of meta-ethnography and theory (and theorizing, as many of us speak about the role of theory in qualitative research)? Luis then set off a chain of events that led to this book. He and I began musing about the role of theory on qualitative research and what Dwight Hare and I had not understood when we wrote *Meta-Ethnography* (Noblit & Hare, 1988). I was also fortunate in that the noted Thai scholar Rattana Buosonte was interested in these ideas and came to the University of North Carolina to work through them with me. He sponsored an international conference in 2014 at Naresuan University where I, Summer Pennell, and Hillary Parkhouse were able to update our understandings of meta-ethnography for a new audience. All this pushed Luis and I to move on this book.

Like so many scholars today, Luis and I work via networks—some we share and some that are unique to each of us. However, one network that we shared had been working on identity studies over many years, and some of these same scholars were also conducting meta-ethnographies through a work group at the University of North Carolina at Chapel Hill. We reached out to this network and found interest in taking part, and people began to shift their work toward this project. Luis and I owe a debt of gratitude to the authors here for both shifting their work to be part of this and for their tolerance with a project based in shifting sands of our understanding of both meta-ethnography and identity theory.

Luis, in the first chapter, recounts how we came to understand identity theory. I do the parallel here for meta-ethnography.

META-ETHNOGRAPHY'S ORIGIN

There is not space in this chapter to write a history of research methods and qualitative methods in particular. However, it is important to locate meta-ethnography's origins. The original book idea was conceived in the mid-1980s in the midst of the qualitative-quantitative paradigm wars and other crises in thought. While qualitative methods, understood as observation, had been the basis of the early social, cultural, and psychological sciences, as quantitative methods developed scholars argued qualitative approaches were not "scientific." For many years, qualitative research, as we now know it, struggled to maintain itself outside of anthropology. However, by the 1960s, qualitative research experienced a resurgence in popularity in part brought on by the notion that qualitative research created the ideas that could later be "tested" via quantitative research. In larger part, though, qualitative research "came back" because of what was called the "legitimation crisis" (Habermas, 1975) of the West. As is well known, the 1960s and 1970s in the United States were characterized by civil rights, anti-war, and youth protest movements. These movements questioned the ideas that legitimated governments. Further, social scientists came to be seen as part of the legitimation process—and thus were not to be trusted. "Objectivity" came to be seen as a "god trick" (Haraway, 1988), representing the dominant groups' perspectives. But in any case, the challenges to intellectual (as well as other) authority led to considerable contestation between quantitative and qualitative methods—the "paradigm wars" (Gage, 1989). Since then qualitative research has burgeoned and is the approach of choice of those who wish to understand how social and cultural life works, how what seem to be objective facts are socially con-structed, and what taken-for-granted assumptions undergird both.

Anthropology had long been concerned with speaking across cultures and had called this effort *ethnology*. With ethnology, the goal was general theories beyond the cultures from which the practices were extracted. In the end, though, ethnol-ogy was a way of establishing the superiority of Western thought and giving it dominion over the ideas of other groups. Hymes, in discussing an ethnology of education ethnography, also set the stage for a primary and devastating critique that would, a few years later, undercut the ethnological project. He wrote: "One way to describe anthropology is to say that it has divided the world into names—names of peoples, languages, cultures—that it has made legitimate objects of knowledge" (Hymes, 1980, p. 4). Anthropology's "crisis of representation" in the mid-1980s led to reading ethnology's goal of achieving a greater understanding as another form of Western dominance (Marcus & Fisher, 1986).

The critique of Marcus and Fisher (1986) was devastating to both ethnography and ethnology—but in the politicized paradigm wars, qualitative research, even given the colonial origins of ethnography, was ironically positioned as represent-ing the "emic" or grounded perspectives of the people.

META-ETHNOGRAPHY IN PRACTICE

As Dwight Hare and I developed our ideas around meta-ethnography, we were fully engaged in the aforementioned "wars" and "crises"—even if we did not fully understand their ultimate implications. At that time we were able to speak about fields of study and to focus on interpretations (not objective findings), as well as a translation theory of synthesis rather than an aggregative theory such as that used with meta-analysis. Meta-ethnography posits that interpretations need to be synthesized. Meta-ethnography, in the end, constitutes additional layers of inter-pretation. Further, meta-ethnographic syntheses are not simply an aggregation of the interpretations already made in the studies being synthesized. Instead, meta-ethnography sees synthesis as involving translation—the translation of the whole interpretations (we like to think of these as storylines) of each study (not the indi-vidual themes, concepts, or elements) into one another.

As with all qualitative research, the results are not generalizable to wider popu-lations. In the place of generalization, meta-ethnography seeks a *specification* of what the studies as a whole are about and then goes deeper into the meanings evi-dent in this specified realm (Hughes & Noblit, 2017). The synthesis process may result in new interpretations and new questions (beyond those contained in the studies included in the synthesis), which reveal the value of the synthesis itself. But we must be clear: meta-ethnography does not automatically yield new "third order" interpretation (Ecker & Hulley, 1996, 2000). Sometimes studies, when put together, are replicative. This is important to know. It tells us that different scholars and different contexts are producing similar accounts. We may conclude that we have a "settled" interpretation. A settled interpretation may tell us that research has sufficiently understood the phenomenon of interest, but it also may mean that it is time for qualitative researchers to dig deeper and unpack the phenomenon of interest in different ways, deploying different theory, positionality, and/or perspectives. While there are many who want research synthesis to yield a more definitive truth, it is not our experience that this is what results. Research—and science—do not work that way. Every finding leads to new questions, and every synthesis does likewise.

In meta-ethnography, there is a tension between identifying the salient themes/concepts/metaphors that can reduce the account to a manageable level and preserving the salient contexts in which these themes/concepts/metaphors make sense. Translating full storylines is more complex than concept by concept but well worth the effort. At times, the focus on storylines recast what seems to be a similarity or difference (when focusing on individual themes/concepts/metaphors) into a different understanding that belies the surface similarities or differences of the individual themes/concepts/ metaphors. Such translations make fuller use of the interpretations provided in the studies and allow a more complete synthesis as well.

The nature of the translation itself was, and is, based on Turner's (1980) *Sociological Explanation as Translation,* in which he examines comparative explanations. Turner argued that one society's practices, and the concepts used to describe such practices, may vary from those of another society. In making comparisons, then, one may either use a concept from one society or create a new concept to enable the translation between the two accounts. In this, explanation is a form of translation, and "an adequate translation would yield us claims that had the same implications" (p. 53) in both accounts. Synthesis as translation starts with a puzzle asking where one study says *x*, what is another study saying? Addressing this puzzle requires formulating an analogy between the studies. As we consider more studies, we may find that the translation/analogy offered with the initial studies does not hold up. In this, Turner argues that it is necessary to examine settings and contexts to make a translation that works across the studies. "Our goal will be to find a rule, or an analogy, that will not break down" (p. 56).

Meta-ethnographic synthesis, then, involves the process of "setting, rejecting, and replacing puzzles" and providing the "grounds and considerations" (Turner, 1980, p. 57) for such. The process involves setting a puzzle, exploring "the surrounding customs, practices and circumstances," and describing the "practices and circumstances" as analogies or "game variations" (p. 57). This process is clearly more involved than that employed in many meta-ethnographic studies, which end with identifying how the themes are similar or different across studies. Synthesis as translation would see this as simply the grounds for setting the puzzle and starting the process of translating studies into one another. Noblit and Hare (1988) posit there are at least three forms of such translations: reciprocal (studies are directly translatable into one another), refutational (studies contradict one another), and line of argument (studies have overlap but when compared reveal the studies are addressing different aspects of a larger explanation than any one study posits). These are not necessarily mutually exclusive. Reciprocal translations can be subsets of lines of arguments and so on.

Further, meta-ethnography was built on an understanding of language and interpretation as essentially metaphoric. That is, when humans (and scholars are not exceptions) explain or describe something, they use concepts and images that already exist in the language, and thus the application of these words or concepts makes them metaphors—"as if" characterizations. When Margaret Mead (1928) talked about the culture of Samoa, it was not literally true that men governed the day and women governed the night—rather *if* we understood Samoa culture this way we would have insight into its nature. It was *as if* day and night explained metaphorically the culture in ways we, in our culture, could make sense of. Not all qualitative researchers are as metaphorically eloquent as Margaret Mead, but all use metaphors drawn from other domains of language and life to characterize that which they wish to explain. Unfortunately, we must conclude from reading a host of meta-ethnographies to date that both the understanding of interpretive story-lines and concepts/themes as metaphors and synthesis as translation has proven quite challenging to scholars. We hope this volume will help those conducting meta-ethnographies to accept these challenges more readily, even if their execution remains difficult.

Many other things have changed since Dwight Hare and I wrote *Meta-Ethnography* as well. First, and most obviously, qualitative research has "taken off" in popularity. It has moved well beyond anthropology and sociology into a wide range of disciplines, including education, nursing, allied health, and other fields. There are new journals and countless methodological innovations. The numbers of qualitative studies in any year is literally countless. Thus the need for synthesis has become more evident as time passes. Further, those doing syntheses in this expanding context of the expansion have found our original focus on ethnographies not necessary. We originally focused on ethnographies because they were the "gold standard" qualitative research in the 1980s. However, it is now clear that this standard was not defensible. Researchers have found case study approaches, narrative and life history approaches, participant observation approaches, and so on all have something to recommend them. Thus pragmatically meta-ethnography is no longer limited to ethnographies. Using meta-ethnography with all forms of qualitative research has proven successful. We hold to the term not to limit what research can be synthesized but rather to signal a synthesis approach that is interpretive (and critical, which we come to next) and using a translation theory of explanation. Synthesis approaches that emphasize "findings," focus on individual themes or concepts, and aggregate instead of translate studies, we would argue, end up reducing studies rather than interpreting them as a set in relation to one another.

Finlayson and Dixon (2008) reviewed qualitative meta-synthesis for researchers in nursing. In their review, they correctly noted that our book did not comment on search procedures necessary and issues of study quality in relation to inclusion or exclusion. It is clear that the common practice used in health research is to couple a systematic review with meta-ethnography. This has notable advantages of course. It enables a reasonable claim to be including all relevant studies and thus to be able to speak broadly about a field of studies. Yet it is also clear that a purposive sampling of studies may be appropriate (Finfgeld-Connett & Johnson, 2013; France et al. 2014). Clearly, there are many search procedures possible, and in this volume the reader will see authors use purpose as the driver that leads to the search—which then may be understood as something like exhaustive. We say "something like exhaustive" because while the authors did search widely, they were doing so as part of a larger process that may be called *specification*. While Luis and I are ecumenical on issues of quality in study selection, we think quality checklists based on ideas of good methodology and research procedures need to be justified on the basis that they are not excluding on genre rather than quality. The criteria used for quality deserve interrogation in themselves and authors should be explicit about the kinds of qualitative research that is excluded when quality is used as an inclusion/exclusion criteria. The authors in this volume did not employ formal quality assessments. They were purposive about finding studies that (a) focused on identity and/or identity theory, (b) were critical in orientation, and (c) were loosely about youth (up to 24 years of age was a starting guideline). These were less hard criteria than ways of specifying what they in the end were going to speak about through their respective meta-ethnographies. For example, Martin and Locklear in their chapter in this volume were dismayed by the deficit nature of many of the studies they found on Native American youth. They then excluded the deficit studies based on their increasing specified purpose of speaking about the construction of a positive identity for American Indians. *Specification* suggests that while initial purpose drives the search, the purpose is altered, or specified, by what the search reveals. This then pushes back against the proposal common in the literature that a good research question is set in the beginning. Our authors had an intent that was complex, and as they pushed the complex purposes through the search, they specified what they were about in the synthesis. Luis and I want to be clear. We are not saying the correct approach to meta-ethnography is what we have described. It is one approach that speaks against being overly prescriptive about search processes.

Another major shift since the 1988 volume concerns the use of theory in qualitative research. At the time of that volume, theory was in the midst of a sea change. On the one hand, grounded theory, which held to an inductive logic, was dominant in several fields, such as sociology, education, and nursing. Yet it was also true that critical theory had emerged as a challenge to functionalism, and indeed the 1988 volume engaged this theoretical difference in the example of a refutational synthesis. In anthropology, the "crisis of representation" (Marcus & Fisher, 1986) had come to a head, a point also recognized in *Meta-Ethnography*. While much more can be said about these times, the essential point was soon to be clear to qualitative researchers in general—research was not value-neutral but rather expressed ideological beliefs about the nature of the world. Moreover, functionalist approaches were found to be grounded in an imperialistic gaze and justified the power of elites. By the late 1980s, critical ethnography had emerged as a powerful and revealing genre of qualitative research.

Since then critique has become a central theoretical logic of social research as critical feminist, critical race, LatCrit, tribal critical, critical whiteness, queer critical, critical disability (and so on) theories became dominant lenses for qualitative research. Paterson, Thorne, Canam, and Jillings (2001) in their development of "meta-study" as a qualitative synthesis approach recognized the emerging importance of theory, and we are thankful for their efforts and encourage scholars to engage their approach. Their approach made theory one of the syntheses to be conducted in a meta-study. For us, however, theory and interpretation are intimately intertwined. Thus our approach is to engage theory as central to interpretation and storyline (and to positionality as well) and less as a separate sphere of research activity. The original intent for meta-ethnography to understand a field of studies means today that theory must be engaged in synthesis. However, qualitative synthesis has been largely captured by notions of "evidence-based" practice, which turns synthesis away from ideas and theory. We hope in this volume to return meta-ethnography to the focus on fields of research themselves, and today that means engaging theory and critique as part of synthesis. We wish to be clear that we do not hold this approach as more important or appropriate than a focus on practice but rather hope to reinvigorate a focus on fields of study and theory.

The crisis of representation in anthropology also led to a reconsideration of who is speaking in ethnographic texts. It became apparent that the ethnography was the author's account, not an account of the participants. Clearly, the participants' accounts were part of the author's account but the author used them to her or his own ends. By the late 1980s, many qualitative studies included a "the researcher as instrument" section, but as the fuller implications of the crisis of representation led to "new ethnography" (cf. Goodall, 2000), authors were experimenting with many ways to reveal their hands in the construction of the ethnography. This, of course, was helped greatly by feminist ethnographers who drew on "standpoint" epistemology (Collins, 1990) in ways that not only changed ethnographic practice but served as a wholesale critique of natural science approaches to the social sciences. Today, a qualitative researcher routinely speaks of her or his positionality (Goodall, 2000; Noblit, Flores, & Murrillo, 2004) in rather complex ways. Theoretical stances are part of positionality as are all perspectives the researcher brings into a qualitative study. Shifts in qualitative research practice since our 1988 book now argues that both theory and positionality are part of the interpretation and that those doing the synthesis need to explicate their positionality and how this interpolates with the synthesis they offer (Doyle, 2003). This volume pushes in both of these directions.

META-ETHNOGRAPHY IN EDUCATION

We have chosen to focus this volume on the relationship of meta-ethnography with theory and theorizing. There are many reasons for this, but our primary reason is that meta-ethnography is, at base, about the nature of knowledge. Further, Luis and I share a concern about the instrumentalism that undergirds evidence-based practice. Gregson, Meal, and Avis (2002), for example, have argued for rejecting the naïve realism that undergirds the idea of truth as correspondence to reality that characterizes much of quantitative meta-analysis. Given that we are dealing with qualitative meta-synthesis here, we do not review their full argument but rather focus on their point that "a narrow epistemology, which gives exclusive precedence to scientific rationality, is not, in itself, sufficient to answer important questions about how we ought to practice" (p. 26). Gregson and colleagues argue that deciding what to do is not only the result of weighing objective knowledge, in part because practice has its own expertise of "intuitive and reasoned decision-making that employs a variety of hard and soft evidence" (p. 26), under conditions of incomplete evidence where application of knowledge is uncertain and in a value-laden context with competing priorities of client, organization, law, and society. This means that knowledge is only one part of the "complex and intricate reasoning" that is practice. Knowledge certainly cannot automatically be said to trump ethics or law, for example. As importantly, the response of the client to the practice of medicine or education is an interpretive accomplishment, meaning that clients respond and react to practice as well as accept it. We can go on, but our purpose here is simply to point out that scholarship needs to do its homework on practice itself before it is used to recommend practice, a point made in reference to qualitative synthesis as well in Thorne et al. (2004).

Nevertheless, we must acknowledge a very real irony in the history of meta-ethnography. Uny, France, and Noblit (2017) argue that it was the emergence of evidence-based health-care research in the United Kingdom that led to the steady growth in the number of meta-ethnographies published (118 in 2014 and 2015 alone according to France et al., 2015). In education, meta-ethnography has been less tied to ideas of evidence-based practice—and there are many fewer studies.

It is not clear why meta-ethnography has been less popular in education compared to health, but there were several developments that have consumed the energies of qualitative researchers in education. First, qualitative research in education by the late 1980s was in the process of elaborating a range of approaches to qualitative research, what Guba and Lincoln (1994) termed the "competing paradigms of qualitative research" (p. 105): positivism, post positivism, critical theory, and constructivism. Second, the critical turn, in particular, was especially compelling and pushed against notions of utilitarianism in which research synthesis in general was implicated. Third, the "culture wars" over reading instruction and the value of literature and social studies (and now even science) meant that educational policy and practice had been politicized, and qualitative research was often positioned in opposition to efforts to force schools to comply uniformly with state-required educational reforms (Noblit & Pink, 1987). This politicization of education has meant that educational researchers, regardless of methodology, are even today somewhat tentative in their relation to evidence-based practice. Finally, neither Noblit nor Hare began a research program around meta-ethnography and instead returned to their established programs of research. Had they done so, this may have changed the trajectory of meta-ethnography. There are no doubt other reasons, but it is clear that meta-ethnography did not catch on with the qualitative researchers in education. However, there are signs that in education meta-ethnography is now coming into its own, including the 2017 special issue of *Ethnography and Education* on meta-ethnography (Kakos & Fritzsche, 2017). We think it is helpful to recount how meta-ethnography has been described and used in education as a way to situate the contributions of this volume.

Davies (2000) reviewed various research synthesis approaches and aligned synthesis with assessing the "effectiveness of educational policy and practice" (p. 366), while noting that in the UK there was considerable interest in research synthesis, including the then recent establishment of the Campbell Collaboration for applied social science that paralleled the Cochrane Collaboration for health. He noted that the elaboration of qualitative methods had resulted in a heterogeneity of qualitative approaches and theoretical perspectives that "may be greater with qualitative research" (p. 371). He also noted that the applicability of syntheses is more limited given that classrooms vary year to year and are complex social organizations. "Teachers, learners, parents, and educational managers tend to have particular and context-specific concerns about education" (p. 374) that must be integrated with evidence. Of course, this requires a different conception of teaching than as a follower of correct instructional practices as evidenced by "what works" and other approaches to evidence-based educational practice. Here Davies acknowledges the utilitarian press on research and synthesis while complicating the same relationship.

Rice (2002) used meta-ethnography to synthesize studies about professional learning communities' collaboration process. Case studies of the collaboration process were synthesized to yield 12 themes organized under four categories. Situational factors included the unwillingness to collaborate, prior relationships and attitudes, and the difficulty in obtaining sustaining funding. Structural dimensions included the lack of formalization, issues of parity and control, and the importance of the principal. The main process dimension involved miscommunication, while the relational dimension included interorganizational strain, conflicting goals between organizations, initial distrust and skepticism, the importance of key individuals, and the importance of informal meetings. The study resulted in a set of practical recommendations and the line of argument that it was the relations dimension that captured most of the issues in collaboration.

Doyle (2003) used a meta-ethnographic study for methodological purposes, finding limitations in the approach and suggesting enhancements that included explaining how the author of the meta-ethnography is situated in the study and text, moving to an augmented grounded theory approach, employing the language of the authors of the original studies in the translation, theorizing how the studies relate, providing audit trails, and member checks. Substantively, her meta-ethnography of educational leadership yielded three patterns: "commitment to a vision, power with an essence, and congruency of actions" (p. 338). She also sees in meta-ethnography the "possibility to empower" by "amplifying voices," "facilitating praxis" (p. 339), weakening "hierarchical roles" and extending "borders" "to communicate across groups" including disciplinary groups (p. 340).

Rice (2002) and Doyle (2003) both created syntheses that were rather close to the studies synthesized. Doyle did push the methodology in novel ways, including incorporating the synthesizer's positionality into the text, and enabled it to have wider implications in the politics of knowledge that surround education.

Savin-Baden and her colleagues published two articles on higher education that emphasized meta-ethnography as an interpretive endeavor and signaled a push to return to Noblit and Hare's (1988) idea that synthesis could be more than what the original studies contained. Most importantly, they also incorporated the synthesizers' positionality into the texts, were critical in orientation, and problematized the pursuit of similarity over difference in meta-ethnographies. Savin-Baden and Major (2007) used interpretive meta-ethnography to examine how innovative approaches to learning influence the understandings faculty have of their teaching, using problem-based learning in higher education as the case in point. In an interpretive approach, they argue that their interpretive stance needed to be explicit and that this same stance led to data being reinterpreted as part of the synthesis. Also in standing against conventional notions of validity in qualitative research, they engaged with four "honesties": "situating ourselves in relation to our participants," "voicing our mistakes," "situating ourselves in relation to the data," and "taking a critical stance towards research" (p. 837). Unlike earlier authors in education, they were explicit about using synthesis to develop a second-order interpretation and then worked to develop third-order interpretations that went beyond a summary of the findings of the original studies. Four overarching themes developed: changes in role perception (e.g., moving from lecturer to facilitator); changes in perspectives about the nature of authority and control (repositioning to maintain control, to offer control and to relinquish control); shifts in views about the nature of disciplinary knowledge (e.g., perceiving disciplines in novel ways, breaking down artificial boundaries within the discipline and across disciplinary lines); and changes in perception about the nature of teaching and learning (teaching for understanding, as shared practice, and as research). They concluded: "What the synthesis added was the importance of facilitating change in academic identities and in confronting issues of power and control" (p. 850).

Savin-Baden, McFarland, and Savin-Baden (2008) in another interpretive meta-ethnography of learning and teaching in higher education examined the relationship across practice, transfer, and community. They explicitly focused on literature that problematized and clarified the relations between the three main concepts; literature that explored different practitioner, policy, and development understandings and the tensions evident among them; areas where existing knowledge is not being used; and locating needed further research. Again, the interpretive meta-ethnography developed both second-order and third-order themes—pushing beyond what the original studies found. Their findings were complex and detailed as they moved from first order to second order and then to third order. In the end, the meta-ethnography revealed that "issues of pedagogical stance, disjunction., learning spaces, agency, notions of improvement and communities of interest all help to locate the overarching themes and hidden subtexts that are strong influences on areas of practice, transfer and community" (p. 225). They note that interpretive meta-ethnography allows a new interpretation to be constructed, but "the difficulty with this approach is that there is a tendency to privilege similarity (and sometimes difference) because the process of sense making across studies tends to focus on ordering and cohesion rather than exploring conflicting data sets and contestable positions" (p. 225). We find their work largely commensurate with this volume. We hope they find us taking their work but one step further.

This focus on difference, positionality, and critique, though, was not picked up in all of the later meta-ethnographic studies in education. For example, Tondeur et al. (2012) used meta-ethnography to study strategies to prepare preservice teachers to integrate technology into instruction. The focus was on the content and delivery methods that best prepare preservice teachers for effective technology integration. Twelve themes resulted. In relation to the preparation of preservice teachers, aligning theory and practice, using teacher educators as role models, reflecting on the attitudes about the role of technology in education; learning technology by design; collaborating with peers, scaffolding authentic technology experiences, and moving from traditional assessment to continuous feedback were all key themes. At the institutional level, technology planning and leadership, co-operation within and between institutions, staff development, access to resources, and systematic and systemic change efforts were all key themes. The key themes were seen as linked and difficult to address separately but were also rather close to those in the individual studies and framed similarly in terms of promoting technology integration without positionality or critique being evident.

While also not picking up on positionality and critique, Jamal et al. (2013) conducted a systematic review and meta-ethnography of school environment and student health that found considerable complexity and led to a reconsideration of theory as well. Four "meta-themes" (p. 4) resulted in a line of argument that (a) aggressive behavior and substance use are elements of status and social relations in adolescents, (b) problematic health behaviors were evident in unsupervised "hotspots" (p. 6) of the school, (c) good relationships with teachers are important but school organization and policies are constraints for these, and (d) unhappiness in school lead students to "escape" (p. 7) school in unauthorized ways. These findings, they suggest, led to a refinement of human functioning and school organization theory that put student social networks and agency in interaction and contention with school organization.

The focus on theory as well as positionality, critique, and difference can be found in Beach, Bagley, Eriksson, and Player-Koro (2014). They synthesized a set of studies of teacher education in Sweden that addressed two competing historical policy tendencies: (a) unification of the profession with a professional and research based knowledge base and (b) a return to a more dualist, age- and grade-based professionalism. Theoretically they also were demonstrating the value of Bernstein's theories (cf. Bernstein, 2003) in understanding how teacher education is situated in social and political processes and institutions. Their goal was to identify paths of thought that were not as evident in the original studies (and which they had conducted independently). The meta-ethnography revealed that the unification-oriented policies had not been very successful in influencing either practice or teacher professional perspectives. Thus the return to dualist policy was a misnomer as unification policies had never been substantiated in practice. They concluded that education policy is more ideological than based in scientific evidence, raising questions about the wisdom of government interventions in teacher education. In this study, the politicized nature of education and research, a critique of utilitarian approaches to policy and practice, an elaboration of the meta-ethnographic approach, the synthesizers' place in the text, and an explicit focus on theory are all full blown.

Baker and Harter (2015) used meta-ethnography to speak rather directly to a controversy in education. They revisited the case studies that undergirded the development of cognitively guided instruction (CGI) in elementary mathematics instruction because of a high-profile critique of the differentiated instruction (which they argued was a "working model of differentiation" [p. 27]). In their meta-ethnography they specified their positionality and perspective, addressed a key theory of educational practice, and engaged the high-profile critique that had recently been lodged. They focused on six case studies that "exemplified teachers' voices around CGI" (p. 29). They discerned three themes of student-centered pacing, alternative forms of assessment, and teacher scaffolding. They then used these themes to reanalyze CGI as "a metaphor of differentiation," which had been critiqued as essentially impossible to implement. They then arrayed the elements of the critic's characterization of differentiation, revealing that teachers were able to effectively achieve what the critic had denied as possible. This article used meta-ethnography to speak to salient debates about educational practice. The authors were explicit about CGI being a "living metaphor" for the more abstract concept of differentiation. The resulting meta-ethnography speaks of a possibility that others deny.

In education, then, we would argue that meta-ethnography has been the least useful when it recapitulates what the original studies had to say, either recategorizing it or endeavoring to assert that this is "what is known." Both of these, of course, can be of interest, but they add little to knowledge. Meta-ethnography, on the other hand, is more useful when it addresses the contexts and nature of educational knowledge, when it is interpretive and/or critical in orientation, when the synthesizers' positionality is actively engaged in the text, when complexity and difference are sought out, and when theory and the history of ideas in an area of research are addressed. In doing so, meta-ethnography gives education another way to consider, critique, and advance ideas, research methods, and the field as an intellectual endeavor. Meta-ethnography places what were done as individual studies in wider contexts and asks scholars to take ownership not only of their ideas but of the contexts in which those ideas are implicated. It challenges educational researchers to take responsibility for that which they assume was outside their domain of action.

IMPROVING META-ETHNOGRAPHY

Meta-ethnography continues to develop and change with each iteration. This is as it should be. Meta-ethnography is a method that should not be fetishized.

That said, there are clear issues in the syntheses that have been produced. France et al.'s (2014) account of "what's wrong with meta-ethnographic reporting" does an admirable job detailing what the reporting is and is not. To overly summarize their review, authors of meta-ethnographies are often not even doing a meta-ethnography per se. Authors assert what they have done, rather than show how they did it. As the papers move from the search to the synthesis, things become more opaque, leading of course to the devastating finding that it was not clear in some 38% of the papers if anything new was offered at all. I know the distinction between normal science, the slow plod of accumulating findings, and the paradigm shift, when what was known before is accounted for in a new way that takes in what was not able to be explained under the normal science regime (Kuhn, 1970), but this makes me wonder why bother with all the sheer hard work of research synthesis if so little is gained in practice?

If meta-ethnography is to be useful, researchers need to step up. Thankfully, France and her colleagues are continuing their work, and this should enable authors to backfill what they should do from what they should be including in their synthesis products. But there is a limit to what they can do in their project. Their team and I have discussed many of the topics covered in this chapter, and this book should be seen as supporting and extending their work. This should not imply their agreement with what we do in this volume. All of us have agreed that there are many meta-ethnographies, and the job at this point is to address critical issues and elaborate differences. Their work with project eMERGe and this book are both parts of this effort.

THIS BOOK

This book examines the relation of meta-ethnography and theory with identity theory as the theoretical case in point. The core of the book is a set of eight meta-ethnographies. Each researcher or team of researchers examined a specific field of studies that addressed identity and/or identity theory; that focused on youth, broadly defined; and that took an explicitly critical approach. Meta-ethnography has not to date explicitly addressed a theoretical domain, nor has it been seen as critique. Both of these are new steps in meta-ethnography's development. The authors worked largely independently, with only some guidance from the editors. Nevertheless, the editors are heartened by what each chapter, and the entire set of chapters, reveals about identity theory in the specified field of study, the role meta-ethnography played in such revelations, and most importantly how the authors theorized with the meta-ethnography they produced. We invite each chapter to be read in terms of all three of these points.

Charles Price and Orisanmi Burton were focused on Black racial identity theory (BRIT). This field of study has been largely quantitative, but they found dissertations had qualitative studies in them that were often never published. They found the nature of BRIT—a stage theory measured by scales—limited the interpretations that were possible and yielded a line of argument synthesis more about methodology and positionality. Moreover, they also found that the qualitative studies of BRIT are moving toward intersectionality, intra-Black relations, and the globalization of Black identity.

Bettez, Chang, and Edwards took on Multiracial identity development and examined pieces in peer-reviewed journals and books. The initial reciprocal synthesis discerned three themes: fluidity of identity, exclusion/isolation, and the salience of place/space. With these in hand, they went on to consider the bases of these themes and argued that paradigms (interpretive or critical) provide refutational lines of argument. Reconceptualizing across the studies, they found two omissions: lack of attention to intersectionality and an absence of attention to whiteness—a whiteblindness.

Ender and Rodriguez decided that in the studies of Latin@ immigration no one had taken the time to consider identity manifestations in specific "gateway" (new immigration) states. They focused on one such state, North Carolina, in which a set of studies had been conducted. In this, they set aside the youth focus in order to better characterize this specific space. They found themes of schooling and ways of knowing, identities in flux, and fuerzas and agency. These led them to characterize Latin@ identity as engaging a supervivenicia that countermanded that Latin@s needed to be helped.

Kolano, Childers-McKee, and King also were interested in specificity. They addressed racialized Southeast Asian American youth identities—critiquing the pan-ethnic model minority stereotype. Their reciprocal synthesis had three prominent themes in peer-reviewed studies: disrupting the institutional influences of racism and colorism, opening up the success narrative for Southeast Asian American youth, and centering Southeast Asian American youth studies within mainstream research on schools. They concluded, though, that the focus on cultural identity belied a structural critique of schooling.

Parkhouse and Pennell focused on intersectional identities of gender, ethnicity, and sexuality in Latina students. Their synthesis focused on three overarching themes that contribute to the identity theory that emerges through these studies: space, performance, and agency. Each of these were multifaceted. There were two intersecting lines of argument: one related to personal agency and the other to collective resistance. They saw identity theory as conceptualizing agency as an individual attribute that was problematic for cultures that are less individualistic than White Americans.

LaGarry and Conder were concerned with White preservice teachers and how they used identity "play" to protect White privilege. Their meta-ethnography was timed such that it became a methodological experiment. LaGarry and Conder used figured worlds theory to develop an extended metaphor of Whites playing games to protect hegemony and a line of argument synthesis. After they completed this synthesis, "second wave studies" were published that revealed that their meta-ethnography anticipated this theoretical shift, an argument for more methodological studies.

Martin and Locklear examined studies on Native American youth identities but were dismayed by the deficit perspective in these studies and the consequent denigration of the youth. In response, they identified studies that were not deficit oriented in order to understand how positive Native American identities are developed. Their line of argument synthesis centered the necessity of language; fighting White education with Indigenous knowledge systems; and identity battles against racism, discrimination, and colonization. These youth want adult relationships that sponsor their cultures.

Hatt portrays a rather different sense of intersectionality by focusing on studies of smartness and identity in schools. She discovers three key themes: epistemologies of schooling, learning as production of identity, and teacher power in student identities. Identity in these studies was multiple, but schooling locked down identities in key ways. The studies analyzed how identities of smartness were formed, racialized, classed, and gendered but rarely addressed resistance and struggle. She argues for a shift toward defining learning as identity production. Identity is not a precondition to learning.

We end the book with a final chapter that examines the relationships between theory (and theorizing) and meta-ethnography. In this chapter, we also offer some modest proposals for how to proceed for both identity theory and meta-ethnography.

REFERENCES

Baker, K., & Harter, M. (2015). A living metaphor of differentiation: A meta-ethnography of cognitively guided instruction in the elementary classroom. *Journal of Mathematics Education at Teachers College, 6*(2), 27–36.

Beach, D., Bagley, C., Eriksson, A., & Player-Koro, C. (2014). Changing teach education in Sweden: Using meta-ethnographic analysis to understand and describe policy making and educational changes. *Teaching and Teacher Education, 44*, 160–167.

Bernstein, B. (2003). *Class, codes and control. Volume 4, The structuring of pedagogic discourse.* London: Routledge.

Britten, N., Campbell, R., Pope, C., Donovan, J., Morgan, M., & Pill, R. (2002). Using meta-ethnography to synthesise qualitative research: A worked example. *Journal of Health Services & Research Policy, 7*(4), 209–215.

Collins, P. (1990). *Black feminist thought.* Boston: Unwin Hyman.

Davies, P. (2000). The relevance of systematic reviews to educational policy and practice. *Oxford Review of Education, 26*(3–4), 365–378.

Doyle, L. H. (2003). Synthesis through meta-ethnography: Paradoxes, enhancements, and possibilities. *Review of Qualitative Research, 3*(3), 321–344.

Ecker, B., & Hulley, L. (1996). *Depth oriented brief therapy: How to be brief when you were trained to be deep, and vice versa.* San Francisco, CA: Jossey-Bass.

Ecker, B., & Hulley, L. (2000). The order in clinical "disorder:" Symptom coherence in depth oriented brief therapy. In R. A. Neimeyer & J. Raskin (Eds.), *Constructions of disorder* (pp. 63–89). Washington, DC: American Psychological Association.

Finfgeld-Connett, D., & Johnson, E. D. (2013). Literature search strategies for conducting knowledge-building and theory-generating qualitative systematic reviews. *Journal of Advanced Nursing, 69*(1), 194–204.

Finlayson, K., & Dixon, A. (2008). Qualitative meta-synthesis: A guide for the novice. *Nurse Researcher, 15*(2), 59–71.

France, E. F., Ring, N., Noyes, J., Maxwell, M., Jepson, R., Duncan, E., . . . Uny, I. (2015). Protocol-developing meta-ethnography reporting guidelines (eMERGe). *Review of BMC Medical Research Methodology, 15*(1), 103.

France, E. F., Ring, N., Thomas, R., Noyes, J., Maxwell, M., & Jepson, R. (2014). A methodological systematic review of what's wrong with meta-ethnography reporting. *Review of BMC Medical Research Methodology, 14*(1), 119.

Gage, N. (1989). The paradigm wars and their aftermath. *Educational Researcher, 18*(7), 4–10.

Goodall, H. (2000). *Writing the new ethnography.* Lanham, MD: Alta Mira.

Gregson, P., Meal, A., & Avis, M. (2002). Meta-analysis: The glass eye of evidence-based practice. *Nursing Inquiry, 9*(1), 24–30.

Guba, E., & Lincoln, Y. (1994). Competing paradigms of qualitative research. In N. Denzin & Y. Lincoln (Eds.), *Handbook of qualitative research methods* (pp. 105–117). Thousand Oaks CA: SAGE.

Habermas, J. (1975). *Legitimation crisis.* Boston: Beacon Press.

Haraway, D. (1988). Situated knowledges: The science question in feminism and the privilege of partial perspective. *Feminist Studies, 14*(1), 575–599.

Hughes, S. A., & Noblit, G. W. (2017). Third guiding process: synthesizing new-self insights with MICA. In S. Hughes (Ed.), *Autoethnography: Process, product and possibility for critical social research* (pp. 110–142). Los Angeles, CA: SAGE.

Hymes, D. (1980). Educational ethnology. *Anthropology and Education Quarterly, 11*(1), 3–8.

Jamal, F., Fletcher, A., Harden, A., Wells, H., Thomas, J., & Bonell, C. (2013). The school environment and student health: A systematic review and meta-ethnography of qualitative research. *BMC Public Health, 13*(1), 798.

Kakos, M. & Fritzsche, B. (2017). Meta-ethnography E&E. *Ethnography and Education, 12*(2), 129–133.

Kuhn, T. (1970). *The structure of scientific revolutions.* Chicago: University of Chicago Press.

Marcus, G., & Fisher, M. (1986). *Anthropology as cultural critique.* Chicago: University of Chicago Press.

Mead, M. (1928). *Coming of age in Samoa: A psychological study of primitive youth for Western civilization.* New York: William Morrow.

Noblit, G., Flores, S., & Murrillo, E. (Eds.). (2004). *Post-critical ethnography: Reinscribing critique.* Cresskill, NJ: Hampton Press.

Noblit, G., & Hare, D. (1988). *Meta-ethnography: Synthesizing qualitative studies.* Thousand Oaks, CA: SAGE.

Noblit, G., & Pink, W. (Eds.). (1987). *Schooling in social context: Qualitative studies.* Norwood, NJ: Ablex.

Paterson, B., Thorne, S., Canam, C., & Jillings, C. (2001). *Meta-Study.* Thousand Oaks, CA: SAGE.

Rice, E. H. (2002). The collaboration process in professional development schools: Results of a meta-ethnography, 1990–1998. *Journal of Teacher Education, 53*(1), 55–67.

Savin-Baden, M., & Major, C. H. (2007). Using interpretative meta-ethnography to explore the relationship between innovative approaches to learning and their influence on faculty understanding of teaching. *Higher Education, 54*(6), 833–852.

Savin-Baden, M., McFarland, L., & Savin-Baden, J. (2008). Learning spaces, agency and notions of improvement: What influences thinking and practices about teaching and learning in higher education? An interpretive meta-ethnography. *London Review of Education, 6*(3), 211–227.

Thorne, S., Jensen, L., Kearney, M., Noblit, G., & Sandelowski, M. (2004). Qualitative metasynthesis: Reflections on methodological orientation and ideological agenda. *Qualitative Health Research, 14*(10), 1342–1365.

Tondeur, J., van Braak, J., Sang, G., Voogt, J., Fisser, P., & Ottenbreit-Leftwich, A. (2012). Preparing pre-service teachers to integrate technology in education: A synthesis of qualitative evidence. *Computers & Education, 59*(1), 134–144.

Turner, S. (1980). *Sociological explanation as translation.* Cambridge, UK: Cambridge University Press.

Uny, I., France, E., & Noblit, G. (2017). Steady and delayed: Explaining the different development of meta-ethnography in health care and education. *Ethnography and Education, 12*(2), 243–257.

3

Meta-Ethnography

*An Exploratory Inquiry into Black Racial Identity Theory
and Qualitative Research*

CHARLES PRICE AND ORISANMI BURTON ∎

I advance it therefore as a suspicion only, that the blacks, whether originally
a distinct race, or made distinct by time and circumstances, are inferior
to the whites in the endowments both of body and mind . . . . [D]ifferent
species of the same genus, or varieties of the same species, may possess
different qualifications.
—THOMAS JEFFERSON (1781/1999), *Notes on the State of Virginia*

More than two centuries have passed since Thomas Jefferson published his ideas
about race. During the past four decades, we have developed productive ways to
study and explain race and are continually improving our strategies and theories.
There is consensus, for example, that race is a socially constructed belief system
about human differences and similarities. Furthermore, there is growing recognition that racial identity gives life to and actualizes the category of race because
people enact their understandings of race through their identities.[1]

We encourage studying and theorizing racial identity through field-based qualitative research. We advocate context-sensitive and experience-near studies of
racial identity informed by people's life experience and their *own* understandings
of what it means to live as a racial being. According to Jeffers, Ray, and Hallett
(2010), much of the ethnography of race is about racial discrimination and racial
inequality, what they describe respectively as deficit and relational approaches.
We bring another focus into view: Black racial identity and the influences that
shape it. There is a dearth of qualitative research on race informed by racial

identity theory. For example, the research and theorizing of William Cross Jr. and of Robert Sellers and his colleagues present multidimensional theoretical and empirical conceptualizations of race and racial identity. Our chapter uses meta-ethnography to focus on Black racial identity theory (BRIT) and relevant studies that utilize qualitative research.

We argue that theoretically informed qualitative study of Black racial identity can provide a detailed account of the intersections among race, racial identity, and other identifications. We make a case for qualitative study of race and racial identity, outline major BRIT, and explore recent qualitative dissertation research that speaks to Black racial identity theory.[2] Qualitative research allows us to get "close" to race; it offers us an opportunity to grasp the interaction among White hegemony, racial categories, and racial identities. We adapt George Noblit's and R. Hare's (1988) meta-ethnographic strategy to interpret, translate, and synthesize the dissertations.

We use the term "Black" for the sake of consistency as well as a political statement: we write Black in upper case to signal it as a real thing. We define Black as inclusive of people who describe themselves as Black and/or African-descended.[3] Our chapter focus is restricted to Black people in the United States.

Our meta-ethnographic line of argument is that qualitative (especially ethnographic) studies informed by BRIT allow us to theorize racial identity in ways closer to how people experience it—in relation to a multiplicity of identifications. Intersectionality, for example, is an interpretive paradigm that claims that people have multiple and intersecting identities: racial identity is informed by gender, class, sexuality, religion, and so on. Such complexity, however, is neglected when researchers partition identifications into experience-distant variables or test for "strength" among discrete variables. To offer an example, a qualitative approach informed by intersectionality or the "simultaneity of identities" (Holvino, 2012) would allow us to understand how one can be simultaneously Black, woman, lawyer, mother, and Rastafarian. However, we do not intend to construct qualitative and quantitative as neat dichotomies, and we do not argue that one is better than the other. We believe, however, that our theorizing of racial identity would benefit from more qualitative studies informed by BRITs. First, we briefly explain our focus on dissertations and qualitative research. We then address our positionality before providing a sketch of meta-ethnography, BRIT, and our methodology. We then turn to our synthesis of and line of argument about the dissertations.

DISSERTATIONS AND QUALITATIVE RESEARCH INTO BLACK RACIAL IDENTITY

We reviewed dissertations rather than peer-reviewed journal publications for several reasons. Dissertations on Black racial identity are based in original data, research, and analysis, whereas journal publications manifest as a range of forms such as essays, opinions, and theoretical treatises that need not draw upon empirical data. Many of the dissertation authors who engage BRIT eventually will publish on the topic in peer-reviewed journals. Some of the recent dissertation research, such as the studies of relationships between blackness *and* gender identity, raise cutting-edge concerns that ask us to think differently about how Black racial identity is gendered. Moreover, some of the PhD graduates will go on to make substantial contributions to racial identity theory. For example, Charmaine Wijeyesinghe (1992) published a dissertation on biracial identity formation and later published substantial scholarship on racial identity theory (e.g., Wijeyesinghe, 2001, 2012).

Our focus on dissertations makes our contribution to the volume different from others. Many of the dissertations reviewed were published in fields unwelcoming of qualitative research and ethnographic research in particular. Therefore, we defined qualitative and ethnographic broadly to emphasize research that addresses participant experience and that analyzes data collected through participant observation, in-depth interviewing, focus groups, and journaling. The broad definition is important because none of the dissertation authors conducted the long-term field research characteristic of classic notions of ethnography. The selected dissertations contain qualitative orientations that are ethnographic in how they address participant experience, participant meaning-making, and researcher positionality (or reflexivity) in relation to both their participants and research.

Promoting a qualitative strategy for studying racial identity is relevant because of the growth of interest in Black identity in the post–President Obama era, because of the proliferative abstract analyses and representations of race (Hartigan, 1999) and because the "vast majority of research on Black racial identity is quantitative in nature" (Walden, 2008, pp. 78–79).

David Walden (2008), a psychologist who published a dissertation on racial identity formation among Black men, justified his qualitative strategy by pointing out what quantitative research does not address, such as social and historical context or the nuanced and sometimes contradictory quality of human subjectivity:

> the drive for and dilemma of identity formation for Black people as described in narrative format is as follows: The standards of society in which I live are White. All things are compared to White, and all things are judged by their proximity to it. As much as I have been told either implicitly or explicitly by individuals and institutions, especially in this "modern age," that I am equal to or in essence *am* White, I have repeatedly—and sometimes brutally, but always to my disadvantage—discovered this to not be the case. My only choice is to continue to live in ignorance or denial of my identity *as a Black person,* thus consciously becoming either as close to White as I can or unconsciously becoming a caricature of Blackness that has also been defined for me, *or* I can embrace myself as Black and redefine myself and my world in relation to that new identity, in all its confusion and with all its attendant frustration. (p. 25)

The sense of history, emotion, meaning, paradox, and interior dialogue expressed by Walden is vital to understanding racial identity and race but reaches beyond the ambit of quantitative methodologies. Qualitative research is concerned with how people generate meaning and interpret experience and how varied situations and histories influence how individuals come to understand themselves as Black.

The value of a qualitative approach to race and racial identity is unlikely to be obvious to scholars untrained in the methodology. Education leadership and policy researcher Levester Johnson (2004), for example, blundered into a "strange" but compelling world of qualitative methodology in his study of how biracial college students understand themselves as racialized people:

> The road to determining the research design and methodology for this study was one of discovery. Like "Alice in Wonderland" or Dorothy following the yellow brick road to "The Wizard of Oz," the design portion of this study introduced me to numerous new and different characters. These characters have challenged my beliefs and concepts of truth, widened my perspective and knowledge of research techniques, and offered a new audio system for the silenced voice of biracial people to be heard. (p. 29)

The better we understand race, perhaps the better we can become at dealing with it in sensitive and smart ways. We must understand and explain how people become racialized beings.

AUTHOR POSITIONALITY

Explaining positionality—a researcher's experience and stance in relationship to his and her epistemology, favored interpretive paradigm, and methodological choice(s)—is increasingly expected in qualitative research. Our preceding quote of Walden gives example to the importance of readers' awareness of an author's positionality. When Price first read the quote, he erroneously assumed that Walden identified as Black given his tone and first-person voice. Price discovered that Walden identified as White.

Does an author's positionality matter? Yes. It ought to tell readers something about an author's stance, theoretical commitment, and politics. It should help us interpret a scholar's research. Walden displays his awareness of and sensitivity toward the experience of race from a Black standpoint, something different from his own positionality as a White male. His awareness of and sensitivity toward race and blackness inform his research and interpretations.

Our positionality can bias our epistemology when we do not reflect on how our experience shapes what we know and why we believe what we believe (Takacs, 2003). Ideally, we should be open to alternative views and endeavor to step beyond our cherished convictions. We all bring our experience and "theoretical concerns and [prior] commitments" to our research (Emerson, Fretz, & Shaw, 2011, p. 199).

A scholar can perhaps attain a broader grasp of the trustworthiness (or "rigor") of a given study if he or she has access to an author's motivation, intellectual commitment, and identity (Stringer, 2014, p. 92).

Briefly, we share our positionality.

Charles. I was born in New York City to an African American mother and West Indian father. My mother sent me at an early age to live with her parents in rural South Carolina where official racial segregation continued until 1972. I recognized that I was not White, and faintly, I recognized that many of the Whites I observed had a monopoly on "good things" like nice homes, choice tracts of land, and the opportunity to vacation. College was my first peek into the intimate lives of flesh-and-blood White folk. The wealth of some of my White student peers stirred an unsettling awareness within me. Their wealth made me recognize my mother's tenuous working-class status and the atrocious poverty of the rural community where I grew up. I gradually realized my miseducation, in Cross's (1995) sense of the term: limited or distorted knowledge of Black history and culture, and therefore, scant awareness of historical injustice and inequity. I developed an interest in social justice and in Black history, culture, and identity. My interest in race and identity evolved out of my experience as a man who identifies as and has been marked by American Society as Black.

Orisanmi. A few days after I was born in 1981, my mother and father hosted a naming ceremony in my honor. Close friends and family attended it, many of whom were artists, educators, and activists. They packed into our apartment in Boston, Massachusetts, to participate in a divination ritual, rooted in the method of Lukumi, a particular strand of African Traditional Religion, traceable to the Yoruba people of southwestern Nigeria. My given name, Orisanmi, which roughly translates to "beautiful destiny," was selected from this ritual. I was born into a household for which the valorization of Black identity was never in question. My parents, who are both artists and educators, were politicized during the 1960s and 1970s. As their child, I grew up exposed to a wide array of books, photographs, plays, and conversations that left little room in my mind for doubt about the richness of Black culture. But growing up in Massachusetts and later in Charlotte, North Carolina, my unique name forced me to grapple with my identity and with how to communicate it to others, who often questioned me. People had a hard time pronouncing my name, and, as a youth, I often wished it was common, like everyone else's. Because of my name, people often assumed that either I or my parents were "from" Africa. When people heard my last name and found out that I was "just" African American, they sometimes became disappointed or even hostile, questioning me about my parents' intentions. Over time, I have come to embrace the contradiction presented by my African first name and my "slave name."

Finally, we should mention that Charles was Orisanmi's dissertation advisor. We are Black men trained in anthropology—one older, one younger—who have an intellectual and a political commitment to understanding race and racial identity. A primary motivation for collaborating on this chapter was to draw attention to the barely tapped potential of combining experience-near qualitative research with BRIT. We now turn to summarize our conception of meta-ethnography and our research design.

META-ETHNOGRAPHY AND THE STUDY
RESEARCH DESIGN

Meta-ethnography is a strategy for synthesizing qualitative research and translating the conceptual metaphors of individual studies into each other (Noblit & Hare, 1988). Translation is an act of interpretation. Meta-ethnography is integrative research, an amalgamation of texts. A meta-ethnographic analysis seeks to create patterns across cases that generate a novel interpretation based in a new synthesis of the individual cases. Meta-ethnography is a means to generating a higher order of analysis—a third order of interpretation—by translating the content and meanings of each case into a shared framework (Britten et al. 2002, p. 213). A third level of analysis catapults meta-ethnography beyond mere literature review or meta-analysis (Doyle, 2003). A meta-ethnography asks us to choose cases that provide an opportunity to learn, to translate the concepts of the cases into a dialogue among the cases (Doyle, 2003).

Research Questions and Text Selection

We met several times in person and by Internet to develop our study of dissertations that use qualitative methods to engage BRIT. After independently browsing academic journal articles and books on Black identity, we shared with each other what we discovered during our research. The initial search confirmed our hunch. Although the number of non-dissertation academic publications on BRIT have grown during the past two decades, there are few publications that employ qualitative methods in relation to BRIT. Therefore, we developed the following research questions: (1) What qualitative methodology and methods do dissertation researchers utilize in conjunction with BRIT? (2) What interpretive paradigms do dissertation authors use? (3) What are the methodological and theoretical themes across the dissertations? (4) What are the conclusions of dissertation authors who combine BRIT with qualitative research?

Guided by these questions, we identified the dissertations (the cases), focusing on how authors used BRIT, the authors' interpretive paradigm, the qualitative method(s) employed, and the findings. We created a grid that identifies the major components of interest for each dissertation (discussed later). During the inquiry we identified and synthesized combinations of qualitative method and interpretive paradigm, neglected areas of research, and extensions and critiques of BRIT.

We searched the Proquest Dissertations and Theses Global database, seeking recent qualitative research dissertations. We defined "recent" as a decade. Therefore, we searched dissertations published between the years 2003 and 2013; this constituted one of our "boundaries" (e.g., Doyle, 2003, p. 329; we began the research in 2014). The strategy that we used to begin the research was to identify dissertation abstracts that contained the phrases "Black identity theory" or "racial identity theory" (we enclosed search terms in quotations). The phrases turned up few hits (2 and 20, respectively). We revised our inquiry to search the phrases "African American identity," "Black identity," "blackness," and "racial identity." We abandoned "blackness" and "racial identity" because they returned too many hits (559 and 1,103, respectively), most having nothing to do with BRIT. Although "African American identity" returned 93 hits, we abandoned the search because very few abstracts mentioned BRIT. It is worth noting that we could not rely upon a dissertation's title to communicate whether it substantially engaged BRIT and qualitative research. After gaining a handle on the range of published dissertations, we determined to search the database for dissertation abstracts with the term "Black identity." The search returned 212 hits.

Coding, Analysis, and Trustworthiness

The abstracts were numbered and saved in a digital folder created through the Proquest site. By reading each of the 212 abstracts, we determined whether a dissertation had a qualitative component *and* whether it gave attention to BRIT. Of the 212 results, we eliminated those dissertations that did not have a qualitative component, those that did not in some way give focused attention to BRIT, and those focused on populations outside of the United States ("focused attention" meant that the dissertation contained at least one paragraph that discussed BRIT in relation to the dissertation research. Some dissertations mentioned BRIT in a mere sentence or two). This left us with 52 dissertations. For example, we eliminated the dissertation *Black Is Beautiful: Body Image in Black Women* (Shearon 2008). Although it is an interesting dissertation concerned with Black identity, body image, and race, it does not address BRIT. We narrowed down the criteria to focus on those most relevant to the research questions: main ideas of the dissertations; methodology and methods; interpretive paradigm; researcher positionality; and extensions and critiques of BRIT. These categories in effect served as codes. We created a spreadsheet that coded the 52 dissertations (available upon request), focusing on particular key concepts or metaphors. We used phrases such as "nigrescence," "qualitative," "ethnographic," and "Black identity" to scan the abstract, methodology, theoretical framework, and conclusion sections of each dissertation. Upon scrutiny of the 52 dissertations, we determined that some did not substantially address BRIT or substantially develop the qualitative component (i.e., both BRIT and qualitative research were not central to the purpose of the research itself). We eliminated these dissertations, reducing the pool to 13 dissertations. We created a second spreadsheet that lists the coded dissertations.

Our strategy for determining which dissertations to include turned out to be less precise than we imagined when we began the research (e.g., how much BRIT or qualitative analysis was sufficient). Noblit and Hare (1988) note that during a meta-ethnographic analysis the focus will shift as the analyst works to translate metaphors, identify compatibilities and incompatibilities, and create a line of argument (p. 35). However, as the research developed, we gained a sense of how to consistently translate the content within our codes and key concepts, noting, for example, how interpretive paradigms address gender.

A SKETCH OF MAJOR BLACK IDENTITY THEORIES

Racial identity theories assume that racial formations—"races" and the cognitive, sociocultural, and institutional structures that make their existence possible—vary in how members experience and understand race (Adams 2001; Wijeyesinghe & Jackson, 2012). Racial identity theories focus on specific racial formations, primarily in the United States, cognizant of the interconnections among the different formations (e.g., Omi, 1994). BRIT, for example, implicates White racism and White cultural hegemony in the various expressions of Black identity.

Origins of BRIT

BRIT emerged as a response to three concerns: scholarship that assumed that Black people were plagued by pathological tendencies, White researchers who developed models of identity and behavior based in their analysis of Whites but projected as universal, and Black social movements that shifted conceptions of blackness.

After World War II, growing numbers of Black Americans rejected undiscerning notions of a path to citizenship predicated on assimilation into spheres of White hegemony in workplaces, schools, media portrayals, and so on. The civil rights and Black power movements, in different ways, thrust Black identity on America's center stage. The former attempted to humanize African Americans and make them entitled citizens of the United States while the latter encouraged Black pride and Black self-love. Sherif and Sherif (1970), Thomas (1971), Cross (1971), and Hall, Cross, and Freedle (1972) were among the first to publish scholarship addressing the growing shift toward positive Black racial identity awareness. For nearly two decades, BRIT models explained Black identity attitudes in relation to racism. However, times change, and so too have the workings of racism and race. The early BRITs were important, but they neglected the diversity of Black identifications, the quotidian functions of Black identity, the impact of globalization on Black identity, and that many factors other than White racism animate Black identity.

Major Black Identity Theories

There are four major theorists of Black racial identity: William Cross Jr., Bailey Jackson III, Janet Helms, and, recently, Robert Sellers (and his colleagues). We deem them major because they established the parameters and content of BRIT and because they are widely cited. Therefore, another boundary of our meta-ethnographic inquiry required that a study address the work of at least one of these theorists. Of the major BRIT theorists, Cross's scholarship is most widely used.

William Cross's formulation of BRIT was initially described as the "Negro-to-Black conversion" (Cross, 1971), and later, nigrescence, the psychology of becoming Black (Cross, 1978, 1993). Cross defined nigrescence as a metamorphosis in which a part of a person's self-concept—Black racial awareness—is singled out and transmuted in ways that facilitate positive assessment of blackness, internalizing the emergent consciousness so that it eventually functions as a consistent part of the person's self-concept. The metamorphosis also involves a revision both of one's reference groups and worldview. Nigrescence is an "identity transformation" that involves a person's tussle with reconciling discrimination, deracination, and miseducation while creating a valorized Black self-concept that is historically and culturally informed (Price, 2009).

During the mid-1990s, Cross revised his Nigrescence theory. We use the revised theory to describe the five states of nigrescence: pre-encounter, encounter, immersion-emersion, internalization, and commitment. Price (2009, p. 115) uses "process" rather than "stage" to describe identity states. Pre-encounter describes a person whose self-concept does not mark blackness as especially salient among his or her various identities. Encounter characterizes an unsettling racialized experience(s) that leads a person to feel a need to transform his or her self-concept. Immersion-emersion designates the transition from the pre-encounter identity to the transformed (or redefined) identity. During immersion-emersion, a person is involved in an identity transformation that entails redefining and privileging Blackness. Internalization involves a person making the transformed identity a "natural" part of his or her self-concept and self-presentation. Internalization-commitment is attained when a person feels comfortable with and committed to the transformed identity. While the stage language of nigrescence theory suggests a linear developmental teleology, Cross (1995, 2001) emphasizes the fragility and open-endedness of nigrescence. Nigrescence is always subject to disruption, is never totally consummated, and is sometimes totally abandoned.

Jackson developed a model of BRIT independent of Cross (though they have cross-fertilized each other's thinking). Jackson calls his theory Black identity development. Jackson's and Cross' models share much in common, indicating some agreement among theorists on the major facets of BRIT (e.g., Blackness co-exists with other salient identifications). The two differ in how they explain Black identity development, however. Jackson for example, continues to emphasize the role of racism in Black identity development whereas Cross and others acknowledge racism but give it less prominence.

Jackson's (2012) revised BRIT has five stages: naïve, acceptance, resistance, redefinition, and internalization. Jackson revised his model to include a new stage (naïve) in order to emphasize culture and meaning-making, to situate Black identity formation within a global framework, and to broaden the analysis to explain Black racial identity development during childhood. The influence of preadolescence and childhood is not explicit in the other BRITs.

The naïve stage is the state of identity development of preschool children where difference is unlikely to make children "feel fearful or hostile, inferior or superior" (Jackson, 2012, p. 40). Race is unlikely to influence the self-concept of such children, though they may recognize difference. The acceptance stage is based in the assumption that as children age, they learn race ideologies. Children learn that race is associated with particular values (e.g., whiteness and beauty, blackness and stigma) and that there are consequences associated with race. Eurocentric frames of reference shape young people's understanding of culture, history, race, and so on. During acceptance, young people's racial beliefs are likely to be unexamined, and the stigmas associated with blackness may loom large in some young people's experience: poor school performance, police brutality, Black-on-Black crime, incarceration, and single parenthood, to list a few examples. Between their teens and 20s, Black people consciously and unconsciously make choices about how to relate to White, Black, and other people. Acceptance makes possible the stage of resistance (stage 3). That is, a person may decide to subject to *critical* scrutiny the beliefs of the acceptance stage. Resistance is characterized by a person's critical awareness of White racism; commonly it involves anger and frustration, sometimes so great that people are unable to move beyond it. What a person faces is making choices whether to disengage from White society and White people or whether circumstance or preference dictates selective interaction with White society and White people. The challenge of redefinition (stage 4) is to define oneself "independent of White people and the dominant White culture" (Jackson, 2012, p. 44). People experiencing stage 4 actively define themselves as Black and privilege interaction with like-minded Black people. During redefinition, people search for a paradigm that justifies their concern with blackness and their critique of whiteness. They may come to identify as Rastafari, Nation of Islam, Black Panther, or some other formulation that expresses Black consciousness. Jackson sees internalization as the penultimate stage of Black identity development. It involves integrating one's previous experience with the revised identity. People no longer feel a need to "explain, defend, or protect their Black identity" (Jackson, 2012, p. 45). From a developmental point of view, internalization signifies a "healthy" identity when a person is able to imagine blackness and Black people as positive rather than degraded, and when they are able to bridge cultural and racial difference without feeling threatened. Indeed, some people may create a multifaceted self-concept, integrating identifications such as Black, British, woman, Christian, and Jamaican.

Janet Helms (1990c) is known for her White racial identity development research. However, she is an important contributor to BRIT (Helms, 1990b), in particular conceptualizing the notion of stages as worldviews or statuses (Walden, 2008, p. 74). Helms (1990a) argues that theories of Black identity have two strands: a Black client-as-problem (BCAP) and nigrescence (1990a, p. 9). The two approaches evolved from different concerns and have different implications. The BCAP notion questioned the dearth studies of the strengths of Black personalities and the notion that post–civil rights Blacks would become unruly and would behave violently toward Whites (Helms, 1990a, p. 10). Much of Helms's contribution is empirical research seeking to create tools such as racial identity scales that analyze racial identity rather than developing a distinctive formulation of BRIT. Therefore, space considerations preclude our providing further detail on Helms's models.

A recent contribution to BRIT is the multidimensional model of racial identity (MMRI; Sellers, Smith, Shelton, Rowley, & Chavous, 1998). Sellers and colleagues argue that the MMRI addresses the heterogeneity of blackness while also addressing how people inject meaning into their conception of Black identity. The MMRI is based on four assumptions: (a) identities are "situationally influenced" but also exhibit stability and mutability, (b) people have multiple identities that are "hierarchically ordered" (based on self-definitions), (c) self-evaluations of Black racial identity should be privileged (although ascription of blackness must not be ignored), and (d) a focus on identity and meaning is preferable to a focus on developmental paths (pp. 23–24).

The MMRI focuses on four dimensions of Black identity: salience, centrality, regard, and ideology. Salience asks how important Black identity is in a given situation. Centrality addresses how a person defines him- or herself in terms of race. Unlike salience, centrality is treated as "relatively stable across situations" (Sellers et al., 1998, p. 24). Regard speaks to how a self-identified Black person evaluates other Black people. Ideology involves ascertaining people's attitudes and beliefs concerning what constitutes proper Black behavior or, said differently, how Black people should act in certain situations. The notion of ideology involves four philosophies: nationalist; oppressed, assimilationist, and humanist (the MMRI assumes a person can hold more than one of these philosophies).

The dissertations included in this study are informed by the BRITs described here, applied to particular problems such as how Black identity functions in predominantly White institutions of higher education. In particular, most of the dissertations acknowledge or draw on nigrescence theory. In the following section, we discuss the themes we identified and our interpretation of the themes.

RESULTS: DISSERTATION THEMES AND SYNTHESES

The key metaphors for this study are the terms and concepts used by dissertation authors to describe, organize, and analyze their research. We interpret these metaphors across the dissertations. Our line of argument coalesced around the dissertations' main ideas, qualitative mechanics, interpretive paradigm, and the positionality of the authors. However, we take care to offer quotes and examples from specific cases as a way to intersperse the voice of the authors' interpretations with our interpretations.

The qualitative applications of BRIT by dissertation researchers varied. Examples include analysis of how well nigrescence theory explains the racial experience of Black men (Rice, 2004; Walden, 2008); achievement and Black racial identity in higher education institutions (Baber, 2007; Carson, 2003; Hill, 2008); Black women's identity formation (Christal Johnson, 2013; Harris, 2004; McNickles, 2009); biracial identity and blackness (Johnson, 2004), Black teachers and tokenism (Hasberry, 2013); and how Black adolescents experience race (Campbell, 2013; Johnson, 2006; Jones, 2012). The primary qualitative methods the authors use are the in-depth interview (semistructured, focus group interview), journaling, and observations. The size of the study populations ranged between 2 and 28. Typically, the authors engaged established BRIT theorists within the context of one or more interpretive paradigms. Interpretive paradigms employed by the authors include BRITs, critical race theory (CRT), Black feminism, and a conception of experience akin to phenomenology.

Schools and colleges of education and departments of psychology produced most of the dissertations, namely eight and three, respectively. Perhaps this pattern traces to the influence that theorists Cross (community psychology) and Jackson (education) had on the formation of BRIT. The two other dissertations were products of social work (Johnson, 2006) and communications (Johnson, 2013). Anthropology and sociology, disciplines with venerable qualitative traditions, contributed no dissertations during the boundary period (Price's [2001] anthropology dissertation employs a life narrative methodology and nigrescence theory to a purposive sample of elder Rastafari people in Jamaica).

Qualitative Methodology and Methods

The qualitative mechanics (design, methods, and interpretive paradigm) of the dissertations were inspired by the desire of dissertation authors to use firsthand accounts to address the meaning-making and lived experience dimensions of Black racial identity. Walden's (2008) mixed-method design, for example, sought to understand the "lived experience" of Black males in the United States in relation to the explanations of Black identity formation proffered by nigrescence theory. Johnson (2006) found a qualitative approach apropos of understanding how 16- to 19-year-old Black girls handled the death of a murdered peer and how race influences their resilience: "Those who have lived the experience are best suited to provide emic data in this knowledge-building process" (p. 78). Johnson concluded, "Meaning-making played a crucial role in how adolescents recover from the traumatic loss of a friend to murder" (p. 176). Given her focus on Black girls, Johnson created a hybrid BRIT that drew heavily from nigrescence theory as well as from developmental and gender identity literature.

The primary methodologies employed are the mixed-method design, the case study, and grounded theory. All of the dissertations employed a mixed-method design, and all employed semistructured interviews. The common strategy was a combination of at least one qualitative method with a questionnaire or a racial identity scale, such as the MMRI, the Multidimensional Inventory of Black Identity (MIBI), the Racial Attitude Identity Scale-B (RAIS-B), or the Cross Racial Identity Scale (discussed later). Carson (2003, p. 25), for example, combined open-ended interviews with the MIBI. The MIBI is a "submeasure" of Sellers and colleagues' (1998) MMRI.

Interpretive Paradigms: The Case Study and Other Paradigms

An interpretive paradigm does work similarly to what theory does. Both provide systematic explanations for a given phenomenon. We define interpretive paradigm as an epistemology that informs a study's theory, methodology, methods, and data analysis. Two interpretive paradigmatic frames characterize the qualitative BRIT dissertation research. One is a case study methodology that simultaneously functions as an interpretive paradigm. The authors treat the case as a means to understanding and recognizing the limited generalizability of the case. The other approach involves combining two or more interpretive paradigms. Each paradigm speaks to the connection between the research problem, the study population, and the author's beliefs about both. Authors can use an interpretive paradigm to make a political statement in a discipline where researchers are expected to express detachment and objectivity in relation to their research subjects. However, in fields where "unbiased" quantitative research is de rigueur, application of one or more interpretive paradigms in conjunction with mixed methods can allow a researcher to have his or her cake and eat it too. Both measurement and application of a given interpretive paradigm can be a part of the same study.

Case Study

The case study is a favored qualitative methodology among the sampled dissertations. Rice (2004) argued that the case study is important to personality psychology because it allows one to explain the "particulars of the case and its activity in context" (pp. 14–15). Authors utilized the case study in different ways. Levester Johnson (2004), Baber (2007), Hill (2008), Jones (2012), and Hasberry (2013) treated each study participant as a case. Rice (2004) took a different tack by defining his six focus group participants as the case (p. 15). During the interviews, Rice prompted the participants to discuss their life experience and to use personal documents such as photographs to tell stories about themselves. Rice wanted to show that the construct of double consciousness is useful to theorizing Black racial identity. Rice identified three types of double consciousness enacted by his study participants. The "Unadulterated Presentation of Self," for example, is a "form of double consciousness in which the individual negotiates a need to maintain fidelity to how and who one is within a universal context of racism" (p. 76).

Case study researchers were critical of predetermined categories and pursued learning firsthand from their participants. Through case studies, for example, researchers could show how a positive self-concept was important to Black student success in conjunction with factors such as being prepared to handle racism, being aware of how to use one's Black cultural capital in a predominantly White institution, and being able to be bicultural (Baber, 2007; Carson, 2003; Johnson, 2004).

Hill (2008) created a sample of 74 Black community college students from which he selected eight Black males for focus group interviews and completion of the RAIS-B scale. His goal was to ascertain whether Black identity influences the academic achievement of Black community college students. Hill concluded that race was not that important to the experience of his participants (note that the community college was predominantly Hispanic, not predominantly White or Black), that students were unconcerned with being labeled as "acting White," and that they took their education seriously (p. 90).

Math educator Jennifer Jones (2012) asked how young girls who identify as Black also become girls who "do math." Jones focused in-depth on two girls as independent cases in order to gain detailed insight into relationships between their racial identity and mathematics ability. Combining a version of the MIBI for teens with videotaped interviews treated as storied portraiture, Jones learned that middle school is an important period in the development of Black girls' mathematical ability and interest. Indeed, Jones suggests that positively identifying as Black could be an asset to developing mathematical ability. Speaking comfortably in her vernacular, Jana, one of the case student teens, illustrated the point:

> "I'll be kinda proud like when I see a Black person on top of their game in school and doing their work, getting good grades because that's not what other people see of us . . . the people of other races they see us failing and they see, you know, us being out in the streets . . . you know other people think we're dumb." (Jones, 2012, p. 9)

MULTIPLE INTERPRETIVE PARADIGMS

Another primary paradigmatic strategy involved using more than one interpretive paradigm. Such a strategy provides a researcher with the flexibility both to frame the racial experience of his and her interlocutors as well as take a political stance on issues of race, gender, and equity. Using this strategy, one can play both the "race card" and the "good scholarship card." Interpretive frameworks used in this complementary way include CRT, Black feminism, and grounded theory.

CRT assumes that racism and discrimination are the norm in American society, "not the exception" (Carson, 2003, p. 18). Social justice and the relevant historical, institutional, and policy concerns should be brought to bear in any analysis of race in the United States (Campbell, 2013). Claims of "objectivity, neutrality, color-blindness, and merit are to be challenged," while scholars should value the "experiential knowledge" of people of color and utilize the benefits of narrative and storytelling as a way to communicate and analyze that experience (Jones, 2012, p. 22). Black feminist paradigms allowed researchers to center the experience of Black women in ways that acknowledged the particularities and politics of their experience.

Harris (2004), for example, focused on eliciting an insider's perspective from her Black women participants while also soliciting feedback from them on her interpretations which she incorporated into her analysis (p. 78). Grounded theory is an interpretive framework in how researchers use it as a way to keep their analyses "experience-near." That is, concepts and categories are based on analyses of their data rather than preconceived categories such as those used by BRIT scales. Grounded theory offers the opportunity to give voice to one's interlocutors and to make the categories that they use to understand the world a part of the interpretation of the data (e.g., Johnson, 2006; McNickles, 2009).

Johnson (2006), Carson (2003), and Campbell (2013) singled out CRT as central to their analysis. Johnson combined CRT with theories of racial identity (Cross's in particular) and women's and adolescent identity development. As such, Johnson was able to speak directly to the multiple concerns of her study—how young Black girls deal with race, gender, and the loss of intimate friends. For many Black adolescents, "the journey of self-discovery involves constructing an identity as a member of a socially devalued racial/ethnic group" (pp. 63–64).

Several studies combined CRT, Black feminism, and nigrescence theory. The CRT lens allowed authors to address how history, politics, and public policy influence Black Americans' quality of life. Jones (2012) illustrates how an insider's perspective informed by CRT, Black feminism, and nigrescence theory is useful to conceptualizing race, gender, and educational outcomes, a problem that is often quantitatively framed:

> This approach to understanding the disparities between White and Black students' mathematics participation and achievement differs from studies that focus on test scores as a measure of ability or systemic school inequities. The girls in this study spoke about their experiences, feelings and beliefs about mathematics learning, and reflected on their mathematics and racial identity. By hearing stories in Black adolescent girls' own voice and words, we can learn more about the complexities of their racial and mathematics identity development. (pp. 6–7)

Researcher Positionality

Most of the dissertation authors consciously disclosed their positionality (two did not), or they provided clues about their identities and affinities in their acknowledgments section. Harris (2004) described positionality as "bracketing," suggesting a benefit of disclosure:

> Bracketing is the process by which one makes explicit one's biases, assumptions, and preconceptions. . . . Bracketing makes explicit the framework from which the researcher operates and the biases that inevitably influence findings. With biases and intent made obvious, one can judge the data from the perspective of the researcher. (p. 71)

A few authors offered minimal positionality disclosure even though they acknowledged its value. Campbell (2013) and Johnson (2013), for example, disclosed personal information relevant to their research in acknowledgment and dedication sections. Many researchers discussed their racial and gender identification, some locating their interest in racial identity in their personal experience, seeking to address concerns that gained their attention before they became scholars. Researchers varied in the positionality depth and detail that they provided, from intimate (Jones, 2012) to a perfunctory statement about "theoretical bias" tucked into an abstract (Hill, 2008).

The location in the dissertation where authors made their positionality statements varied. Locations include the acknowledgment section, the introduction, the methodology section, or spread across a dissertation. We encourage researchers to present their positionality early in a manuscript and to clearly label it.

I already mentioned Jones's (2012) study of adolescent Black girls' racial and mathematical identities. Jones's interest in the topic was academic—increase knowledge of how Black adolescent girls relate to mathematics—and it was personal. In a section titled "Personal Note," at the end of the dissertation, Jones said:

> This dissertation came about because I wanted to know more about the school mathematics experiences, mathematical identity and racial identity of Jana and Tyana. I had been a mathematics teacher and coach in their school district. . . . My daughter had attended middle school and graduated from the high school that Jana and the other girls attended. I developed my own mathematical and racial identity as an African-American girl growing up in a large urban community before moving to the small urban community where Jana and Tyana lived, and where I briefly attended the same high school before graduating from a nearby private suburban high school. (p. 232)

Race, kin, and memories of her own math experience served as conduits that connected Jones to a younger generation of mathematically inclined Black girls. Jones's desire to plumb the depths of the girls' identities and experiences as a way to learn what facilitates their mathematical development necessitated a qualitative component capable of eliciting nuanced experience and beliefs.

Extending and Critiquing BRIT: Limitations and Revisions

Dissertation researchers offered incisive critiques of BRIT. A relevant theme across the studies was authors' suggestions for further developing BRIT. The discrete topics in the dissertations warranting translation were gender and Black identity, United States-centric focus of BRIT, Black-on-Black discrimination, and extending BRIT in ways that align with a qualitative analysis of Black identity.

Gender and Black Identity

There is a critical gap in BRIT: a need to explain empirically how gender and race inform each other as a part of a person's identity. The authors suggest that males and females are socialized differently into racial identification and that this is insufficiently addressed in contemporary BRIT. One explanation for the neglect is the gender-centrism of the BRIT researchers:

> Mostly Black men have written Black identity formation models, with little attention to gender, while female identity models have been written mostly by White women, with little attention to race. Moreover, psychological studies of the gender-role formation of Black women are scarce. . . . Therefore, the identity formation theories in psychology may not address the unique identity formation issues of Black women (Harris, 2004, p. 35).

Gender and racial identity are inseparable; they are simultaneously experienced. Gender must be incorporated into BRIT if we are to make better sense of why some Black women privilege race and others gender: "Development and applications of Black identity models should account for the polyrhythmic, dialectical realities of Black womanhood" (McNickles, 2009, p. 139).

BRITs focus on racial identity and racism when in fact people have multiple identities, and racism alone does not motivate people to positively affirm blackness. Black racial identity theorists are transitioning to address multiple identifications and oppressions through the lens of intersectionality and simultaneity (e.g., Sellers et al., 1998; Cross, 2012; Holvino, 2012; Renn, 2012; Wijeysinghe & Jackson, 2012). Empirically explaining the intersection of racial identity and gender is complicated by the politics of interpretive paradigms such as feminism. Black women research participants, for example, may be uninterested in feminism—including Black feminism—even if they are oppressed. That is, they might not foreground their gendered experience. While intersectionality and simultaneity are useful strategies for analyzing multiple identifications, we must account for the fact that some Black women privilege race while others privilege gender or other identifications. Qualitative research allows us to fathom such paradoxes. Intersectionality may not be the paradigmatic solution that some imagine it can be; it must be carefully operationalized for empirical research. We need more qualitative research into Black identity, intersectionality, and simultaneity. Identities may be intersectional and simultaneous, but people emphasize particular identities and experiences in ways that suggest they can be hierarchically ordered *and* are differently experienced. With Black women's experience of race, for example, dissertation researchers identified the importance of relationships to women's Black racial identity development: "Relationships shape racial identity development as much as or more than experiences with oppression. The [study] participants seemed to develop their sense of Blackness and of being Black women more from relationships than from oppression or interaction with Whites" (Harris, 2004, p. 227). Explaining such gendered and raced differences in socialization and racial identity awareness deserves more attention.

US-Centric Focus of BRITs

BRITs draw primarily on the experience of African American college students in the United States. Harris (2004) raised the issue of how applicable BRITs are to people outside of the United States. BRIT may well be relevant to situations in which Black people are the majority, not the minority, as in some Caribbean and African nations. Even though nigrescence theory will require modification to address the content of a pre-encounter state of African-descended people in majority Black societies (e.g., Price, 2009), nigrescence theory remains relevant because factors such as deracination, miseducation, discrimination, and racism create the conditions that can make blackness a salient identification. Valorizing Black identity, for instance, can be a meaningful undertaking in situations where blackness and Black people are denigrated.

Intra-Black Discrimination and Biracial Identity and Blackness

BRIT theorists are only beginning to tackle how Black folk assess each other's blackness, how and why Black people discriminate against each other, and how such intrablack interaction influences one's self-concept. The MMRI can address intrablack discrimination because it addresses situations (Sellers et al., 1998), and Cross (2012) recently has tackled intrablack concerns of buffering, bonding, and bridging with his Black Enactment Transaction Model. It is likely that research into this issue will continue to develop.

BRIT's focus on blackness does not provide for understanding biracial people who can be pushed to emphasize one racial heritage while downplaying the other. Johnson (2004) combined in-depth interviews and field notes (recorded during interviews) with a survey that collected "background" information. The study focused on four people (cases). Ultimately, Johnson developed a biracial model based on one Black and one White parent. An important finding was that the biracial students acknowledged their parents as the "most significant influence on [their] identity and racial identity development," with the mother being the most influential (pp. 97–98). This challenges the notion that biracial people are highly susceptible to the influence of people who pressure them to privilege one parent's cultural heritage over the other. Note that such findings vary from but are relevant to the conclusions of meta-ethnographic analyses that emphasize the fluidity of biracial identity, the impact of monoracial identifiers on biracial folk, and the value that such folk place on safe spaces (e.g., Bettez et al., 2017).

BRIT: Engaging Qualitative Analysis

Racial identity scales disembody racial identity because they are not experience-near and because they depend upon predetermined categories. In this sense, quantitative approaches function like race as category. For example, the RAIS-B "examines the racial identity attitudes of students without inquiry as to why they might self-identify as Black as opposed to African American" (Hill, 2008, p. 62). That is, we need to understand how and why people identify racially and how they develop the identity that exists at the point of the research intervention. Said differently, the quantitative emphasis elides how people *become* Black and *sustain* and *negotiate* a sense of Black identity in various situations. When a researcher asked a teenage subject about her view of Black people, she quipped, "What kind of Black people"? (Jones, 2012). The young woman's question is supremely important. It suggests that she has a multilayered conception of Black people that the Black racial identity scales are unable to capture in the ways possible with qualitative methods. Black people may talk about themselves and each other in monolithic ways while simultaneously holding multifaceted views of blackness that do not rest easily with the rhetoric. Qualitative inquiry is relevant to drawing out and addressing such paradoxes that are, we hypothesize, common to people's conceptualization of blackness.

One obvious implication of our meta-ethnographic excursion is that we need more qualitative studies that utilize BRITs in analyzing Black racial identity. We learned that BRITs are evolving to incorporate complexities such as the influence of intersectionality, intrablack relations, and globalization on Black racial identity. However, encouraging more scholars to use qualitative-BRIT approaches would help us better design such studies and would help us better explain the complexities involved in how people experience and enact Black racial identity. Although we foreground qualitative methodology, we encourage mixed-method strategies, such as employing questionnaires or scales that are ethnographically generated. The foundational meta-ethnography platform erected by Noblit and Hare (1988) has evolved into a diverse body of research. Meta-ethnography has become more useful as scholars have identified the shortcomings and benefits of the methodology and have elaborated upon how to carry out such study. Meta-ethnography pushed us to think systematically about the relationships among different studies and allowed us to usher the studies into an intentional dialogue. We benefitted from the fact that, like speech, meta-ethnography offered a set of conventions for making the dialogue work.

One could argue that quantitative BRIT dissertations explain interpretations—of coded questionnaire responses, for example. To the extent that this is the case, the interpretations are interpretations of experience-distant and predetermined categories. But what if one of our interlocutors tells us that he is more than Black? That he is a Black man and a Rastafarian? Should we stick to race and neglect the religious identification because we did not account for it in the research design? Ideally, a qualitative approach builds an understanding out of the experience and behavior of participants, requiring interpretation of experience-near categories or processes. Meta-ethnography asks us to generate a dialogue among the interpretations that transforms into another level of interpretation different from the preceding two.

CONCLUSION

Theoretically informed qualitative study of Black racial identity can provide a detailed account of the intersections among race and racial identity. Through context-sensitive and experience-near studies of racial identity, we can better grasp and unravel thorny questions about identity formation itself, such as the relations between racial identity and gender. BRIT is a relevant starting point for the qualitative study of Black identity. Since the 1970s, scholars have developed a substantial body of theory explaining Black identity. The corpus of BRIT has become increasingly sophisticated and nuanced. BRIT informed research is typically quantitative and thus limited in its ability to identify and communicate the nuances of racial identity and race as people experience it on a regular basis. BRIT scholars cling to methods and methodologies that inhibit a fuller understanding of how race as category becomes race as identity, how people act as racial beings. Qualitative research offers a different perspective on race and Black identity formation and hence can enrich and extend BRIT. We applied Noblit's and Hare's (1988) meta-ethnography methodology to recent published qualitatively oriented dissertations that address Black racial identity theory. We analyzed BRIT theories and theorists in order to situate our analysis of the dissertations. We wanted to show how they use, elaborated, and critiqued BRITs.

We wanted to learn why and how authors justify qualitative study of Black racial identity, how they conceptualized their methodology, how they used interpretive paradigms, and how they addressed their positionality. What could we learn from these studies? We were reminded of the importance of positionality to qualitative research. This is especially the case with race and racial identity where a person's experience matters, especially his or her standpoint in relation to race and racial identity. As men who identify as Black, we have a stake in how we study and theorize Black racial identity. We know the diversity of Black experience—for example differences among our generations—and we want to more effectively theorize and communicate such diversity and experience.

The qualitative mechanics of the dissertations suggest directions for future qualitative research: continue to collect and analyze experience near data through interviews, participant observation, personal documents, journaling, and similar methods; use of multiple interpretive paradigms; specify positionality; and extend BRITs in qualitative directions such as addressing the intersections of race, gender, and age, and how people are socialized into Black identity. Based on our meta-ethnographic inquiry, we can imagine a qualitatively grounded theory of Black racial identity able to explain the variations in how people use and experience blackness, and how blackness intersects with or dominates other identities. Dissertation authors are pushing the envelope on developing experience-near and theoretically informed accounts of race and racial identity. We should follow and extend their examples.

NOTES

1. Race and racial identity operate within hierarchal institutions and structures that can exert determining force on people's lives.
2. The dissertations are published by institutions of higher education in the United States.
3. Our definition includes, minimally, people of the Caribbean and the continents of Europe, Africa, and South and North America. We recognize that blackness involves more than self-definition. Race is also ascribed through stereotyping, social interaction, and institutional records, to offer a few examples. Self-definition (or achievement) and ascription work together, forming a throbbing tension felt, for instance, in how a person might feel pride in blackness but angered by negative stereotyping of Black people.

REFERENCES

Adams, M. (2001). Core processes of racial identity development. In C. L. Wijeyesinghe and B. W. JacksonIII (Eds.), *New perspectives on racial identity development: A theoretical and practical anthology* (pp. 209–242). New York: New York University Press.

Baber, L. (2007). *First year experiences of African American students at a predominantly white institution: Considering influence of ethnicity and socioeconomic status through cultural capital theory* (Doctoral dissertation). Pennsylvania State University, State College.

Bettez, S., Chang, A., & Edwards, K. (2017). Multiracial youth identity meta-ethnography: Moving from themes of fluidity, exclusion, and space to uncovering paradigmatic impact and the dangers of whiteblindness. In L. Urrieta & G. W. Noblit (Eds.), *Cultural constructions of identity: Meta-ethnography and theory.* New York: Oxford University Press.

Britten, N., Campbell, R., Pope, C., Donovan, J., Morgan, M., & Pill, R. (2002). Using meta-ethnography to synthesise qualitative research: A worked example. *Journal of Health Services Research & Policy, 7*(4), 209–215.

Campbell, J. (2013). *Urban African American youth language choice in voice: A counter narrative* (Doctoral dissertation). Mills College, Oakland, CA.

Carson, L. (2003). *The ethnic and academic identities of African-American college students: External influences and internal dichotomies* (Doctoral dissertation). University of California, Berkeley.

Cross, W. Jr. (1971). The Negro-to-Black conversion experience. *Black World, 20,* 13–27.

Cross, W. Jr. (1978). Black families and black identity. *Western Journal of Black Studies, 2*(2), 111–124.

Cross, W. Jr. (1993). *Shades of black: Diversity in African American identity.* Philadelphia, PA: Temple University Press.

Cross, W. Jr. (1995). The psychology of nigrescence: Revising the cross model. In J. Ponterotto, J. Casas, L. Suzuki, & C. Alexander (Eds.), *Handbook of multicultural counseling* (2nd ed., pp. 93–122). Thousand Oaks, CA: SAGE.

Cross, W. Jr. (2001). Encountering nigrescence. In J. Ponterotto, J. Casas, L. Suzuki, & C. Alexander (Eds.), *Handbook of multicultural counseling* (2nd ed., pp. 30–44). Thousand Oaks, CA: SAGE.

Cross, W. Jr. (2012). Enactment of race and other social identities during everyday transactions. In C. Wijeyesinghe & B. Jackson (Eds.), *New perspectives on racial identity development: Integrating emerging frameworks* (2nd ed., pp. 192–210). New York: New York University Press.

Doyle, L. H. (2003). Synthesis through meta-ethnography: Paradoxes, enhancements, and possibilities. *Qualitative Research, 3*(3), 321–344.

Emerson, R., Fretz, R., & Shaw, L. (2011). *Writing ethnographic fieldnotes* (2nd ed.). Chicago: University of Chicago Press.

Hall, W., Cross, W., & Freedle, R. (1972). Stages in the development of Black awareness: An exploratory investigation. In R. Jones (Ed.), *Black psychology* (pp. 156–165). New York: Harper & Row.

Harris, J. (2004). *Black women's identity from a Black feminist perspective: The interaction of race and gender* (Doctoral dissertation). Southern Illinois University, Carbondale.

Hartigan, J. (1999). *Racial situations: Class predicaments of whiteness in Detroit.* Princeton, NJ: Princeton University Press.

Hasberry, A. (2013). *Black teachers, White schools: A qualitative multiple case study on their experiences of racial tokenism and development of professional Black identities* (Doctoral dissertation). University of Nevada, Las Vegas.

Helms, J. (1990a). An overview of Black racial identity theory. In J. Helms (Ed.), *Black and White racial identity: Theory, research, and practice* (pp. 9–32). New York: Greenwood Press.

Helms, J. (1990b). Introduction: Review of racial identity terminology. In J. Helms (Ed.), *Black and White racial identity: Theory, research, and practice* (pp. 3–8). New York: Greenwood Press.

Helms, J. (1990c). Toward a model of White identity development. In J. Helms (Ed.), *Black and White racial identity: Theory, research, and practice* (pp. 49–66). New York: Greenwood Press.

Hill, R. (2008). *Hanging out on Crenshaw: Examining the role of racial identity on the academic achievement of Black students at a Southern Californian community college* (Doctoral dissertation). University of Southern California, Los Angeles.

Holvino, E. (2012). The "simultaneity" of identities: Models and skills for the twenty-first century. In C. Wijeyesinghe & B. Jackson (Eds.), *New perspectives on racial identity development: Integrating emerging frameworks* (2nd ed., pp. 161–191). New York: New York University Press.

Jackson, B. (2012). Black identity development: Influences of culture and social oppression. In C. Wijeyesinghe & B. Jackson (Eds.), *New perspectives on racial identity development: Integrating emerging frameworks* (2nd ed., pp. 33–50). New York: New York University Press.

Jeffers, G., Ray, R., & Hallett, T. (2010). The vitality of ethnographic research on race. In S. Hillyard (Ed.), *New frontiers in ethnography* (pp. 19–45). (Studies in Qualitative Methodology 11). London: Emerald Press.

Jefferson, T. (1999). *Notes on the state of Virginia.* New York: Penguin Books. (Original work published 1781)

Johnson, C. (2006). *When friends are murdered: A qualitative study of the experience, meaning and implications for identity development of older adolescent African American females* (Doctoral dissertation). Bryn Mawr College, Bryn Mawr, PA.

Johnson, C. (2013). *Recognizing racial publics: An exploration of racial identity and community among Black women in understanding obesity* (Doctoral dissertation). University of Oklahoma, Norman.

Johnson, L. (2004). *"Other": Biracial students in the college environment* (Doctoral dissertation), Indiana University, Bloomington.

Jones, J. (2012). *Case stories of mathematical and racial identity among Black girls in a small urban school district* (Doctoral dissertation). Rutgers University, New Brunswick, NJ.

McNickles, J. (2009). *Interracial marriage and Black women's racial identity: Polyrhythmic voices and realities* (Doctoral dissertation). National-Louis University, Chicago.

Noblit, G. W., & Hare, R. (1988). *Meta-ethnography : Synthesizing qualitative studies*. Beverly Hills, CA: SAGE.

Omi, M. (1994). *Racial formation in the United States: From the 1960s to the 1990s* (2nd ed.). New York: Routledge.

Price, C. (2001). *No cross, no crown: Identity formation, nigrescence, and social change among first and second generation Rastafarians in Jamaica* (Doctoral dissertation). City University of New York Graduate School, New York.

Price, C. (2009). *Becoming Rasta: The origins of Rastafari identity in Jamaica*. New York: New York University Press.

Renn, K. (2012). Creating and re-creating race: The emergence of racial identity as a critical element in psychological, sociological, and ecological perspectives. In C. Wijeysinghe & B. Jackson III (Eds.), *New perspectives on racial identity development: A theoretical and practical anthology* (2nd ed., pp. 11–32). New York: New York University Press.

Rice, D. W. (2004). *Race self complexity and success: How is double-consciousness represented in the identity construction of six African-American adolescent males?* (Doctoral dissertation). Howard University, Washington, DC.

Sellers, R. M., Smith, M. A., Shelton, J. N., Rowley, S. A., & Chavous, T. M. (1998). Multidimensional model of racial identity: A reconceptualization of African American racial identity. *Personality and Social Psychology Review, 2*(1), 18–39.

Shearon, S. (2008). *Black is beautiful: Body image in Black women* (Doctoral dissertation). Howard University, Washington, DC.

Sherif, M., & Sherif, C. (1970). Black unrest as a social movement toward an emerging self identity. *Journal of Social and Behavioral Sciences, 15*(3), 41–52.

Stringer, E. (2014). *Action research* (4rd ed.). Thousand Oaks, CA: Sage Publications.

Takacs, D. (2003). How does your positionality bias your epistemology? *Thought and Action,* Summer, 27–38.

Thomas, C. (1971). *Boys no more: A Black psychologist's view of community*. Beverly Hills, CA: Glencoe Press.

Walden, D. (2008). *"I'm not gonna let you define me": A qualitative investigation of racial identity development in Black men* (Doctoral dissertation). Fielding Graduate University, Santa Barbara, CA.

Wijeyesinghe, C. (1992). *Towards an understanding of the racial identity of bi-racial people: The experience of racial self-identification of African-American/Euro-American adults and the factors affecting their choices of racial identity* (Doctoral dissertation). University of Massachusetts, Amherst.

Wijeyesinghe, C., & Jackson, B. (2012). *New perspectives on racial identity development: Integrating emerging frameworks* (2nd ed.). New York: New York University Press.

4

Multiracial Youth Identity Meta-Ethnography

Moving from Themes of Fluidity, Exclusion, and Space to Uncovering Paradigmatic Impact and the Dangers of Whiteblindness

SILVIA C. BETTEZ, AURORA CHANG, AND KATHLEEN E. EDWARDS ■

INTRODUCTION

A meta-ethnography expands the depth and breadth of understanding we have about a topic and endeavors to derive a "holistic interpretation" from these multi-perspective texts (Noblit & Hare, 1988, p. 10). This chapter describes the findings from a meta-ethnography of research accounts about Multiracial identity development in young adults. We worked collaboratively to understand what these articles revealed on a grander scale about Multiracial experiences, and certain themes came to the fore: (a) fluid identities, (b) isolation from "monoracial" (people who identify with a single race) individuals and communities, and (c) the importance of place/space for Multiracial people. Our analysis also "surprise[d] us with new understandings of existing social conditions" (Doyle, 2003, p. 325). Specifically, these surprises included (a) a lack of attendance to intersectionality in both participants' identities and authors' positionalities and (b) the absence of attention to Whiteness and White supremacy in discussing Multiraciality, a discursive strategy we are calling *Whiteblindness*. Ultimately we argue that researchers' paradigmatic perspectives and theoretical frameworks impact the framing of problems and solutions related to understanding and working with Multiracial people. Specifically, we claim that Whiteblindness affects interpretations of Multiracial research.

Positionality Statements and Research Paradigm

Doyle (2003) argues that "meta-ethnographers need to ascertain where they are situated" (p. 331). Given that one of our ultimate conclusions from the synthesis was the lack of attention to authors' positionalities and its implications, we name our positionalities and articulate the paradigm from which we work in this chapter.

Silvia. Being mixed is a core part of my identity. I was born in Bogotá to a Colombian mother who was born and raised in Bogotá and a White French-Canadian father who was born and raised in Massachusetts; however, we moved to the United States when I was less than a year old and, with the exception of second grade when we returned to Bogotá for one year, I spent most of my formative years in suburbs of Boston. I felt and was reminded (by peers) of our "difference" as a lower-middle-class interracial family in predominantly White, mostly upper-middle-class towns. When I arrived at college, Multiraciality was rarely discussed, and I struggled to articulate the fullness of my racial/ethnic positionality until I was introduced to the book *Borderlands/La Frontera* by Gloria Anzaldúa (1987), which inspired me to co-found a group for mixed folks on campus and write an undergraduate thesis based upon interviews with women who identified as mixed. This passion for research with/about mixed-race women continued as I returned to graduate school, and I later published a book on the topic titled *But Don't Call Me White: Mixed Race Women Exposing Nuances of Privilege and Oppression Politics* (Bettez, 2012).

Aurora. My Multiraciality has always played a central role in my life though I was not always aware of its impact on my identity production. Born in Guatemala of parents with Italian and Chinese heritages, we immigrated to the United States when I was five years old. I have lived in the California Bay Area most of my life where my ethnically ambiguous features were not uncommon. In college, however, I felt pressured to choose a monoracial identity mainly due to the racially segregated campus. It was during this time that I became aware of the politics of Multiracial identity. Eventually, I wrote my dissertation, *Racial Queer: Multiracial College Students at the Intersection of Identity, Education and Agency* (Chang, 2010), and have published several articles about Multiracial identity.

Kathleen. I grew up in a lower-middle-class, White household in the Midwest. My parents were part of the first generation in my extended White Appalachian family to move out of western Kentucky. My early introduction to the social constructions of race and racism was intimately connected to socioeconomic class and the broader structural history of Appalachian racial politics. Because of a deep commitment to social justice work, my scholar-activism centers on popular education in informal educational spaces with people who are regularly oppressed by the entrenched status quo. While my work does not specifically focus on Multiraciality, what I have learned regarding race informs my scholar-activism.

Critical paradigm. This project is the first time the three of us worked together. Through our research practices of reflecting deeply about our own positionalities,

analyzing these multiple texts, and co-constructing our textual themes, we recognized that we were working from a very particular paradigm. We each claim
a variety of epistemological perspectives (e.g., constructivist, critical, poststructuralist, borderland, feminist) in our larger bodies of work. Yet having each been
trained in cultural foundations of education, we collectively approached this
meta-ethnography primarily from a critical perspective with social justice aims.
"Critical social justice recognizes inequality as deeply embedded in the fabric of
society (i.e. as structural), and actively seeks to change this" (Sensoy & DiAngelo,
2012, p. xvii).

Methods

Noblit and Hare (1988) explain that meta-ethnography is a "rigorous procedure
for deriving substantive interpretations of any set of ethnographic or interpretive
studies" (p. 9), which involves "a sophisticated understanding of the nature of
comparison and interpretation, a meticulous yet creative rendering of the texts
to be synthesized, and reciprocal translations of the meanings of one case into
the meanings of another" (p. 10). In this section of the chapter, we describe our
research questions and process for selecting texts.

Research questions. The purpose of this edited book—how identity theory is
deployed in the study of difference—directed our research questions. We identified two major questions along with some subquestions:

1. How are identity theories being deployed in qualitative studies of mixed
   race youth?
   a. What themes across the studies are revealed regarding mixed race
      youth identities?
   b. What patterns arise regarding the connections between authors'
      epistemological leanings and the theories chosen?
   c. What patterns arise between the authors' theories and interpretations?
2. What is revealed in the collective that may be obscured when each
   individual study is independently evaluated?

Text selection. Our text selection began with a broad interdisciplinary search
through a variety of academic databases (e.g., ERIC, ProQuest, JSTOR, and
EBSCO). Since Multiracial research is an emerging area of scholarship[1], we limited the search to publications post-1980 (and our search ended in 2014). We used
a wide range of search terms in combination with each other (e.g., ethnography,
mixed race, Multiracial, biracial, education, young adult, youth, student, identity
theory, intersectionality, higher education, college). We eliminated research not
conducted in the United States since this is a study of Multiracial identity in a
US context; cross-cultural research would have been an additional and unneces-
sary research layer (Noblit & Hare, 1988, p. 14). Other "predetermined boundary
conditions" (Doyle, 2003, p. 328) for selecting texts were that (a) it was qualitative

research, (b) research participants were 26 or younger, (c) the publication venue was a peer-reviewed journal or book, and (d) the research setting was traditional formal education (i.e., K-12 and higher education). From the broad initial search, we narrowed down the texts by reviewing abstracts and other portions of the publication to identify research questions and methods as well as information about the participants. At this stage, we also looked at the references used in promising texts. The final stage of the selection process comprised deeper review of the texts, which had been narrowed down to 23, looking for publications that centered Multiracial identity development in the research. Ultimately we chose eight publications that provided a purposive selection (Doyle, 2003). These texts are listed in Table 4.1. This table represents a concise collection of the most salient points that we considered in our meta-ethnography. While we selected US-only research, there is worthwhile ethnographic research occurring in other countries (e.g., Ifekwunigwe [U.K.], 1999; Mahtani [Canada], 2001). Much of the Multiracial literature focuses on adults (older than 26), and even within the literature that fit our chapter's parameters, most of the research is about college students; in eight of our nine texts, the participants are in college. An encouraging finding for the future of Multiracial research is that a number of promising texts were dissertations (e.g., Montgomery, 2010; Strmic-Pawl, 2012). These studies were asking complex and nuanced questions and expanding participants to include *Multiracial* persons as well as biracial persons. Of the participants in current studies, many of them included individuals who had one White parent and another parent who was of color.

Coding, analysis, and trustworthiness. We collectively engaged in an iterative coding and analysis process. The coding involved marking portions of texts by creating "a word or phrase that symbolically assign[ed] a summative, salient, essence-capturing, and/or evocative attribute" (Saldaña, 2009, p. 3). Throughout this process we searched for "salient language" or what Doyle (2003) calls "key descriptors" (p. 333). We engaged in discussion about our codes, potential categories, and emerging themes. Glesne (2011) explains that "Holloway and Jefferson (2000, 55) identify four core questions that researchers should ask themselves as they work through their data. Each question is linked to the trustworthiness of analytical questions" (p. 210). In our discussions we asked each other and ourselves these (and other) critical questions:

1. What did you notice?
2. Why do you notice what you notice?
3. How can you interpret what you notice?
4. How can you know that your interpretation is the "right" one? (Glesne, 2011, p. 201)

Silvia returned to the coding document and organized the codes into 11 categories and added these categories: methodologies, theories, audience, and positionality. Aurora and Silvia then swapped articles, coding them all for the 16 identified categories. Individually, we listed related quotes under each code, ultimately creating a full document of categorized codes with quotes.

Table 4.1 ELEMENTS OF THE STUDIES

Title	Paradigm	Methods	Participants	Main Ideas/Findings	Audience	Theories/Conceptual Frameworks	Author Positionality
Brunsma, Delgado, & Rockquemore (2013)	Critical	Survey of biracial experience and semi-structured in-depth interviews	231 survey respondents and 24 interviewees; all Black-White Multiracial college students	Current research leaves our understanding of Multiracial identity incomplete because often dualistic when "race identity . . . is multifaceted" (p. 499); identity matrix (social, political, cultural, physical, and formal); importance of studying the *identities* of Multiracials instead of Multiracial identity	Multiracial researchers	Identity matrix (Collins, 2000; Crenshaw, 1991); notion of "liminality" (Turner, 1969); social identity theory; identity theory; identity capital theory; internationally negotiated selves (Mead, 1934; Goffman, 1959; Blumer 1969)	Not discussed
Chang (2014)	Critical	Counterstories; ethnographic interviewing	25 Multiracial college undergraduates	Agentic Multiracial identity production via complexly negotiated positionalities within varying contexts	K-16 educators	Figured worlds (Holland et al., 1998); facultad (Anzaldúa, 1987); oppositional consciousness (Sandoval, 2000)	Thoroughly discussed and integrated (see p. 26)

Jones (2011)	Who are we? Producing group identity through everyday practices of conflict and discourse	Interpretivist	Case study; ethnographic field work with a university mixed-race student organization	A mixed-race student group of approximately 100 members, 50 of who were considered active	Collective identity development is socially constructed and micropractices are essential to group formation; group identity vs. individual identity	Multiracial Activists and Researchers	Collective identity theory (Brown, 1998; Coser, 1956); refers to Bonilla-Silva's (2003) idea of triracial construction, arguing against it (p. 155).	Not discussed
Kellogg & Liddell (2012)	"Not half but double": Exploring critical incidents in the racial identity of Multiracial college students	Interpretivist	Individual interviews (two per participant); diaries, artifacts, and focus groups	14 Multiracial participates at two coeducational, predominantly White institutions (seven from each institution); 11 women, 3 men	Identified four sorts of critical incidents in the development of a Multiracial identity	Higher education professionals and researchers	Multiracial identity models that recognize fluidity, not linearity (e.g., Rockquemore & Brunsma, 2002; Root, 1990, 2001); critical incidents (Flanagan, 1954)	Positionality discussed in methods section (pp. 526-527)
Literte (2010)	Revising race: How biracial students are changing and challenging student services	Interpretivist / Critical	(a) in-depth, semistructured interviews (n = 60), (b) focus groups, (c) archival collection, and (d) observation (p. 122)	Biracial students and race-oriented student services staff at two California universities (n = 60)	There can be a disconnect between higher education institutions' and students' understanding of race. Institutions often assume monoracial backgrounds for students of color. Programming, departments' self-portrayal, and funding allocations should be assessed to make sure they are reaching all students of color, multi- and monoracial.	Higher education student services	Racial formations theory (Omi & Winant, 1994) and double consciousness (Du Bois, 1903/1999)	Not discussed

(continued)

Table 4.1 CONTINUED

	Title	Paradigm	Methods	Participants	Main Ideas/Findings	Audience	Theories/ Conceptual Frameworks	Author Positionality
Pollock (2004)	Race bending: "Mixed" youth practicing strategic racialization in California	Critical	Three-year participant research with ethnographic interviews, natural observations, informal discussions	High school in California, students and instructors	Students strategically used or challenged race labels to work toward equitable access to resources even as they recognize complexity of race in other situations--called *race-bending*	Multiracial researchers	She builds "upon prior theories of the everyday (re) production and challenging of social structures" (p. 33).	Positionality is considered in methods (pp. 34)
Renn (2000)	Patterns of situational identity among biracial and Multiracial college students[a]	Interpretivist	Semistructured interviews, written responses, archival research with observations of the campus, focus groups at each university (3–4 students per group)	24 biracial or Multiracial participants at three private universities (15 women, 9 men)	Sense of belonging is highly influenced by campus-peer culture. Develops a "conditional model" explaining construction of Multiracial campus spaces based on individual needs, peer culture, and campus demographics	Higher education professionals and researchers	Qualitative grounded theory (Glaser & Strauss, 1967) framed by postmodern racial identity theory (Root, 1996)	Positionality is considered with regard to analysis (p. 404)

| Rockquemore & Arend (2002) | Opting for White: Choice, fluidity, and racial identity construction in post-civil rights America | Critical | Life maps, in-depth interviews (1–3 hours) | Two case studies from 259 biracial survey participants | Suggest that Multiracial people will create a buffer class of "honorary Whites" (Bonilla-Silva, 2003) in the growing tri-racialization, but not without reservation. Finds the Latin-Americanization framework useful to anticipating new ways of thinking about race | Multiracial researchers | Triracialization / Latin Americanization of race (Bonilla-Silva, 2003) | Not discussed |

[a] Renn has a book on this research, but we selected her article because it seemed incomparable to look at a 250-page publication alongside 20- to 30-page publications.

In addition to reading the original eight articles, other articles furthered our thinking process. We each read Doyle's (2003) article about conducting a meta-ethnography; this became a central part of our dialogues regarding meaning making. As new ideas emerged, Kathleen continued to conduct literature searches, adding to our repertoire of information; we each read, for example, theoretical (versus qualitative-based) articles by Chang (2016) and Rockquemore, Brunsma, and Delgado (2009). Aurora and Silvia also drew upon the theoretical work that had informed our previous research on Multiracial people and relied upon aspects of what Delgado Bernal (1998) calls "cultural intuition" (p. 563). As self-identified Multiracial people who have engaged in extensive reading, writing, and research on the topic of Multiraciality, our personal experience, professional experience, knowledge of the related existing literature, and collective engagement in the analytical research process (pp. 564–566) all informed our meaning making.

For the final stage of our coding and analysis process, Silvia searched for patterns and connections, ultimately condensing the categories (and related quotes) into three overarching themes; Rossman and Rallis explicate the move from categories to themes: "Think of a category as a *word or phrase* describing some segment of your data that is *explicit,* whereas a theme is a *phrase or a sentence* describing more *subtle and tacit* processes" (p. 282, emphasis added; as cited in Saldaña, 2009, p. 13). In our final coding process step, Silvia returned to the original documents searching for related information on each theme that may have been overlooked in the other stages of the coding process. During this step Silvia checked in periodically with Aurora and Kathleen to gather feedback on the connections between the codes, categories, and themes, making this a collective meaning-making process of "translating the stories into one another" (Noblit & Hare, 1988, p. 28).

As we continued to move from the theme identification, to dialogues, to the writing process and back again, we shifted more specifically to synthesis; this is when meta-ethnographers juxtapose key descriptors, use comparative strategies on the translations to interpret across studies, and present their synthesis typically in a written format (Doyle, 2003, p. 335). Thus, ultimately, the entire process was iterative with a combination of cyclical coding, analysis, and interpretation buttressed by collective critical question posing, by each of us to each of us, about the codes we created, the categories we settled upon, the themes that emerged, and the synthesis we generated.

Chapter Framework

The remainder of this chapter is divided into three main sections. First, we represent the eight texts and their most salient components in a table (see Table 4.1) and then identify themes raised amongst the studies regarding Multiracial people's experiences related to identities. Through our coding and analysis process, we identified patterns across the collective studies of general experiences shared by many, perhaps most, Multiracial participants. However, the heart of meta-ethnographic work requires synthesizing not only the data themes represented across the studies but also conducting an "interpretation of interpretations through a new lens" (Doyle, 2003, p. 330). Thus, in the next section, we focus on the results of our analysis and synthesis regarding the theories and research paradigms of the various studies. Finally, we conclude the chapter by highlighting what we believe to be the most salient contributions of our interpretations and naming the implications of our findings for future research on the topic of Multiracial youths' identities.

COMMON MULTIRACIAL YOUTHS' EXPERIENCES ACROSS THE STUDIES

Table 4.1 is a concise collection of each text's most salient elements that we considered in our analysis as well as additional elements that will provide context for readers.

Among the articles we reviewed, the authors' findings revealed general experiences shared by a significant portion of the Multiracial participants. We identified three main themes in the collection of texts related to such shared Multiracial experiences: (a) the prevalent experiences of fluid identities, (b) exclusion by/from "monoracial" (meaning people who identify with a single race) individuals and communities, and (c) the importance of place/space for Multiracial people.

Fluid Identities

Authors of all the included studies raise the issue of "fluid identities." Participants' experiences with fluid identities were positioned as both challenging and agentic. For example, Jones (2011) states, "What is distinctive about multiracials—their fluidity and diversity—also serves to simultaneously disrupt their sense of collectivity" (p. 141). Jones, whose work examines collective group identity, finds that although "the fluidity and diversity within mixedness often made members uncomfortable and unable to conceive of themselves as a group"(p. 146), ultimately they developed "a sense of group identity by using what they felt was most resonant about their own Multiracial experience" (p. 147). One (of three) main unifying collective Multiracial experiences was that of "racial fluidity." This fluidity, however, manifests as both a challenge and as a space of agency among Multiracial people in the articles.

Fluid identities as a challenge. In addition to disrupting attempts to coalesce as a group of Multiracial people (Jones, 2011), other challenges related to fluid identities arose for Multiracial people across the studies. These challenges included false assumptions about their identities, pressures to identify in particular ways, and trouble with self-naming. Kellogg and Liddell (2012) explain, "Because Multiracial students' racial background was not easily identified by their physical attributes, it was often assumed by fellow students, faculty and staff, and community members" (p. 532). These assumptions sometimes resulted in Multiracial students hearing discriminatory remarks about a group to which they belong, feeling confusion about how to identify, and defending their "racial legitimacy" (Kellogg & Liddell, 2012, p. 534). Literte (2010) shares this quote from a student named Carmela, who is Black and Panamanian, "I was . . . frustrated with this experience of being told that I did not belong, as well as the experience of being told who I should be" (p. 126). In several of the studies, data reveal that having fluid identities can lead to significant challenges; however, in numerous other studies, having fluid identities was positioned as a strength.

Fluid identities as possibility and agency. Chang (2014) is the author who most explicitly discussed the agentic potential of fluid identities. She argues that Multiracial students assumed both relational and positional identities, which they asserted by "engaging in improvisational activity, the predominant form of agency in one's identity production" (p. 38). Students navigated fluid identity construction by drawing upon a Multiracial "cultural intuition," which is not only a "survival tool" but also a particular kind of "Multiracial common sense" that can "be used agentically as a tool of resistance against the White supremacy which underlies the fact that there are monoracial storylines to begin with, where whiteness remains the referent" (p. 38). Brunsma, Delgado, and Rockquemore (2013) also highlight fluidity as it relates to agency and resistance in their description of two participants who claimed to be "biracial;" they state, "Joshua and Desmond show how agency provides fluidity with regard to formal identification as they are able to choose the third space of liminality as resistance to dominant racial hierarchies" (p. 420). Although other authors did not highlight fluid identities as explicitly agentic, many reveal participants' growing sense of self over time and reconsiderations of identities in ways that demonstrated increased understandings of both themselves and others.

Fluid identities as disruption to normative ideologies. In addition to posing challenges and opening possibilities, experiencing and enacting fluid identities also disrupts two often made assumptions related to identities. First:

> This approach disrupts the perception that there is an end stage to identity development. As identities change based on the relational nature of specific situations, there is no way to essentialize Multiracial identity—this analysis invites new ways of thinking about identity development that are both flexible and purposive. (Chang, 2014, p. 32)

Much identity theory and scholarship is based upon identity development models that are linearly progressive and have purported end stages; the participants' fluid identities challenge these models.

Second, fluid Multiracial identities challenge monoracialism. Literte (2010) sums this up in her literature review by stating, "The traditionally dominant theoretical strain in the literature argues that Multiracial identity progressively challenges monoracialism because it creates racial fluidity, correctly identifies people, and discourages racism" (p. 118). Pollock (2004) echoes this in her work: "The students kept returning over the course of the conversation to expose race groups as infinitely malleable and multiple" (p. 39). Pollock argues that students in her study did not break apart race categories altogether, but they participated in what she terms *race bending*. Thus, Multiracial participants' experiences and articulations of fluid identities disrupt linear, unidirectional identity development models and challenge conceptions of monoracialism.

Exclusion by/from "Monoracial" Groups/Individuals

Discussions of challenges by monoracial people[2] to Multiracial individuals' legitimacy permeate the interviews. The incidents shared almost always involved people of color as those who challenged Multiracial people's legitimacy and right to belong in people-of-color spaces; discussions of White people excluding Multiracial people were noticeably absent—our conclusion discusses this absence in more detail. Sometimes participants shared specific incidents of being excluded and/or challenged by people of color; in several articles, exclusion emerges as a main theme (see Jones, 2011; Kellogg & Liddell 2012; Literte, 2010; Renn, 2000). Kellogg and Liddell state, "Many participants described incidents when they were challenged by their peers—typically peers of color—for not being Asian, Black, Latino, or Native American enough" (p. 534). Although several participants across the studies experienced exclusion, other times participants described a fear of being excluded rather than actual experiences of exclusion as a reason to avoid entering or remaining in particular spaces for students of color. For example, Renn (2000) explains, "Several students told or wrote about times when they had entered a meeting of a group of monoracial students of color and people had looked at them questioningly, as Jennifer put it, as if to say, 'Are you *sure* you belong here?'" (p. 407). Thus, "experiencing mixedness as outsiders to monoracial identity" (Jones, 2011, p. 151) emerged as a Multiracial shared experience.

Two storylines emerge within these exclusion discussions. First, Multiracial individuals are positioned as being limited in their abilities to identify and make connections with people of color. Within larger critiques of passing, Multiracial people are put in an impossible situation: No matter what choices are made, someone will position the choices as wrong. Multiracial individuals are susceptible to critique for trying to insert themselves in "monoracial" communities of color. Literte (2010) included a quote by Leah, a student of Chinese and Black ancestry: "If I go to a 'Black' event, people always look at me, like 'What is she doing here? Does she think she's Black?'" (p. 126). Second, people of color in this theme of "exclusion" are, by default, positioned as the villains, often without a discussion of the larger context that could play into why people of color might challenge Multiracial peoples' claims to particular identities and spaces. Jones (2011), for example, concludes, "University Mixed [the Multiracial campus group] was able to construct an 'oppressor' to galvanize its members' feelings of collectivity and to frame it as a shared oppressive experience around which all Multiracial members could rally" (p. 151). The "oppressors" in this story are the monoracial people of color and communities that "marginalize" Multiracial people. Jones frames her conclusion around the ways in which the Multiracial participants bonded as "wounded minorities," which "served to engage members in the daily practice of articulating the meaning of, and commitment to, a collective mixed-race identity" (p. 153).

Desire for Multiracial Space and Claiming a Space of Agency

The discussions of exclusion lead to a third shared experience: a desire to belong, a need for particular Multiracial "spaces," and claiming spaces of agency. In half of the articles, this idea of space centers on the straightforward creation or mainte-nance of groups for Multiracial people and/or the need to be accepted by others. The other half of the articles either complicate the idea of a singular Multiracial group by incorporating socioeconomic class or other intersectional factors and/ or present a shift from focusing on the limits of acceptance to highlighting the strategic claiming of space by discussing Multiracials' maneuvers within varying, embedded contexts.

The concept of space is central to Renn's (2000) work. In fact, Renn identi-fies "the notion of space" (p. 405) as one of her two main themes. "On all three campuses, students spoke of finding space—both physical and psychological— to fit in" (p. 405). Renn explains that "permeability of boundaries around communities was a major factor in determining which spaces students would choose to occupy" (p. 413). Students at the Carberry campus, where boundar-ies were "the most rigid," created a new cultural space through a Multiracial group, Spectrum.

> Repeatedly . . . Participants told stories of feeling comfortable, of fitting in, or of finding a space in Spectrum. Unlike other organizations in the Third World community [collection of monoracial people of color student groups and programs], Spectrum [the Multiracial organization] was a space where students could identify however they chose. (p. 408)

At Ignacio, students felt that they could affiliate with AHANA (the campus short-hand for both students of color and student of color groups) but had to either claim allegiance with one group or have no allegiance with any. Renn found that Woolley had the most permeable boundaries. In this context Multiracial students felt like they could be both a part of monoracial student of color groups while still holding Multiracial identities. On all campuses, finding spaces of belonging mattered.

In the conclusion of their work regarding "critical incidents" in Multiracial par-ticipants' lives, Kellogg and Liddell's (2012) findings "confirmed Renn's research addressing the importance of space" (p. 537). Jones's (2011) work centers on the collective identity development of Multiracial students. Through her research of the Multiracial campus group during a time of transition, she finds that they "were able to identify a baseline of common experiences around which they could build a collective identity;" this space proved important to the participants (p. 155). Literte (2010), who conducted research on campuses that did not have Multiracial organizations, finds that participants desired programming for biracial students; "Many biracial students feel that they will not have a 'place' within these student services [for students of color], although they desire one" (p. 128). Thus desire and appreciation for spaces where one could be accepted as Multiracial and connect with other Multiracial people are collectively prominent findings.

The works of Pollock (2004), Rockquemore and Arend (2002), Brunsma et al. (2013), and Chang (2014) surface as distinct from the other authors' strong emphasis on a desire for Multiracial space. This is due in large part to the nature, context, and perspective of their work as well as the context of participants' lives. Pollock's (2004) work on everyday race talk is set in a highly diverse high school, which was distinct from the other studies conducted with college-aged youth. Pollock argues that Multiracial youth "strategically employed simple 'race' categories to describe themselves and inequality orders, even as they regularly challenged these very labels' accuracy" (p. 30). Although Pollock does not discuss the socioeconomic status of the students, we gather, from the amount of quotes regarding students' concerns over "equality," that there are more pressing socioeconomic class issues related to lack of access to resources. Pollock explains that Michael, the student of self-proclaimed "hecka races," had to "pick a culture within an adult run structure of distributing financial aid" (p. 44). On his transcript, Michael was identified as "Other White," and he remarked, "I can't get anything with that, even though I live in the projects or whatever" (p. 45). Notably, explicit discussions of intersectionality were often absent from the collection of texts we studied. Yet, positionality beyond race and the sociopolitical context both matter.

Although Rockquemore's (1999) larger research project entailed over 230 survey respondents and 24 interviewees, she wrote articles that focused on a few respondents. For example, we know that the majority of her participants identified primarily as biracial, but in her co-authored article with Arend (2002), they focus on the only two participants who claimed a primary White identity on their survey responses—albeit in the interviews one consistently referred to herself as "biracial." Thus discussions of desiring a space to be Multiracial were absent. However, in contrast to the majority of the other articles, Rockquemore and Arend foreground discussions of intersectionality by highlighting other aspects of the two women's lives and identities including the fact that they lived in predominantly White, affluent communities and had highly traditionally-educated parents. Thus we see the impact of intersectionality in both Pollock's (2004) findings and Rockquemore and Arend's (2002) work. While the need for Multiracial space does not surface in the ways present in most of the other articles, the need to belong, as impacted by contextual factors, remains.

The importance of contextual factors is also highlighted in Brunsma et al. (2013) when the authors argue that a singular Multiracial identity is insufficient to understanding the complexity of Multiraciality. Rather, borrowing from Crenshaw's (1991) and Collins's (2000) ideas of intersectionality, the authors suggest that

Multiracial identity is contextually influenced by social, political, cultural, physical, and formal factors; thus people may adopt a plurality of Multiracial identities. The authors find that this intersection of race and context is experienced as a third space of liminality by the Multiracial students, where they are able to access a "multifaceted toolkit" (Brunsma, Delgado, & Rockquemore, 2013, p. 499) of strategies to deploy depending on the context. Although Brunsma et al. do not use the term *space* specifically, they are articulating "the strategic and agentic formation, maintenance and navigation of a [fluid] identity for Multiracials" that is based on how Multiracial people read the spaces in which they are embedded (p. 499).

Space is a central theme in Chang's (2014) work. However, her work is distinct from many others because she frames discussions about claiming Multiraciality as sites of agency versus a longing for belonging: "This claiming of a Multiracial identity is not solely a borderland of racial deviance, per se, but also a space of agency" (p. 29). Drawing upon Holland, Lachicotte, Skinner, and Cain's (1998) work, Chang names Multiracial people's articulations of Multiraciality as "the space of authoring" (p. 38). This is a space of power.

> An atravesado/a occupies spaces and language that are meant to be silenced and unarticulated yet the atravesado/a feels an urgency to speak his/her truth. The process by which students of color assume and assert a Multiracial identity over time, in an effort to understand their positionality, shapes how some Multiracial students become racial atravesados/as. (p. 29)

The atravesados/as enact agency, which allows them to not only claim Multiracial spaces but also has the potential to be "a source of coalition building between and among different racial groups" (p. 38).

Thus, in this theme of "space" and "a desire to belong," we see a predominant thread among half of the articles (Jones, 2011; Kellogg & Liddell, 2012; Literte, 2010; Renn, 2000): Participants desire spaces to belong as Multiracial people. Within these articulations, most often this desire for and creation of Multiracial space focuses on the limits of acceptance rather than agentic possibilities. Pollock's (2004) and Rockquemore and Arend's (2002) works stand in contrast because they highlight participants' claims of monoracial identities, versus Multiracial identities, as maneuvers to belong and access opportunities. Finally, Brunsma et al.'s (2013) and Chang's (2014) articles highlight claiming space as a form of agency. Chang states explicitly that participants are engaged in authoring as spaces of agency. Brunsma et al. discuss how liminality provides opportunities for strategic and agentic formation of multifaceted Multiracial identities.

Meta-ethnography, through the ability to identify themes across the included articles, paints a larger picture of the collective experiences of participants, which can enhance our understanding of a topic, in this case the experiences of Multiracial young adults. Through our work we identified three major themes across the articles of shared Multiracial experiences. As we uncover what we believe to be the authors' intended messages, other—perhaps unintended—storylines emerge.

THEORETICAL AND PARADIGMATIC APPROACHES
AND IMPLICATIONS

The themes and paradigms that arose via our analysis illustrate both similarities and variations across the chosen studies. However, our interest is not so much in the themes and paradigms themselves. Rather, we consider their origination, production, selection, and telling as well as any light we might be able to shed on their overall substance and meaning. As Doyle (2003) points out, "Enhanced meta-ethnography forces researchers to analyze and interpret not only the product of their research, but also the process" (p. 341). We know that themes do not emerge from a blank slate. Embedded within these themes are theoretical and paradigmatic foundations that guide the selection and identification of such themes, both for the original researchers and for the meta-ethnographers. How our positionalities impact our epistemologies is central to our process and to the product.

In an effort to more clearly see outside the bounds of our own perspectives and to democratize our meta-ethnographic dialogue and analysis, we recognize that our ways of knowing the world and, in this particular case, our identities, fundamentally shape our analysis. In this section, we discuss and situate the studies' theories and paradigms.

Theories

The theories used to ground the included studies vary tremendously. Traditionally, Multiracial identity work has been discussed within psychological identity development theory models (e.g., Kerwin, Ponterotto, Jackson, & Harris, 1993; Kich, 1992; Nakashima, 1992; Poston, 1990; Renn, 2004; Root, 1992; Wijeyesinghe & Jackson, 1992). Although none of the included authors interpret their work primarily through these models, most discuss them. Many authors took a basic interpretivist approach to the work, using little theory to situate their interpretations. From an interpretivist approach, the findings and interpretations match much of what we stated previously: They are explanations of how mixed people negotiate their identities. From that, the implications become what many might consider common sense (e.g., creating safe spaces, allowing people to check more than one box on forms asking for racial data, experiencing feelings of isolation and exclusion from monoracial communities, and negotiating multiple worlds). All of the authors were in agreement that race is socially constructed, and they also acknowledged the paradox of how the constructions of race have real implications in people's lived experiences.

Through our analysis of the theoretical underpinnings and paradigmatic approaches of the various studies, we observed that not only did many of the studies seem lacking in theoretical richness but embedded in the research designs, although not specifically stated, were paradigmatic notions. While many of the studies use theories to frame their studies, they lack strong argumentation in asserting larger implications and discussions of Multiraciality in general. The interpretivist studies tended to be mostly descriptive, focusing more on the micro experiential aspects of Multiracial individuals and less on the macro sociopolitical, cultural, and epistemological contexts that produced such experiences. As we analyzed the researchers' interpretations and related theories, patterns emerged along paradigmatic lines regarding the substance of the research findings and implications.

Paradigms

"A paradigm . . . is a framework or philosophy of science that makes assumptions about the nature of reality and truth, the kinds of questions to explore, and how to go about doing so" (Glesne, 2011, p. 5). Because paradigms inform the very theories, questions, and processes in our research, they have a strong impact on our final interpretations. Thus we spend some time here discussing the two paradigms that we think are employed in these various studies. We then attempt to draw connections between the research paradigms employed and the explicit and implicit theoretical choices and implications. Upon analyzing the studies, we found that they were divided along paradigmatic lines that strongly influenced the ways in which researchers positioned themselves and their Multiracial participants and, in this way, the overall politicization of Multiracial identity. The studies fell into two basic paradigms: interpretivist (Jones, 2011; Kellogg & Liddell, 2012; Literte, 2010; Renn, 2000) and critical (Brunsma et al., 2013; Chang 2014; Pollock, 2004; Rockquemore & Arend, 2002).

The interpretivist paradigm generally seeks to understand knowledge and adopts the notion that knowledge and reality are social constructions and, therefore, relative and multiple. "Researchers in this paradigm attempt to gain increased knowledge regarding their study by interpreting how the subjects perceive and interact within a social context" (Lincoln, Lynham, & Guba, 2011, p. 110). A critical research paradigm, however, takes researchers "beyond describing 'what is,' the intention of interpretivists, and toward describing, 'what could be'" (Glesne, 2011, p. 9).

Similar to interpretivists, the critical paradigm holds that knowledge is a social construction. A critical paradigm further complicates this by asserting that knowledge is also *political*—there are "historically situated structures that have a real impact on the life chances of individuals . . . [leading] to differential treatment of individuals based on race, gender, and social class" (Hatch, 2002, p. 16). The critical paradigm raises questions to heighten awareness of injustices and initiate change. "The 'foundation' for critical [researchers] is . . . social critique tied in turn to raised consciousness of the possibility of positive and liberating social change" (Lincoln et al., 2011, p. 119). Here we review the paradigms used within the studies in an attempt to demonstrate how the two different paradigmatic camps provide refutational lines of argument with one another.

Interpretivist paradigm. Renn (2000) uses qualitative grounded theory (Glaser & Strauss, 1967) as the interpretive framework. Renn offers "a conditional model to explain the construction of public Multiracial space on campus and ask how it might be applied in other situations" (p. 400). Ultimately she argues that to create public Multiracial spaces three conditions must be present. She states, "individual needs create the desire for identity-based spaces, peer culture determines access to existing spaces, and campus demographics create the critical mass (or lack thereof) necessary to sustain a community" (p. 416). In her conditional model, Renn adopts the stance that Multiracial students indeed comprise a legitimate collective group, advocating that if "they [Multiracial students] cannot belong to existing monoracial groups, and if there is a critical mass of Multiracial students willing to organize, then students will create and maintain their own space" (p. 416).

Kellogg and Liddell (2012) subtly associate their research with Multiracial identity models that "position identity as contextual, and as negotiated and defined within relationships" (p. 525) to explain their incorporation of the "critical incident technique, developed by Flanagan (1954)" (p. 526) that emphasizes the importance of context and phenomena. "Critical incidents are defined as descriptions of experiences that students believe had significant influence on their racial identity" (p. 526). They rely heavily on interpretivism to guide their analysis: "Because participants were asked to make meaning of reported incidents and their racial identity, an interpretivist, or constructivist, paradigm framed the study. . . . This framework allowed identity to be understood as not only a social construction, but also contextually specific" (p. 526). Kellogg and Liddell identify four types of incidents that Multiracial students experienced in a variety of contexts including "(a) Confronting race and racism, (b) responding to external definitions, (c) defending legitimacy, and (d) affirming racial identity" (p. 529).

Jones (2011) uses collective identity theory (Brown, 1998; Coser, 1956) to contend that collective identity development is socially constructed and micro practices are essential to group formation. We find it significant that she also challenged Bonilla-Silva's system of triracial stratification in the United States, noting,

> Bonilla-Silva specifically suggests that whites will create this status but that multiracials (among others) will come to embrace this category and its benefits. Bonilla-Silva (2003, p. 937) indicates that "honorary whites may be classifying themselves as 'white' or believing they are better than the 'collective black.' If this is happening, this group should also be in the process of developing white-like racial attitudes befitting their new social position and differentiating (distancing) themselves from the 'collective black.'" (p. 155)

She counters Bonilla-Silva's theory by offering a data analysis:

> By using racial and ethnic group political strategies, my respondents undermine this assessment, indicating that they exhibit significant agency in the process of racialization, choosing to understand themselves as minorities

rather than aspire toward whiteness, which in many cases is readily available to them. Indeed, I find that experiences of hostility from monoracial minorities only serves to strengthen their sense of themselves as a minority group. Moreover, because multiracials are currently a very young population overall, this study may serve as an indicator for how multiracials will come to situate themselves socially and politically in the process of organizing and concretizing their identities as adults. (Jones, 2011, p. 155)

Jones's analysis is problematic for a variety of reasons: (a) her assessment that her respondents exhibited significant agency in the process of racialization seems to provide a narrow understanding of the larger racial politics at play, (b) her depiction of monoracial minorities as hostile toward Multiracial minorities fails to contextualize the overarching White/people of color racial politics operating within these interactions, and (c) her claim that Multiracials are a young population is inaccurate; while the US Census may consider them a young population, Multiracial people have always been present (Chang, 2016; DaCosta, 2007).

Literte (2010) seems to straddle the interpretivist and critical paradigms through her use of racial formations theory (Omi & Winant, 1994) and double consciousness (Du Bois, 1903/1999) to understand how biracial students are changing and challenging student services' definitions of race. Literte (2010) does contextualize race with her discussion of the political discourse between neoconservatives' co-option of Multiraciality as colorblindness and civil rights leaders' objections to the use of Multiraciality for fear of taking political steps backward.

However, her theorization is not as strong as those within the critical paradigm. Specifically, she fails to take intersectionality and positionality, both the participants' and her own, into account in her rendering of the study's findings. Next we turn to the studies that employed a critical paradigm.

Critical paradigm. Brunsma et al. (2013) set the stage for critically thinking about, researching, and analyzing the study of Multiracial identity. In their article, they problematize the development of methodological and theoretical complexity in the study of racial identity, "allowing scholars to think about the various *identities* of Multiracials, the possibility of and conditions enabling an emergent Multiracial consciousness, as well as the socio-cognitive structure and active deployment of identity matrices across other social groups" (p. 481). Specifically, Brunsma et al. include Crenshaw's (1991) idea of an interlocking oppressions matrix, stating that "thinking about Multiracial identities as a matrix sheds light on the intersection of different forms of Multiracial identities and experiences. It also accounts for a contextual fluidity in how individuals deploy and understand this subjectivity" (p. 482).

Like Jones (2011), Rockquemore and Arend (2002) also utilized Bonilla-Silva's (2003) notion of the triracial stratification of race in their theoretical analyses, albeit in a different way. Rockquemore and Arend support the notion that Multiracials will occupy a middle position, serving to split the US racial hierarchy into thirds by deeming Multiracials, among others, as honorary Whites. They use Bonilla-Silva's (2003) theory of colorblindness to frame the post-racial mythology that exists around Multiracial identity. Rockquemore and Arend further utilize Bonilla-Silva's three-tiered racial hierarchy that "simultaneously masks the persistence of racial inequalities while fundamentally changing the way individuals understand themselves and others in terms of racial categories" (p. 50) to support their argument that the growing Multiracial population

> demonstrates a break from historically rooted binary models of racial categorization, implying an erosion of the one-drop rule in determining who is Black, and an expansion of the rules of whiteness that reduce the absolute need for "racial purity," and instead imply socioeconomic standards and cultural assimilation as the price of admission. (p. 61)

In this way, Rockquemore and Arend frame their study in a highly complex way, grounding it in theory and contextualizing it within a sociopolitical understanding.

Pollock (2004) discusses the everyday reproduction and challenging of social structures to show that "'races' are indeed a mind-boggling oversimplification of human diversity" (p. 48) but that young people still continue to use "every-day race talk" (p. 32) in order to make meaning of the racial and economic inequalities of everyday life. For example, she explains that "'mixed' youth [she] came to know over several years of teaching and fieldwork in California . . . exposed daily a paradoxical reality of U.S. racialization. . . . We don't belong to simple race groups, but when it comes to inequality, we do" (pp. 31–32). In this way, Pollock grounds her research and situates her findings within a critical analysis of race-based politics.

Chang (2014) employs Holland et al.'s (1998) theory of identity production and their concept of figured worlds coupled with Anzaldúa's (1987) notion of borderlands to frame Multiracial students' narratives, adopting the perspective that one has the capability of actively participating in different cultural worlds within one's socially constructed and scripted social position. Chang's theoretical framework supports the notion that "the study of Multiraciality can be utilized as a tool of resistance, even a subversive instrument, in solidarity with traditional monoracial narratives and against discourses that fail to capture Multiracial experiences" (p. 29). Her analysis embraces the critical paradigm, describing resistance as a tool of social justice efforts. Chang also problematizes the notion that Multiracial students are powerless by looking at the nuanced ways in which their situational identities emerge. She argues that Multiracial students assume both relational (positioned relative to others) and positional (connected to power, privilege, and status) identities and points to the ways in which the students' intersectional complexities inform their behaviors in various situations, relaying that there are various elements at play—some with room for agency and others mediated through societal factors outside of their control. Chang emphasizes that Multiracial identity is anything but simple, pointing specifically to the duality of her participants' Multiracial identities:

> While Multiracial college students . . . suffered ostracization at times, they also . . . embraced the uniqueness of their racial/cultural fusion and gained a

certain competency or as Anzaldúa (1987) more aptly puts it, la facultad. For the participants in this study, la facultad served as a survival mechanism, a sixth sense that developed as a response to others' racism, homophobia, sexual violence, and general intolerance. (p. 28)

Chang claims that Multiracial college students, while ostracized, also find themselves empowered, drawing from their facultad and creating their own space of survival and agency.

Our analysis of the interpretivist and critical paradigms within this meta-ethnography point to the potential—even if unintended—consequences of studying issues of race without a critical lens. Even with a critical lens, we miss important and even foundational issues because of our own limits, meaning we need to engage in critical self-reflexivity of our own self-identified positions as critical scholars.

Reconceptualizing Multiracial Identity Research in Relation to Broader Structures

While we synthesized the studies, we engaged in a "reconceptualization across studies" (Doyle, 2003, p. 323). Certainly, we identified similarities and differences within the studies but, more than that, we identified two glaring omissions from most of the articles: (a) the lack of attendance to intersectionality in both the discussion of Multiracial students' identities and in the positionality of the authors and (b) discussions of Whiteness and White supremacy. We address these two thematic omissions here.

Intersectionality. Doyle (2003) indicates, "Writers who explain their 'place in the text' make their meta-ethnographies comprehensible by showing readers that they understand not only how they expand by telling, but also how they constrain by deciding what is told" (pp. 336–337). We found that, for the most part, the authors of the selected studies did not place themselves in the text with regard to their positionalities. The authors' social identities remained opaque, as did the intersectional nature of the participants' identities. Intersectionality (Crenshaw, 1989) and the resulting "matrix of domination" (Collins, 2000) refers to the idea that multiple identities (such as race, class, religion, gender, ethnicity, ability, sexual orientation) contribute to systematic injustice and inequality for marginalized groups in an intersectional manner—interacting with one another, rather than acting independently from each other. Intersectionality becomes particularly important when studying Multiracial identity because of the multiple social identities that impact Multiracial people's experiences as illustrated by phenotype, class, language, national origin, and the like (Bettez, 2012). What is lost when researchers discuss Multiracial identity without integrally incorporating intersectionality? And, given the serious attention paid to identity, what does it mean for authors who fail, superficially include, or barely allude to their own intersectional positionalities within the context of their studies? As critically oriented scholars,

we mark our critical stance by acknowledging that "race continues to be a significant factor in determining inequity in the United States" (Ladson-Billings &
Tate, 1995) and recognizing the existence of White supremacy, defined by Sensoy
and DiAngelo (2012) as "the academic term used to capture the all-encompassing
dimensions of White privilege, dominance, and assumed superiority in society"
(p. 188).

Whiteblindness. Given the robust conversation surrounding race and
Multiraciality specifically, we find that collectively, the studies we selected suffer
from what we term as *Whiteblindness*. As a way of teasing out this concept, we
reference Bonilla Silva's (2003) explanations of colorblindness to draw a contrast
and identify a referential point for its use. Bonilla Silva contends that "whites have
developed powerful explanations—which have ultimately become justifications—
for contemporary racial inequality that exculpate them from any responsibility
for the status of people of color" (p. 92). He goes on to describe "color-blind racism" as "an ideology, which acquired cohesiveness and dominance, in the late
1960s [that] explains contemporary racial inequality as the outcome of nonracial
dynamics" (p. 92). Similar to Bonilla Silva's line of argument, except inverted, we
suggest that the studies in this meta-ethnography also developed powerful, albeit
implicit, explanations for the issues around Multiraciality, often removing all
association with White supremacy, a notion undeniably present in the somewhat
hidden discourse of Multiracial politics. This is what we term *Whiteblindness*, that
is, an intentional or unintentional failure to acknowledge—and thereby consider
implications—that all notions of racial identity and contentions around racialization are filtered through and permeated with White supremacist ideology. While
"colorblindness" is frequently discussed in relation to White people's conscious or
unconscious silence around race as it relates to people of color (e.g., "I don't see
race"), in these articles the participants and the authors often discussed the relationship between Multiracial individuals and ("monoracial") people of color, interactions with people of color are forefronted. However, discussions of Whiteness,
both interactions with White people and White supremacy are largely absent in
the majority of the articles, particularly those written from an interpretivist perspective. It is this absence of discussion that we are naming Whiteblindness.

The "surprise" in our meta-ethnography revolved around all of the voices—
authors' and participants'—apparent Whiteblindness. Collectively, we seemed
to run in circles around the centrality of Whiteness within the discourses of
Multiraciality, either avoiding it, misrepresenting it, or being engulfed within it
like fish in water. As we collaboratively processed the themes during one of our
online analysis meetings, the realization of Whiteblindness was almost epipha-
nous. Our cultural intuition and understanding of the topic raised nagging
questions regarding many of the authors' interpretations. We made statements
such as "something seems to be missing" or "something is troubling about the
authors' interpretations." Then Aurora asked, "Where is the conversation about
Whiteness in all of this and how it frames the work?" Silvia exclaimed "That's
it!" In Silvia's work with mixed-race women, constructions of Whiteness as it
relates to White supremacist ideology had emerged as a central theme. Why

hadn't we noticed the absence of discussions of Whiteness? Why were we noticing it at that moment? What did this lack of clarity say about the individual studies and the meta-ethnography as a whole? What did this Whiteout say about our "place in the text[s]" (Doyle, 2003, p. 331)? This led us back to re-examine the theories and paradigmatic leanings to better understand when, where, and why discussions of Whiteness were present or absent and what role the intersectionality of participants and authors might have played in the Whiteblindness of the texts.

FROM A RECIPROCAL TO A REFUTATIONAL SYNTHESIS

Through the process of conducting this meta-ethnography, we engaged in multiple layers of discovery as we collectively worked in the cyclical coding, analysis, and writing process. Reflecting upon this process, we consider our work to be dialogical; we moved between analysis and synthesis in our interpretations of the collective body of works. "Schlechty and Noblit conclude that an interpretation may take one of three forms: (1) making the obvious obvious, (2) making the obvious dubious, and (3) making the hidden obvious" (as cited in Noblit & Hare, 1988, p. 17). As we searched for answers to the research question "What themes across the studies are revealed regarding mixed-race youth identities?," our analysis led us to the original understandings described in our section of the "common Multiracial experience youths' experiences across the studies." This process of our interpretation resulted primarily in "making the obvious obvious." In our uncovering of themes, we found that there were lines of arguments in the findings related to Multiracial experiences and identities. In virtually all the articles, discussions arose related to (a) fluid identities, (b) exclusion by and/or isolation from monoracial people and communities of color, and (c) a desire for Multiracial space, to be accepted as Multiracials. Noblit and Hare (1988) explain, "When ethnographies are roughly about similar things, the synthesis takes the form of each case into the other cases" (p. 38). In our initial analyses and interpretations, it seemed that we might have a reciprocal synthesis.

However, as we delved deeper into understanding the connections between authors' paradigmatic leanings, their selected theories, and the resultant interpretations, a new pattern emerged. We found generally researchers' paradigmatic perspectives and theoretical frameworks impact the framing of problems and solutions related to understanding and working with Multiracial people. Authors who operated from interpretivist constructivist paradigms tended to situate their work in various identity theories that led to what we would call descriptive, individual-based (versus macro-structural) interpretations and implications. Authors who claimed critical stances in their work resulted in contextualized interpretations of how Multiracial experiences are situated in larger sociopolitical contexts. Thus we uncovered what Noblit and Hare (1998) would term a refutational synthesis. Noblit and Hare explain:

Refutations are a specific form of interpretation. In one sense, a refutation is an interpretation designed to defeat another interpretation. In another sense, all interpretations have the form of a proposal about the way things are. To the extent that the interpretation claims to be reasonable, it implies a critique of other possible interpretations: an implied refutation. Implicit refutations, in some ways, are the most problematic in that they require a determination of the essential nature of the explanations, as well as whether reciprocal synthesis is possible. In the process of making this determination, we, in essence, transform an implied refutation into an explicit one. (p. 48)

These refutations were not explicit; the authors were not speaking to each other in refutational ways. In fact, as previously mentioned, much of what was shared in terms of data between the studies was reciprocal; common mixed-race experiences were revealed. The interpretations, however, of the meanings of those experiences varied. Thus we ultimately found ourselves, as the meta-ethnographers, "making the hidden obvious."

Although general themes emerged, we also found that context matters, including the structural context (college vs. high school), the relational or individualized context, and positional sociocultural contexts of power. In most of these articles, the participants' stories are set against a monoracial standard context that sometimes went unnamed, which can reify a false monoracial framework. As researchers studying (multi)racial experiences, it is incumbent upon us to note both the intended and unintended consequences of our work as situated within larger privilege and oppression politics.

We agree with Ladson-Billings's (2005) statement, "The real issue is not necessarily the black/white binary as much as it is the way *everyone* regardless of his/her declared racial and ethnic identity is positioned in relation to Whiteness" (p. 116). These ways that we are positioned are highly impacted by the matrix of domination (Collins, 2000); if we wish to promote social justice, we cannot afford to operate from a Whiteblind perspective, meaning one that fails to acknowledge the impact of White supremacist ideology on racial identity and racialization. Ultimately, those of us doing this work need to understand that our interpretations of Multiracial youths' identity-based experiences can produce and create or suppress and silence. We must reflexively ask ourselves about our interpretations, "how projections of [Multiracial] identity-based meanings both enable and limit . . . thinking and being" (Schippert, 2006, p. 283) related to racial politics and White supremacy.

NOTES

1. Maria P. P. Root's book *Racially Mixed People in America,* written in 1992, was the first academic publication about multiraciality. Until then only a few personal narratives had been published. Other early and significant texts include

Rethinking "Mixed Race" (Parker & Song, 2001) and *"Mixed Race" Studies: A Reader* (Ifekwunigwe, 2004).

2.   Please note that we do not wish to reify the myth of racial purity. Monoracial, in this context, refers to individuals who self-identify with a singular race.

REFERENCES

Anzaldúa, G. (1987). *Borderlands/la frontera: The new mestiza.* San Francisco, CA: Spinsters/Aunt Lute.

Bettez, S. C. (2012). *But don't call me White: Mixed race women exposing nuances of privilege and oppression politics.* Rotterdam, Netherlands: Sense.

Blumer, H. (1969). *Symbolic interactionism: Perspective and method.* New York, NY: Prentice Hall.

Bonilla-Silva, E. (2003). *Racism without racists: Color-blind racism and the persistence of racial inequality in the United States.* Lanham, MD: Rowman & Littlefield.

Brown, W. (1998). Wounded attachments: Late modern oppositional political formations. In J. B. Landes (Ed.), *Feminism, the public and the private* (pp. 448–474). New York: Oxford University Press.

Brunsma, D. L., Delgado, D., & Rockquemore, K. A. (2013). Liminality in the multiracial experience: Towards a concept of identity matrix. *Identities: Global Studies in Culture and Power, 20,* 481–502.

Chang, A. (2014). Identity production in figured worlds: How some multiracial students become racial atravesados/as. *Urban Review, 46,* 25–46.

Chang, A. (2016). Multiracial matters—disrupting and reinforcing the racial rubric in educational discourse. *Race Ethnicity and Education, 19*(4), 706–730. doi:10.1080/13613324.2014.885427

Collins, P. H. (2000). *Black feminist thought: Knowledge, consciousness, and the politics of empowerment.* New York: Routledge.

Coser, L. A. (1956). *The functions of social conflict.* New York: Free Press.

Crenshaw, K. (1989). Demarginalizing the intersection of race and sex: A Black feminist critique of antidiscrimination doctrine, feminist theory and antiracist politics. *University of Chicago Legal Forum, 1989,* 139–167.

Crenshaw, K. (1991). Mapping the margins: Intersectionality, identity politics, and violence against women of color. *Stanford Law Review, 43,* 1241–1299.

DaCosta, K. M. (2007). *Making multiracials: State, family, and the market in the redrawing of the color line.* Stanford, CA: Stanford University Press.

Delgado Bernal, D. (1998). Using a Chicana feminist epistemology in educational research. *Harvard Educational Review, 68*(4), 555–579.

Doyle, L. H. (2003). Synthesis through meta-ethnography: Paradoxes, enhancements, and possibilities. *Qualitative Research, 3,* 321–344.

Du Bois, W. E. B. (1999). *The souls of black folk.* Edited by H. L. Gates & T. H. Oliver. London: Norton. (Original work published 1903)

Flanagan, J. C. (1954). The critical incident technique. *Psychological Bulletin, 51,* 327–358.

Glaser, B., & Strauss, A. L. (1967). *The discovery of grounded theory: Strategies for qualitative research.* Chicago: Aldine.

Glesne, C. (2011). *Becoming qualitative researchers: An introduction* (4th ed.). Boston: Pearson Education.

Goffman, E. (1959). *The presentation of self in everyday life*. New York, NY: Doubleday.

Hatch, J. A. (2002). *Doing qualitative research in educational settings*. New York: State University of New York Press.

Holland, D., Lachicotte, W. Jr., Skinner, D., & Cain, C. (1998). *Identity and agency in cultural worlds*. Cambridge, MA: Harvard University Press.

Ifekwunigwe, J. O. (Ed.). (1999). *Scattered belongings: Cultural paradoxes of race, culture and nation*. London: Routledge.

Ifekwunigwe, J. O. (Ed.). (2004). *"Mixed race" studies: A reader*. London: Routledge.

Jones, J. A. (2011). Who are we? Producing a group identity through everyday practices of conflict and discourse. *Sociological Perspectives, 54*(2), 139–162.

Kellogg, A. H., & Liddell, D. L. (2012). "Not half but double": Exploring critical incidents in the racial identity of multiracial college students. *Journal of College Student Development, 53*, 524–541.

Kerwin, C., Ponterotto, J. G., Jackson, B. L., & Harris, A. (1993). Racial identity in biracial children: A qualitative investigation. *Journal of Counseling Psychology, 40*(2), 221–231.

Kich, G. K. (1992). The developmental process of asserting a biracial, bicultural identity. In M. P. P. Root (Ed.), *Racially mixed people in America* (pp. 304–317). Newbury Park, CA: SAGE.

Ladson-Billings, G. (2005). The evolving role of critical race theory in educational scholarship. *Race Ethnicity and Education, 8*(1), 115–119.

Ladson-Billings, G., & Tate, W. F. (1995). Toward a critical race theory of education. *Teachers College Record, 97*, 47–68.

Lincoln, Y. S., Lynham, S. A., & Guba, E. G. (2011). Paradigmatic controversies, contradictions, and emerging confluences, revisited. In N. Denzin & Y. S. Lincoln, (Eds.), *The SAGE handbook of qualitative research* (4th ed., pp. 97–128). Thousand Oaks, CA: SAGE.

Literte, P. E. (2010). Revising race: How biracial students are changing and challenging student services. *Journal of College Student Development, 51*(2), 115–134.

Mahtani, M. (2001). "I'm a blonde-haired, blue-eyed black girl": Mapping mobile paradoxical spaces among multiethnic women in Toronto, Canada. In D. Parker & M. Song (Eds.), *Rethinking "mixed race"* (pp. 173–190). London: Pluto Press.

Mead, G. H. (1934). *Mind, self and society*. New York, NY: Doubleday.

Montgomery, M. R. (2010). *Being raced, acting racially: Multiracial tribal college students' representations of their racial identity choices* (Doctoral dissertation). Retrieved from ProQuest database (3440164)

Nakashima, C. (1992). An invisible monster: The creation and denial of mixed-race people in America. In M. P. P. Root (Ed.), *Racially mixed people in America* (pp. 162–180). Thousand Oaks, CA: SAGE.

Noblit, G. W., & Hare, R. D. (1988). *Meta-ethnography: Synthesizing qualitative studies*. Newbury Park, CA: SAGE.

Omi, M., & Winant, H. (1994). *Racial formation in the United States: From the 1960s to the 1990s*. New York: Routledge.

Parker, D., & Song, M. (2001). *Rethinking mixed race*. London: Pluto Press.

Pollock, M. (2004). Race bending: "Mixed" youth practicing strategic racialization in California. *Anthropology & Education Quarterly, 35*(1), 30–52.

Poston, W. S. C. (1990). The biracial identity development model: A needed addition. *Journal of Counseling and Development, 69*(2), 152–155.

Renn, K. A. (2000). Patterns of situational identity among biracial and multiracial college students. *The Review of Higher Education, 23*(4), 399–420.

Renn, K. A. (2004). *Mixed race students in college: The ecology of race, identity and community on campus.* Albany, NY: SUNY Press.

Rockquemore, K. A. (1999). *Race and identity: Exploring the biracial experience* (Doctoral dissertation). Retrieved from ProQuest database (9935366)

Rockquemore, K. A., & Arend, P. (2002). Opting for White: Choice, fluidity, and racial identity construction in post-civil rights America. *Race & Society, 5,* 49–64.

Rockquemore, K. A., & Brunsma, D. (2002). Socially embedded identities: Theories, typologies and processes of racial identity among Black/White biracials. *Sociological Quarterly, 43,* 335–356.

Rockquemore, K. A., Brunsma, D. L., & Delgado, D. J. (2009). Racing to theory or retheorizing race? Understanding the struggle to build a multiracial identity theory. *Journal of Social Issues, 65*(1), 13–34.

Root, M. P. P. (1990). Resolving "other" status: Identity development of biracial individuals. *Women & Therapy, 9,* 185–205.

Root, M. P. P. (Ed.). (1992). *Racially mixed people in America.* Thousand Oaks, CA: SAGE.

Root, M. P. P. (1996). *The multiracial experience: Racial borders as the new frontier.* Thousand Oaks, CA: SAGE.

Root, M. P. P. (2001). Factors influencing the variation in racial and ethnic identity of mixed-heritage persons of Asian ancestry. In T. Williams-Leon & C. L. Nakashima (Eds.), *The sum of our parts* (pp. 61–70). Philadelphia, PA: Temple University Press.

Saldaña, J. (2009). *The coding manual for qualitative researchers.* Thousand Oaks, CA: SAGE.

Sandoval, C. (2000). *Methodology of the oppressed.* Minneapolis: University of Minnesota Press.

Schippert, C. (2006). Critical projection and queer performativity: Self-revelation and teaching/learning otherness. *Review of Education, Pedagogy, and Cultural Studies, 28,* 281–295.

Sensoy, Ö., & DiAngelo, R. (2012). *Is everyone really equal? An introduction to key concepts in social justice education.* New York: Teachers College Press.

Strmic-Pawl, H. (2012). *"What are you?" Multiracial identity and the persistence of racism in a "post-racial" society* (Doctoral dissertation). Retrieved from PsycINFO database (2013-99090-058).

Turner, V. (1969). *The ritual process: Structure and anti-structure.* Ithaca, NY: Cornell University Press.

Wijeyesinghe, C. L., & Jackson, B. W. (1992). *New perspectives on racial identity development: A theoretical and practical anthology.* New York: New York University Press.

5

Beyond Survival

A Portrait of Latin@ Identity in North Carolina

TOMMY ENDER AND ESMERALDA RODRÍGUEZ ∎

INTRODUCTION

Research on the new Latin@[1] South notes that because Latin@s have historically been absent from the southeastern region of the United States, the increased Latin@ migration of the past 25 years has created profound and important shifts in the sociocultural, historical, and political structures of the region. The increased visibility has also led to growing political hostility and rejection toward these communities, as evidenced by legislative initiatives such as Georgia's HB 87 and North Carolina's HB 786. Both initiatives called for draconian laws against Latin@ immigrants residing in both states. Latin@s moving into states such as North Carolina, Georgia, Arkansas, and Tennessee have also faced challenges of identity, community, and access to resources (Hamann, Wortham, & Murillo, 2002). Latin@s within these settings exist in a liminal space because it is not always clear where they fall in the Black/White dichotomy of the region. As a result, Latin@s have disrupted ethnic, cultural, and social norms.

For this chapter, we illustrate Latin@ identity in one southern state: North Carolina. We constructed a meta-ethnographic synthesis based on qualitative research conducted in Latin@ communities within the state (Hamann, Wortham, & Murillo, 2002). This chapter will engage the reader in understanding our critical approach in developing this meta-ethnography. We first discuss the physical setting and our connections with it as Latin@ graduate students. We then explain our case selection, coding, and analysis schema. We then engage with the selected cases, followed by our synthesis. Lastly, we discuss our interactions with one of the scholars involved in this meta-ethnography, Dr. Sofia Villenas, in an epilogue. We learned how Latin@ identity is both situational and complex.

Physical Setting

Space and place matter. Identifying as members of the Latin@ communities in
North Carolina, we attempt to develop "new interpretations" of the research we
selected for the synthesis (Doyle, 2003, p. 325). Our synthesis continues the analysis (France et al., 2014) articulated by the original authors and original studies.
Our work is important in helping explore the nuances of what it means to be
Latin@ in North Carolina in the 21st century while establishing connections to
a broader body of research. In order to understand the role of Latin@s in North
Carolina, it is necessary to understand the significant population changes within
the state.

Population numbers and estimates indicate that the population growth of
Latin@s in North Carolina will continue at an exceptional rate. Using population data from the year 2000, Suro and Singer (2002) found that the Research
Triangle area experienced a "Hispanic hyper growth," meaning that the Latin@
population grew more than 300%. North Carolina experienced a 110% increase
in the Latin@ population during the first decade of the 21st century (Office of the
Governor, 2010). Approximately 805,000 people identified as "Hispanic," which
was the 11th largest Latin@ population in the United States (Motel & Patten,
2012). The US Census Bureau (2015) estimated that the Latin@ population
would continue to rise. It projected an increase of approximately 80,000 Latin@s
into North Carolina for the 2014 calendar year alone. Constructing a meta-
ethnography on Latin@ identity in North Carolina helps promote awareness and
understanding of the complex issue of Latin@s living in this state (France et al.,
2014). Part of the development of a meta-ethnography is establishing our positionalities (Doyle, 2003).

Positionality Statements

We are both PhD students at the School of Education, University of North
Carolina at Chapel Hill (UNC), as well as founding graduate student members of
the Latin@ Education Research Hub. Being involved in this program has granted
us access to individuals who graduated from this program and their research.
We have connected with scholars such as Dr. Marta Sánchez, Dr. Luis Urrieta,
and Dr. Sofia Villenas. Each scholar has provided valuable insights in developing
this study. All three scholars, along with Dr. Enrique Murillo, Dr. Susana Flores,
Dr. Margarita Machado-Casas, Dr. Janet Lopez, and Dr. Jason Mendez, completed
dissertations at UNC. Their work not only allowed Latin@ communities to have
voices in the research but also established the foundations for future engagements
with Latin@ communities.

This meta-ethnography comments on issues of power and oppression, as well
as planting seeds of empowerment within Latin@ communities. Part of this push
for critical Latin@ research is reflexivity not just on our positions as researchers

but reflexivity on the body of research itself. This meta-ethnography, in a way, moves us toward a reflexive practice on North Carolina–based Latin@ scholarship. Fine (1994) asserts that, as researchers, "We need to position ourselves as no longer transparent, but as classed, gendered, raced, and sexual subjects who construct our own locations, narrate these locations, and negotiate stances with relations of domination" (p. 76). North Carolina is an important Latin@ center of culture, space, and power in the United States; however, we found that researchers continued to use the term "new" to describe the North Carolina Latin@ community. We disagree with the use of the term "new" because it brings a sense of novelty to the experiences of Latin@s in this area (North, 2013).

The persistence of "new" also encourages deficit perspectives because the term disables Latin@ communities, implying a reliance on dominant powers for help (M. Sanchez, personal communication, 2015). Yet, Latin@s have been settling in this region for over 30 years. In the process, we have disrupted the racialized dichotomies and created new discourses (Urrieta & Villenas, 2013). Resiliency and agency have helped Latin@s navigate various institutions of power and oppression in North Carolina. Latin@s in North Carolina have grown cultural roots based on *supervivencias* (Trinidad Galvan, 2011)—a desire to not just survive but also grow and thrive.

We have intentionally invoked the "I/we" in our articulations of North Carolina Latin@ communities within this chapter. Researchers, in order to critically engage with the narratives, must drop the veil that separates us from our research. It is important to acknowledge our positionalities and interrogate our identities as members of the emerging Latin@ community in North Carolina. Not only do we interrogate ourselves, but we also choose to intentionally bring our epistemologies into the research process. This self-reflexivity allows us to position ourselves not just as witnesses but as participants in the very social structures we wish to explore (Foley, 2002; Noblit, Flores, & Murillo, 2004).

Tommy. I moved to North Carolina from California to teach public school. The son of a Colombian mother and Panamanian father, I was born and raised in the New York City metropolitan area. Growing up in that area, I experienced the diversity of being a Latin@. My best friend is Dominican while other friends were Honduran, Ecuadorian, Puerto Rican, and Argentinian. I developed an awareness of unique differences among Latin@s. In moving to North Carolina, understanding those differences guided my interactions with the local Latin@ communities.

I taught in the public schools system. But I did more than just teach social studies; I disrupted the system. I organized teacher/parent nights specifically for the Latin@ communities after convincing school administrators of its importance. I spoke with Latin@ communities at urban community centers about navigating the public school process as an attempt in finding space within this system. I brought in Latin@ community leaders to speak to my predominantly White classes. Unfortunately, I kept seeing countless Latin@ students entering a school system not adequately prepared to serve them. As a result, they failed academically, behaviorally, or both. Even though I engaged in activities that allowed Latin@s to empower themselves in this area, I often got the sense that others viewed Latin@s from a deficit perspective.

Once I entered graduate school, I started coming across research studies that examined the experiences of Latin@ students. These studies, unfortunately, confirmed my impressions from my teaching days: researchers framed these experiences from a deficit perspective (dropout, violence in schools, low test scores, etc.). As I entered the dissertation phase of my education, I realized the importance of changing the research dynamics in a conservative setting such as social studies research. I have been studying a Latin@ social studies educator in North Carolina. Her epistemologies and pedagogies have both inspired and challenged my work as a Latin@ scholar. As a result, Esmeralda and I are challenged to create a new narrative of the Latin@ experience in North Carolina (Villenas, 2002).

Esmeralda. I moved to North Carolina for graduate school. While I am undoubtedly part of this emerging community of Latin@s, I admit that it took me a while to realize it. The daughter of Mexican immigrants, I was born and raised on the physical border of Texas and México, in a region known as the Rio Grande Valley. I grew up in a hybrid culture that did not distinguish what was of the United States and what was México. I was born into a historically established Mexican community and was immersed in its cultural productions.

My status as the lone Chicana across all of the education graduate programs and my isolation from other Latin@s in the North Carolina area led me to mistakenly view the emerging Latin@ communities as something I was not a part of. I moved into a space (graduate school) that has a small but established Latin@ history or community. I was invisible in the sense that I was not always represented in the populations inhabiting these spaces and the fact that Latin@ issues continued to be marginalized in my courses. However, placed in sharp contrast against a predominantly White institution, my Mexicanidad, epistemology, and critical consciousness also made me hyper-visible. In many of these academic spaces, I was *the only* Latina voice and body. This placed me in a position of being both student *and* teacher to both my peers and professors—a position that I have come to resent over time. This is not to say I did not have allies or that I experienced outright resistance from individuals. Rather, it has to do with the physical, emotional, and spiritual tolls that arose from feeling alone and isolated from my people. I realize now that my own experiences of isolation and cultural longing are reflected in the very work I sought to analyze in this meta-ethnography. However, just as the works discussed in this chapter show, I too have engaged in strategies of resistance and resiliency. In fact, it was my Chicana feminist scholarship, cultural isolation, and longing that led me to step out of the ivory tower and into a middle school English as a second language classroom. While arguably not conducive to maintaining my graduation timeline, it did become necessary for me to thrive as a Chicana educator and scholar. Enacting my agency and autonomy over how I embody and practice my epistemologies and activism is in service to my *supervivencia*.

Case Selection

We engaged in a review of research focused on the Latin@ population in North Carolina from January 2005 to January 2015. In order to locate research-based pieces, we searched certain databases from February 2015 to March 2015: EBSCOHOST, Articles +, and Google Scholar. We used the keywords Latino, Latina, Hispanic, Latino North Carolina, Latina North Carolina, Hispanic North Carolina. The searches revealed 11 papers. Two studies were eliminated because of a mixed-methods research design, while the third study obtained data from a survey. The fourth study viewed Latinxs in North Carolina from a deficit perspective and was excluded. We wanted to be faithful to studies that relied on interviews as the main qualitative method.

In the spirit of transparency, most of the authors of the chosen pieces are graduates of the UNC School of Education. Our searches were also intentional in that we had some prior knowledge on some of the pieces we wished to include. However, we did not specifically target these scholars.

Coding and Analysis

We developed a template, based on Noblit and Hare (1988), in order to code and analyze the selected papers. The following sections were included in the template:

1. Methodology
2. Theory
3. Research Site and Participants
4. Main Ideas
5. Themes and Search Terms
6. Thoughts and Observations

The template attempted to establish our position within this complex topic and research (Doyle, 2003). We took into account our own research peda-gogies and experiences and sought to develop a unique voice. We also cre-ated transparency with our approach. We acknowledged our academic and personal identities. We also understood our own epistemologies. The meta-ethnography piece has the potential to inform theory, research, and policy (France et al., 2014).

It is also important to discuss the role of technology in developing this meta-ethnography. We utilized technology to our advantage in analyzing the selected works. We worked on a cloud-based document in order to overcome issues of distance and work commitments outside this research. Within the document, we created a table to organize our findings. We also communicated through a chat program on this document. This technique allowed us to engage with one another without having to be physically present.

RESULTS

We identified seven papers for this meta-ethnography. We discuss each paper and then explain the themes we developed in the synthesis.

Villenas (2001) documented the experiences of Latina mothers settling in a rural town in North Carolina. In working with these mothers, Villenas helped frame these experiences as ones of strength and power. The mothers articulated numerous experiences of prejudice and discrimination from their White neighbors.

Villenas (2001) argued that the lives of the immigrant Latin@ families in her study intersected with the economic demands of globalization. As a result, researchers have not "paid serious attention to the 'racial and ethnic character of the massive distributive transformation that globalization has set in motion'" (p. 5). North Carolina companies specifically advertised employment opportunities to these families simply out of desire for profit. They did not pay attention to the physical and symbolic violence these families experienced in traveling to the United States. They also did not pay attention to the institutional racism existing in "areas of housing, employment, and police surveillance" (p. 7).

This article critically examined the Latin@ experience in North Carolina through a Chicana/feminist theoretical framework. These mothers spoke out against the White dominant narrative of being weak. The mothers posited common sense, life experiences, and the home as important markers in redefining the specific notion of being educated. Second, Villenas (2001) identified mothers from El Salvador, Guatemala, and Mexico to share their experiences, thus changing the dominant Southern White belief that all Spanish speakers are Mexican. Lastly, Villenas connected these mothers to new spaces that "figured prominently" in the conversations about the "Latino problem," such as health care services and education (p. 8).

Villenas (2002) drew from her two-year ethnographic study "to examine the cultural/racial dynamics and creative resilience of Hope City Latino families in [the face of] conflictual debates about Latino family education" (p. 18). She unpacked the deficit public discourses surrounding the designated faults and needs of the Latin@ community. Importantly, however, Villenas decided to highlight how Latin@ families practiced agency defining and enacting child-rearing practices that they deemed important for the moral upbringing of their children. In her observations of Hope City, Villenas found that Latin@s were often constructed as "workers," there to serve those in power. US-born White and Black individuals portrayed Latin@s as a people in need of help. This positioned Latin@s as "social service clients" rather than people with agency and power.

This notion of Latin@s as clients was a symptom of larger deficit frames that designated Latin@ people as culturally flawed. Thus the focus on services targeting families and child-rearing practices was a result of the idea that White ways of raising children were the *right* ways. However, for Latin@ families, child-rearing was not just a way of cultural and tradition maintenance but also an explicit naming of moral and ethical values that they thought were not always reflected in US society and culture. Along these lines, parents practiced *educación* where their teaching focused on instilling a moral education using *consejos*[2] to impart values of *respeto*[3] and *buen comportamiento*.[4]

Context was incredibly important to this ethnographic study as Villenas (2002) not only showed community responses to the emerging Latin@ population in the mid-1990s but was also able to illustrate how families continued *and* reinvented their culturally specific pedagogies to fit their needs in this new context. An example of this is a parent's decision to instill a certain level and kind of *confianza* between herself and her children. She pointed out that she did not want her children to fear her and instead wished to instill trust through mutual respect—something she pointed out was different from how she was reared in her home country. The transformation they felt was necessary because there was an expressed need to maintain vigilance in this new context, which they were both new to. However, it was important for Villenas to point out that these transformations and departures from traditional notions of *educación* were not just responses to a new context but specific acts of agency. This agency, she argues, is something that needs to be recognized and respected.

Murillo (2002) studied the dynamics between the established White residents of "Sunder Crossings, Rodham County" (pseudonym) and the Mexican/Latin@ laborers and their family members living in a North Carolina town as it underwent a demographic change in the late 1990s. Murillo purposely redirected his focus to include White residents because, often, "'race' is equated with subordinate groups" (p. 219). He connected cultural and social capital with the power of being white. The incorporation of White voices brought new viewpoints into the themes of "getting a good education" and "protecting the family" viewed by Latin@s in North Carolina.

These viewpoints revealed the negative thinking of the White residents and the prejudice experienced by Latin@s. Murillo (2002) found how education, policy, and identity all intersected for both groups and located his research in the issue of race within the Southern context. For Whites, Latin@ identity connected with criminality or violence. The arrival of Latin@s signified the "end of their 'very friendly city'" (p. 226). Police in dialogue with community members associated gangs as part of the general Latin@ culture. As a result, they pledged to work to lower the crime rate associated with these individuals. Murillo also captured Whites' laments concerning the use of school resources to accommodate newly arrived Latin@ students by educators. The educators remarked on school administrators' and policymakers' resistance toward Latin@s. These examples reflected the adjustment from the traditional Black–White dichotomy to a system of "fear and exclusion" brought by the sudden and massive arrival of Latin@s to this area (p. 217).

For Latin@s, being culturally and physically different from their White neighbors contributed to their struggles. Latin@s experienced the false promises of new socioeconomic opportunities offered by the companies of Rodham County. Latin@s encountered a lack of available and affordable housing. They remarked about how landlords consistently raised the price of rent while doing minimal or no maintenance work. Murillo (2002) also found that Latin@s lacked political support. This was evident when it came to educational issues for Latin@s. Many Latin@ students, lacking knowledge in the English language, struggled with a "largely monolingual curriculum" (p. 223).

Lopez's (2007) dissertation work was conducted a few years after Villenas's (2001, 2002) and Murillo's (2002) ethnographic work in the same North Carolina town. Lopez points out that while many oppressive systems and deficit cultural constructions of Latin@s remained, she also found that the town had significantly changed over time in the sense that there was more infrastructure in place to support the Latin@ community. Her research extends the previous studies by the institutionalized barriers faced by undocumented Latin@ youth in the educational system.

Lopez's (2007) study centered the counternarratives of five Mexican origin undocumented students also living in Sunder Crossings. Lopez worked with high school teachers to identify students who were "college ready." While working with White teachers, she found that these educators were instrumental in acting as institutional agents and brokers between Latin@ students and the educational system. Teachers were able to use their knowledge and cultural capital to facilitate the navigation of graduation requirements and the college application process. Many of these teachers expressed a critical consciousness regarding the undocumented status of their students and the broken immigration and educational systems that barred them from accessing higher education. These teachers are a contrast to the institutional agents described in Villenas's (2001, 2002) and Murillo's (2002) work a decade prior. However, it is important to recognize that Lopez did note other teachers' propensity to also view students in a subtractive and deficit manner. These perspectives targeted and further marginalized parents and their motivations for bringing their children to the United States. One example of this was a teacher who believed that parents only brought their children to the United States to work—a belief that stands in contrast to the students' own reason for immigrating: to get a good education and thus to achieve social mobility that would not have been possible in Mexico.

The undocumented Latin@ students in Lopez's (2007) study recognized how the world of the school and the world of the home were sometimes at odds. Students reported that while their parents always pushed them to succeed in school, rarely did they encourage higher education. All the while, those in honors classes had received the message that everything was in preparation to attend college. Another way these two worlds were seemingly at odds was that school emphasized that students were a "blank slate where everyone could qualify for a college education, while at home the emphasis on being well educated included being a good son/daughter and being able to respect and take care of your family" (p. 110). Institutionalized barriers, such as the lack of in-state tuition for undocumented youth, prevented these students from accessing higher education.

Lastly, Lopez (2007) highlighted the different kinds of resistance and agency that students employed in navigating a racist xenophobic educational system. For example, regarding language, students expressed the importance of learning

English. While this emphasis might bring up issues of uncritical assimilation and cultural betrayal, students described English-language attainment as a way to create success for themselves. At the same time, these students continued to maintain and honor their Mexican cultures outside the school setting. Some students also practiced a transformative resistance (Solórzano & Delgado Bernal, 2001) in relation to their status as undocumented students. These students developed and *acted* on their critical consciousness by participating in rallies and public critiques of the broken immigration system.

Ko and Perreira (2010) examined the experiences of Latin@ adolescents in emergent communities in North Carolina. The authors understood the lack of qualitative research on the "migration and acculturation experiences of first-generation youth" (p. 466). They also realized that even fewer research studies existed on the migration and acculturation experiences of Latino youth. Ko and Perreira interviewed 20 first-generation Latin@ adolescents. They focused on how these youths characterized "their migration and acculturation experiences, how migration affects their normative development, and how they adapted to the challenges of international migration and settlement in a new country" (p. 467).

Ko and Perreira (2010) utilized three major theoretical thoughts in executing their research: acculturation theory, cultural-ecological theories of child development, and Sluzki's stages of migration framework (p. 468). Ko and Perreira selected these three theories as tools in rejecting the traditional deficit perspectives used by previous researchers in studying immigrant youth. The authors wanted to empower the youth through their actions. Ko and Perreira looked for examples of youth engaging in cultural straddling.

Through hours of interviewing, where the youths switched between Spanish and English, the authors came to understand three important aspects of their occurrences: the premigration experience, the migration experience, and the postmigration experience. Within each experience, Ko and Perreira (2010) allowed the participants to articulate their own thoughts and experiences in moving to the United States. They did this because they wanted the participants to drive the research.

The participants mentioned some social and personal issues important to them. A number of them spoke to a more pronounced attempt at gender equity in the United States. The participants also rationalized the parent and child separation that occurred during these experiences as good/necessary. Lastly, the majority of participants identified isolation and unhappiness that resulted from transitioning to life in the United States. Providing spaces within the research for the participants' voices revealed the difficulties, and the promises, of living in the United States.

Machado-Casas (2012) explored the cultural and sociolinguistic identities of transnational Indigenous Latin@ immigrants (ILIs) and how they developed strategies of cultural and social survival. While the larger study consisted of 230 participants, this particular piece used the experiences of three participants to illustrate how ILIs engage their pedagogies of the chameleon. Machado Casas's participants included Iza, an Indigenous Otomí woman from Mexico. She was raising children in North Carolina, a place she had lived in for six years at the time of the study. Maria was a K'iché woman from Guatemala who had been living in the United States for seven years. She was raising children in the United States, in addition to having one child in Guatemala. Manuel—the only male referenced in this article—was a Náhualt/Pipil father from El Salvador who had been in the United States for five years. All three had attended some school—though the extent of their formal education was vague.

Machado-Casas (2012) developed the framework of pedagogy of the chameleon to highlight how Indigenous people were able to use "coyote tools" to create fluid identities. These practices allowed them to adapt to different contexts for the purposes of physical, cultural, and social survival. In particular, she highlighted how their multilingualism (English/Spanish/Native languages) was an important tool for their survival. In addition, Machado-Casas explored how ILIs redefine traditional notions of transnationality. *Traspasando fronteras* is not always a physical act. Rather, with the growth in technology and the participants' imperatives to maintain contact with their international communities, and by crossing borders via virtual and linguistic spaces, ILIs have transformed transnational experiences into experiences of empowerment in resisting the dominant culture.

The effects of colonialism are entrenched in the everyday life experiences of Indigenous people, including Indigenous Latin@s. All the participants referenced in this study spoke an Indigenous language, and they often noted that it was an integral part of their identity. It was important for the participants to maintain their Indigenous language because it promoted cultural survival. Language as a tool of survival was best exemplified in the ways and reasons the participants used their multilingualism. While the invisibility of ILIs has led to the erasure of Latin@ intergroup diversity when employed by the ILIs, invisibility often served as a form of protection and survival. Along these lines, Machado-Casas (2012) likened the participants' use of their multiple languages (Indigenous, Spanish, and English) to taking on disguises for this very purpose.

In addition to multilingual strategic disguises, participants also employed multicultural disguises. Due to Latin@ anti-Indigenous racism and prejudice, María developed multiple identities in order to "protect" herself. Iza further underscored this in-group marginalization by revealing that life in the United States represented the first time she was able to pass as Mexican—an identity that while marginalized in the United States provided more power to her in the Mexican community. While Machado-Casas (2012) referred to these strategies as tools, the pedagogies of the chameleon was more than a strategy—it was a way of being since it delineated access, mobility, and protection.

Lastly, Machado-Casas (2012) highlighted how indigeneity and transnationalism redefined Latinidad. While Trueba (2004) defined transnationals as people who have frequent mobility across physical borders, the participants in this study—while limited in physical transnational travel due to their undocumented status—also engaged in transnationalism. For example, language played an important role in crossing these virtual spaces. Multilingualism—Indigenous languages,

Spanish, and English— gave them the tools to be active in their various communities in the United States and countries of origin.

Wilson, Ek, and Douglas (2014) studied the cultural and sociopolitical circumstances influencing the actions of Latin@ immigrant youth as they transversed educational borderlands. They examined three aspects: geopolitical, institutional, and home community. However, their study examined educators either assisting or hampering Latin@ students. In selecting these positions, the researchers studied how these spaces intersected when immigrant students used them to cross borders in the United States.

The authors posited their research aims via border theories. Specifically, they cited notions of border and border crossing as spaces "occupied by groups who are viewed as different from dominant groups in power" (Wilson et al., 2014, p. 3). This led to the dominant groups, in this case White people, establishing legal practices and cultural cues that oppressed other groups into submission, most notably Latin@s. The authors also argued that, within these spaces, the dominant groups characterized these others as "alien and undeserving" (p. 4).

Wilson et al. (2014) also examined the role of identity within the setting of differences. Specifically, they understood identity construction occurring within these contexts. According to them, "identity is relational and one typically constructs themselves as 'I' and those different from them as the 'other'" (p. 4). This approach led the authors to examine the role of schools in designating identities. The authors came to the understanding that in order for educators to redirect these oppressing actions, they needed to lead proactive cultural discussions in the classroom. These actions, according to the researchers, came with major risks, such as resisting school authority and circumventing curricula.

The authors found, through interviews with North Carolina educators, that educators "do not have long-term experience" serving Latin@ groups, in comparison with California, the other state examined in this research (Wilson et al., 2014, p. 14). As a result, North Carolina educators failed to move outside of their privileged spaces and continued to view Latin@ immigrant students from deficit perspectives. The educators often used the "tripped wire metaphor." According to the authors, this signified a colorblind approach that failed to acknowledge the strengths of underrepresented groups. The authors also found that the intense emphasis on testing and accountability in schools contributed to the educators' intolerance of Latin@s. Educators cited the rigorous standards of Academic Yearly Progress (AYP) as a major factor. According to one participant, one student could put "AYP in the toilet" (p. 16). The test results from these Latin@ immigrant students then led to other educators viewing them as deficient learners. The community also echoed these viewpoints. One participant, the parent-teacher organization president, lamented the community's view of one of the schools in the study. She commented how often she heard the comment "Ewww, you work there?" from community members (p. 17). Because of these narratives, the authors called for educators to disrupt their settings through acts of empathy and translational approaches in the classroom.

SYNTHESIS

We developed a new set of meanings from the examinations of qualitative research into Latin@ communities in North Carolina: "Education: Schooling and Ways of Knowing," "Identities in Flux," and "Fuerzas and Agency." These meanings, as illustrated in Figure 5.1, demonstrate the third-level synthesis of the coding process, which indicates the introduction of new knowledge into the existing research (Savin-Baden et al., 2008). The following themes came from detailed rereadings and coding exercises of the literature examined: education, *fuerza* (strength), and North Carolina Latin@ identity. While these themes also intersected with one another at different junctions in the research, their recapitulation warranted detailed, individualized analysis. A fourth-order interpretation of these intersecting concepts led us to a discussion of *supervivencia* in which we argue that education, *fuerzas*, and identity functioned together to show that these communities are doing more than just surviving in these new North Carolina Latin@ spaces: they are creating new discourses and forging spaces.

EDUCATION: SCHOOLING AND WAYS OF KNOWING

A number of pieces looked at how the school itself reflected a barrier for Latin@s in North Carolina. Wilson et al. (2014) noted how the importance of education was rooted in the public school space in North Carolina. With educators entrenched within the domain of the traditional political power, Latin@ immigrant youth "seeking access" often encountered struggles within these spaces (p. 15). Yet they uncovered educators who were willing to cross their own intersectional borders in order to disrupt the system. One educator commented how interactions with

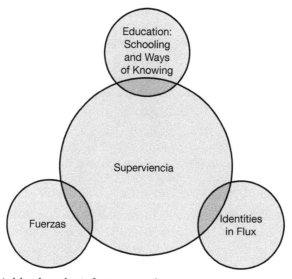

Figure 5.1. Third-level synthesis from our readings.

Latin@s would not only "erase borders" but also "foster inclusion" among all students within the school setting (Wilson et al., 2014, p. 18).

Buena educación. Three articles described the importance of *buena educación*. For Latin@ communities, education begins in the home setting, not in the traditional school setting. Machado-Casas (2012) identified Latin@s' home language(s) as examples of *buena educación*. Latin@s used both the Native and acquired languages as sources of currency for survival and understanding in an unfamiliar setting (Machado-Casas, 2012). Villenas (2001) saw common sense as an extension of *buena educación*. Latina mothers prepared their children entering the US school setting with knowledge of morality and a hard-work ethic. This approach empowered Latin@s when the White community continually identified deficiencies such as illiteracy or lack of motivation in Latin@ students.

Villenas (2002) also saw the power of *respeto*, since it reflected the core definition of *buena educación*. *Respeto* valued the profoundness of developing human relationships and "the valuing of the wisdom of older family members" (p. 23). Developing *buena educación* allowed Latin@s to establish collective agency in a setting that encouraged individualism. Lopez (2007) identified the importance of "being a good son/daughter and being able to respect and take care of your family" (p. 110). These elements of *buena educación* allowed Latin@s to not only take control of their experiences but also to survive in a new setting.

IDENTITIES IN FLUX

Identity, arguably, is implicit in these studies. Using our own experiences of moving to North Carolina as Latin@s, we believe that identity plays a significant role in how we navigate the various spaces we occupy (educational, political, social, etc.). Next we discuss how Latin@s in North Carolina developed intersectional identities, borderlands identities, and identities as agency and resistance.

Intersectional identities. All of the studies identified conflict as a significant and constant occurrence for Latin@s in North Carolina. In examining these experiences, we saw how Latin@s developed identities as responses to those conflicts. Murillo (2002) connected identity through the development of "survival skills" (p. 224). Developing these survival skills allowed Latin@s to forge identities on their own terms, not on the dominant power's terms. This approach counteracted the more patronizing approach, employed by churches and other community groups, of having Latin@s enter an already established social network with entrenched norms (Murillo, 2002). Machado-Casas (2012) highlights important nuances in Latin@s' experiences by pointing to the experiences of Indigenous Latin@ communities. For example, Manuel's identification of "safe" and "unfriendly" spaces were underpinned by his *camaleonidad*—his abilities to weave in and out of Indigenous communities, broader Latin@ spaces, and White-dominated spaces in North Carolina (Machado-Casas, 2012, p. 543).

Identity was also created as a form of cultural resistance and reaffirmation to being in North Carolina. Villenas (2001) chronicled Latina mothers who, in developing new identities in North Carolina, retained a significant part of their original identities. One mother, Rocio, said, "for someone who is Mexican, right, we have to teach them [children] our country's customs. It's to our advantage. Well, here there are people with a lot of vices" (Villenas, 2001, p. 18). Ko and Perreira's (2010) study similarly depicted this reaffirmation. One Latina student, Isabel, declared that, as Latin@ youth, "we needed to keep our traditions. I don't want to be like an American [White] or like other people. This is how I was born, and this is how I want to remain" (p. 485).

Lopez (2007) identified a much stronger infrastructure in place in North Carolina. Intake centers, advocacy groups, and a dual-language elementary school helped settle Latin@s into the area. As a result, Wilson et al. (2014) argued that while schools could still assign identities to Latin@ students, the same students, through their own agency, now "resist the dominant group's efforts to define, assimilate, and/or negate them" (p. 5). Some students, like Carmen and Frances, recognized that going to college was a part of their identity; a student like Fidel, however, understood his undocumented status might prohibit him from attending higher education even though he worked hard to do well academically (Lopez, 2007). Ko and Perreira's (2007) study found similar experiences. One student, Fernandina, said that many Latin@ students felt disheartened by the lack of educational options after high school. She asked why would Latin@ students try to finish high school "if I can't go to college? Why would I do this if people out there are already expecting me to quit because I'm Hispanic?" (pp. 485–486). On the other hand, Alonso believed it was important to all Latin@ students to "keep all their options open" (p. 486).

Borderland identities. It was clear to us that many Latin@s in North Carolina developed borderland identities. According to Anzaldua (1987), individuals who moved across a variety of borders, such as those of geography, gender, and race, were considered border crossers. The notion of a border-crossing identity spanned all of our studies (Kier Lopez, 2007; Ko & Perreira, 2010; Machado-Casas, 2012; Villenas, 2001, 2002; Wilson et al., 2013). Wilson et al. specifically identified three specific types of borders Latin@s navigated through: geopolitical, institutional, and home community borders. Machado-Casas established that Latin@s crossed both concrete and abstract spaces in North Carolina. She discovered how Indigenous Latin@s, after crossing political borders, utilized languages to cross borders they could not "really see" (p. 544). Developing an additional identity allowed Latin@s to contest the spaces they faced as they settled in the United States.

Wilson et al. (2013), however, argued that White communities created hurdles out of deficit-based views toward Latin@s. The communities continued reliance on low test scores among Latin@ students and an understanding of language acquisition difficulties hindered their "ability to thrive in schools" (p. 18). Ko and Perreira (2010) identified the difficulties of establishing a borderland identity in school settings. A number of Latin@ students they interviewed greatly expressed the challenges of connecting home cultures with the school. One student, Carlos, called this challenge "a friction between 'I'm Mexican and I want my traditions to continue being valid' and 'I'm American and I want my traditions also to continue being valid'" (p. 481). Another student, Fernandina, stated the difficulties of trying to figure out who she was: "we have to change but keep what our parents taught us in some way" (p. 481).

Identity as agency and resistance. We also came to understand the cultivation of identity through chameleon-like survival strategies. According to Machado-Casas (2012), Latin@s maintained strong connections with their home communities while residing in the United States. For example, they still participated in elections and land purchases (Machado-Casas, 2012). In addition, Latin@s maintained connections with fellow country persons. Being chameleons, especially for Indigenous Latin@s, allowed them to converse in their native language, Spanish, and/or English in North Carolina. One Latin@, Iza, exhibited this powerful identity: "So we talk to people in Otomí or Spanish to find out about the places where the houses are but also we need to speak English when we go to the bank or deal with people at the (realtor's) office" (p. 544) This multilingual, multinational strength granted Latin@s agency and currency in a setting that placed their survival at risk (Machado-Casas, 2012).

Machado-Casas (2012) further added that developing an identity as a chameleon worked to combat the "internalized inferiority" felt by Latin@s (p. 546). We can surmise that this specific identity type applied also to the Latina mothers interviewed by Villenas (2001). For example, Carmen asserted her intelligence because "she was fully aware of how Hispanos were being negatively positioned in Hope City" (p. 14). Another mother, Marisela, positioned her stories "against the deficit framing of Latina mothers as poor educators judged against the norms of 'superior' Western ways of rearing children" (p. 15). In another study, Villenas (2002) identified Latin@ parents who "strategically created boundaries" in direct response to the deficit framing created by the dominant public rhetoric (p. 28). Latin@s negotiate their identities without losing touch of their roots or succumbing to the deficit narratives of White, American culture.

Lastly, Latin@s used identity as resistance in the public schools. Wilson et al. (2014) identified educators as privileged members, since they suppressed Latin@ student advancement. Lopez (2007) described how Frances continually advocated for herself when it came to grade-level placement. Frances was confident in her past educational experiences and presented US school officials with Mexican school transcripts. Yet she encountered resistance. School officials "finally got tired of me. So they let me into the junior classes; they got tired of me going there every day and bothering them" (Lopez, 2007, p. 137). Ko and Perreira (2010) illustrated how Latin@ students embodied their home identities in the face of school discrimination. One student, Erica, was "very proud" to be Mexican and "very proud" of her customs, even when she and other students were constantly harassed by school officials (Ko & Perreira, 2010, p. 485). These acts of resistance allowed Latin@ students to feel empowered in an environment that often invalidated them (Wilson et al., 2014).

Fuerzas

In selecting the pieces for this meta-ethnography, we were conscious of the varying types of research and foci of these studies. Some of these researchers focus on students and the educational system and others on families or community members; Murillo's (2002) stands aside in that it draws mostly from ethnographic observations to paint a picture of the climates in which Latin@ communities were living. In essence, we had different perspectives addressing the question of "What is it like to be Latin@ in North Carolina?" from different angles. These different articles allowed us to envision the North Carolina Latin@ community in a well-rounded way.

In our analysis of the pieces, we found that in the face of oppression and community tensions, Latin@s have exhibited incredible *fuerzas*. This resiliency manifested in moments of agency where Latin@s showed that they were not only living their lives here, but they were living them with dignity—a trait often ignored by those in power, like police officers who proclaim that violence is a "cultural thing" for Latin@s (Murillo, 2002). In fact, when we were first conducting our analysis of Murillo's article, titled "How Does It Feel To Be a 'Problem'?" Ender expressed concern over the seemingly pessimistic nature of the piece in that it really highlighted the negative community response toward Latin@s. He questioned whether this piece fit in with our initial hopes to use critical work that also lent itself to finding moments of resistance and hope. However, Rodríguez advocated for the inclusion of this piece as it served to highlight the incredibly negative constructions and odds these Latin@s were facing. Coupled with the other pieces in the meta-ethnography, it stands to show that *despite* the realities of marginalization, "othering," and even persecution, studies like Villenas (2001, 2002), Lopez (2007), Machado-Casas (2012), Ko and Perreira (2010), and Wilson et al. (2014) illustrate the *fuerzas* exhibited by Latin@s.

On parenting, for example, despite being viewed as bad mothers, a woman in Villenas's (2002) study proclaimed that "no importa que se críen acá, van a tener las mismas costumbres de uno" (It doesn't matter that they are being raised here; they are going to have our same customs). This mother recognized the value of her teachings despite the messages that sought to not just devalue but also erase her agency as a mother. This inner *fuerza* was also exhibited by younger generations as well. For example, a young woman in Ko and Perreira's (2010) study said,

I like how I am. I don't want to be like an American [White] or like other people. I don't need that, I feel. This is how I was born, and this is how I want to remain. For example, I hear my mom or someone else say, "If they steal a purse you need to steal a purse also?" "If they want to smoke are you going to smoke because that is what they do?" No. And that is certain. You don't do that just because you want to be like them. It won't go well. (p. 485)

In fact, in this statement, the student is expressing the same critiques and concerns the parents are vigilant and wary of in Villenas's study. This *fuerza* and desire to flourish helped the youth in Ko and Perreira's work to surpass the traumas of immigration and excel in school. The creation of *hybrid* identities as described in Wilson et al. (2014), the will to honor transnational responsibilities as described in Machado-Casas (2012), and the demonstrations of activist identities as noted by Lopez (2007) all demonstrate *fuerza*. These themes and the strategies associated with them culminate to create a culture of *supervivencia,* which Trinidad Galvan (2011) described as "survival and its beyondness"—a desire to thrive.

CONCLUSION: EMERGENCE OF *SUPERVIVENCIA*

Drawing from Trinidad Galvan's (2011) conceptualization, Urrieta, Mendez, and Rodríguez (2015), define *supervivencia* as "a state beyond mere survival encompassing the full intricacies of people of color's everyday survivance, including unending resourcefulness, creativity, and resiliency despite difficult conditions" (p. 13). We argue that the themes and examples articulated in this chapter exemplify strategies of living dignified, full lives while also forging new communities and spaces to call our own. We first took note of the importance of survival whilst reading Machado-Casas (2012). We found that the ideas of cultural, emotional, and physical survival were incredibly important components of life in North Carolina. We kept finding that survival was intricately tied to identity and ways of knowing and teaching. We also discovered that the word "survival" did not denote the agency and strategizing that took place in order for people to live full, meaningful, and dignified lives, all the while reinventing what it meant to be Latin@.

This focus on the agency and strategy piece of survival contradicts the arguments that Latin@s are needy people waiting to be helped. In fact, it is clear that the piece that focuses on youth situates these young people as aware of their positions within these social structures. As delineated in the epilogue section, there is an awareness of communities and a burgeoning sense of activism that not only creates community and lays down roots but, because it is happening in relation to a particular historical moment (new Latin@ diaspora), also helps develop a sense of political consciousness. This consciousness is not just found within the data in the articles but also in the work being produced by critical scholars engaging in research in the new Latin@ diaspora. While not as vast as the historically established critical Latin@ work that comes from areas like the Southwest, this kind of research *does* exist in "new" Latin@ diaspora spaces like North Carolina. What sets this field apart from the work from the Southwest, for example, is that while it invokes fleshed-out concepts like *educación* and transnationalism, it also seeks to (re)define them.

Globalization plays a significant role in (re)defining these concepts. Historically, the development of the Southwest United States comes from Spanish, Mexican, and Indigenous influences. For example, Trueba (2004) based his definitions of transnationalism—which entailed frequent physical mobility across international borders—out of research in Texas. North Carolina is rooted in English influences. Yet, as Machado-Casas (2012) argued, changes in technology and communication have created a different type of transnationalism. Latin@s preserve connections to the home country in different ways, such as the reliance on technological approaches such as mobile-to-mobile texting, messenger apps, and social media. Within these new social elements, Latin@s create new spaces. Creative reimaginations of possibility and hope for living are at the heart of *supervivencia*.

We learned how *supervivencia* differs from survival in North Carolina. It is characterized by a desire and will to thrive in the face of oppression. These desires and will are enacted through creative and resourceful acts of agency. The

Latin@ communities described in these works are living lives that go beyond mere survival—beyond just getting by. They are grounding themselves in old knowledge generationally passed down from ancestors and communities past. Additionally, in finding themselves in new diaspora spaces, they are also creating new ways of knowing and complex Latin@ identities. In this context, then, *supervivencia* itself takes on an additional quality in the creation of an empowering "new-ness" that is rooted in old knowledge and practices.

These ethnographies and their authors underscore this by the continued re-definition of Latin@ cultural and academic concepts. This meta-ethnography enabled us to discern an implicit identity theory in the research in this specific context and to develop new levels of interpretations. *Supervivencia* synthesizes the original studies and gives new meaning to the new Latin@ diaspora and Latin@ identity in North Carolina. Going back to the transparency we discussed earlier in the chapter, we discovered more about ourselves as Latin@s in North Carolina.

We realized that we added an additional layer to this meta-ethnography: our experiences as Latin@ doctoral students. We acknowledge access to scholarship on our communities. Yes, we crossed numerous borders, and faced struggles as Latin@ doctoral students. We encountered similar questions Urrieta (2009) faced in graduate school: Why do we keep having to define and defend our Latin@ identities to non-Latin@s? Why do we feel tired? We realized the uniqueness of our experiences. However, instead of viewing our positions with detriment, we saw ourselves as agents of change. We do not engage with hit-and-run research tactics that continue to plague communities of color. Our established relation-ships with the various Latin@s communities in the area provide us with *el agua* (water) to continue our journeys into the academy. This meta-ethnography not only confirms the complex identities developed by Latin@s but also provides the energy for future research into understanding how Latin@s rely on these identi-ties in defying xenophobia.

EPILOGUE

We had the privilege of speaking with Dr. Sofia Villenas as we developed this chapter. We gained valuable insights on three topics: her thoughts on Latin@s in North Carolina today, her reflections from conducting the two studies we included in this meta-ethnography, and her thoughts on the future of Latin@s in North Carolina.

First, she acknowledged that many things have changed since the completion of her work in North Carolina in the mid-1990s. Latin@s have access to health-care providers within the community. In addition, the school system now works with the community in providing educational services to Latin@s. However, problems still exist for Latin@s in North Carolina. According to Villenas, the biggest issue is the lack of leadership positions for Latin@s. One can look at the political struc-ture within North Carolina and see that Whites continue to occupy congressional, senatorial, and state governmental positions.

Second, Villenas reflected on her experiences in working with the Latin@ community in North Carolina. She recognized the lack of a "road map" in conducting her research. She recalled public health scholars conducting research on Latin@s in North Carolina. However, other than herself and Enrique G. Murillo Jr., no other educational scholars worked with the Latin@ communities at that time. She also recalled how no educational spaces or opportunities existed during her time in Hope City. In essence, she trail-blazed the path for scholars like us.

Lastly, she holds out hope for the second-generation Latin@ community members in North Carolina to level the playing field and create equitable situations for Latin@s. She believes that second-generation Latin@s understand their historical and collective situations. She also believes they have a sense of pride in themselves. If second-generational Latin@s lack these two attestations, then substantial changes will not take place.

We are now entering the third decade of Latin@s living in North Carolina in large numbers. Yet minimal research exists that reflect the political empowering of Latin@s in this state. The experiences of Latin@s that Villenas (2001, 2002), Murillo (2002), Lopez (2007), Ko and Perreira (2010), Machado-Casas (2012), and Wilson et al. (2014) studied could be applied to other new Latin@s diasporas occurring in the United States. For example, Villenas considered Utah as a "re-new-ed" diaspora, given the historical and contemporary contexts of Latin@ presence in that state (personal communication, April 23, 2015).

To conclude, we go back to our initial argument that context matters. This diaspora matters. It is important to step away from monolithic depictions of what it means to be a Latin@ living in the United States. Latin@s' experiences in North Carolina reinforce some of what we already know from places like the Southwest, but they also actively dismantle other generalizations and allow us to re/write new re/definitions. It is important to take note and explore these nuances.

NOTES

1. Latin@ indicates gender inclusivity, a move that disrupts the Spanish language reliance on gender separation for nouns.
2. Narrative advice—often embedded in stories of struggle.
3. Respect.
4. Good behavior.

REFERENCES

Anzaldua, G. (1987). *Borderlands/La frontera: The new mestiza.* San Francisco: Aunt Lute.
Doyle, L. H. (2003). Synthesis through meta-ethnography: Paradoxes, enhancements, and possibilities. *Qualitative Research, 3*(3), 321–344.
Fine, M. (1994). Working in the hyphens: Reinventing self and other in qualitative research. In N. Denzin & Y. Lincoln (Eds.), *Handbook of qualitative research* (pp. 70–82). London: SAGE.

Foley, D. E. (2002). Critical ethnography: The reflexive turn. *International Journal of Qualitative Studies in Education, 15*(4), 469–490.

France, E. F., Ring, N., Thomas, R., Noyes, J., Maxwell, M., & Jepson, R. (2014). A methodological systematic review of what is wrong with meta-ethnography reporting. *BMC Medical Research Methodology, 14*(119), 1–16.

Hamann, E. T., Wortham, S., & Murillo, E. G. Jr. (2002). Education and policy in the new Latino diaspora. In S. Wortham, E. G. Murillo Jr., & E. T. Hamann (Eds.), *Education in the new Latino diaspora* (pp. 1–16). Westport, CT: Ablex.

Ko, L. K., & Perreira, K. M. (2010). "It turned my world upside down": Latino youths' perspectives on immigration. *Journal of Adolescent Research, 25*(3), 465–493. doi:10.1177/0743558410361372

Lopez, J. K. (2007). *"We asked for workers and they sent us people": A critical race theory and Latino critical theory ethnography exploring college-ready undocumented high school immigrants in North Carolina* (Doctoral dissertation). University of North Carolina, Chapel Hill.

Machado-Casas, M. (2012). Pedagogías del camaleón /Pedagogies of the chameleon: Identity and strategies of survival for transnational indigenous Latino immigrants in the US south. *The Urban Review, 44*(5), 534–550. doi:10.1007/s11256-012-0206-5

Motel, S., & Patten, E. (2012). Latinos in the 2012 election: North Carolina. Retrieved from http://www.pewhispanic.org/2012/10/01/latinos-in-the-2012-election-north-carolina/

Murillo, E. G. Jr. (2002). How does it feel to be a "problem"? "Disciplining" the transnational subject in the American South. In S. Wortham, E. G. Murillo Jr., & E. T. Hamann (Eds.), *Education in the new Latino diaspora* (pp. 215–240). Westport, CT: Ablex.

Noblit, G. W. Flores, S.Y., & Murillo, E.G. (2004). *Postcritical ethnography : Reinscribing critique.* Cresskill, NJ: Hampton Press.

Noblit, G. W., & Hare, R. D. (1988). *Meta-ethnography: Synthesizing qualitative studies.* Newbury Park, CA: SAGE.

North, M. (2013). *Novelty: A history of the new.* Chicago: University of Chicago Press.

Office of the Governor. (2010). Demographic trends of Hispanics/Latinos in North Carolina. Retrieved from http://www.alpesnc.org/uploads/1/1/7/4/11741227/deomographic_trends_of_hispanics-latinos_in_nc.pdf

Savin-Baden, M., McFarland, L., & Savin-Baden, J. (2008). Learning spaces, agency and notions of improvement: What influences thinking and practices about teaching and learning in higher education? An interpretive meta-ethnography. *London Review of Education, 6*(3), 211–227. doi:10.1080/14748460802489355

Solórzano, D., & Delgado Bernal, D. (2001). Critical race theory, transformational resistance, and social justice: Chicana and Chicano students in an urban context. *Urban Education, 36,* 308–342.

Suro, R., & Singer, A. (2002). *Latino growth in metropolitan America: Changing patterns, new locations.* Washington, DC: Brookings Institute.

Trinidad Galvan, R. (2011). *Relatos de supervivencia: Desafios y bienestar en una comunidad transmigrante Mexicana.* Mexico: UAEM—Universidad Autonoma del Estado de Mexico.

Trueba, E. (2004). *Immigrants and transnationals at work.* Lanham, MD: Rowman & Littlefield.

Urrieta, L. (2009). *Working from within: Chicana and Chicano activist educators in whitestream schools.* Tucson: University of Arizona Press.

Urrieta, L., Méndez, L., & Rodríguez, E. (2015). "A moving target": A critical race analysis of Latina/o faculty experiences, perspectives, and reflections on the tenure and promotion process. *International Journal of Qualitative Studies in Education, 28*(10), 1149–1168. doi:10.1080/09518398.2014.974715

Urrieta, L., & Villenas, S. (2013). The legacy of Derrick Bell and Latino/a education: A critical race testimonio. *Race Ethnicity and Education, 16*(4), 514–535. doi:10.1080/13613324.2013.817771

US Census Bureau. (2015). *North Carolina QuickFacts from the US Census Bureau* [Data File]. Retrieved from http://quickfacts.census.gov/qfd/states/37000.html

Villenas, S. (2001). Latina mothers and small-town racisms: Creating narratives of dignity and moral education in North Carolina. *Anthropology & Education Quarterly, 32*(1), 3–28. doi:10.1525/aeq.2001.32.1.3

Villenas, S. (2002). Reinventing educación. In S. Wortham, E. G. Murillo Jr., & E. T. Hamann (Eds.) *Education in the new Latino diaspora* (pp. 17–36). Westport, CT: Ablex.

Wilson, C. M., Ek, L. D., & Douglas, T. M. O. (2014). Recasting border crossing politics and pedagogies to combat educational inequity: Experiences, identities, and perceptions of Latino/a immigrant youth. *The Urban Review, 46*(1), 1–24. doi:10.1007/s11256-013-0246-5

6

Spaces in Between

A Meta-Ethnography of Racialized Southeast Asian American Youth Identities

LAN QUACH KOLANO, CHERESE CHILDERS-MCKEE,
AND ELENA KING ∎

INTRODUCTION

Noblit and Hare (1988) state that "a meta-ethnography is complete when we understand the meaning of our lives and the lives of others" but that getting to that place is "somewhat complex" (p. 81). Through the writing of this chapter, we recognized that complexity and sought to use meta-ethnography as a means to showcase and interpret the diversity of identity construction in Southeast Asian American youth. Initially, we approached this chapter as a way to explore the ways in which Asian American youth identities writ large have been constructed in the United States. However, given the complex diversity within this racial group, we quickly acknowledged the need to narrow our analysis and focus on the experiences of youth identity from different Southeast Asian American communities that have permeated and changed the post–Vietnam War, US demographic landscape.

The US Office of Management and Budget (1997, Section D) defines Asian as people having origins in "the Far East, Southeast Asia, or the Indian subcontinent." Although Asia includes hundreds of diverse ethnic groups and numerous countries and territories, there are only six major Asian "races" or national-origin groups listed as checkboxes on the census form, including Asian Indian, Chinese, Filipino, Japanese, Korean, and Vietnamese (Perez & Hirschman, 2009). Also noteworthy is the checkbox on the census for "Other Asian" where census respondents can write in a specific national origin. In the 2000 census, the nine largest groups written in under "Other Asian" included Cambodian, Hmong, Laotian, Pakistani, Thai, Bangladeshi, Indonesian, Sri Lankan, and Malaysian (Perez & Hirschman, 2009). According to Yu (2006), "Asians are arguably the least homogeneous of all racial groups and Asian Americans possess an unusually wide range of social characteristics marked by diverse ethnic, social class, and immigrant experiences" (p. 327).

Discourse on Asian American experiences has focused on those with the largest numbers, creating one collective identity and thus constructing one dichotomous grand narrative for the Asian American student. Studies on Vietnamese youth for example—particularly in urban communities in California—have been racialized as "both *model minority* and *gang-banger* because of the substantial number of Asian American youth gangs" (Lam, 2015, p. 2). More recent studies have emerged that highlight the experiences and struggles of Southeast Asian American youth, yet some fail to push against dominant constructions of Asian identity as "model minority," "hardworking," and "high achieving" or "dropouts, gangsters, and welfare dependents" (Ngo & Lee, 2007, p. 416).

We begin this meta-ethnography by first acknowledging the heterogeneity that exists within the Asian American population, which is comprised of distinct ethnic or cultural subgroups, all with unique languages, writing systems, and histories (Asian Pacific American Legal Center, 2004; Ong & Leung, 2003). We then chose eight qualitative studies that focused on one or more Southeast Asian groups that attempted to highlight identity in ways that complicated essentialized, surface understandings of Asian culture/ethnicity. In this chapter we use meta-ethnography as a methodology to understand how Asian identity, particularly of youth within Southeast Asian American communities, has been constructed within the larger historicized label of Asian American and discourses of success. Through this meta-ethnography, we explore the spaces of identity in between those constructed by researchers within the past 15 years that include but are not limited to *Gangsta, Model, Fresh off the Boat (FOB), White-washed, or Honorary.* This collection of qualitative work on Southeast Asian Americans specifically illuminates the identity building youth enacted as they struggled to both dispel and live up to the model minority myth.

Positionality

As educational researchers with shared interests but diverse experiences, we share similar yet divergent lenses—allowing greater depth, perspective, and multiplicity in our approach to meta-ethnography. While we all identify as critical educators, our positionalities and subjectivities have been (and continue to be) shaped and tempered by the experiences and contexts in which we navigate. From the onset of this project, we felt the difficulty of navigating the tenuousness of describing any racial/ethnic group—especially one as culturally and linguistically diverse as the Asian American community. As we approached this meta-ethnography, we did so with trepidation, acknowledging to one another that describing Asian identity felt inherently problematic for us. We wondered how we would navigate the issue of theming and analyzing studies on Southeast Asian American identity when we inherently resisted the idea of aggregating groups with varying experiences of race, class, and history into one racialized group called "Asian." Also, as critical educators and former English as a second language (ESL) teachers, we have witnessed the ways in which the prevalence of stereotypical notions of Asianness (smart/demure or gangster/delinquent) have negatively influenced teachers' beliefs about, expectations of, and treatment of Asian students.

Glesne (1992) describes that "being attuned to positionality is being attuned to intersubjectivity, how the subjectivities of all involved guide the research process, content, and ideally, the interpretations" (p. 158). Positionalities allow researchers to acknowledge the multiplicity of identities they occupy as fluid and as markers of relational position that change with each new context, not as specific qualities (Beverly, 2011). Although our positionalities have been informed by our unique differences and experiences, we have all been shaped by our role as ESL teachers working with diverse racial and linguistic communities. Our personal experiences as insiders, outsiders, or a complex mixture of both allowed us to engage in this iterative research project as women and as critical educators.

Lan. "What are you?" in some form has been a question cast by almost everyone I have encountered in both my personal and professional life. It is a question about identity and asked of people "in the margins," and people of color by those outsiders looking in—often curious about ethnic heritage or place of origin. I have occupied a variety of educational spaces that have deeply informed my professional interests in diverse Southeast Asian American communities of color. These spaces include the public school classrooms I sat in as an immigrant child learning English as a second language as well as those high-needs classrooms in which I taught. I arrived in the United States at the age of four and began kindergarten one year later with my native English-speaking peers. I see race/language/class and gender identities through the eyes of a refugee from Vietnam. I see myself now as the hybridized Asian American within two worlds—as both insider and outsider at the same time. I look at education through a critical lens with the acknowledgement that my personal journey from immigrant to educator deeply informs how I see the world.

Cherese. My positionality as a Black woman who is the proud aunt of three mixed-race (Lao-Black) youth, a former ESL teacher, and a critical feminist educator shapes the lens with which I view this work. My memories of teaching ESL in poor, urban, and "majority minority" schools are filled with a complex mixture of emotions that range from frustration, anger, and sorrow to pride, excitement, and joy. I have experienced the mental, emotional, and physical grind of convincing students to "buy in" to a myth that I no longer bought into myself as well as the trickiness of walking that fine line between empowering students to think critically and inciting them to anger and frustration at the unfairness of the educational system. I recognize that my race, citizenship status, working-class, rural upbringing, and educational opportunities have afforded me a complex mix of privileges and oppressions. Yet, the contours of identity are more fluid and nuanced than what our various identity "boxes" denote. While these boxes ground and sustain during difficult times, they also constrain and often attempted to inscribe on our bodies who we should be, what we should think, how we should act, and how we should relate to others.

Elena. During my childhood in rural North Carolina with outsider parents—my mother a second-generation Greek from the Bronx and my father a second-generation Eastern European-Jew from Brooklyn—I learned that I was an *other*. If I had been raised in New York, I would not have been an *other*, but in the South, I was a minority and I was different. However, I had choice with my otherness. I learned early on that people knew I was different, but they did not know *what* I was. As a child, I strategically chose how to present myself to others. However, it was not until I began studying to become an ESL teacher that I was able to delve deeper into understanding where my beliefs developed. It was through teaching ESL and later researching how teachers view their immigrant students that I began to think about identity through both a critical and a sociocultural-historical lens. It is through these lenses that I position myself as insider/outsider and view the world of hybrid, transitional identity formation.

Research Questions

In this meta-ethnography we address the following research questions: (1) How are "Southeast Asian Americans," defined, understood in the current selected studies, and racialized as a collective? (2) What narratives are constructed in schools about Southeast Asian American youth? (3) How have Southeast Asian American youth embraced or resisted being framed as model minorities? We analyze the work of qualitative researchers who have examined how identities have been shaped by and for Asian Americans in the United States in an effort to better understand Southeast Asian American youth identity. In doing so, we acknowledge the unique factors affecting the process of identity and assert that these identities are fluid and complex—influenced by historical, social, and cultural contexts that are distinct in diverse communities. Through meta-ethnography as methodology, we show the nuances, complexities, and contradictions of identity formation while opening up spaces of possibility for future understandings of this uniquely diverse group.

We contextualize this meta-ethnography by historicizing what it means to be Asian in the United States, highlighting the diversity within this panethnic label, and complicating this image by focusing on Southeast Asian American youth. Moreover, this work explores how raced, classed, and gendered hierarchies of oppression have shaped the way Southeast Asianness is researched, studied, and talked about. In this chapter we focus on the synthesized translations of studies on Southeast Asian American youth, interpretations, and contributions to literature about Southeast Asian American studies. From the results of our analysis, synthesis, and interpretations of eight studies about Southeast Asian American youth, we discuss three prominent themes: disrupting the institutional influences of racism and colorism, opening up the success narrative for Southeast Asian American youth, and centering Southeast Asian American youth studies within mainstream research on schools. In exploring these interpretations, we offer recommendations for reframing future research on Southeast Asian American youth identities.

METHODOLOGY

Text Selection

Here we outline the processes by which we established trustworthiness in text selection, coding, analysis, and synthesis. Initially we made purposeful decisions for the inclusion and established clear exclusion criteria for each of the studies that we reviewed. Each study had to (a) frame the research qualitatively and (b) focus on an Asian population.

Yet, reflective of our critical research paradigm, we were personally troubled by our research and experience of the silencing and marginalization of Southeast Asian American youth in schools across the nation. Therefore, we focused our review on work conducted in the United States on immigrant groups, English-language learners, and 1st-, 1.5-, and 2nd-generation youth from Southeast Asian American communities.

Our approach to text selection was multipronged. We focused on peer-reviewed, research-based inquiries found in certain databases: ERIC, EBSCO Host, JSTOR, PschINFO, and Education Research Complete. We first explored the studies that included "Asian," "Asian American," "Asian immigrant," and "identity" in the title. These general terms yielded results that spoke about the experiences of the largest Asian groups that included largely successful Chinese and Korean communities. We read those that were quantitative in nature in order to understand how Asian identity has been framed within the domains of psychology and education. While we found several studies that spoke broadly about Asian American identity as a collective, we were interested in selecting studies that dealt with the histories, struggles, and educational contexts of specific Southeast Asian American communities—particularly those that have been excluded from current educational discourse and have been silenced by pervasive constructions of Asian as successful and model minority. Thus we searched for Southeast Asian American identity and individual subgroups within the Southeast Asian American community and further limited our search to include only qualitative and/or ethnographic studies with keywords that included combinations of the following: Asian identity, Asian education, Southeast Asian, Asian American, Vietnamese, Hmong, Cambodian, Lao, Burmese, and Thai. After several meetings to discuss the findings, we chose 30 publications, all published in the past 15 years, for preliminary analysis. As we continued to read, write, discuss, reread, and rewrite, the recursive nature of qualitative inquiry helped us narrow the scope of this meta-ethnography until we purposefully chose a total of eight articles for further analysis. In Table 6.1, we outline the research contexts of each study, theoretical lenses used, and the positionality of the authors.

Coding, Analysis, and Synthesis

Noblit and Hare (1988) proposed meta-ethnography, which "synthesizes the substance of qualitative research" as an alternative to meta-analysis, which "synthesizes the data" using work within the field of education (p. 81). In this seminal

Table 6.1 RESEARCH CONTEXTS

Author	Vo-Jutabha, Dinh, McHale, & Valsiner (2009)	Stritikus & Nguyen (2007)	Lee (2001)	Nguyen & Brown (2010)	Ngo (2009)	Chiu (2007)	Tang & Kao (2012)	Chhuon & Hudley (2010)
Title	A qualitative analysis of Vietnamese adolescent identity exploration within and outside an ethnic enclave	Strategic transformation: Cultural and gender identity negotiation in first-generation Vietnamese youth	More than "model minorities" or "delinquents": A look at Hmong American high school students	Making meanings, meaning identity: Hmong adolescent perceptions and use of language and style as identity symbols	Ambivalent urban, immigrant identities: The incompleteness of Lao American student identities	Americanization against academics: Racial contexts and Lao American youths in a New Hampshire high school	Ethnicity, gender, and the education of Cambodian American students in an urban high school	Asian American ethnic options: How Cambodian students negotiate ethnic identities in a US urban school
Theoretical Framework	Grounded theory/ social constructivist	Feminist and sociocultural	She "reviews the data through the economic forces, relationships with the dominant society" (p. 505).	Sociocultural	Poststructural/ postcolonial	Critical	Equity pedagogy framework	Social constructivist
Methods	Thematic and grounded narrative analysis of journal writings	A part of a larger two-year qualitative study utilizing ethnographic techniques that focused on the social and academic adjustment Vietnamese immigrant students	1½-year ethnographic study	Interview-based study	A part of a larger yearlong ethnographic study	10-month ethnographic study	Qualitative, interview-based study	Qualitative interview-based study

(continued)

Table 6.1 CONTINUED

Author	Vo-Jutabha, Dinh, McHale, & Valsiner (2009)	Stritikus & Nguyen (2007)	Lee (2001)	Nguyen & Brown (2010)	Ngo (2009)	Chiu (2007)	Tang & Kao (2012)	Chhuon & Hudley (2010)
Positionality	Team consisted of some American-born Vietnamese	1.25-generation Vietnamese immigrant students (22 focal students from a larger pool of 30 [half male and half female])	Third-generation Chinese American woman	Primary author's ethnic identity as a Southeast Asian woman	Immigrant from Southeast Asia	Asian American woman who is "significantly older" than the teens in the study and does not speak Lao (p. 11)	Tang is a Cambodian American female, who as a young child fled Cambodia. Kao is a US-born Taiwanese American male	Chhuon is a Cambodian American. Hudley is an African American
Context	Southern California's "Little Saigon" Vietnamese	Northwest Newcomer Center, Greenfield High (predominately White), Englewood High (predominately mixed), two schools in Vietnam	Southern California's "Little Saigon" Vietnamese	Peripheral school context	Dynamic high school	Millshore Junior and Senior High ESOL Room	Large high school with a large Cambodian population in Southern California	Comprehensive high school schools-within-schools program (academic and standard tracks)
Main Participants	46 Vietnamese youth ages 15–18	1.25-generation Vietnamese immigrant students (22 focal students from a larger pool of 30 [half male and half female])	46 Vietnamese youth ages 15–18	Semistructured interviews with 25 Hmong adolescents age 12–18	1.5- and 2nd-generation Lao students	9 Lao American students (6 boys and 3 girls)	2 administrators, 4 teachers, and 10 ninth-grade Cambodian American students (5 boys and 5 girls)	52 Cambodian students, 15 teachers, 5 counselors, 2 school psychologists, 1 librarian, 2 teacher's aides

work, they use Strike and Posner's (1983) definition of synthesis as "an activity in which separate parts are brought together to form a whole" (p. 346) and Turner's (1980) theory of social explanation as undergirding principles to consider when trying to build understanding rather than simply aggregating the data. According to Noblit and Hare (1988), researchers can use three different methods of synthesis to conduct meta-ethnographies. These include *reciprocal translational analysis, refutational synthesis*, and *lines-of-argument synthesis*. Reciprocal translational analysis requires that the studies are similar enough to be "added together" and thus can be understood "in terms of each other" (p. 47). In contrast, refutations are interpretations that are created to contrast or contradict. Thus this form of synthesis must consider the competing arguments or contradictions that exist between studies. When analyzed using the lines-of-argument synthesis, the researcher uses all of the information to build a more accurate or "whole" through inference-conceptualized clinical inference or grounded theorizing (Noblit & Hare, 1988, p. 62). Noblit and Hare assert, "to be truly ethnographic, the synthesis must take into account the implied relationship between the competing explanations" (p. 47). Within the body of literature on Southeast Asian immigrants and Southeast Asian American youth, we found the process of reciprocal translational analysis between individual studies beneficial in understanding the studies in relation to one another.

From the eight studies chosen, we individually coded the articles with larger recurring metaphors that emerged—including those such as *fresh off the boat, white-washing, model minority, gangsta, high achieving*, and *dropout*. We then worked collaboratively to collapse, analyze, and translate the coded data into themes that describe the identity formation of and by Southeast Asian Americans living in the United States. In Table 6.2, we outline the initial metaphors gleaned from the eight qualitative studies collected.

At the beginning of our analyses, we found it reasonable to argue that these studies could be added together in some form, as they were focused on similar issues of identity and struggle. Many of the researchers argued that Southeast Asian American youth resisted traditional constructions of identity and thus the studies could be understood as translations of one another. However, a more in-depth look at the findings also revealed the complexity of the nature of the identities being constructed. Regardless of how youth identities were studied, most were still framed within a duality of contradiction—either students were framed as model minority or dropouts and gangsters. Noblit and Hare (1988) encourage researchers to assess the emic metaphors that emerge from the studies and determine whether or not they are appropriate. In our initial synthesis, metaphors across the eight studies included model minority versus failure; racialized identity markers: honorary, FOB, white-washed, and blackened; influences of school-class culture; and gendered differences in youth school experiences. After synthesizing the metaphors by translating the studies into one another, we narrowed our focus to second-order thematic interpretations: resisting binaries, the presence of institutional racism and colorism, and positive and negative influences of schools. After translating and synthesizing common metaphors uncovered throughout this process, we reframed the interpretations by exploring three additional concepts: disrupting the institutional influences of racism and colorism, opening

Table 6.2 Themes/Metaphors

Author	Vo-Jutabha, Dinh, McHale., & Valsiner (2009)
Title	A qualitative analysis of Vietnamese adolescent identity exploration within and outside an ethnic enclave
Themes of Race/Culture	Here one of the students resists his Asian culture by adding Spanish to his narrative. He fights with his parents about using the language and "being" Vietnamese; "his parents expect him to speak Vietnamese and associate with Vietnamese friends (particularly females). The relationship with his family is already strained given his dislike of the Vietnamese culture, but it is greatly affected by how much opportunity he has to meet his parents' expectations and becomes worse when he creates greater distance from his parents by learning a language besides English or Vietnamese" (p. 684).
Themes of Identity	Focus on narratives of family values, tradition, and success, including the model minority narrative; students expressed a belief in particular beauty standards and particular careers that denoted success. 'Living near Little Saigon and the Asian metropolis has made me afraid of Asian grown-ups in general. If you do something wrong they look at you . . . If I lived somewhere else, I wouldn't feel so ashamed of myself for not being in touch with my Viet culture" (p. 680).
Structural Critique	Area they live in prevents the exploration that they desire (e.g., lack of diversity, lack of experiences in nonenclave students) or supports growth (e.g., feels comfortable with being Vietnamese in enclave students) (p. 679). The surrounding communities strongly shaped the identities these students felt and maintained
Overall Argument/ Conclusions	"Our analyses substantiated not only that ethnic identity was influencing other domains, but also that exploration within a variety of different domains was reciprocally and simultaneously affecting exploration in others" (p. 686), creating a cyclical nature of identity building.
Author	Stritikus & Nguyen (2007)
Title	Strategic transformation: Cultural and gender identity negotiation in first-generation Vietnamese youth
Themes of Race/Culture	Students were segregated in the international hall, which contributed to feelings of isolation
Themes of Identity	Students in the newcomer school had a space to discuss US culture and reminisce about Vietnam; Students expressed themes of isolation, assimilation with clothing, language barriers, and contrasting gender-relational differences between Vietnam and the United States
Structural Critique	The ways in which youth "navigate the social and physical spaces at Greenfield High and Dao at Englewood High are indicative of the racial, ethnic, and linguistic isolation that the Vietnamese immigrant youth experience in their mainstream high schools. The initial language barrier that separates the immigrant students and their native-born peers eventually leads to a more sustained racial and ethnic divide as few meaningful exchanges take place between the students" (p. 878).

Table 6.2 CONTINUED

Overall Argument/ Conclusions	Authors describe that the ways in which students "define cultural, ethnic, and academic identities is influenced by how they interpret gender—a social category that shifts across different spaces and interacts with other social categories in complex and often contradictory ways" (p. 889).
Author	Lee (2001)
Title	More than "model minorities" or "delinquents": A look at Hmong American high school students
Themes of Race/Culture	"A lot of Americans think that all Asians eat dogs and cats. They don't. They think all Hmong are on welfare. We aren't . . . . I just feel like some White people neglect me" (p. 521).
Themes of Identity	Students who identified too strongly with Hmong culture were dismissed as "FOB" or "FOBBIES." The ESL teachers saw their jobs as to help integrate the students to mainstream classes, but "students remained socially segregated" (p. 515).
Structural Critique	There was a sharp divide between how people saw the newly arrived Hmong "good kids" and the Americanized second-generation Hmong "the bad kids." Some students were "often overlooked because they were quiet and teachers assumed they were working hard . . . thus the stereotype of the hard-working, quiet, model-minority worked against the students' best interests" (p. 515). Ultimately, many of the students felt that outside of the ESL classrooms, the teachers (majority White) just did not like them.
Overall Argument/ Conclusions	This research indicated that the binary good/bad, traditional/ Americanized dichotomy was seen only by outsiders. The students felt that their identities were much more complex with groups of students in both the 1.5- and 2nd-generation categories finding success and failure in school and in flux between Hmong and American identities.
Author	Nguyen & Brown (2010)
Title	Making meanings, meaning identity: Hmong adolescent perceptions and use of language and style as identity symbols
Themes of Race/Culture	The term "fob" is associated with being low class and "really Hmong"; students also used the term "og," which had a similar connotation.
Themes of Identity	Students were proud of their Hmong identity and wanted to reinforce it by using the language. There were strong ties between language and identity; fobby versus Americanized or preppy was defined by dress and how well youth knew Hmong language and culture.
Structural Critique	Students expressed discomfort in school and described Americans as smart; students felt confident in ESL class only

(continued)

Table 6.2 CONTINUED

Overall Argument/ Conclusions	"Hmong adolescents in this study utilize language and style behaviors to create cultural boundaries, which are then used to define their peer group and social identities. Together, language and style are used to categorize peers into the following categories: (1) those overly embedded in Hmong culture (fobby), (2) those overly adherent to American culture (Americanized), and (3) those who balance both Hmong and American culture" (p. 862).
Author	Ngo (2009)
Title	Ambivalent urban, immigrant identities: The incompleteness of Lao American student identities
Themes of Race/Culture	Disrupts the binary and argues for an ambivalence in how students see themselves.
Themes of Identity	Students sought to rebuild identities and to resist binaries of "good/ bad, ancestral country/United States, oppositional framing"; "male students were expected to exhibit . . . 'gangster-fronting behaviors' in order to be respected—or at the least to not be denigrated as gay. Simultaneously, however, the response to Lao male students who incorporated urban style into their identity is one of bewilderment. Here, discourses of what it means to be male and what it means to be Asian American collided and competed" (p. 210).
Structural Critique	The teachers in this study employed narratives of students "between two worlds" and "in limbo" (p. 209); however, the students' identities—like many adolescents—were in flux and complicated. They were able to articulate a complex set of ideas of who they were but were seen as "dualisms" and "contradictory" by their teachers.
Overall Argument/ Conclusions	"Likewise, when immigrant students struggle with the lure of gangs, how to afford trendy clothes they want, or getting enough meals each day, these issues are at once about being disenfranchised, an urban youth and an immigrant" (p. 216).
Author	Chiu (2007)
Title	Americanization against academics: Racial contexts and Lao American youths in a New Hampshire high school.
Themes of Race/Culture	"Media-inspired hip hop cool, with its close association to Blackness, allows the Lao American boys I observed and interviewed to refashion themselves out of earlier cultural constructions that cast them as quiet meek amenable- as the model minority" (p. 3). "All of the boys would quickly reject any affinity with African Americans for they implicitly understand gradations of racial acceptance in being Anglo or African American. They prefer recognition of their difference through their ethnicity as Lao Americans and not through a correspondence to blackness" (p. 15).

Table 6.2 CONTINUED

Themes of Identity	"The adoption of strong Lao pride" (p. 3). "Lao American students supplement their Asian American identities (regarded by the majority as feminized, nerdy, weak, and backwards) with gang symbols to compensate for their lack of self-esteem, not their possession of it, and to accommodate to U.S. gender norms" (p. 16).
Structural Critique	"They [teachers] did not inquire into racial assumptions they themselves and the wider academic institution possessed that might influence social attitude, personal pedagogy, and thus Lao Americans' self-identity and academic success" (p. 13). "An institutional 'Culture of Avoidance' by teachers" (p. 18).
Overall Argument/ Conclusions	"This [identity] shift has been detrimental to their academic success, rending significance and urgency to the educational implications of this study on identity, racialization, and academic success" (p. 3). "Americanization and academics need not be mutually exclusive. But their inextricability from institutionally constructed racial contexts demands scrutiny if faculty, staff, and administration persist in dichotomizing 'those' academically at-risk Lao-Americans from 'our' pedagogical and institutional contexts" (p. 20).
Author	Tang & Kao (2012)
Title	Ethnicity, gender, and the education of Cambodian American students in an urban high school
Themes of Race/Culture	Cambodians described as "stupid" and "dark" by Chinese peers (p. 13). Non-Cambodian Asians held prejudices about Cambodian peers, expressed anger at being mistaken for Cambodians. Discrimination from Chinese and Vietnamese affected Cambodian students willingness to interact in the classroom. One participant aligned himself with Black and Latino peers for protection from Chinese and Vietnamese peers.
Themes of Identity	Students were often misidentified as Chinese; students wanted to be seen as "model minorities"; felt marginalized by other Asians. Little analysis of the role of gender on Cambodian student identity as the authors proposed to discuss; Teachers perceived dichotomy of the quiet obedient Cambodian student versus the gangster who was typically racialized as male
Structural Critique	Cambodian students were invisible in the school context to the point that teachers were not sure how many Cambodian students they had in classes and had little to no understanding of Cambodian culture; students were reticent to ask for help. Teacher/student relationships and cultural expectations prevent Cambodian students from educating their teachers when cultural missteps occur; teachers were unaware of the unique needs of their Cambodian students. Teachers assumed they were "model minority" and thus did not need help. When they did acknowledge Cambodian student difficulties, teachers blamed problems on home culture

(continued)

Table 6.2 CONTINUED

Overall Argument/ Conclusions	Youth were conflicted by what was expected of them at home versus expectations of school; Cambodians were marginalized within the larger Asian population and assumed to be a model minority only when they were assumed to be non-Cambodian; Schools failed to meet both the academic and social needs of Cambodian students
Author	Chhuon & Hudley (2010–2011)
Title	Asian American ethnic options: How Cambodian students negotiate ethnic identities in a US urban school/ethnic and panethnic Asian American identities: Contradictory perceptions of Cambodian students in urban schools
Themes of Race/Culture	Ghetto versus white-washed dichotomy; difference in identity perception in magnet versus humanities track courses.
Themes of Identity	Students in humanities sometimes pretended to be smart to fit the "model minority" stereotype; students in the magnet program felt lumped by teachers and said teachers were surprised when they found out students were Cambodian and successful.
Structural Critique	Teachers see students as either/or—either a successful Asian model minority or an unsuccessful Cambodian minority. When students succeed, teachers do not know that they are Cambodian. When students do not succeed, teachers blame their lack of school success on being Cambodian.
Overall Argument/ Conclusions	The "lumping" of Asians, the invisibility of Cambodians, and the negative perception/racism of teachers toward Cambodians.

up the success narrative for Southeast Asian American youth, and centering Southeast Asian American youth studies within mainstream research on schools.

SYNTHESIZING TRANSLATIONS OF THEMES

Resisting Binaries

Model minority versus failure. The model minority–failure binary represented a prominent theme across the studies analyzed (Chhuon & Hudley, 2010, 2011; Chiu, 2007; Lee, 2001; Ngo, 2009; Tang & Kao, 2012). Despite the unique cultural differences found in the Asian community, in educational spaces, Southeast Asian American youth were categorized, stereotyped, and labeled as a relatively homogeneous group or marginalized and silenced by the assumptions of the model minority stereotype. The Southeast Asian American participants in nearly all of the selected studies found that their schools imposed an often contradictory view of all Asians as model minorities and yet at the same time spoke about Southeast Asians (Cambodian, Hmong, Vietnamese, or Laotian) as failures, characterized by poor achievement and gang behavior (Chhuon & Hudley, 2010, 2011; Chiu, 2007; Lee, 2001; Ngo, 2009; Tang & Kao, 2012).

Southeast Asian American youth expressed mixed feelings about being part of a successful race or "model minority." Gina, a Cambodian student experiencing difficulty in her classes, explained: "the stereotype is probably, like, something that maybe helps us . . . because like last week this girl was like 'C'mon, just help me do this, you all are all smart'" (Chhuon & Hudley, 2011, p. 694). However, students like Gina were either deemed "culturally invisible" (p. 696), as teachers assumed they understood content material because of their Asianness, or "described as poor, welfare dependent, and involved in gangs" (p. 690). Similarly, one Cambodian youth in Tang and Kao's (2012) study described: "When we do group work, the other students in the class would tell the teachers that they want to be in my group because I'm Asian and Asians are supposed to be smart. . . . And when I don't do well, they blame me and said, 'You're really not Asian, you're just Cambodian'" (p. 10). This quote exemplifies the recurring theme that membership in certain Southeast Asian American ethnic groups is associated with failure both by teachers and peers. Ngo (2009) described one academically successful Lao youth as not embracing the "discourse of school achievement unequivocally . . . [Chintana] did not want to be a labeled a 'nerd'" and distinguished herself from another Lao student who she described as a nerd who "does like a lot of other extracurricular activities outside of school" (p. 212). In contrast, Kett, another Lao youth in Ngo's (2009) study, described his dilemma of trying to take school more seriously but explained that, "it's just other kids want to draw you into the [negative] things they be doing" (p. 215). These examples show that youth negotiate their identities in ways that complicates the false dichotomy of the model versus failure binary.

Identity and gender. In three of the articles analyzed (Ngo, 2009; Stritikus & Nguyen, 2007; Tang & Kao, 2012), researchers employed critical and feminist approaches to describe Asian participants' experiences with gender identity and role expectations. In showing the nuances of identity formation as "site[s] of struggle in multiple contexts" (Park, 2008, p. 174), we highlight the individual agency of Asian American participants to negotiate and navigate race, culture, and gender roles. Tang and Kao (2012) contended that the boys they interviewed described a stronger encouragement for education and college, while the girls were expected to focus more on familial responsibilities. While gendered differences in the role of education did not arise in the other studies, both Ngo and Stritikus and Nguyen found instances of gender roles being strongly influenced by American culture. Stritikus and Nguyen described their male participants as "seeing girls 'becoming American' as 'distasteful'" (p. 887). They distinguished their own and other male students' changes as "surface level (appearances, dress, and hair)" (p. 887). In contrast, male students described females' transformations, including their thinking about relationship and gender roles, as "deep and lasting" (p. 887). Also, Ngo described gender-specific behavior of male youth: "Male students were expected to exhibit . . . 'gangster-fronting behaviors' in order to be respected—or at the least to not be denigrated as gay" (p. 210). In these instances, males felt the need to adopt an urban American style and affectation in order to be seen as cool (Ngo, 2009; Stritikus & Nguyen, 2007).

Disrupting identity as a binary. Despite gender-specific influences on identity and the insidious presence of model minority myth, authors described accounts of youth who conceptualized their identities in ways that crossed fixed boundaries. Authors suggested that a binary, "either-or" mentality overly simplified the identity-forming process for immigrant Southeast Asians and Southeast Asian American youth. Some authors suggested a *both-and* perspective (Chhuon & Hudley, 2010, 2011; Ngo, 2009; Stritikus & Nguyen, 2007; Tang & Kao, 2012; Vo-Jutabha, Dinh, McHale, & Valsiner, 2009) that allowed Southeast Asian Americans to include "both ethnic roots and mainstream [American] values" (Park, 2008, p. 556). Ngo described this *both-and* perspective in the analysis of her data. She stated, "what was paramount in the identity struggles of my Lao participants cannot be framed within discrete, binary discourses that put the ethnic identity of the students at one end of the spectrum and another identity at the other end" (p. 216). In Ngo's work, by complicating the binaries and writing in terms of intersections, the dualistic categories were erased as more complex narratives unfolded. Lee (2001) contended that it was only the teachers in her study that saw students in a good/bad, traditional/Americanized dichotomy and that the youth described their identities as much more fluid. Vo-Jutabha et al. described their analysis as providing "support for the contention that categorizing differences based on fixed status cannot accurately portray the developmental processes of immigrant adolescents" (p. 686) and that the space that these youth occupied influenced their identity narrative in complex ways. This complication of identities permeated the analysis conducted in this meta-ethnography.

Through the use of interviews and participant observations, authors attempted to frame identity-building as an active, contextualized process to offer a more nuanced understanding of ways in which youth navigate the stereotypes of "homogenized Asianness" (Kibria, 2000, p. 84). Notions of immigrant populations being bicultural or "insert ethnicity here"-American (such as Asian-American or Korean-American) implies a splitting in half and equal fusion between two cultures. The *bi* prefix creates a false image of immigrants coming to the United States and striking a perfect balance of traditional and American values. In synthesizing these studies, we sought to view Southeast Asian American youth identities through the lenses of spatial terms like borderlands (Anzaldúa, 1987), the interstitial (Bhabha, 1999), and the heterogeneity created of this space-making (Gonzalez, 2011). These more aptly described hybridizations create a new entity formed from the spaces or borders between the two cultures and is, in a sense, more personal and contextual. Understanding hybridization acknowledges the fluidity of identity and the ways in which identity formation is influenced by societal structures within the context of current and past histories (Ngo & Lee, 2007).

Racism and Colorism: Honorary, FOB, White-washed or Blackened

Asian Americans have historically either been positioned as good or bad (Ngo, 2009) and framed within a dichotomous or White–Black racial context (Lee, 2006). Authors explained that, for Asian Americans who have achieved success in school and reinforced notions of what it means to be model, they somehow achieve an honorary status, or as Tuan (1998) described it, an *honorary Whiteness*. In a memoir that offers another perspective, Liu (1998) writes,

> I never asked to be white. I am not literally white. That is, I do not have white skin or white ancestors. I have yellow skin and yellow ancestors, hundreds of generations of them. But like so many other Asian Americans of the second generation, I find myself now the bearer of a strange new status: white, by acclamation. Thus it is that I have been described as an "honorary white," by other whites, and as a 'banana' by other Asians . . . to the extent that I have moved away from the periphery and toward the center of American life, I have become white inside. (p. 34)

However, studies of youth from certain Southeast Asian American communities suggest that a White identity or honorary whiteness status could never be achieved, even among second-generation Southeast Asian American youth, and may not even be desired. Chhuon and Hudley (2010) articulated that "accusations of being 'white-washed' were levied at Cambodians hanging out with white Americans and other Asian youth represented disdain for those who did not take sufficient pride in their Cambodian heritage" (p. 353). However, even these supposedly "white-washed" youth were not fully accepted as American and were simply seen as "good Asians" by their teachers. Southeast Asian American youth's perspectives on honorary whiteness seemed to reside in the idea that biculturals retain a link to their ethnicity and may never be able to fully join the White world. They charged those who attempted to do so, the so called "white-washed," as deluding themselves. Our analysis suggests that youth may have assumed essential differences between Whites and Asians, and that as non-Whites, they could never really be American (Pyke & Dang, 2003, p. 157).

In the studies analyzed, *Fresh off the Boat* immigrants, or FOBs, contrasted sharply to their white-washed counterparts. This binary revolves around length of time in the United States as well as perceived adoption of "White" culture. The disassociation with FOB is an attempt by Asian American youth to disidentify not with Asianness but with "foreign-ness" (Lee, 2001; Nguyen & Brown, 2010). In essence, FOB refers to being too ethnic or low class and white-washed refers to being too assimilated (Nguyen & Brown, 2010). Chiu (2007) described that it "was cool to be Asian as long as one possessed such material accoutrements . . . ripped T-shirt, do-rag, and a Honda Accord" (p. 16). Authors suggested that youth preferred to reside somewhere within the bicultural middle, where they could claim both an ethnic and Americanized identity. In essence, biculturals were "defined by what they were not: neither a 'FOB' nor 'white-washed'" (Pyke & Dang, 2003, p. 157). Youth in this middle ground sought to change their appearance in an appropriation of hip-hop culture that rendered them "cool" by both White and Asian peers (Chiu, 2007). The Cambodian youth interviewed by Tang and Kao (2012) tried to "blend in" as they felt marginalized by their Asian peers who "looked down on" and "poked fun at" Cambodians: "I guess by the things they say, they think they [Chinese] are better off than Cambodians," reported one student in the study (Tang & Kao, 2012, p. 12).

In Lee's (2001) ethnography on Hmong students in a school with a tradition of high academics and a school culture of "whiteness," she asserts that both 1.5- and 2nd-generation Hmong Americans continued to be marginalized within a White school context. Yet, within this context, students struggled with their own ethnic identities. Second-generation students who were able to emulate their White peers in terms of high academic and social achievement were never fully included and self-identified as "Americanized" Hmong rather than "American."

Other studies indicated that often Southeast Asian Americans are racialized as "collective black" (Bonilla-Silva, 2004, p. 931). While all authors in the analyzed studies described racialization, only two explicitly raised themes suggestive of the collective black hypothesis. Chiu (2007) notes that Lao American participants rejected any association with African Americans, yet employed a "media-inspired hip hop cool, with its close association to Blackness, [which] allow[ed] the Lao American boys . . . to refashion themselves out of earlier cultural constructions that cast them as quiet meek amenable—as the model minority" (p. 3). Similarly, Ngo (2009) recounts teacher participants' descriptions of Lao American male students' "gangster-fronting" behavior and theorizes that youth "created identities that were in such juxtaposition with dominant 'received wisdom' of how they *should* look and act as Asian boys that it created confusion among other students and teachers" (p. 210). The arguments provide further credence to the notion that Southeast Asian American youth push back against fixed, static, binary concepts of identity in favor of more fluid constructions.

School Influences

Authors suggested that educators' perceptions of "Asian" or particular ethnicities within the Asian subgroup influenced Southeast Asian American youth identities. The youth in Stritikus and Nguyen's (2007) study began their US school career in a Newcomer school, where they were allowed an opportunity to navigate newly emerging ideas of what it meant to be Vietnamese in the United States. However, once they moved to the comprehensive high school, they felt that school was a place in which they were invisible and felt lonely, finding only a small amount of solace in the ESL wing of the school. For immigrant and second-generation students, schools—and teachers in particular—contribute both passively and actively to either perpetuating forms of inequality or providing students access to the cultural capital that promotes success (Conchas, 2010; Franquiz & Salazar, 2004; Gibson, 1998; Valenzuela, 1999). The students in several of the analyzed studies felt that teachers and peers overly relied on the model minority construct to position them as hard-working and consistently successful in school settings (Chhuon & Hudley, 2011; Lee, 2001; Stritikus & Nguyen, 2007; Tang & Kao, 2012). This stereotype, on the surface, may be mistakenly seen as a positive one, but there are two major flaws in the construct. First, the construct denies pervasive institutional racism in the United States that raises structural barriers that may impede success for persons of color (Chiu, 2007). Second, it silences the concerns of Asian American youth who are marginalized and experience poverty (Lee, 2001). For example, Tang and Kao (2012) revealed that when Cambodian students were mistaken for other (non-Cambodian) Asians in their school context, teachers held higher expectations that they would excel academically. Rather than disappoint their teachers, they often remained silent about both their ethnicity and their academic struggles (Tang & Kao, 2012).

The context of the school environment emerged as a prominent theme in influencing the Cambodian students in Chhuon and Hudley's (2010, 2011) studies. The school, which was segregated by the honors magnet program and the regular education track, created a space in which Cambodian students, particularly higher achieving youth, often blended into the larger panethnic Asian community. The teachers in the school who identified Cambodian students as less academically successful often were not able to identity their Cambodian students in their honors classes. For them, these successful students were *just Asian*. Cambodian students in the magnet school received the benefits associated with the model minority rather than the negative stereotypes associated with being Cambodian. Identifying as Cambodian represented a stigmatized label—an identity that teachers felt was characterized as less intelligent and more likely to participate in less academic, career-track classes. Because the school was split into two tracks: the academic magnet and the career track, identity formation of Asian students at the school was influenced by the ways in which they were tracked and subsequently treated (Chhuon & Hudley, 2011). The magnet and academic track teachers lumped their Cambodian students as "Asians," according to their panethnic identity, and often failed to realize which students in their classes were Cambodian.

Similarly, the teachers in Tang and Kao's (2012) study were also unaware of the ethnicities of their Asian American students: "I know it's sad, but I can't even tell you if the Asian students in my class [are] Khmer or Chinese or Vietnamese. I know that the student is Asian, has an Asian last name, and looks Asian" (p. 9). While the Cambodian students chose to embrace the panethnic term *Asian* in school because they perceived it as a path to a positive academic identity, the deficit thinking of the teachers in Tang and Kao's study combined with tensions between school and familial expectations negatively influenced Cambodian students' educational outcomes. For the Cambodian students in Chhuon and Hudley's (2010, 2011) study, "the Asian American label meant that teachers and students would view them as high achievers, rather than as academic strugglers" (Chhuon & Hudley, 2010, p. 350). However, this positive panethnic school identity positioned Cambodian youth in opposition to other Cambodian peers in the non-honors track, and the honors Cambodian students were often accused of being *white-washed*. In contrast, although "Cambodian students in the career academies [lower tracks] were viewed as low achieving students," they were able to "maintain their ethnic integrity" (Chhuon & Hudley, 2011, p. 692). The school's role in forcing students into a binary of *either* Cambodian *or* successful reduced students' abilities to create a positive cultural identity. Students in the career academic tracks held less negative views of their Cambodian identity. Most associated being Cambodian with having other Cambodian friends and having a less rigorous school track. Some acted out or identified with urban youth culture and had an anti-school attitude, while others did well in their academics to counter the anti-academic stereotype of Cambodians "to prove the haters wrong" (p. 355).

Ngo (2009) stresses that educators need to understand how "we position students" (p. 217). She asks, "How are schools teaching and addressing issues of culture and identity? . . . How are immigrant students reworking, contesting, and constructing 'culture' and 'cultural identity?'" (p. 206). When these questions are ignored or when educators attempt to construct whole *truths* for individual students, they run the risk of creating the dichotomy of Asian versus American, as in "this is how Asians need to be taught" rather than acknowledging the way in which "society intersects with their experiences as adolescents and urban students" (Ngo, 2009, p. 216). Chiu (2007) reiterated this point when she argued that "the problem is not to re-culturize them [second-generation Lao students] (or transform them back into the model minority), but rather to find avenues that offer them agency without unduly distinguishing them from non-Lao students" (p. 21) in order to provide access to a "default college-prep curriculum for all students" (p. 21).

REFRAMING SOUTHEAST ASIAN AMERICAN IDENTITY RESEARCH

The presence of various histories and contexts influences both the story of diversity within the Asian American community as well as the struggle for Asian solidarity as a cohesive racial group. The process of interpreting our analysis of multiple studies allowed us to explore the questions we first posed: How are Southeast Asian American youth defined, understood in the current studies, and racialized as a collective? What narratives are constructed in schools about Southeast Asian American youth? How have Southeast Asian American youth embraced or resisted being framed as model minorities? Through our meta-ethnography of studies on Southeast Asian American youth identity we argue for a reframing of studies of Southeast Asian American identity that provides a more nuanced critique of the influence of institutional racism and colorism, more complexly explores narrowly defined ideas of academic success, and centers Southeast Asian American studies within both Asian American studies and mainstream educational studies.

Disrupting Racism and Colorism

While most of the studies in question critiqued the influence of the model minority myth, many authors mentioned, but did not fully explore, the workings of racism and colorism. Some authors spoke about institutional barriers (Chiu, 2007; Lee, 2001; Nguyen & Brown, 2010; Stritikus & Nguyen, 2007), yet institutional racism was present but largely unnamed in the studies. In our initial synthesis of the metaphors found in the eight studies, we included a "structural critique" category in order to consider what evidence exists that points to social forces that influence Southeast Asian American youth identity. Although we list "themes of race/culture," "themes of identity," and "structural critique" as separate categories for the purpose of gleaning specific arguments from each study, within our holistic interpretation of the synthesis, these three categories interact complexly in shaping the overall picture of influences on Southeast Asian American youth identities.

For youth participants in the analyzed studies, acculturation into panethnic Asianness occurred within and was influenced by school structures. The main critique of schools focused on the isolation of immigrant, 1.5- and even 2nd-generation Southeast Asian American students based on English-language proficiency (Chiu, 2007; Lee, 2001; Nguyen & Brown, 2010; Stritikus & Nguyen, 2007). Stritikus and Nguyen described the initial language barrier as leading to "sustained racial and ethnic divides" (p. 878). Lee, likewise, described the social segregation of FOB students who were in ESL classes and their more Americanized or mainstreamed peers. Chhuon and Hudley's (2010–2011) analysis critiqued the divide between students in academic and nonacademic tracks. Chiu spoke out beyond language segregation to expose the "culture of avoidance" in her focus school stating that commentary by staff in the school "exposes racist sentiments" (p. 19).

Though some of the authors described Southeast Asian American youth identity within a cultural framework of immigrant, first (1.5 or 2nd) generation, Asian, and/or Southeast Asian American, there were underlying threads that pointed to the ways in which youth were racialized based on dominant perceptions that particular ethnicities had somehow taken up "blackness" (Chiu, 2007) in their speech, behavior, or attitudes. The remark (made to a Cambodian student by a non-Asian peer), "You're really not Asian, just Cambodian" speaks volumes in describing the experiences of Southeast Asian American youth across the studies analyzed (Tang & Kao, 2012, p. 10). Upon initial analysis, this comment seems to confirm Southeast Asian American youth struggle with the discrimination inherent in the model minority stereotype in which their academic struggles make them somehow less Asian—less good, beneficial, ideal, and "just" Southeast Asian. Yet, upon further analysis, we viewed the ways in which characterizations of Southeast Asian American students aligned with racist and colorist narratives already firmly entrenched within the school social environment. These narratives, whether reflective of a US racial hierarchy or borrowing from a global racial hierarchy that existed prior to immigration, influenced both the identity formation of Southeast Asian American youth as well as the ways they were treated by teachers and peers. While race and culture were conflated in many of the studies analyzed, some authors specifically theorized about racialized characterizations of Southeast Asian American students (Chhuon & Hudley, 2010–2011; Chiu, 2007); yet we suggest that the ways in which Southeast Asian American youth have been racialized requires additional study. First, whiteness was present throughout the synthesis and emerged in several ways: acting White, White as successful, and ethnic identity as a rejection of whiteness. Although concepts of *whiteness* and *blackness* were apparent in the studies, authors explicitly said very little about Southeast Asian American direct interaction with Black and White peers but described youth interaction with Asian peers. One participant in the Tang and Kao study mentioned aligning himself with Black and Latino peers for protection against Chinese students, but little was articulated about how interracial relationships affect Southeast Asian American youth identity. Also, while some researchers described teacher stereotypes about Southeast Asian American youth, little was mentioned about teacher race/ethnicity and the resulting influences on students.

Second, some Southeast Asian American students became racialized as collective Black (Bonilla-Silva, 2004; Chiu, 2007), which reflects an underlying assumption that Asian youth, when faced with the US racial hierarchy, will either be placed high (honorary White) or low (collective Black). Yet we found important concepts missing from this explanation including the influence of colorism in Asian communities and how colorist narratives interact with social class, nationality, and gender. Jones (2013) argues that colorism is significant for Asian and Asian American communities and works to "further intragroup divisions and hierarchies" (p. 1120). She goes on to describe

> Because much prior research on skin color has focused on African Americans, it has been tempting to conclude that skin color gets its meaning from race and indeed that colorism is primarily a subset of racism.... However, preferences for lighter skin also exist in Japan, China, and other parts of Asia. Are these preferences of recent origin, suggesting that they may be developing as Eastern and Western cultures collide, or are they more ancient in origin, suggesting that some color preferences may exist independently of, and indeed may pre-date, the development of racist ideologies? (pp. 1120–1121)

Therefore, future research of Southeast Asian American youth identity should consider both the racial and colorist influences on identity from both a US social context as well as a global perspective. In synthesizing these metaphors, we found underlying deficit perspectives in the ways that teachers described Southeast Asian American youth in the organization of the wider academic institutions and in the social status of these students in schools.

Opening Up the Success Narrative

Interpretations of the studies in this meta-ethnography suggest that the "ideal" for Southeast Asian American youth would be to navigate a tricky balance between maintaining a cultural/ethnic self while also conforming to mainstream norms of success. In essence, success for Southeast Asian American students seemed narrowly defined. Authors described maintenance of the cultural/ethnic self in terms of youth speaking their native language; expressing association or affinity for Asianness, Southeast Asianness, being Hmong, Lao, and so on; or wearing particular clothing, dress, or style. Success narratives, in many of the studies, included speaking English, performing well in school, and assimilating into the "positive" qualities of being Americanized.

While scholars have long critiqued the model minority theory, and many of the studies in this meta-ethnography proposed a more fluid and complex description of Southeast Asian American youth identity, the idea of the model minority remained intricately linked to the narrative of success for Southeast Asian American youth. The model minority stereotype, which has long been critiqued as a method of suppressing the struggles of certain facets of the Asian American community, such as Southeast Asian Americans, also functions to gloss over the still-present discrimination and violence experienced by Asian Americans as a racial group (Chang, 1993). At the same time, the model minority stereotype, with its tendency to hide the history of discrimination and racial violence against Asian Americans (Chang, 1993), is inextricably linked to the formation of Asian identity. Reminiscent of Butler's (1990/1999) work in which she likens identity categories to "regulatory regimes" that limit and exclude the current and future development of the subject, we note the discursive power of the model minority stereotype on Asian American identity performances—even as Southeast Asian American youth may have actively struggled against it through the appropriation of hip-hop culture or the maintenance of their ethnic identity. If identity is fluid, changing, and contextual, then despite our initial urge to completely dismiss the model minority stereotype as a myth, we eventually acknowledged that perhaps it continued to recur in the literature because of the intricate ways in which it has influenced Asian American identity and/or the researchers studying Asian American identities.

Whether described explicitly or clothed in the guise of a "success narrative," the influence of the model minority myth stands as a reminder of structural forces of power and oppression and their ability to inscribe static, essentialized identities. Therefore, by acknowledging the influences of colorism and institutional racism on Southeast Asian American students, there exists greater opportunities to disrupt fixed ideas about identity categories, illuminate ways that identity categories become essentialized, and create spaces for describing how political solidarity occurs both within Asian American communities and between Asian Americans and others.

Centering Southeast Asian American Youth Studies

As scholars who identify with, work, and live closely with marginalized communities, we firmly recognize the importance of scholars of color writing about communities of color. As we considered the positionalities of authors in the analyzed studies, we uncovered three main findings. First, while the lead authors may have identified as Asian or even Southeast Asian American, some did not share the culture or language of their participants. Statements of positionality varied from a one-sentence statement of ethnicity to a lengthier explanation of the influence of researcher positionality on the findings presented. Second, we noticed interesting patterns in the journals in which Southeast Asian American studies were published. While we found literature reviews and large quantitative studies on Asian Americans in mainstream educational journals, most of the ethnic group-specific, case study–oriented, qualitative work on Southeast Asian Americans was more likely to be published in the *Journal of Southeast Asian American Education and Advancement* and less likely to be published in mainstream journals. Third, we realized that, even within our own research team, our lead author was Southeast Asian American and that the other two authors, though they had engaged with the Southeast Asian American community, had not previously published work specifically on these groups. Our critical orientations prompted us to further analyze our musings on author positionality and publication outlet and include them in our overall meta-ethnographic interpretations.

We were curious about the narratives of Asian American scholars doing this work, particularly those engaged in cross-ethnic/racial work. We pondered the absence of White scholars discussing Asian-American issues. We speculated about the absence of Southeast Asian American youth in the mainstream educational literature, particularly within literature describing issues faced by students of color. In response to some of our questions, we reference literature written about scholars of color in academia. Padilla (1994) writes about the challenges of ethnic minority scholars who want to conduct and publish ethnic-related research. He argues that there exists an overprevalence of research (in mainstream journals) that compares a particular ethnic group to Whites, thus eliding intragroup variability and ethnic knowledge. Padilla goes on to argue that "We must resist the erroneous idea that only the guild journals are peer reviewed and thus the most prestigious in which to publish," yet he also emphasizes that "ethnic research should not be viewed as only an appendage to 'mainstream' educational research" (p. 25). Turner (2003) writes about the benefits and risks of moving from marginalization to incorporation for faculty of color in academia, and writes that, for some, "maintain[ing] their unique identity is a tension" described by some scholars as a "lived contradiction" that is impossible to navigate "without compromise" (p. 114). Turner quotes Gonzalez in saying, "to increase the probability that new problems will be addressed in the sciences, there is a need to increase the number of scholars likely to find those problems interesting. Doing so will eventually have an impact on an institution's research agenda" (p. 117).

Taking these observations into account, we celebrate Asian researchers for writing about Southeast Asian American identity and acknowledge the long-fought battles that scholars of color have fought to be recognized as experts in studying their own communities. Also, we acknowledge the value of insider perspectives and applaud the intra- and interracial/cultural collaborations that some of the research teams, including our own, represented. At the same time, we feel that the interpretations of this meta-ethnography illuminate gaps in mainstream educational scholarship, particularly in scholarship that purports to address the issues faced by marginalized youth in the nation's schools. Southeast Asian American youth have largely been silenced and invisible in educational studies of urban schools, students of color, and students experiencing poverty (for a notable exception see Lee's [2004] article, "Up against Whiteness: Students of Color in Our Schools). With this meta-ethnography, we hope to begin a conversation about challenging mainstream educational scholarship to work toward centering the social, racial/cultural, linguistic, and gendered concerns of Southeast Asian American youth.

IMPLICATIONS FOR IDENTITY THEORY

Scholars have acknowledged the influence of school and social structures on Southeast Asian American youth, and many have pushed back against linear, simplistic understandings of Southeast Asian American youth experiences. In our analysis of the eight studies in this meta-ethnography, we sought to both highlight and expand existing understandings of Southeast Asian American identity by illuminating underlying themes of racism/colorism, showing how students' embrace fluidity in their identities, and critiquing school structural barriers faced by Southeast Asian American youth. We suggest that the interpretations in this meta-ethnography hold implications for future studies of Southeast Asian American youth, studies of the wider panethnic Asian group, and other youth of color studies as well. Many of the studies analyzed in this meta-ethnography focused on cultural identity and could perhaps be critiqued for the overreliance on cultural explanations of school success or failure. In contrast, we argue for a stronger structural critique of school institutions that pull from racist, classist, and nativist narratives and "box" students into narrowly prescribed racial/cultural roles.

A study of Southeast Asian American youth identities represents a unique opportunity to study youth identity formation at the intersections of gender, social class, immigration, race/culture, color, US racial hierarchies, global racial hierarchies, and past/present histories of interracial-interethnic conflict within the Asian diaspora. In doing this analysis, we sought to complicate the narrative of Asian identity found in one-dimensional research studies that present Asian identity solely in terms of acculturation/assimilation statistics and achievement. We began with a strong desire to portray a deep, complex story of Southeast Asian American youth identity, but we too struggled against the labels associated with essentialized Asianness and the prevalence of equating Asian with foreignness and perpetual immigrant status. Although youth in the analyzed studies represented everything from first- to third-generation Asian, we unexpectedly fell into the trap of conflating *immigrant* and *Asian*, even in our terminology. How would we refer to youth in our meta-ethnography? As Southeast Asian youth? As Southeast Asian immigrant youth? As Southeast Asian American youth? Although we could dismiss these concerns as minor editorial decisions to be made, we acknowledged something deeper at work in our naming difficulties that reflected back to the challenge of theorizing about Southeast Asian American youth identities. As we explored the ways in which identity has been framed for Southeast Asian American youth, we found descriptions of identities that were contextual, fluid, and somewhat unstable for some youth. As we journeyed through the literature, initial fixed boundaries and categories began to blur as we delved into the varying histories and experiences of distinct communities (Southeast Asian American, Asian American, Asian immigrant, Cambodian, Hmong, etc.) and their individual and collective struggles around, race, class, language, and gender. Reminiscent of what some have called the tension between critical and poststructural approaches to conceptualizing identity (Alarcón, 1990; Mann, 2013), scholars in studies we included tended to approach Asian identity from either a bicultural perspective (individuals are a mixture of ethnic group and American) or a postmodern/poststructural perspective (identity as ambiguous and contradictory). We suggest that a greater understanding of how the fluid continuum of Asian American identity has been shaped by history, context, and agentic subjects requires a discussion of *both/and* instead of *either/or.*

CONCLUSIONS AND IMPLICATIONS OF META-ETHNOGRAPHIC RESEARCH

Meta-ethnography represented the method by which we analyzed and synthesized various studies on Southeast Asian American identity. Yet our goal in utilizing this method was more complex than simply aggregating and interpreting the findings. In situating ourselves in this research and finding our "place in the text" (Denzin & Lincoln, 2000, p. 1051; Doyle, 2003, p. 331), we acknowledged the influences of our own positionalities and research lenses, grounded in critical and social justice ideologies, in the meta-ethnographic interpretation put forth in this chapter. In being transparent about our relationship with the interpretive process, we align our thinking with Doyle's (2003) articulation of meta-ethnography as a "process for rethinking and expanding democratic practices into research" (p. 338). She explains this process by stating

> Meta-ethnography offers the possibility to empower. Meta-ethnography expands the conversation about qualitative synthesis as methodology to one that furthers the cause of democratic principles because it offers new conceptualizations of how knowledge as power may be transgressed. Numerous case studies tell valuable stories . . . but, because of narrowed beliefs about research, these voices typically are silenced beyond the boundaries of each individual case. Embedded in each of these case studies may be ideas that lead to new conceptualizations about the whole that can contribute to understanding. . . . Meta-ethnography empowers by amplifying voices. (p. 339)

The concept of meta-ethnography as a vehicle for highlighting the voices and experiences of Southeast Asian American youth greatly appealed to us as critical educators. Therefore, we argue that the centering of marginalized voices represents an important goal that might be pursued through meta-ethnography. In analyzing narratives that highlighted Southeast Asian American youth's fluid, complex identities, we hoped to problematize the marginalization of Southeast Asian American studies in the mainstream educational literature while still showing the common threads of racialization and oppression that influence the pan-ethnic group as a whole. Synthesis through meta-ethnography represented an ideal study method for capturing the specificity of studies on individual Southeast Asian American communities, allowing individual *voices* to be heard, while drawing out larger themes and narratives about Southeast Asian American youth as a collective group.

In conclusion, we contend that Southeast Asian American youth navigate their identities in ways that are complex, fluid, contextual, and historically and socially constructed. We recognize that the literature on Asian American identity is broader, more expansive, and more complex than what could be explored in a single chapter. Yet, through our individual positionalities and collective research lenses, we endeavored to put forward a critical analysis of a select body of research in hopes of contributing to existing studies and pushing forward future theories of Southeast Asian American youth. Whether communities are described according to individual ethnic groups (i.e., Hmong, Laos, Cambodian, or Vietnamese) or racialized as Asian Americans as a whole, the complexity and contextual nature of identity formation risks being obscured without a discussion of the influence of structural, historical, and political forces that act on identity as well as the agency of individuals to resist, reshape, and recreate their identities.

REFERENCES

Alarcón, N. (1990). Chicana feminism: In the tracks of "the" native woman. *Cultural Studies, 4*(3), 248–256.

Anzaldúa, G. (1987). *Borderlands/la frontera: The new mestiza.* San Francisco, CA: Aunt Lute.

Asian Pacific American Legal Center. (2004). The diverse face of Asians and Pacific Islanders in Los Angeles County 2004. Los Angeles, CA: United Way of Greater Los Angeles.

Beverly, M. G. (2011). *Viewing positionality through the lens of first-time qualitative research students.* Paper presented at the annual meeting of the Seventh International Congress of Qualitative Inquiry, University of Illinois at Urbana-Champaign Illini Union, Urbana.

Bhabha, H. (1999). *The location of culture.* London: Routledge.

Bonilla-Silva, E. (2004). From bi-racial to tri-racial: Towards a new system of racial stratification in the USA. *Ethnic and Racial Studies, 27*(6), 931–950. doi:10.1080/0141987042000268530

Butler, J. (1999). *Gender trouble.* New York: Routledge. (Original work published 1990)

Chang, R. S. (1993). Toward an Asian American legal scholarship: Critical race theory, post-structuralism, and narrative space. *California Law Review, 81*(5), 1241–1323.

Chhuon, V., & Hudley, C. (2010). Asian American ethnic options: How Cambodian students negotiate ethnic identities in a U.S. urban school. *Anthropology & Education Quarterly, 41*(4), 341–359. doi:10.1111/j.1548-1492.2010.01096.x.

Chhuon, V., & Hudley, C. (2011). Ethnic and panethnic Asian American identities: Contradictory perceptions of Cambodian students in urban schools. *The Urban Review: Issues and Ideas in Public Education, 43*(5), 681–701. doi:0.1007/s11256-010-0172-8

Chiu, M. (2007). Americanization against academics: Racial contexts and Lao American youths in a New Hampshire High School. In C. C. Park, R. Endo, S. Lee, & X. L. Rong (Eds.), *Asian American education: Acculturation, literacy development, and learning* (pp. 1–24). Charlotte, NC: Information Age.

Conchas, G. (2010). Structuring failure and success: Understanding the variability in Latino school engagement. In R. Saran & R. Diaz (Eds.), *Beyond stereotypes: Minority children of immigrants in urban schools* (pp. 155–182). Boston: Sense Publishers.

Denzin, N. K., & Lincoln, Y. S. (2000). The discipline and practice of qualitative research. *Handbook of Qualitative Research, 2*, 1–28.

Doyle, L. H. (2003). Synthesis through meta-ethnography: Paradoxes, enhancements, and possibilities. *Qualitative Research, 3*, 321–344.

Franquiz, M. E., & Salazar, M. (2004). The transformative potential of humanizing pedagogy: Addressing the diverse needs of Chicano/Mexicano students. *High School Journal, 87*(4), 36–53.

Gibson, M. A. (1998). Promoting academic success among immigrant students: Is acculturation the issue? *Educational Policy, 12*(6), 615–633.

Glesne, C. (1992). *Becoming qualitative researchers: An introduction.* White Plains, NY: Longman.

Gonzalez, N. (2011, February). *Immigration and migration: Ethnography in education in dynamic times and spaces.* Paper presented at the Annual Ethnography in Education Research Forum, Philadelphia, PA.

Jones, T. (2013). Significance of skin color in Asian and Asian-American communities: Initial reflections. *University of California Irvine Law Review, 3*, 1105–1123.

Kibria, N. (2000). Race, ethnic options, and ethnic binds: Identity negotiations of second-generation Chinese and Korean Americans. *Sociological Perspectives, 43*(1), 77–95. doi:10.2307/1389783

Lam, K. D. (2015). Racism, schooling, and the streets: A critical analysis of Vietnamese American youth gang formation in Southern California. *Journal of Southeast Asian American Education and Advancement, 7*(1), 1–16.

Lee, S. J. (2001). More than" model minorities" or" delinquents": A look at Hmong American high school students. *Harvard Educational Review, 71*(3), 505–529.

Lee, S. J. (2004). Up against whiteness: Students of color in our schools. *Anthropology & Education Quarterly, 35*(1), 121–125. doi:10.1525/aeq.2004.35.1.121

Lee, S. J. (2006). Additional complexities: Social class, ethnicity, generation, and gender in Asian American student experiences. *Race Ethnicity and Education, 9*(1), 17–28.

Liu, E. (1998). *The accidental Asian: Notes of a native speaker.* New York: Random House.

Mann, S. A. (2013). Third wave feminism's unhappy marriage of poststructuralism and intersectionality theory. *Journal of Feminist Scholarship, 4*, 54–73.

Ngo, B. (2009). Ambivalent urban, immigrant identities: The incompleteness of Lao American student identities. *International Journal of Qualitative Studies in Education, 22*(2), 201–220. doi:10.1080/09518390701770936

Ngo, B., & Lee, S. (2007). Complicating the image of model minority success: A review of Southeast Asian American education. *Review of Educational Research, 77*(4), 415–453. doi:10.3102/0034654307309918.

Nguyen, J., & Brown, B. B. (2010). Making meanings, meaning identity: Hmong adolescent perceptions and use of language and style as identity symbols. *Journal of Research on Adolescence, 20*(4), 849–868. doi:10.1111/j.1532-7795.2010.00666.x

Noblit, G. W., & Hare, R. D. (1988). *Meta-ethnography: Synthesizing qualitative studies.* London: SAGE.

Office of Management and Budget. (1997). Revisions to the standards for the classification of federal data on race and ethnicity. Retrieved from https://www.whitehouse.gov/omb/fedreg_1997standards

Ong, P. M., & Leung, L.-S. (2003). Diversified growth. In D. Arguelles (Ed.), *The new face of Asian Pacific America: Numbers, diversity, and change in the 21st Century* (pp. 7–16). Berkeley, CA: Asian Week & UCLA Asian American Studies Center Press.

Padilla, A. M. (1994). Ethnic minority scholars, research, and mentoring: Current and future issues. *Educational Researcher, 23*(4), 24–27.

Park, J. (2008). Second-generation Asian American pan-ethnic identity: Pluralized meanings of a racial label. *Sociological Perspectives, 51*(3), 541–561. doi:10.1525/sop.2008.51.3.541

Perez, A. D., & Hirschman, C. (2009). The changing racial and ethnic composition of the U.S. population: Emerging American identities. *Population and Development Review, 35*(1), 1–51. doi:10.1111/j.1728-4457.2009.00260.x

Pyke, K., & Dang, T. (2003). "FOB" and "whitewashed": Identity and internalized racism among second generation Asian Americans. *Qualitative Sociology, 26*(2), 147–172. doi:10.1023/A:1022957011866

Strike, K., & Posner, G. (1983). Types of synthesis and their criteria. In S. Ward & L. J. Reed (Eds.), *Knowledge structure and use* (pp. 343–362). Philadelphia, PA: Temple University Press.

Stritikus, T., & Nguyen, D. (2007). Strategic transformation: Cultural and gender identity negotiation in first-generation Vietnamese youth. *American Educational Research Journal, 44*(4), 853–895. doi:10.3102/0002831207308645

Tang, K., & Kao, D. (2012). Ethnicity, gender, and the education of Cambodian American students in an urban high school. *Journal of Southeast Asian American Education and Advancement, 7*(1). doi:10.7771/2153-8999.1045

Tuan, M. (1998). *Forever foreigners or honorary Whites: The Asian ethnic experience today.* New Brunswick, NJ: Rutgers University Press.

Turner, S. P. (1980). *Sociological explanation as translation.* New York: Cambridge University Press.

Turner, C. S. (2003). Incorporation and marginalization in the academy: From border toward center for faculty of color? *Journal of Black Studies, 34*(1), 112–125.

Valenzuela, A. (1999). *Subtractive schooling: U.S.-Mexican youth and the politics of caring.* Albany, NY: SUNY Press.

Vo-Jutabha, E. D., Dinh, K. T., McHale, J. P., & Valsiner, J. (2009). A qualitative analysis of Vietnamese adolescent identity exploration within and outside an ethnic enclave. *Journal of Youth and Adolescence, 38*(5), 672–690. doi:10.1007/s10964-008-9365-9

Yu, T. (2006). Challenging the politics of the "model minority" stereotype: A case for educational equality. *Equity & Excellence in Education. 39*(4), 325–333. doi:10.1080/10665680600932333

7

Tools of Navigation

A Meta-Ethnography of Latina Students, Gender, and Sexuality

HILLARY PARKHOUSE AND SUMMER MELODY PENNELL ∎

INTRODUCTION

Identity is inherently intersectional (Crenshaw, 1991). Youth are in a constant state of identity negotiation, both in and outside of school, and this negotiation draws on race, ethnicity, class, gender, sexual orientation, as well as other dimensions. It is only in the past 30 years or so that research has attended to the intersectionality of identity. Research on ethnic identity became more prevalent in the late 1980s (Phinney, 1993), while research on gender identity (such as Rubin, 1975) and queer identities (Turner, 2000) gained popularity in the 1990s. In this meta-ethnography, we focus on conceptualizations of identity as revealed through qualitative studies on Latina[1] students' identities, particularly in relation to gender and sexuality as well as race and ethnicity. As these studies demonstrate, Latinas' conceptions of their gender and/or sexuality are shaped by their racial and ethnic identities. However, ethnicity is not a fixed determinant of Latinas' relation to these roles, as seen in the studies by Tijerina-Revilla (2004, 2009), Cruz (2006, 2008), and Ek (2009a; 2009b). Latina high school and college students, particularly Latina queer youth, explored their identities in complex ways while questioning norms from both their own backgrounds and the dominant culture.

Context

The decision to focus on gender and sexuality in Latina students came out of our interest areas. At the time of the research study, we were both doctoral students in education interested in social justice. Parkhouse taught high school for six years in the Dominican Republic and then in a Dominican neighborhood in

New York City. Equity in education for Latinx high school students is now one of her research interests. Pennell's research interests center on queer students and queer theory. As White, cisgender scholars, we approach this work in light of Anzaldúa's (1987) call that White scholars "come to see that they are not helping [Latinxs] but following our lead" (p. 85) As interpretivists, we also wish to emphasize that this meta-ethnography is but one of many possible interpretations of the literature on gender and sexual identities in Latina students. We approached this research to investigate the following question: What insights for identity theory are suggested in the qualitative research on Latina students/Latina students' experiences related to gender, sexuality, and ethnicity?

METHODS

Text Selection and Search Procedures

When we first began this work, our focus was broader and we had not narrowed our focus to Latinas only. Our initial criteria for inclusion were that studies needed to (a) be ethnographic, (b) focus on Latina/os, (c) select participants who were students, and (d) use identity theory to investigate the participants' conceptions of both their race/ethnicity along with their gender and/or sexuality.

In order to find ethnographic studies about Latinxs in school settings that included an examination of gender and or sexuality, we first conducted broad searches using several databases: ERIC, Sociological Abstracts, and AnthroSource. We chose these databases to draw from anthropology, sociology, and education, fields in which ethnography is utilized as a research method for studying students. In each database, we searched for a variation of ethnography (sometimes using the truncated ethnograph* depending on the individual databases search functions) and identity and Latina and education. (In the ERIC database, we did not include the "education" search criteria). We also substituted gender, sexuality, queer, lesbian, or gay for "identity" to catch more results. Additionally, we substituted "Latino" for "Latina" and also searched for "Chicana" or "Chicano." We found different results with these searches, as some authors used the term Chicana but not Latina.

We found that there were more ethnographic studies focusing on gender and/or sexuality among females (Latinas or Chicanas) than among males (Latinos or Chicanos). For this reason, we dropped studies with males as primary subjects from our inclusion criteria. Some of the remaining studies do include male subjects, but in each case they are compared to females (Barajas & Pierce, 2001; Wortham, 2002). We also eliminated studies that fit the search criteria of Latina student participants but did not problematize identity, gender, or sexuality via theory and only discussed identity in the everyday use of the word. Some studies on Latinas were further eliminated because they were not based in school settings or did not include education in their foci (Garcia, 2012; Mann, 2013; Mendoza-Denton, 2014) or because they did not problematize or explicitly set out to contribute to identity theory (Garcia, 2009a, 2009b; Sanchez, 2009). We did not find studies about elementary or middle school students that fit our search criteria, so the studies reviewed here focus on high school and college students.

These inclusion guidelines resulted in nine studies, some of which spanned multiple articles. We felt that nine was a suitable number for our purposes given that "qualitative synthesis experts agree that meta-ethnography is best suited to addressing a conceptual question through synthesis of a limited number of conceptually rich studies; to synthesize a very large number of studies a thematic synthesis is often considered more appropriate" (France et al., 2014, p. 3). Using only nine studies allowed us full immersion in all facets of the study—conceptual, empirical, positional, and so forth—immersion that is integral to the meta-ethnographic method (Noblit & Hare, 1988).

Coding and Analysis

We began by coding each article for methods, participants, theories used, and keywords (e.g., "conformist resistance" in Cammarota, 2004). Next, we open-coded one article together and then compared our codes. Whereas literature reviews and other forms of research synthesis tend to focus primarily on findings, meta-ethnography requires reviewers to preserve all contextual features of studies in their syntheses (Noblit & Hare, 1988). Thus we coded the entire articles (e.g., introductions, literature reviews, theoretical frameworks, and discussions), paying particular attention to metaphors and themes. After coding the first article, we agreed upon an initial code list that categorized moments where the researcher described (a) sexuality/gender, (b) the researcher's relationship to participants, (c) nationality/ migrant status, (d) language, (e) race, (f) sub-nationality, (g) space, (h) group identity construction, (i) individual identity construction, (j) school/learning, and (k) performance. We created a spreadsheet and copied direct quotes from each article into columns corresponding to each code.

After this initial coding phase, we read over the coded segments together and realized that there were common subcodes within these primary codes. For this second round of coding, we investigated the previously coded segments for the following elements: (a) queer or gender identities/explorations, (b) immigrant/ Latina, (c) a combination of queer/gender with immigrant/Latina identity explorations, (d) political resistance, (e) personal resistance, or (f) in-between spaces and/or identities. For example, under the initial "language" code, we placed a quote from Ek (2009a, 2009b) where Amalia, her research participant, discussed her purposeful seeking out of Spanish-dominant spaces, such as her church. We additionally coded this section in our second round as "personal resistance." To code segments as multiple subcodes, we color-coded for the subcodes within the existing columns of our spreadsheet. Further examples of our methods and coding strategies can be found in the appendix.

Chapter Framework

Through this iterative coding and recoding process, we were able to narrow down our analysis here to three overarching themes that contribute to the identity theory that emerges through these studies: space, performance, and agency. Before exploring these themes in depth, we first outline each study's theoretical approach and conclusions. The studies are presented in alphabetical order by author's last name. After we present the thematic synthesis (translation of metaphors) of the nine studies, we discuss the line of argument (Noblit & Hare, 1988) that emerged through this synthesis. Finally, we conclude with ideas for future work on identity theory in relation to our meta-ethnography.

THEORETICAL AND PARADIGMATIC APPROACHES OF INCLUDED STUDIES

Barajas and Pierce (2001)

In Barajas and Pierce's (2001) study called "The Significance of Race and Gender in School Success among Latinas and Latinos in College," the authors interviewed Latina and Latino college students and their high school mentees. The older women discussed with the high schoolers the ways in which Latinas were seen negatively by their (mainly White) teachers and how to successfully navigate their schooling experience. The authors pointed out that "universities typically embody the presumption of one-way assimilation for students of color" (p. 860). Barajas and Pierce used Patricia Hill Collins' concepts of "sphere of freedom" and "collective resistance" (p. 863) to describe the spaces created by the women in their mentoring relationships, as well as through the positive environments of family and friends.

Cammarota (2004)

Julio Cammarota (2004) studied gendered academic roles for Latina and Latino youth drawing from his larger ethnography of a barrio in Southern California. He found that Latinas used high academic achievement as a form of resistance to social subordination. Cammarota's theoretical framework primarily centered on resistance theories that have been used specifically for understanding Latinx youth (Delgado Bernal, 2001; Valenzuela, 1999). He argued that the Latinas in his study were engaged in transformative resistance (Solórzano & Delgado Bernal, 2001), because their achievement would empower them to break free from the gender roles that characterized prior generations. He also linked this to their motivation to achieve despite low expectations from teachers (Yosso, 2002).

CULTURAL CONSTRUCTIONS OF IDENTITY

Cruz (2006, 2008)

Cindy Cruz (2006, 2008) conducted a two-year ethnographic study at a high school that served lesbian, gay, bisexual, transgender, and queer (LGBTQ) students. For our meta-ethnography, we used an article from this work, "Notes on Immigration, Youth, and Ethnographic Silence" (Cruz, 2008) and then compared it with her dissertation, *Testimonial Narratives of Queer Street Youth: Toward an Epistemology of a Brown Body* (Cruz, 2006). Her participants were LGBTQ undocumented immigrants, and many were experiencing homelessness. Cruz (2008) found that many students were out to their families and did not struggle with family acceptance of their sexuality, and so their sexual orientation was not the cause of their homelessness. Instead, it was related to their—or their parents'—undocumented status. Cruz (2006, 2008) used Liang's theory of ethnographic silence (how we can learn from what participants *do not* say in interviews) to discuss how she did a "reciprocal reading" (2008, p. 69) of the youth interviews. Because she is Latina and queer, she could understand their coded speech.

Delgado Bernal (2001)

Delgado Bernal (2001) used life history interviews with 32 Chicana college students in California to explore their educational experiences as they related to their cultures and identities. She used a Chicana feminist epistemology and drew on Anzaldúa's (1987) concept of *mestiza consciousness* to understand "how a student balances, negotiates, and draws from her bilingualism, biculturalism, commitment to communities, and spiritualities in relationship to her education" (Delgado Bernal, 2001, p. 627). She used her own theoretical concept of "pedagogies of the home" (p. 624) to analyze specifically the ways in which "the teaching and learning of the home allows Chicanas to draw upon their own cultures and sense of self to resist domination along the axes of race, class, gender, and sexual orientation" (p. 624). She argued that these pedagogies of the home serve as assets with which Chicanas can subtly (and sometimes unknowingly) resist subjugation and challenge dominant expectations about their capabilities.

Ek (2009a, 2009b)

Lucila Ek conducted a case study of a Guatemalan American she called Amalia, following her from age 8 to 21. From interviews with Amalia and her family, as well as observations at school, home, and church, she published two articles (Ek, 2009a, 2009b). One study (Ek, 2009b) focused on the tools Amalia used to negotiate the multiple socializations she faced in high school, at church, and at home. The other (Ek, 2009a) traced how transnationalism influenced her identity over time. Ek argued that Amalia's resistance to being positioned as sexualized, Americanized, and Mexicanized pointed to "the 'improvisations' of agents that constantly change the conceptual and material aspects of figured worlds (Holland et al., 1998) and help them to negotiate the disjunctures of their multiple socializations" (p. 416). Drawing from Anzaldúa, Butler, and Bucholtz, Ek attended to Latina identity construction specifically by acknowledging the importance of language as a tool for identity maintenance and expression and gender performance as a reflection of socialization through cultural activities.

Tijerina-Revilla (2004, 2009)

Anita Tijerina-Revilla conducted a five-year study with Raza Womyn, a student group at the University of California, Los Angeles. We used two of her articles from this study, "Muxerista Pedagogy: Raza Womyn Teaching Social Justice Through Student Activism" (Tijerina-Revilla, 2004) and "Are All Raza Womyn Queer?" (Tijerina-Revilla, 2009). Tijerina-Revilla explained that muxerista is an identity these women created as a way to encompass their ethnic identity, political beliefs, and gender and sexual identities. Muxerista is a variation of *mujeres*, meaning women, with the "x" in place of the "j" to indicate "a connection to Indigenous ancestry/language and anticolonial struggle" (Tijerina-Revilla, 2009, p. 49). The participants related to the concept of borderlands used by Anzaldúa as in Raza Womyn "gender and sexuality roles are vehemently questioned and rejected, even when they are painful *travesias* (crossings)" (Tijerina-Revilla, 2009, p. 50). The group openly integrated queer issues, which shows the influence of Moraga's (1993) *Queer Aztlan*. These methods are used to raise a queer consciousness and a social justice mindset, which also "has a direct effect on these students' retention . . . [as they] create meaning of their education" through the group (Tijerina-Revilla, 2009, p. 92).

Valenzuela (1999)

In "'Checkin' Up on My Guy': Chicanas, Social Capital, and the Culture of Romance," Valenzuela (1999) focused on three heterosexual Latinx high school couples, drawing from a larger ethnography. She found the culture of romance and its impact on Latina identities to be strongly influenced by schooling conditions. To preserve self-worth in the face of de-Mexicanization at their high school, these Latina students found stability in taking on perceived adult roles of caring for males. Valenzuela framed her study with Bourdieu's social capital theory and Holland and Eisenhart's (1990, as cited in Valenzuela) work on the culture of romance in college. To counter the school's "social decapitalization" (p. 61) of Latinxs' linguistic and cultural resources, the Latinas in this study obtained social capital through academically supporting males.

Vetter, Fairbanks, and Ariail (2011)

In "'Crazyghettosmart': A Case Study in Latina Identities," a case study from a larger ethnography, Vetter and colleagues (2011) focused on how one participant, Jessica, negotiated the identities of "crazyghetto" and "smart." In particular, they examined how, "through the negotiation of these 'in-between' spaces, Jessica was able to construct multiple identities within the figured world of school that merged her home and school worlds" (p. 203). For their analysis of the transitional phases Jessica was negotiating, they used Lesko's concept of the "border zone" (p. 186) occupied by adolescents. They also used Butler's performativity in discussing how Jessica "performed as an adult" (p. 203) after her pregnancy and "both performed and resisted the normative constructions of both 'crazyghetto' and 'smart'" (pp. 189–190). The authors also invoked Bhabha's concept of "third space" (p. 189) in relation to Holland's concept of figured worlds and identities (p. 187).

Wortham (2002)

In the book *Education in the New Latino Diaspora: Policy and the Politics of Identity*, Stanton Wortham's (2002) chapter, "Gender and School Success in the Latino Diaspora" explored the identities of Latinas and Latinos in a rural New England town in the late 1990s. Similar to Cammarota, he found that gender significantly impacted the academic orientations and trajectories of his participants. However, Wortham found that traditional Mexican gender roles magnified the trend. He found that Latinas perceived they had the choice of achieving in school or early marriage. At the same time, however, many Latinas who chose the former did so primarily to help their families. In this sense, their adoption of mainstream Anglo values was motivated by their families even as, Wortham argued, this was distancing them from their families. These Latinas had "dual identities . . . to succeed in the mainstream world, but to maintain their cultural traditions at home" (p. 137). Wortham did not explicitly describe his conceptual framework, but he drew on ideas such as working-class anti-school culture (Willis, 1977), oppositional identities (Fordham & Ogbu, 1986, as cited in Wortham, 2002), and dual identities (Gibson, 1988, 1997, as cited in Wortham, 2002).

TRANSLATIONS OF THEMES

As we coded the articles chosen, a number of themes emerged, three of which we elaborate on here: space, performance, and agency. As we coded for agency, we discovered the need for separate categories of individual and collective agency. "Tools for navigation" was a subtheme of agency in many studies, but some uncovered individuals' tools while others highlighted tools shared among groups. Also within the theme of individual agency were subthemes including (gendered) academic resistance and shifting/dual identities.

Space

Space was used in four ways in the studies: physical space of school or home, space to explore sexuality, space to affirm gendered identities, and space to affirm racial and ethnic identities. Frequently authors described participants' spaces as "in-between." In these instances, Latinas had to both navigate the space they were in while simultaneously creating space for themselves to express and explore their identities.

Physical. Physical space was featured most prominently in Cruz's (2006, 2008) work, as the homeless youth she worked with had the pressing concern of where they could safely live. One lesbian young couple lived together in an abandoned house and described to Cruz their constant awareness of physical space as opportunities for shelter and sustenance. One of the pair, Sandy, explained that "lots of places will feed you breakfast and dinner like the local youth drop-in center and runaway youth drop-in center—so we can always get food there. But it's nice to have our own place, for as long as we can handle it" (Cruz, 2006, pp. 112–113). Private, safe physical space was treasured and often unattainable.

Delgado Bernal (2001) also explored the physical (and symbolic) space of home, although, for her participants, home was already present rather than continually sought after. In fact, home was a stable wellspring from which Chicanas drew the cultural assets of bilingualism, biculturalism, spirituality, and commitment to their families and communities. She argued, "pedagogies of the home extend the existing discourse on critical pedagogies by putting cultural knowledge and language at the forefront to better understand lessons from the home space and local communities" (p. 624). When we translated the metaphor/concept of home from the Cruz into Delgado Bernal studies (and vice versa), we saw that home is an integral part of identity and particularly cultural identity regardless of whether or not home is physically present or attainable.

Sexuality. The phrase "safe space" is commonly used in queer circles to denote a physical place that is open and welcoming and a metaphorical place that is emotionally supportive of myriad sexual orientations and gender identities. It is not surprising, then, that the word "space" was used in Cruz's (2006, 2008) and Tijerina-Revilla's (2004, 2009) studies. Cruz (2008) noted the importance of high school teachers having "Safe Zone" stickers on their door or similar visual confirmations for LGBTQ youth to feel they can "tell their stories without fear of reprisal" (p. 69). For Tijerina-Revilla's (2004, 2009) college student muxeristas, a "safe space" was something they intentionally created, as they wanted a space that was open to an exploration of sexuality as well as anti-patriarchal political views. The muxeristas were drawn to Raza Womyn "after experiencing alienation or rejection in predominantly heterosexual or nongender specific organizations" on campus (Tijerina-Revilla, 2009, p. 50). For the women in Tijerina-Revilla's study, these spaces were also constructed to celebrate Latina culture, shown in part by adopting the name muxerista but also to critique the parts of Latina/o cultures they found problematic, namely patriarchy and homophobia.

Gendered identities. These uses of space are in contrast to the other articles, especially Valenzuela's (1999), in which space was not used to explore queer sexualities but to reaffirm a heterosexual sexuality and feminine gender identity. The girls Valenzuela interviewed were attached to their identity as girlfriends and took pride in looking after their boyfriends. It was in this light that Valenzuela evoked "space," stating that it was "girls' lifelong experience with stronger social control mechanisms that resulted in their ability to provide *'safe spaces'* for potentially wayward males" (p. 73). Unlike in the previous section where a safe space was a source of empowerment for women and an opportunity to explore their own desires, in this case it is a source of empowerment for men and a space to explore their desires. Yet even though Valenzuela saw these relationships as exploitative, the girls did not. For them, "romantic relationships provided a secure *loving space* that provided some measure of stability and protection in a difficult and capricious [school] environment" (p. 74). This was also true in Vetter et al. (2011). "Space" was also evoked as a way to reify Jessica's female identity. When Jessica became pregnant, Vetter et al. stated that she "found a space to explore her [pregnancy] story at school" (p. 202). This exploratory space is similar to that in Cruz's (2006, 2008) and Tijerina-Revilla's (2004, 2009) studies, but instead of a space to explore sexualities outside of heteronormativity, for Jessica it became a space to explore her new identity as an adult woman, participating in the gendered ritual of motherhood.

Race and ethnicity. Space was also used in relation to racial and ethnic identities, both Latina and Anglo-American. In discussing the experiences of the Latina college student mentors in their study, Barajas and Pierce (2001) noted that "the white spaces of universities typically embody the presumption of one-way assimilation for students of color" (p. 860). In contrast to these unwelcoming spaces, "safe spaces were created [for the Latinas] in relationships with friends, family, and community including association with other successful Latino students in spaces such as Latino organizations" (p. 869). The Latina high school mentees created a positive space with their mentors, who the authors deemed their "cultural translators." As Barajas and Pierce stated, "these relationships with cultural translators became spaces in which Latinas learn positive meanings and valuations that counter the negative significations operating in schools" (p. 869). The Chicana college students in Delgado Bernal's (2001) study engaged in the same positive meaning-making as a counter to negative expectations through the space of home, rather than within a space at school. This place of racial affirmation was also found in the Raza Womyn's group, as Tijerina-Revilla (2009) characterized the group as a "space to explore . . . other aspects of identity including race/ethnicity, class . . . and immigration status" (p. 56).

In-between. Because all aspects of identities are connected, and because frequently the Latinas in these studies walked between heteronormative/queer and Anglo-American/ Latina/o spaces, the idea of being in-between or in transition came up frequently. This was true in Delgado Bernal (2001), Vetter et al. (2011), and Ek (2009a, 2009b), as each of these researchers analyzed how Latinas attempted to preserve their cultural identities while also navigating American schools and their definitions of success. Delgado Bernal used the concept of borderlands as a "metaphor for the condition of living, between spaces, cultures, and languages" (p. 632). In Vetter et al.'s study, Jessica's "in-between spaces . . . [related to] Jessica's relationship with academics and Jessica's relationship with her social world" (p. 191). Her social "crazyghetto" world was not always conducive to school success, but as this was also important to her, she navigated between her "crazyghetto" and "smart" personas. For Amalia in Ek's (2009a) study, the "tensions between the socializations [in school, church, and at home] create spaces where Amalia enacts her agency and constructs her identities" (p. 405).

Agency

All nine of the studies portrayed agency and resistance, although they varied in degree to which this resistance was located at the individual or group level. For instance, the two case studies described the tools with which Amalia and Jessica resisted positioning by others as sexualized or "crazyghetto"; however, resistance in Tijerina-Revilla's (2004, 2009) and Barajas and Pierce's (2001) studies was achieved collectively and through relationships with others. The methodologies likely play a role here; it is not surprising that studying groups would yield different interpretations of agency than studying individuals. However, what is interesting are the similarities among the forms of resistance, the tools employed, and the shifting nature of the identities constructed through this resistance.

Because we focused on students and experiences within education settings, most studies revealed forms of resistance specific to academic achievement or rejection. Having further narrowed our focus to articles exploring gender and sexuality, we found that academic resistance is gendered and can even be partnered (in romantic relationships). We begin by translating these areas into one another. We then translate the navigational tools employed in the studies and the shifting identities constructed and finally turn to the collective resistance and shared tools that emerged in some of the studies.

Academic resistance. In every study that examined academic success, success was both defined in Anglo-American terms as well as achieved through performance of middle-class Anglo versions of desirable academic behavior. Barajas and Pierce (2001) described this as "one-way assimilation for students of color" (p. 860) and, more specifically, "assimilation to an individualistic and meritocratic understanding" (p. 859). For Amalia, this meant becoming "competitive and aggressive" (Ek, 2009b, p. 411). For Jessica, this meant that she, along with her boyfriend, "resisted those peer activities that conflicted with their academic goals" (Vetter et al., 2011, p. 197). In Jessica's case, resistance occurred in partnership with her boyfriend, a dynamic that set Jessica's resistance apart from that of Amalia. While Jessica's boyfriend "helped her to become who she wanted to be" (p. 196), Amalia avoided the world of romance out of a desire to resist sexualization and focus on academics. However, Jessica's boyfriends "sometimes distracted her from academics" (p. 196). Although Vetter et al. claimed they "never saw Jessica putting her own achievement at risk for her boyfriend" (p. 196) in the same sense that Valenzuela's (1999) participants did, Jessica's relationships "influenced how she wrote herself within the social world of school, sometimes causing her to fall behind academically" (p. 198). Her ability to position herself in "the fig-ured world of school" was more constrained than was Amalia's because of Jessica's investment in the "figured world of romance" (p. 198).

Vetter et al.'s (2011) study differed from Cammarota's (2004), Delgado Bernal's (2001), and Wortham's (2002), however, in that Latinas in the latter three succeeded in isolation from and sometimes in contradiction to Latino males. In Cammarota's study, Latinas engaged in "resistance through achievement" (p. 53) by "proving them wrong" (p. 56), where "them" refers to racist institutions and media repre-sentations, whereas Latinos resisted the policing occurring in schools by cutting class. In Wortham's study, Latinas were not attempting to prove expectations wrong but rather saw academic achievement as a way to help their families and, perhaps, through avoiding early marriage, gain "independence from domestic relations" (p. 133). Similarly, Cammarota found that Latinas hoped their achievement would "herald a new perception of Latinas . . . no longer submissive to men, but respected as equal, capable, and worthy" (p. 63). So in both studies, Latinas' academic success was a tool for resisting traditional Mexican gender roles. Delgado Bernal's Latina participants showed similar patterns of resistance through achievement, but she did not contrast them with their male counterparts like the former two studies did.

On the other hand, Latino males in both studies chose to resist academic assim-ilation but for different reasons. In Wortham's (2002) New England town, males saw little room for upward mobility, reinforcing their inclination toward manual labor, which they viewed as more masculine than white-collar work. Latinos in Cammarota's (2004) study, however, resisted academic assimilation because they were policed and criminalized at school. Thus Cammarota's interpretation was that the males' behavior was more reactive than proactive, although in both cases it is navigation of oppressive institutions that drove the resistance to schooling. In contrast, Latino college students in Barajas and Pierce's (2001) study actu-ally assimilated more to the dominant culture than did Latinas. This was due to the influence of sports involvement and mentorship of coaches, as opposed to Latinas who used group membership to preserve positive ethnic identities.

Valenzuela (1999) highlighted the interactions between Latinas and Latinos in school rather than treating them as separate groups. Through these interac-tions, Latinas were able to support Latinos' academic achievement. Like Wortham (2002) and Cammarota (2004), she found that Latinas performed "a version of femininity that promotes school as a goal" (p. 60). Unlike the males in the previ-ous studies, however, the Latinos here adopted a "pro-school ethos" (p. 74), even though "were it not for the females in these groups, US-born youth would be vir-tually devoid of social capital" (p. 62). In the end, however, the subtractive nature of the school in which Valenzuela conducted her ethnography severely limited the potential for either males or females to reach their academic goals.

In synthesizing these translations, we see that the ways gender and romantic relationships have been shown to interact with academic success depends on the methodology (case study versus ethnography), the context (Cammarota's highly policed high school versus Wortham's working-class New England town), and even the priorities of the individuals studied (Amalia valued school suc-cess over romantic life, while Jessica found academic success through romantic relationships). Although the implications among these studies seem to vary, a line of argument does emerge. Most studies tended to present agency related to school success in the somewhat dichotomous framework of assimilation or resistance to Anglo-defined versions of academic success. Participants assimilated or resisted depending upon the community and school contexts, as well as the gendered identities that formed within these contexts and in the context of ethnic traditions. What is true in every instance is that gender and ethnicity are always at play in academic assimilation or resistance, but when we examine individual cases, self-authorship and the power of agency become more apparent. The next section details specific ways the individuals exercise this agency.

Tools for navigation. The idea of "tools of agency" (Ek, 2009b, p. 416) or tools or strategies of resistance (Delgado Bernal, 2001) is prominent in these two studies, but translating this idea into the other studies reveals that all of the participants leverage some resources to exercise agency, even if they are not always referred to as tools. Delgado Bernal's participants "drew from a mestiza consciousness in which their spiritual practices served as tools or strategies of resistance that helped them persist towards their educational goals" (p. 635). They also used bilingualism, biculturalism, and commitments to families and communities as tools to navigate school and achieve dominant conceptions of educational success.

Amalia used "Spanish language" to resist Americanization, "the Guatemalan variety of Spanish" to resist "Mexicanization" (Ek, 2009b, p. 417), and transnationalism to preserve her religious identity. She also used her religious identity, as well as dress, to negotiate "sexualization" (p. 416) at school. Amalia used these tools to "negotiate the multiple socializations to ethnic and gender identities in three primary educational contexts: her home, her Pentecostal church, and her high school" (p. 405). In doing so, Amalia was "improvising identities" (p. 407) in the way Holland et al. (1998) described. Ek also drew on Gee's (2000) notions of discourse identity to explain how these improvisations contribute to identities without "the support of the official institutions" (p. 407).

The other two studies that examined the use of tools on an individual level are Cruz (2008) and Vetter et al. (2011). A transgender participant in Cruz's study used "cross-dressing as an older Latina" (p. 70) for empowerment. In Vetter et al.'s analysis, Jessica used tools "such as reflexivity and humor to negotiate spaces in between crazyghetto and smart" (p. 202). After becoming pregnant, Jessica used "performance of her personal story" to "resist societal positioning that her pregnancy was a problem" (p. 202). The metaphor of positioning serves well to describe Amalia's preservation of her Guatemalan and Pentacostal identities as well. In each of these three studies, participants exercised agency and resistance by leveraging tools such as dress and language or personal narratives to position themselves against dominant and nondominant expectations.

In contrast, the tools analyzed in the other studies were not used by lone individuals. The Latinas in Valenzuela's (1999) and Barajas and Pierce's (2001) studies used "caring" (Valenzula, 1999, p. 66) and "mentoring" (Barajas & Pierce, 2001, p. 867) as tools, both of which require a recipient. In the former, caring for male friends gave Latinas "a sense of self-worth, connectedness, and status" (Valenzula, 1999, p. 66). In the latter, "Latinas navigate successfully through negative stereotypes by maintaining positive definitions of themselves and by emphasizing their group membership as Latina" (Barajas & Pierce, 2001, p. 859). In the first case Latinas derived their self-worth in relation to male partners, whereas in the second, they derived it in relation to other females. The reason for this difference, as suggested by Valenzuela, is that the subtractive nature of her participants' high school limited their access to social capital beyond that provided by their romantic relationships. On the other hand, Barajas and Pierce's participants were involved in mentoring relationships that, among other benefits, provided social capital that could be converted into college access and success and therefore into economic capital.[2] In the case of the latter study, participants' relationships helped rather than hindered their academic accomplishments.

Like Barajas and Pierce (2001), Tijerina-Revilla (2009) conducted her study with a university organization, and therefore the tools highlighted in her analysis are collective, rather than individual. In fact the primary tool *was* the collective "struggle against women's oppression within the Latino/a community" (p. 49). This was conducted through the muxerista consciousness, which "signifies a layering of identities that speaks to the relationship between ethnicity/race, gender, and critical feminist consciousness and engagement" (p. 49). In this sense, the women in Tijerina-Revilla's study not only required other women in order to leverage tools of agency but solidarity with these women was in fact the tool of agency and resistance. The line of argument that emerges here is that where group membership and activism are fostered, such as through university organizations, more feminist and empowering tools of agency are available. Although Amalia and Jessica resisted positioning by others, neither seemed to reach the level of "feminist consciousness and engagement." In fact, when Ek (2009a) followed up with Amalia as a college student, she found that she was now identifying as "American" whereas she had previously identified as "Hispanic or Latina" and, before that, as "Guatemalan" (p. 78). Thus, despite her transnationalism, insistence on reading the Bible in Spanish, and use of the Guatemalan variety of Spanish, Amalia's agentic tools did not prevent some degree of assimilation.

Shifting or dual identities. In analyzing the agency of social actors, a clear distinction exists between those authors who used the conceptions of identity offered by Holland et al. (1998) and Anzaldúa (1987) and those who did not. The former described the identities of their participants in terms such as "fluid, dynamic, and emerging in social practice" (Ek, 2009a, p. 406) or "interlocking" (Tijerina-Revilla, 2009). The latter tended to treat identity as more unitary and static.

Ek (2009a, 2009b) and Vetter et al. (2011) explicitly used Holland et al.'s (1998) social practice theory of identity to analyze their two cases. Ek understood Amalia's actions to "point to the 'improvisations' of agents that constantly change the conceptual and material aspects of figured worlds (Holland et al., 1998) and help them to negotiate the disjunctures of their multiple socializations" (p. 416). An example of a disjuncture is the sexualization that occurred in school versus the messages Amalia received at her Pentecostal church. Amalia thus improvised within the school a response of dressing in loose clothing by leveraging the positive religious identity she had constructed through transnational church attendance. In this way, her identities were dynamic and emerging differently in the social practice of school versus church.

Jessica, too, "improvised her positions within various realms of school to both resist and reconfigure discourses that shaped her identities as a student and adolescent" (Vetter et al., 2011, p. 185). She "continually refigured what it meant to be 'crazyghetto' and 'smart'" (p. 192). Just as Amalia constructed her identity through the disjunctures of her multiple socializations, "Jessica's reflexivity made it possible for her to identify 'small cracks and openings' in the world of school and to exploit them for her own agentive purposes . . . improvisations . . self-directed symbolizations" (p. 195). This suggests Jessica was in control of the construction of and movement between her shifting identities.

On the other hand, the studies using Anzaldúa (1987) also referred to identities as fluid and shifting, but in these agency does not appear quite as forceful. For instance, Delgado Bernal (2001) explained that *mestiza consciousness* is fluid but also stated

> Whether they were conscious of it or not, all the women articulated ways in which they lived and moved in and out of more than one culture. Students most commonly identified a home or "Mexicano" culture and a school or dominant "American" culture. And when I asked what their ethnic identity was the young women self-identified in different ways: 38% as Mexican American, 34% as Mexican/Mexicana, 25% as Chicana, and 3% as Biracial. Students discuss how their biculturalism allowed them to see things in ways that students from the dominant culture might not, and how their biculturalism can help others understand things from a different perspective. (p. 630)

Her uncertainty as to whether they were conscious of their movement between cultural identities suggests less of an agentic control over this movement than we saw in the studies of Jessica and Amalia. What is common across all three studies, however, is that the complex and layered social worlds of Latinas call for multiple and shifting identities.

In contrast, the studies that focused on gender differences in academic achievement offered representations of identities as more constructed by context than by improvisations. For instance, Wortham (2002) described the Latinas and Latinos in his study as "caught between two cultures" (p. 137), the two cultures being the Anglo world of schooling and the Mexican world at home. Their resulting feeling of being *no son de aquí ni de allá* (Goldfarb, 1996, as cited in Wortham, 2002) replaced the notion of multiple and shifting identities with displaced and unidentifiable identities. The closest these Latina students came to improvisations or negotiating disjunctures was the adoption of "dual identities, acting partly Anglo in school and largely Mexican at home" (Wortham, 2002, p. 137). The word "dual" connotes two simultaneous identities, rather than multiple identities that can shift from one moment to the next. The two are also determined by the context, leaving little room for agency to negotiate or improvise responses.[3]

Collective identity. Enlightenment-influenced approaches often analyze identity and resistance at the individual level (e.g., Willis, 1977). However, Indigenous and Latina/o traditions are typically more collective oriented. Four of our studies (Barajas & Pierce, 2001; Delgado Bernal, 2001; Tijerina-Revilla, 2004, 2009; Valenzuela, 1999) examined collective identity. Delgado Bernal's study is distinct from the others in that her participants were not affiliated with one another (as far as we could tell). However, the importance of collective identity arose in that "students spoke of their commitment to their families and communities as a source of inspiration and motivation to overcome educational obstacles" (p. 632).

Barajas and Pierce (2001) found interesting distinctions between gender differences in the groups Latina/os identified with and resulting differences in their perspectives on school. They found that "Latinas navigate successfully through negative stereotypes by maintaining positive definitions of themselves and by emphasizing their group membership as Latina" (p. 859). Group membership was also important to Latino males; however, their groups tended to be sports teams, which resulted in their adoption of a more competitive, individualistic approach to school. As a result, they had "less positive racial and ethnic identities than the women" (p. 861).

The Latina college students converted these positive ethnic identities into social capital for their high school mentees. For instance, one mentor explained that her priority was "to help them understand why they are seen as different in school and to establish a real relationship with them" (Barajas & Pierce, 2001, p. 867). In contrast, if the Latino males "challenged or resisted stereotyping, it was through their success as individuals, rather than through connections to other Latinos" (p. 870). Thus gendered variation in individualism versus collectivism not only affected the mentors' positive ethnic identities but may also have trickled down to the mentees' identities and approaches to school as well. Although Cammarota (2004) and Wortham (2002) reported the opposite finding (that Latinas showed greater assimilation to Western individualism), they did not describe how social capital distribution among the groups affected or were affected by this difference in degree of assimilation. Valenzuela's (1999) female participants did confer some social capital to their male friends; however, this was limited by their subtractive schooling context.

Because Tijerina-Revilla (2004, 2009) studied an activist organization, it follows that her analysis was much more collective oriented. The Raza Womyn members she studied engaged in group resistance "to achieve sexual, political, educational, cultural, social and self determination" (2004, p. 86). The muxerista consciousness developed through activism with the Raza Womyn organization allowed the individuals as well as the group to achieve "transformational resistance" (p. 83). Through this consciousness, members were able to construct and preserve complex ethnic and sexual identities. For instance, several were finally able to claim sexual identities in their "own terms" (2009, p. 54), and one participant chose a trinational label of "GuaNica"—"'Guanaco' is the term used to refer to people from El Salvador, and 'Nica' refers to her Nicaraguan heritage; thus GuaNica is the blending of the two" (p. 90). The acceptance offered by the group allowed the women to "connect to community (female and male), culture, language, and the struggle for justice" (p. 91) and to understand the shifting identities that accompany these.

Performance

Performance was another theme found in the articles, usually used in relation to navigating gender or other roles. It was absent in Tijerina-Revilla (2004, 2009), Barajas and Pierce (2001), Wortham (2002), Delgado Bernal (2001), and Cammarota (2004). In Cruz (2006, 2008), Vetter et al. (2011), Valenzuela (1999), and Ek (2009a, 2009b), the participants had to "perform" their identities as they were figuring them out.

These performances manifested in different ways depending on the context. For Cruz's (2006) participants, this performance related to their homelessness. In discussing the problems homeless youth face, Cruz stated, "the embodied performance of queer youth narratives must be seen in tandem with a materialist analysis and its connection to larger effects of global capitalism" (p. 172). Their performance was written on their body: evidence of malnourishment, signs of tiredness, bruises, and so on. This was the only study to talk about the body so specifically, again because of the context—these students' bodies were the most threatened.

Similar to the uses of space and agency, performance was also used as a way to navigate between worlds. Vetter et al. (2011) found that Jessica "both performed and resisted the normative constructions of 'crazyghetto' and 'smart'" (pp. 189–190). They also found that Jessica's "'tough' performance gained her status within her social world" and that her "assertiveness . . . was a performance in which she attempted to author herself as a smart Latina student" (p. 195). Once Jessica became pregnant, they noted that she was "performing as an adult" (p. 203) as she took on the role of mother and caretaker. Jessica used performance to navigate her transitions from her social life to her school life and from childhood to adulthood.

In Valenzuela (1999), performance was used to reify gender roles, similar to the way space was used. After describing an incident of a girl acting distraught over her boyfriend potentially missing class, Valenzuela explains that she had "performed a version of femininity [that] also gave [her] a sense of self-worth" (p. 66). Valenzuela used performance for all of the girls she interviewed, explaining that "when young women provide support to their male friends . . . they enact or perform a version of femininity that promotes school as a goal" (p. 60).

Ek (2009a, 2009b), used performance to illustrate how Amalia resisted these sexualized gender roles, in contrast to Valenzuela's (1999) study. This was most apparent during her *quinceañera*. Ek (2009a) cited Mendoza-Denton (2008) to point out that "makeup paints gender on girls' bodies. In this way, the quinceañera was very much a performance complete with costume and makeup" (p. 415). Amalia resisted this sexualized performance by purposefully acting childlike. She also did not like the "school's performances of gender identities [which] included tight, revealing clothes, and being in heterosexual couples" (2009a, p. 414). Because of her Pentecostal religious beliefs, Amalia was not interested in this particular performance and, as discussed earlier, chose to intentionally act childlike and wear clothing that was more conservative.

In these ways, performance was evoked in the studies that described Latinas who were figuring out their identities. It is not surprising that these studies dealt with high school, not college, students. Because these students were younger, perhaps they were more concerned with their "performances" of gender and sexuality. Amalia had a strong sense of religious self and so resisted the sexualized performance of her peers. Cruz's (2006) study is the only one where performance is used to describe physical markings on the body and not behavior or clothing. As stated previously, this is because of the context and the unfortunate circumstances Cruz's participants faced. Overall, it seems that the word "performance" was used by the researchers if they perceived that their participants were trying to fit in, working out their identities for themselves, or playing a social role.

LINE OF ARGUMENT

As perhaps appropriate for a meta-ethnography examining the intersectionality of identities, we identified two intersecting lines of argument: one related to personal agency and the other to collective resistance as demonstrated by Latina high school and college students across these nine studies. The authors represented their participants as having varying degrees of agency as well as varying commitments to collective, transformative resistance. Figure 7.1 displays the relative position of the participants on each of these two axes. The quotes provide a key metaphor or theme that captures our reasoning behind the decision to place the study in that particular position on the grid.

For the muxeristas in Tijerina-Revilla's (2004, 2009) study, the deeper exploration of sexuality, in addition to gender identities, contributed to Latinas' self-determination and liberation from racial and patriarchal subordination, in addition to academic subordination. As the line of argument we found aligns with queer theory's tenets of questioning norms, limits, and boundaries (Britzman, 1995), we hesitate to use the word "conclusion." To continue our queer turn, we might instead ask how questioning gender and sexuality norms leads to further questioning of other forms of subordination.

For studies concerning gender only (as opposed to gender and sexuality), participants typically did not question gender norms; rather, they were focused on school and racial discrimination. Indeed, the most common form of resistance (and use of agency in general) among all studies was to defy negative stereotypes about the academic capabilities of Latinxs. The Latinas in the Barajas and Pierce (2001) study collectively resisted racist norms through their mentoring relationships so that they achieved personal gains as well as gains for their community. In Cammarota's (2004) study, the Latinas resisted these norms both for the gain of their immediate community as well as future Latinxs.

Heterosexual Latinas in the other studies also attained traditional academic success but with less of an underlying drive to "prove them wrong" (Cammarota, 2004, p. 65), with "them" referring to those who held negative stereotypes of Latina academic capabilities. For the Latinas in Valenzuela's (1999) study, academic

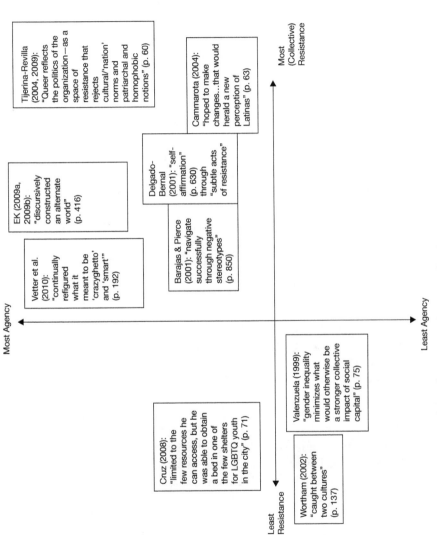

Figure 7.1 Intersecting lines of argument: Agency and resistance.

success garnered them social capital through the help they could offer male peers, while for those in Wortham's (2002) study, it allowed Latinas "to earn some independence from domestic relations" (p. 133). In these cases the motivation was linked to a desire to either partner with males or have the autonomy to choose not to marry, neither of which is related to societal transformation or even transformation of academic norms.

For the studies that included queer participants, there was a broader questioning of social norms, including heteronormativity and the privileging of Anglo-American values. This was most prominent in Tijerina-Revilla's (2004, 2009) study, because the women were questioning patriarchal and racial politics within their own racial groups and questioning the traditional cultural norms in which their campus climate and home lives were situated. Thus these muxeristas were not only challenging negative stereotypes and Anglo-American definitions of success through their own academic achievement, but they were oriented toward broader societal transformation of race-based oppression as well as patriarchy, heteronormativity, and neocolonialism. Perhaps the more dimensions of identity are explored, the more one is able to identify the ways in which both specific cultural institutions, as well as structures in general, constrain identity and agency. This may in turn lead to broader and more transformative forms of social resistance than would a more focused exploration of racialized academic or gender norms.

CONCLUSIONS AND IMPLICATIONS

From our line of argument, we are left with the impression that when Latina students examined both gender and sexuality, as well as societal expectations of each, this led to greater examination of and resistance to other oppressive structures. This included structures in dominant Anglo-American culture, as well as the Latinas' home cultures. Thus we posit that, given the intersectionality of identity, individuals who examine and question how these identities are shaped may engage in academic and social resistance to multiple and interlocking forms of normativity.

Juxtaposing studies of heteronormative gender expectations against studies of queer Latinxs allowed "what was hidden to become apparent" (Noblit & Hare, 1988, p. 75) in terms of identity formation and agency among Latinx students. Within these studies, Latinas who conformed to gender roles tended also not to question narrow definitions of success as solely related to academic achievement. Latinos, who also conformed to gender roles, did resist this narrow definition of success, but they did so through pursuing goals outside of school. However, within the studies in which Latinas transgressed gendered expectations, these youth found ways to persist in their education without assimilating or reproducing dominant racial/ethnic or gender norms. This meta-ethnography can be seen as a call for more studies that explore inter- and intragroup differences in Latinx communities and incorporate intersectionality. When examining the intersectionality of race/ethnicity with gender and sexuality, future studies using identity theory could examine how participants' questioning one or two aspects of their identities (in this case sexuality and gender) can lead to further questioning of other aspects of personal and cultural identities.

Given this, what then are the implications for identity theory? We are left with more questions than answers. Due to the secondary nature of our research, we do not know if the researchers saw something in their data that made them turn to identity theory during their analysis, or if they were interested in identity theory from the outset and used that interest to shape their research design. We also wonder how the use of theorists such as Holland and colleagues (1998) shapes the degree of agency perceived in the participants, particularly in contrast with the use of Anzaldúa's identity theories. Agency tends to be located at the level of the individual in many of these studies—a Western conceptualization that may be problematic when used with cultures that do not hold individualism in the same regard as Anglo-American cultures do. However, we also wonder if researchers were inclined to focus on participants' agency as a reaction to prior research, which had underestimated the agency of people from marginalized populations.

We do not want to suggest that there is a binary between agency/non-agency, or individual agency/collective agency, or even Western and Latinx cultures. As the participants in these nine studies showed, they were capable of moving in and out of different worlds. This very movement, combined with their own examination of their movements within and between identities, led to a further examination of structures. The Latinas in these studies were able to move from a personal examination to a structural one. This shift is difficult, and these participants' multiple identities, as Latinas, Americans, students, friends, mothers, girlfriends, church members, and so on are what allowed them to make this shift. We would argue, as others have (Moya, 2002), that their identities advantaged them to see structural inequalities over people who may see themselves as monocultural. The students in Tijerina-Revilla's (2004, 2009) study were making changes and forming groups from their intense examination of their identities and relationships to structural oppressions and social justice themes of intersectional work toward equality. As Anzaldúa (1987) wrote about *la mestiza*, "she has discovered that she can't hold concepts or ideas in rigid boundaries. The borders and walls that are supposed to keep the undesirable ideas out are entrenched habits and patterns of behavior; these habits and patterns are the enemy within" (p. 101). The muxeristas, and other Latinas throughout these studies, intentionally sought to break free of rigid, stereotyping boundaries to create their own paths.

Future ethnographic studies may be interested in exploring Latinx identities from an intersectional perspective to see what other ideas participants explore regarding how they fit into their own and the dominant culture. What might happen if other, non-Western concepts and theories centered on identity were explored? We feel there is ample room to explore concepts of collective identity and agency, using Anzaldúa (1987) as a theoretical lens. These studies may uncover more benefits and complications of participants whose lives are intersectional and thus may, from their very experiences, have a more abstract and deeper knowledge of identity and dominant structures than that offered via theories bound by Western, heteronormative, patriarchal, and rationalist frameworks.

APPENDIX

Steps	Examples
Determine interests.	• Parkhouse: Latinx populations • Pennell: gender and sexuality
Combine interests for initial topic focus (if working collaboratively).	• Latinx population focus • Studies that specifically discuss participants' concepts of gender and/or sexuality • Schooling (any level) • Researchers discussed participants' identity using theory, rather than simply talking about their identity as demographic categories
Search for studies • Conduct searches in library databases. • Use a combination of search terms and record them to prevent repetition. • Gather all articles that are ethnographic studies that meet topic criteria.	• We searched in ERIC, Sociological Abstracts, and Anthrosource • Terms included Latina, Latino, Chicana, Chicano; queer, lesbian, gay, bisexual, transgender • We had about 20 articles at this stage
Eliminate studies	We eliminated these studies: • Focus on males (only a few studies focused on males, so we decided to focus on females) • Studies that did not discuss what participants *thought* or *felt* about their racial/ethnic identities • Studies that did not discuss what participants *thought* or *felt* about their gender and/or sexuality • Studies that did not focus on school/academic settings
Update research topic based on curating the search results.	We kept nine studies that included the following: • Latina girls/women • Participants discussed feelings about race • Participants discussed feelings about gender or sexuality • High school or college students
First read: skim, look for what is interesting, check that it works for the study.	
Second read: read more carefully; copy and paste selections into a table: methods, theories, participants, and keywords/ideas. More articles can be eliminated at this stage.	See Figure 7.2

Steps	Examples
Coding:	• Some of our open codes were race, gender, power
• Code the articles like a data set.	• In vivo code: "safe space"
• Use open coding and "in vivo" coding.	
Make a chart for the codes. If qualitative software for the previous step was used, the program may create these.	• See Figure 7.3
Determine relationships:	
• What major themes do the studies have in common?	• We compared two studies at a time to better see the relationships
• What themes do not appear in multiple studies?	• See Figure 7.4.
Translate studies into one another.	• Key metaphors: From Cruz (2008): "safe space"
• Identify key metaphors.	
Determine the type of translation.	• Not reciprocal overall. But one example of reciprocal metaphors was "in-between space" (Vetter et al., 2011) and "interstitial spaces" and "transboundary" (Cruz, 2008)
• **Reciprocal:** Do the metaphors match?	
Determine the type of translation.	• Not refutational overall. But one example of refutational metaphors was "dangerous disclosure" (Cruz, 2008) versus "resistance through achievement" (Cammarota, 2004)
• **Refutational:** Do the metaphors dispute or contradict one another?	
Determine the type of translation.	• Yes. The use of metaphors shifted based on age or sexual minority status of participants
• **Line of argument:** Do the metaphors build on each other?	• Example: "space" Valenzuela was used by Latinas to support their boyfriends in culturally specific ways, while "safe space" in Cruz's (2008) reflected a more basic need from the participants for physical and emotional safety
Synthesize translations. Find subthemes.	• Our themes were space, agency, and performance

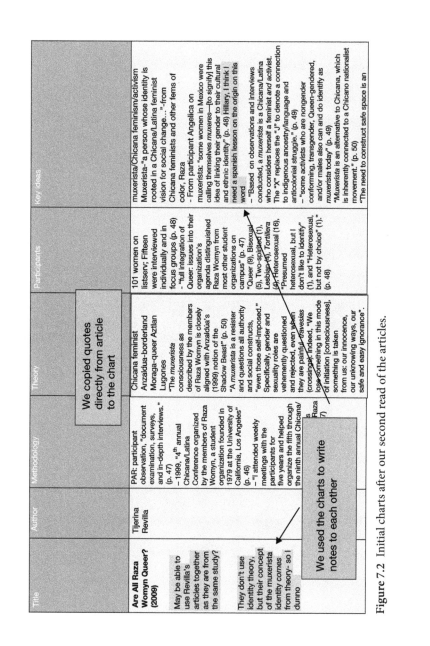

Title	Author	Methodology	Theory	Participants	Key ideas
Are All Raza Womyn Queer? (2009) May be able to use Revilla's articles together as they are from the same study? They don't use identity theory, but their concept of the muxerista identity *comes* from theory- so I dunno	Tijerina Revilla	PAR: participant observation, "document examination, surveys, and in-depth interviews." (p. 47) - 1999, "4th annual Chicana/Latina Conference organized by the members of Raza Womyn, a student organization founded in 1979 at the University of California, Los Angeles" - "I attended weekly meetings with the participants for five years and helped organize the fifth through the ninth annual Chicana/Raza ?)	Chicana feminist Anzaldua-borderland Moraga-queer Aztlan Lugones "The *muxerista* consciousness as described by the members of Raza Womyn is closely aligned with Anzaldua's (1999) notion of the Shadow Beast" (p. 50) "A *muxerista* is a resister and questions all authority and social constructs, "even those self-imposed." Specifically, gender and sexuality roles are vehemently questioned and rejected, even when they are painful *travesias* (crossings). Indeed, "We lose something in this mode of initiation [consciousness], something is taken from us: our innocence, our unknowing ways, our safe and easy ignorance".	101 women on listserv; Fifteen were interviewed individually and in focus groups (p. 48) - "full integration of Queer: issues into their organization's agenda distinguished Raza Womyn from most other student organizations on campus" (p. 47) "Queer (9), Bisexual (5), Two-spirited (1), Lesbian (1), *Tortillera* (4), Heterosexual (16), "Presumed heterosexual, but I don't like to identify" (1), and "Heterosexual, but not by choice" (1)." (p. 48)	muxerista/Chicana feminism/activism Muxerista-"a person whose identity is rooted in a Chicana/Latina feminist vision for social change..."-from Chicana feminists and other fems of color, Raza - From participant Angelica on muxerista: "some women in Mexico were calling themselves *muxeres*—[to signify] this idea of linking their gender to their cultural and ethnic identity" (p. 48) Hillary, I think I need a spanish lesson on the origin on this word – "Based on observations and interviews conducted, a *muxerista* is a Chicana/Latina who considers herself a feminist *and* activist. The "X" replaces the "J" to denote a connection to indigenous ancestry/language and anticolonial struggle." (p. 49) – "some activists who are nongender conforming, transgender, Queen-gendered, and/or males also can and do identify as *muxerista* today" (p. 49) "Muxerista is an alternative to Chicana, which is inherently connected to a Chicano nationalist movement." (p. 50) "The need to construct safe space is an

Callout boxes: "We copied quotes directly from the article to the chart" and "We used the charts to write notes to each other"

Figure 7.2 Initial charts after our second read of the articles.

	A		D	E	F	G	H	I	J	K	
1	blue = sexuality/gender; orange = race/ethnicity; purple = both; green = political resistance; yellow = personal resistance; bold font = in-between		Revilla 2004	Revilla 2009	Vetter, Fairbanks, Ariail, 2010	Valenzuela 1999		Within the "identity" category we found subthemes of: sexuality/gender, political resistance, race/ethnicity, and personal resistance.			
				"[Marina] no longer felt pressured to proclaim a Queer identity. Instead, she felt supported, understood, and able to take steps toward claiming her sexuali identity on her own terms" (p. 54)	"Jessica improvised her positions within various realms of school to both resist and reconfigure discourses that shaped her identities as a student and adolescent" (p. 185)		"assimilation may entail positive as well as negative consequences, some that may be damagin to students' sense of identity and self-esteem as a racial ethnic minority" (p. 860)	The text is quotes from the articles.			
48	Individual Identity (construction/labeling, etc.)		"revolutionaries or revolucionarias" (p. 89)			"Betty has her 'act together'" (p. 67)					
	Individual identity was a broad category		"Guanica" El Salvador and Nicaraguan p. 90	"Raza Womyn not only engaged in activism and consciousness-raising about multiple, interlocking identities, but it also pushed members to reconstruct their sense of self and identity" p. 60	Holland-figured identities p. 187	"Norma justifies her investment in her boyfriend's school work by saying that if she does not help him, 'Chach will definitely drop out of school	"Jennifer's 'awakening' can also be seen as a part of her experience				

Figure 7.3 Thematic chart.

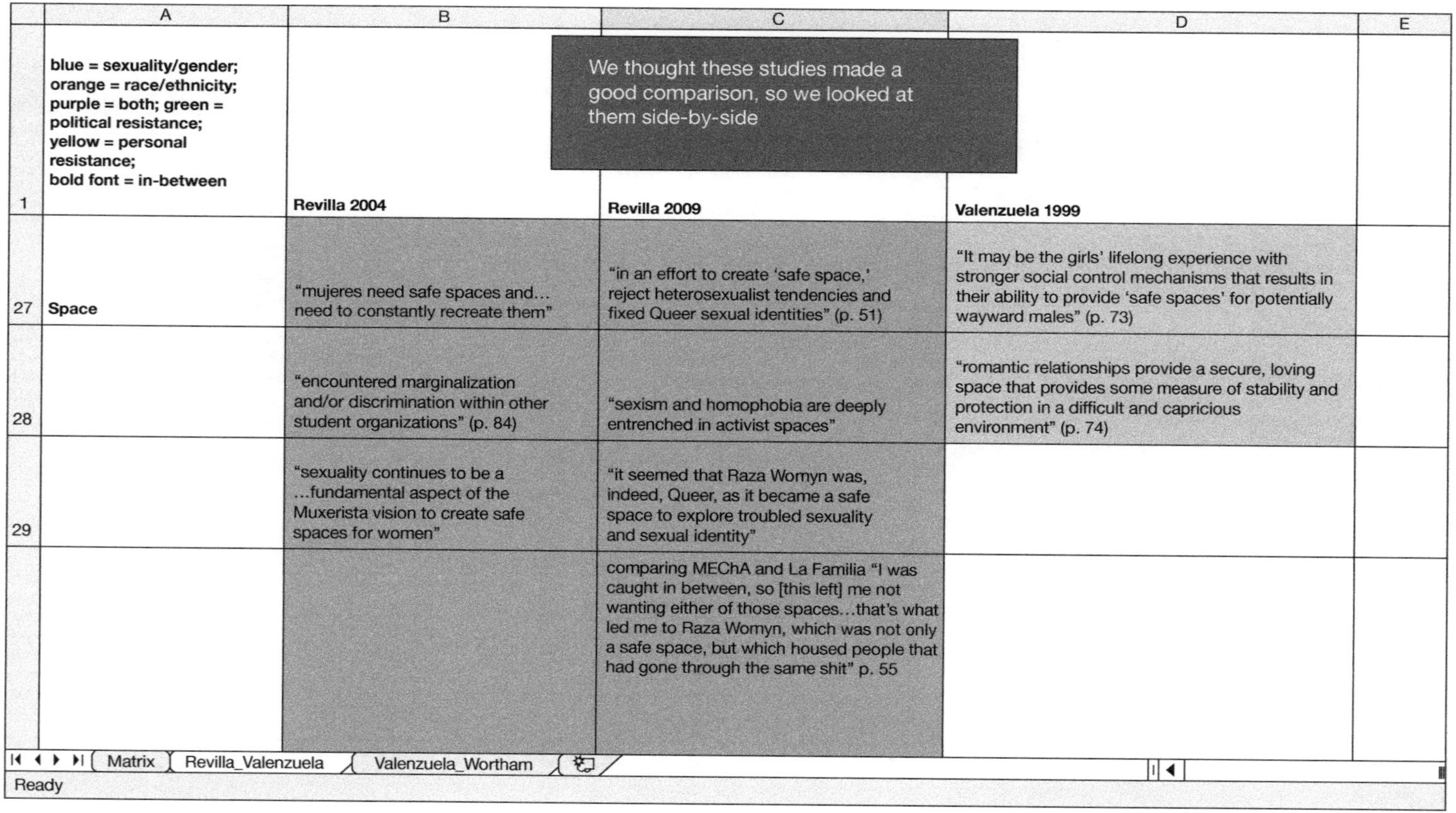

	A	B	C	D	E
1	blue = sexuality/gender; orange = race/ethnicity; purple = both; green = political resistance; yellow = personal resistance; bold font = in-between	Revilla 2004	We thought these studies made a good comparison, so we looked at them side-by-side Revilla 2009	Valenzuela 1999	
27	Space	"mujeres need safe spaces and... need to constantly recreate them"	"in an effort to create 'safe space,' reject heterosexualist tendencies and fixed Queer sexual identities" (p. 51)	"It may be the girls' lifelong experience with stronger social control mechanisms that results in their ability to provide 'safe spaces' for potentially wayward males" (p. 73)	
28		"encountered marginalization and/or discrimination within other student organizations" (p. 84)	"sexism and homophobia are deeply entrenched in activist spaces"	"romantic relationships provide a secure, loving space that provides some measure of stability and protection in a difficult and capricious environment" (p. 74)	
29		"sexuality continues to be a ...fundamental aspect of the Muxerista vision to create safe spaces for women"	"it seemed that Raza Womyn was, indeed, Queer, as it became a safe space to explore troubled sexuality and sexual identity" comparing MEChA and La Famillia "I was caught in between, so [this left] me not wanting either of those spaces...that's what led me to Raza Womyn, which was not only a safe space, but which housed people that had gone through the same shit" p. 55		

Matrix   Revilla_Valenzuela   Valenzuela_Valenzuela   Valenzuela_Wortham

Ready

Figure 7.4 Comparing two studies to determine the relationship.

NOTES

1. We use Latina or Latina/o in this chapter when discussing the cited studies to reflect the authors' language choices. When not talking about the studies specifically, we use Latinx to reflect current community and activist practices at the time of writing, to indicate an intentional break from the gendered Latina/o.
2. Tara Yosso (2005) has since critiqued this Bourdieuiean framework of capital, arguing that it neglects many forms of cultural wealth that students of color possess (e.g., aspirational, navigational, familial, linguistic).
3. We should note that Wortham did not detail how his positionality as a White male researcher may have influenced his analysis.

REFERENCES

Anzaldúa, G. (1987). *Borderlands: La frontera* (Vol. 3). San Francisco, CA: Aunt Lute.

Barajas, H. L., & Pierce, J. L. (2001). The significance of race and gender in school success among Latinas and Latinos in college. *Gender & Society, 15*(6), 859–878.

Britzman, D. P. (1995). Is there a queer pedagogy? Or, stop reading straight. *Educational Theory, 45*(2), 151–165.

Cammarota, J. (2004). The gendered and racialized pathways of Latina and Latino youth: Different struggles, different resistances in the urban context. *Anthropology & Education Quarterly, 35*(1), 53–74.

Crenshaw, K. (1991). Mapping the margins: Intersectionality, identity politics, and violence against women of color. *Stanford Law Review, 43*(6), 1241–1299.

Cruz, C. (2006). *Testimonial narratives of queer street youth: Toward an epistemology of a brown body* (Doctoral dissertation). University of California, Los Angeles. Retrieved from ProQuest Dissertations & Theses.

Cruz, C. (2008). Notes on immigration, youth, and ethnographic silence. *Theory into Practice, 47*, 67–73.

Delgado Bernal, D. (2001). Learning and living pedagogies of the home: The mestiza consciousness of Chicana students. *International Journal of Qualitative Studies in Education, 14*(5), 623–639.

Ek, L. (2009a). "*Allá en Guatemala*": Transnationalism, language, and identity of a Pentecostal Guatemalan-American young woman. *The High School Journal, 92*(4), 67–81.

Ek, L. (2009b). "It's different lives": A Guatemalan American adolescent's construction of ethnic and gender identities across educational contexts. *Anthropology & Education Quarterly, 40*, 405–420.

France, E. F., Ring, N., Thomas, R., Noyes, J., Maxwell, M., & Jepson, R. (2014). A methodological systematic review of what's wrong with meta-ethnography reporting. *BMC Medical Research Methodology, 14*(1), 1–16.

Garcia, L. (2009a). Love at first sex: Latina girls' meanings of virginity loss and relationships. *Identities: Global Studies in Culture and Power, 16*(5), 601–621.

Garcia, L. (2009b). "Now why do you want to know about that?" Heteronormativity, sexism, and racism in the sexual (mis)education of Latina youth. *Gender & Society, 23*(4), 520–541.

Garcia, L. (2012). *Respect yourself, protect yourself: Latina girls and sexual identity.* New York: NYU Press.

Gee, J. P. (2000). Discourse and sociocultural studies in reading. *Handbook of Reading Research, 3*, 195–207.

Holland, D., Lachicotte, W., Skinner, D., & Cain, C. (1998). *Identity and agency in cultural worlds.* Cambridge, MA: Harvard University Press.

Mann, E. S. (2013). Regulating Latina youth sexualities through community health centers discourses and practices of sexual citizenship. *Gender & Society, 27*(5), 681–703 doi:10.1177/0891243213493961

Mendoza-Denton, N. (2014). *Homegirls: Language and cultural practice among Latina youth gangs.* Hoboken, NJ; John Wiley.

Moraga, C. (1993). Queer Aztlán: The re-formation of Chicano tribe. In *The last generation: Prose and poetry* (pp. 145–174). Boston: South End Press.

Moya, P. M. (2002). *Learning from experience: Minority identities, multicultural struggles.* Berkley: University of California Press.

Noblit, G. W., & Hare, R. D. (1988). *Meta-ethnography: Synthesizing qualitative studies.* Newbury Park, CA: SAGE.

Phinney, J. S. (1993). A three-stage model of ethnic identity development in adolescence. In M. E. Bernal & G. P. Knight (Eds.), *Ethnic identity formation and transmission among Hispanics and other minorities* (pp. 61–79). Albany: State University of New York Press.

Rubin, G. (1975). The traffic in women: Notes on the "political economy" of sex. In R. Reiter (Ed.), *Toward an anthropology of women* (pp. 157–210). New York: Monthly Review Press.

Sánchez, P. (2009). Even beyond the local community: A close look at Latina youths' return trips to Mexico. *The High School Journal, 92*(4), 49–66.

Solórzano, D., & Delgado Bernal, D. (2001). Examining transformational resistance through a critical race and LatCrit framework: Chicana and Chicano students in an urban context. *Urban Education, 36*, 308–342.

Tijerina-Revilla. (2004). Muxerista pedagogy: Raza Womyn teaching social justice through student activism. *The High School Journal, 87*(4), 80–94.

Tijerina-Revilla. (2009). Are all Raza Womyn queer? An exploration of sexual identity in a Chicana/Latina student organization. *NWSA Journal, 21*(3), 46–62.

Turner, W. B. (2000). *A genealogy of queer theory.* Philadelphia, PA: Temple University Press.

Valenzuela, A. (1999). "Checkin' up on my guy": Chicanas, social capital, and the culture of romance. *Frontiers, 20*(1), 60–79.

Vetter, A. M., Fairbanks, C., & Ariail, M. (2011). "Crazyghettosmart": A case study in Latina identities. *International Journal of Qualitative Studies in Education, 24*(2), 185–207.

Willis, P. E. (1977). *Learning to labor: How working class kids get working class jobs.* New York: Columbia University Press.

Wortham, S. (2002). Gender and school success in the new Latino diaspora. In S. Wortham, E. G. Murillo Jr., & E. T. Hamman (Eds.), *Education in the new Latino diaspora* (pp. 117–141). Westport, CT: Ablex.

Yosso, T. (2002). Critical race media literacy: Challenging deficit discourse about Chicanas/os. *Journal of Popular Film and Television, 30*(1), 52–63.

Yosso, T. J. (2005). Whose culture has capital? A critical race theory discussion of community cultural wealth. *Race Ethnicity and Education, 8*(1), 69–91.

8

How "Identity Play" Protects White Privilege

A Meta-Ethnographic Methodological Test

ALISON LAGARRY AND TIMOTHY CONDER ■

INTRODUCTION

Just as meta-ethnography seeks to preserve and highlight the context of individual studies, meta-ethnographic analyses themselves have specific temporal, political, and theoretical contexts. When sets of studies are analyzed using meta-ethnography as methodology, the analysis takes place at a particular time in history. In a sense, the products of meta-ethnography are time- and date-stamped. They represent a snapshot of the political atmosphere of that time and are analyzed through the lens of the theory and literature available in that context.

For every meta-ethnographic analysis, the data set consists of published studies that fit particular search parameters set by the researcher. We note that, by the nature of publishing in academia, data sets are constantly changing. Thus any meta-type analysis must allow room for the scholarly conversation to continue beyond the "moment" of a particular meta-ethnographic analysis.

We completed the initial analysis for this meta-ethnography in early 2013. Our findings set up a particular *line of argument*, appropriate to the studies that fit our parameters for inclusion at that time. In the fall of 2016, we noted that a special issue of the *International Journal of Qualitative Studies in Education* (volume 29, issue 8) took up the topic of White identity studies with preservice teachers (PSTs), and theorized "second-wave White teacher identity studies." This publication presented an opportunity for us to explore how meta-ethnographic analyses can be "tested" methodologically, beyond initial findings, to take into account the contextual temporality of this work. In our case, our line of argument *anticipated* the shift in approach, tone, and theory in the literature and practice regarding

White teacher identity studies with PSTs. We see this as a "test" of the value of meta-ethnography for understanding the trajectories of fields of study.

To demonstrate our methodological process, we have included our initial meta-ethnography as it was written in May 2013. We have also included the methodological test addendum to discuss how we considered new studies and what those findings might mean for the line of argument we derived in 2013. In the addendum, we consider how new studies and theoretical understandings have the potential to confirm, disconfirm, or extend the findings of our meta-ethnographic analysis. Additionally, we explore the potential of meta-ethnography to describe and predict slow-moving shifts in thinking and scholarship.

HOW "IDENTITY PLAY" PROTECTS WHITE PRIVILEGE: THE 2013 "TAKE"

The phrase "play well with others" is a familiar, if not stereotypical, refrain in teacher discourse. The concept of play can certainly include whimsical, undirected interaction. But our experience with sports and board games reminds us that "play" can also invoke intentionalities, motives, and goals both positive and negative. Another example of this is the strategic social climber or the obsessive networker, who utilizes their connections and the associated privilege for personal gain. In our study of ethnographies about the performance of racial identity among White PSTs, we found that the strategies used to protect the associated privilege were often based in constructions of personal identity. As White students are challenged to examine their White racial identity, they may find their implication in hegemonic power structures to be disjunctive from their personal sense of "goodness" that led them to teaching. Reactions to this discovery often provoke strategic responses that are highly invested in defensive moves that protect White privilege and obscure their complicity in the dominance of whiteness.

The initial meta-ethnography, conducted in 2013, examines the play between identity and the protection of White privilege. We believe that, when analyzed, the seven selected articles[1] represent a line of argument that writes identity into a field of research in which dominant hegemony persistently obscures identity. The practice of meta-ethnography is deeply sensitive to parameters of inclusion and exclusion of studies. In this chapter we provide a methodological narrative of our search process, as well as the criteria for inclusion in the analysis. We also include a brief summary of each of the included studies, followed by a discussion of our translation of the articles into one another.

AUTHOR POSITIONALITY

Tim Conder is a PhD candidate in cultural studies at the University of North Carolina. He identifies as a White straight cisgender male from a rural working-class background. The study of White identity protection and White teacher identities, including a critical examination of his own privileged background, touches many portions of his professional background and research interests. As a pastoral leader deeply involved for decades in ecumenical faith-based community organizing for justice and a researcher on the relationship of moral ideologies and participation in social justice activism, he is deeply interested in how privileged identities are maintained, adapted, and transformed. His teaching at an elite primarily White university has yielded a window into White students with caring instincts enmeshed in the protection of privilege and his own journey through this same challenge.

Alison LaGarry is a clinical assistant professor of education at the University of North Carolina at Chapel Hill. She identifies as a White straight cisgender woman, also from a rural working-class background. Her interest in studying White teacher identity stems from her own reflections and experiences as a music teacher working in schools where students of color made up the majority of the student population. Currently, Alison works with PSTs in school practicum placements and also has served as instructor for a Social Justice in Education course required for teacher candidates.

As White colleagues in a program in education, we are committed to continuing our own examinations of the privileges gained from being members of the dominant race. We believe that we are guilty of many of the strategies for protecting or obscuring privilege that are found in these studies. We are also committed to the understanding that our identities are constantly under construction and in no way claim that our journey to racial sensitivity is complete. This study has been useful to us in reflecting on our own practices as scholars and leaders.

METHODOLOGY

Research Questions

In honing our approach to this meta-ethnographic analysis, we considered several different parameters to drive our data collection process. We knew we wanted to examine literature on racialized identity among White teachers and, based on preliminary searches, narrowed this specifically to PSTs. Students completing coursework and practicum requirements in teacher licensure programs occupy a unique location; they learn about theory and methodology at the same time they are working in school placements. Often, the practical demands of teaching serve to obfuscate the important racial identity work that may help White PSTs better understand systemic inequities and consider the positionalities of their own students. To examine this unique location in more depth, we formulated the following two research questions:

1. What does the literature say about the performance of racialized identities among White PSTs?
2. What are the relationships, if any, that emerge when the findings of the studies are considered as an analytical unit? (i.e., translated into one another)?

The structure of the two questions is unique to meta-ethnography in that the literature is positioned as the unit of examination. Ultimately, translation of studies into one another is a way of identifying both simple and complex relationships between the findings of each of the included studies, and, therefore, we believe that the second research question could serve any meta-ethnographic analysis.

Search Process and Text Selection

We knew that we wanted to study the performed racial identities of White PSTs and we knew we would need to do some initial keyword searches, followed by a winnowing process that would focus our inquiry through decisions about criteria for inclusion or exclusion of studies. We began by searching the terms "White," "teacher," "PST," and "identity" in databases such as ERIC, Education Full Text, JSTOR, and Google Scholar. These keyword searches produced vast results, with identity used in a common or nontheorized sense. When we attempted to add in other keywords to narrow the return for the search—for example "identity theory" and "race"—only three studies matched our parameters. In consulting with other scholars in a meta-ethnography working group, we noted that our initial searches were less fruitful than theirs and somewhat confounding. While they had designed elaborate schema for searches—searches that returned a reasonable sample of studies—we consistently encountered dead-ends.

We then hypothesized that we had encountered difficulty due to the very nature of our topic. In racial formation scholarship, White racial identity is often perceived as normalized and neutral. White people are often socialized to believe that whiteness is the absence of race. Our hypothesis was reinforced in the three studies that our keyword searches *did* return. These studies all included statements about White PSTs who did not seem to *see* their racial identity. Other terms that authors used in these studies included "invisibility of whiteness," "neutral," and "normalized." In these studies' findings, the authors stated that White racial identity among PSTs represented an area of scholarship that was undertheorized. This undertheorization seemed to contribute to a lack of consistency in the terminology used to describe studies that were, indeed, inquiring into the performance of racial identity among White PSTs.

Confronted with the lack of consistent terminology, we realized that keyword searches in online databases would not return the results we needed for the analysis. Therefore, our primary search method became a process of "scholarly triangulation." We proceeded by examining the reference lists of the studies that seemed to fit our parameters to that point, as well as in theoretical works that specifically discussed White PSTs (Applebaum, 2010; Leonardo, 2009) with scholars who write or are often cited for their work on whiteness as identity or whiteness as critical theory, often studying the education of PSTs. In those reference lists, we scanned for studies with White teachers and then tracked down those studies in online journal databases. This search yielded approximately 20 articles, which we examined and eventually narrowed to the seven that we have included in this chapter.

In examining this new group of articles, we opted to exclude any that mentioned identity but did not engage identity theory specifically. We debated back and forth over one study that engaged narrative in a constructive way but did not relate narrative explicitly to identity. Though we both believe that narrative can be a site of performance of identity construction, it was not theorized as such in this study. There were also a number of studies that hit several of our search parameters—White, identity, teachers—but were not specifically about PSTs. Thus we limited our studies to seven articles that focused on explorations of whiteness among PSTs and included explicit or implicit examinations of identity construction. Additionally, each of these studies theorized identity in some meaningful way. Information about each of the studies is included in Figure 8.1.

Coding and Analysis

We approached coding first by identifying salient components of each study and organizing these components into a chart. For each study, this chart (Figure 8.1) includes the overall intent of the research, the context and setting, a description of participants, methods used, and theory used. We also included an unnamed category where we planned to summarize the findings of each study. In a sense, this step of the coding process was an extension of data collection and preparing the studies to be translated into one another. By identifying each of the components of the studies, we began to generate an impression of how the findings were already "speaking" to one another. Some impressions jumped out quickly. We realized that almost all of the studies described what could be referred to as strategies or tools that White PSTs deployed to defend their racial privilege. At this point, we opted to use the previously unnamed portion of the table to focus specifically on these tools and strategies.

Many of the codes used to describe tools and strategies were presented as discursive metaphors. Thus we took up these metaphors as analytic units to be translated into one another. We completed this process in person, through an iterative process similar to constant comparison. Some metaphors were easily translated across studies, while others were somewhat related but somewhat distinct in the authors' characterizations. In those cases, meta-ethnographic analysis allowed us to consider the similarities of the strategies but also to consider how the context of each study demanded particularity in describing each metaphor. We describe the portion of the analysis process in detail in the section titled "Defending White Privilege."

At this point in the process, we arrived at a set of defendable translations that showed a convincing *reciprocal argument* (Noblit & Hare, 1988). Through our discussions, we began to view these translated metaphors as a "playbook" of strategies among PSTs for defending White privilege. We began to write an analytic memo describing this playbook and initially felt that to be the culmination of our analytic process. We have included a detailed explanation of translation of themes in the section "Playbook of Protective Strategies: Defending Against the Threat."

	Hytten & Warren (2003)	Warren & Hytten (2004) *Same study as Hytten & Warren (2003)	Marx (2004)	Bollin & Finkel (2006)
Intent:	"How students engage in a class that focuses on the political and social power of whiteness." (pg. 65)	"Our goal is to sketch out the pitfalls, or performative stances of white-ness, promoting a vision of the criti-cal democrat – a stance in relation to whiteness that is on of the more eth-ical and socially progressive stances we can assume." (pg. 322)	"Learn more about their beliefs, the ways that their own racial backgrounds affected their beliefs, and how tenacious these beliefs would be if challenged." (pg. 34)	"describe how curriculum integration of race, class, and gender issues in professional education courses can be implemented and evaluated using Helms' (1990) model of White Racial Identity Formation" (pg. 25)
Setting:	Midwest University, Predomi-nately White, Elective Gradu-ate Seminar–"Education and Culture" - Dept. of Education and Higher Education Admin.	Midwest University, Predominately White, Elective Graduate Seminar– "Education and Culture" - Dept. of Education and Higher Education Admin.	Large, Selective South-Western University. "Second Language Acquisition (SLA)" teach educa-tion class with field component (tutoring ELL students)	West Chester University (Public University, 25 miles from Philadelphia) - classes - field placements (tutoring)
Participants:	**15 Students, 1 Audit** - 8 Doctoral, 7 Master's, 1 professor - 7 men, 9 women – 14 White, 2 African-American	**15 Students, 1 Audit** - 8 Doctoral, 7 Master's, 1 professor - 7 men, 9 women - 14 White, 2 African-American	Typical Class: 80 students, 85% White, and 85-100% Female Participants: 9 White Females from SLA class. (age range: 20-35)	- "Small random sample" (pg. 26) - Teacher Education students
Methods:	- 8 Students Interview prior to class starting - Analysis of 9 written reflec-tions, and a summative reflection - Analysis of field notes taken during class discussions.	- 8 Students Interview prior to class starting - Analysis of 9 written reflections, and a summative reflection - Analysis of field notes taken during class discussions.	- In-depth interviews - Analysis of tutoring journals - Field notes from tutoring observations - Intervention mid-way through experience. - "Objectified" participant dis-course by sharing transcripts of their interviews. (pg.38)	- Structured interviews - Questionnaires - Reaction papers - Student Logs

Figure 8.1 Selected Studies and Code Analysis—2013.

Theory Used:	Nakayama and Krizek (1995) McIntyre (1997)	Conquergood (1985)	- Frankenburg (1993) - Critical Whiteness Studies (CWS) - Tatum (1999) - Critical Race Theory - McIntyre (1997) - Helms (1990)	Helms (1990) - White Racial Identity Development
Tools or Strategies:	"Appeals" * "To Self" (pg. 71) - Discourses of "Connections" (pg. 71), "Self-Absorption" (pg. 72), and "Friends and Family" (pg. 73). * "To Progress" (pg. 74). - Discourses of "Fix-It" (pg. 75), Mark-it (pg. 77), and "Enrich Me" (pg. 78) * "To Authenticity (pg. 78) - Discourses of "others," (pg. 79), "yes, but…" (pg. 80), "scholarly authority" (pg. 82). * "To Extremes" (pg. 83) - Discourses of "the real vs. the ideal," (pg. 83) "niceness vs. conflict," (pg. 83) "voice vs. silence" (pg. 85).	"Faces"– * "The Torpefied" (pg. 325) * "The Missionary" (pg. 327) * "The Cynic" (pg. 328) * "The Intellectualizer" (pg. 329) * "The Critical Democrat" (pg. 330)	*"Whiteness as 'normal,' 'neutral' non-ethnic identity" (pg. 35) *"Association of Color with Deficits" (pg. 35). - "Deficits in Language" (pg. 36) - "Deficits in Families" (pg. 36) - "Deficits in Intelligence and Esteem" (pg. 36). * "Described themselves as 'open-minded, "tolerant,' and without prejudice." (pg. 35) * Racism as overt "hate-mongering" (pg. 41).	*Colorblind/mute -Race "shouldn't make a difference" (pg. 24). - "race means nothing" (pg. 24) - "Separating cultures will only create distress in the classroom." (pg. 26). -While tutoring "I never thought about their color or ethnic group" (pg. 29)

Figure 8.1 Continued

	Pennington (2007)	Picower (2009)	Terwilliger (2010)
Intent:	"How did our White identities affect how we viewed the children of color in our classrooms?" (pg. 95). "How could I encourage White PSTs to look at their role and positioning critically?" (pg. 95)	"How do White preservice teachers conceptualize race and difference and what role do these conceptions play in maintaining existing hierarchies?" (pg. 198)	"How teacher education programs can better prepare teachers to acknowledge how personal identity influences classroom practice." (pg. 14).
Setting:	Field placement – tutoring students in literacy at "Marquez" Elementary School	University teacher education program in New York City, "Multicultural Education" course	University in Central Pennsylvania (PWI), Required Education Course. Field Experience with migrant children
Participants:	Nancy, Katrina, Meg White pre-service teachers enrolled in field, Author: University Teaching Assistant, White Female	-8 White female pre-service teachers, "in their twenties"	-13 White pre-service teachers, undergraduate, 1 male, 12 female. 9 students in age range 20–22.
Methods:	"Authoethnography as a possible method of engaging White PSTs in dialogues about race in schools." (pg. 94). Discussion and Interviews based around Authoethographic Methods (listed below in "Line of Argument")	-Interviews -Transcripts of class sessions -Written Assignments -Grounded Theory (Glaser and Strauss, 1967).	-Surveys -Class Discussion Transcripts -TutoringFieldnotes -Written Reflections -Journal Writings from befor, during, and after field placement. **Feminist, Post-Structural Analysis**

Figure 8.1 Continued

Theory Used:	- Bell (1992) – Critical Race Theory - Frankenburg (1997) - McIntosh (1988) - Reed-Danahay (1997) - Autoethnography	Omi and Winant (1986)– Critical Race Theory Ladson-Billings (1995, 2001) **Grounded Theory**	Butler (1999) "Identities are constructed through repetitive exposure to mainstream discourses." (pg. 15).
Tools or Strategies:	**"Saviors" (pg. 97)** - "I wish you were my mom."-custodial positioning (pg. 97) - "I'm a big healer." (pg. 98) - "war stories" (pg. 98). - "I don't think she sees in her home the value of being kind." (pg. 99) **"White Talk" (pg. 103)** - Deficit views of "Neighborhoods" (pg. 103), "Parents and Older Students" (pg. 104) - "You help anybody who needs help." (pg. 106). "Hyperpoliteness" (pg. 108).	"Tools of Whiteness" (pg. 204) **"Emotional Tools"** (pg. 205) - "I never owned a slave" (pg. 205). - "Stop trying to make me feel guilty." (pg. 205) * **"Ideological Tools"** (pg. 206). - "Now that things are equal" (pg. 206). - "It's personal not political" (pg. 206) - "Out of my control" (pg. 207). - "Just be nice." (pg. 208). - "I can't relate" (pg. 208). **"Performative Tools"** (pg. 209) - "Shh" (pg. 209) - "I just want to help them" (pg. 209). - "I would kiss a minority." (pg. 210)	**"goal of multicultural curricula was to achieve colorblindness" (pg. 19). - "treating your students as if they are one." (pg. 20) - "now this woman is saying she wants to be treated differently?" (pg. 20) - "I feel that the color of one's skin should not make any difference as to what kind of American they are." (pg. 21)

Figure 8.1 Continued

One unique feature of meta-ethnography is that it is decidedly subjective. We, the authors, firmly believe that researcher subjectivity is always implicated in the findings of qualitative analyses of this type. Just as the interpretations in the selected studies were influenced by the authors' experiences and positionalities, our own positionalities influenced our analytic process. As White researchers with experience in the field of education, we were performing our own identities as we analyzed the selected studies on the racial identity of White PSTs.

As we were writing up our analysis on the playbook, we continued to engage in reflexive dialogue with each other about how we had employed these strategies at various times throughout our lives. We found that we recognized that we had some impressions from the data that we felt were significant but not well-represented in our reciprocal playbook argument. We could see that the tools and strategies were a viable finding, but we also noted that these defensive identity performances take place in particular contexts and are motivated by the various frames of meaning that help social actors make sense of their identities. Building on the feeling that we were missing an important piece of the analysis, we drew out a visual representation of the arena where these "identity plays" might be situated. Through this process of reconceptualization, we discovered that the various strategies and tools could be assigned to particular *locations* with a field of practice. These locations signified intentions that were not unitary and were rooted in different understandings of White racial identity. This interpretation allowed us to maintain a higher degree of complexity than the reciprocal argument allowed and led us to interpret a *line of argument* from the data. As Doyle (2003) stated, "Synthesis in meta-ethnography does not mean transferability of similar findings on a case by case basis but rather a reconceptualization across studies" (p. 323). In this way, meta-ethnographic methodology invoked layers of conversation for us where—invoked by our own reflexivity—the conversation became an interpretive research moment.

From that point, we felt that our interpreted playbook was no longer a comprehensive representation of what our selected articles implied. In short, our reflexive dialogue inspired new vision regarding this data that sustained the reciprocal defensive intentions we had observed while moving beyond it to an awareness of the importance of different spaces where these defensive strategies were deployed to protect White privilege. Ultimately we extended our metaphor of defensive "play" to a continuation of that same play in the varied and socially complex space of a schoolyard playground. This extension of our analysis from reciprocal discourse to space resonated with identity theorizations that we elaborate on in the section on theoretical framework. In turn, these findings are detailed in the section "Identity Play: How Whiteness and Identity Play Together."

Trustworthiness

We employed a number of the "enhanced strategies" for meta-ethnography proposed by Doyle (2003). As described already, we established boundary conditions for our case requirements, and we were purposive in selecting cases (p. 327). In the analysis process, we worked together to document and understand the salient features of each case study, determined key descriptors unique to each study, and maintained the language used by the authors. As described earlier, we were able to juxtapose (or translate) metaphors from each of the studies and derived an additional interpretive metaphor.

Several authors, including Doyle (2003) and France et al. (2014), have extended the work of Noblit and Hare (1988) to fill in methodological gaps regarding the trustworthiness of meta-ethnography. We believe that questions of trustworthiness regarding meta-ethnography are dependent on the intended audience. In our case, we hoped to synthesize and reconceptualize theoretical considerations about the nature of performances of racial identity among White PSTs.

Our analysis involved actions typically associated with credibility, such as iterative questioning, member checking, and frequent debriefing. In addition, we engaged with a group of peers who were also invested in exploring meta-ethnography as a methodology and held regular discussions regarding the work, which offered the opportunity for peer scrutiny (Shenton, 2004). We have also described our iterative dialogic interpretation process, what we refer to as *dialogic authorial conversation*. This conversation evokes what would usually be referred to as a member check—returning to studies to confirm our analytic impressions and to see what *else* was being stated. Finally, we found that our analysis drove us to well-established theorizations on the construction of identity.

THEORETICAL FRAMEWORK

Our theorizing of White PST identity, particularly in moving toward conclusive metaphors of "identity play," relied heavily on social practice theories of identity and work on the metatheoretical shift of identity studies toward practice in the work of Dorothy Holland and colleagues (Holland, Lachicotte, Skinner, & Cain, 1998; Holland & Lave, 2001). This shift signaled also in the works of Bourdieu (1977) and de Certeau (1984), and more recently in Butler's (1999) gender performance work, upends previous notions of identity as static and fixed. Identities are then theorized as constantly forming and being reformed by various practices in social environments. Holland and Lave (2001) made a significant contribution to the wave of this shift by prioritizing the role of distinct local spaces (such as the classroom setting for PSTs in education programs) in the formation of intimate, more personal identities by serving as a point of contestation that connects historical stories of struggle (such as the historical struggles regarding racial privilege or the fight for racial equity) with these intimate identities. They name this organic system of culturally producing identities "history-in-person," grand historical struggles translated into intimate identities through the essential intermediation of local spaces. Holland et al. have further elaborated on the contestation and work that occurs in these highly formational local spaces with the concept of figured worlds. Figured worlds are horizons of meaning, often summoned through storytelling and various cultural assumptions that are performed in local spaces.

They are imaginary but not abstract, having real and potent consequences in performance and practice. The reality of these identity-forming local spaces in our lives is that they typically host many colliding figured worlds rooted in a variety of histories and narratives. In these spaces of convergence or collision, positional identities such as race, social status, gender, sexual orientation, and the power ascribed or denied by these positional identities may dictate or influence the impact of various figured worlds within that space. Hence, identity is constantly being contested and can shift significantly as we move into the varied local spaces of our lives. These contributions by Holland and colleagues are deeply significant. They acknowledge that identity formation occurs in multiple frames (historical collectivities, local spaces, and within persons) and accentuate the unique significance of contested spaces when identity had so often been theorized as singly dimensional and static within individuals. This notion of space becomes highly significant in our findings.

In the articles that served as data for our 2013 study, a carefully nuanced figured world of whiteness was commonly and deeply present in the expectations and constructed identities of the PSTs. This cultural world of whiteness is commonly invoked, as expected, as a race-neutral normalcy, an invisibility, simply "the way things are." This theorization of a figured world that offers meaning and shapes identities prepared the ground for our findings on the protection of privilege. But several of these studies revealed even more nuanced imaginaries present in the cultural world of whiteness that overlap with a second figured world, that of the missional nature of teaching. In many cases, PSTs understood their mission to teach in terms of a savior identity and highly associated with moral identities of goodness. When present, this distinct figured world of teaching intent was seamlessly and unconsciously translated into whiteness with some students constructing identities as White savior educators motivated by goodness that was also highly aligned with whiteness. The theorization of cultural worlds offers a strong lens when combining these studies into a meta-ethnography. As we progress to the article summaries, the presence of both of these figured worlds is readily marked in the consideration of these texts.

SELECTED ARTICLES

Bollin and Finkel (2006) explored the racial identity development of undergraduate education students over a three-year time period at a university in Pennsylvania. They lamented that White PSTs "have negative attitudes toward American subcultures" (p. 25). This reality suggests that uncritical curriculum practices can magnify stereotyping and hostile attitudes toward students of color. Their study examined the incorporation of critical diversity materials in the curriculum for White PSTs. They analyzed these data through the lens of Janet Helms' (1990) staged model of White racial identity development.

Helms's (1990) model described the evolving journey of Whites as beginning with a certain obliviousness to the importance of race in society (Stage 1: Contact/

Naiveté) and then moving to a greater perception of this importance and the onset of discomfort due to a growing awareness of their White privilege (Stage 2: Disintegration/Dissonance). In the next stage, Whites try to resolve their privilege by defending White superiority (Stage 3: Reintegration/Defensiveness) and then resort to accepting by intellectualizing racial differences (Stage 4: Pseudo-independence/Liberalism). Ultimately they can become more reflexive about their own racial identity and more immersed in the racial identities of others (Stage 5: Immersion/Self-exploration) and eventually internalize multiculturalism and initiate reflexive learning experiences with other cultural communities (Stage 6: Autonomy/Transculturalism).

Bollin and Finkel (2006) found that after introducing their students to a variety of critical content in the course, they were in a wide range of Helms's (1990) stages, some progressing significantly toward Autonomy and others struggling to exit Contact/Naiveté. The interventions that were often most helpful included instructor modeling of a developed racial identity, positive field placements with ample reflective discussion, and reactions to content presented by their peers in a space for dialogue.

Hytten and Warren (2003) studied the discourse of students enrolled in a class titled "Education and Culture." Because of the elective nature of the class, many of the students who opted to enroll were already committed to issues of diversity and inclusion. The authors sought to explore "how whiteness gets inscribed and reified in our education practices, even as we try to disrupt its normative influence" (p. 66). The authors found that students relied on a number of "appeals" to disable race conversation and protect their whiteness. They identified 12 discourses that students use to engage in discussions about racial issues, categorized into four larger trends or appeals. They note that these appeals can serve in both enabling and disabling ways, though this chapter mainly focuses on disabling discourses that serve to protect White privilege. The four appeals are described next.

Appeals to Self included discourses that personalize issues from course readings or discussion and relate these issues to students' own lived experiences. Hytten and Warren (2003) noted that this type of appeal can be enabling in that it encourages empathy but becomes disabling when students "privileg[e] their own feelings and struggles above all else" (p. 71). *Appeals to Progress* characterized class discussions and reflective writings that privilege action over talk and were accompanied by statements of "missionary-like zeal to make changes immediately" (p. 74). *Appeals to Authenticity* involved students either seeking to consult an "authentic" non-White voice for information about their experiences or providing stories of experience that contradict the experiences of non-Whites—stories that the speaker deems authentic. Finally, *Appeals to Extremes* occurred when students created a strict delineation between "real versus ideal" and position themselves at one of the extreme "poles" of this binary (p. 83). The authors stated that it is necessary for educators to understand the ways that educational discourse can serve to reproduce and protect White privilege. In recognizing these discursive tools and strategies, educators understand the many ways that their students might engage.

Warren and Hytten (2004) was a companion study to Hytten and Warren (2003) in which the authors used Conquergood's (1985) "model of ethical pitfalls in performance ethnography" (p. 323) to construct four common, non-linear "faces" that White students performed when confronted with whiteness. These faces are temporal- and location-specific performances. Using Butler's (1990) position of identity as fluid and performed, the faces "are not essentialized . . . but cultural logics one borrows or takes on in certain communicative contexts" (Warren & Hytten, 2004, p. 323). Students may take different faces in varying occasions.

The four faces were represented in a four quadrant grid that established poles of an "obsessive investment with self" to a "distanced engagement with self" on one axis. The other axis included poles of "active investigation" to "static understanding." Each of the four faces were described "their most extreme manifestations" (Warren & Hytten, 2004, p. 324).

The first is that of a "torpefied" face. The torpefied person, seeing their acts of oppression, is paralyzed by guilt, regret, and embarrassment. This face rests in the quadrant of obsessive investment with self and active investigation. These people are quick to engage persons of color and seek simplified answers to absolve their guilt. The "missionary" face involves an obsessive investment with self but differs in seeking static understandings. The missionary performance is impatient with dialogue and seeks rapid responses to evidences of oppression. The "cynic" face—which occupies the most pessimistic position—embraces static understandings but does so with a distanced engagement of self. Hence, these people are both passive in exploration and personally disengaged, believing the problem of race to be too great to merit a realistic response.

The "intellectualizer" face "finds the subject of Whiteness and antiracist work fascinating" (Warren & Hytten, 2004, p. 329). These people are persistent in reading, learning, and discussing this content with those that they encounter. Intellectualizers are located in the quadrant of active investigation but also have a distanced engagement with self. They see whiteness as a hip, academic opportunity.

Against these four common faces, Warren and Hytten (2004) advocate and recommend the posture of the "critical democrat," which is placed in the center of their grid, in balance between obsessive engagement of self and distanced engagement as well as active investigation and static understandings. The authors advocate critical democracy as a way to "mov[e] toward a position of flux, an ethical retraining of the mind, body, and spirit to rehear, to reimagine" (p. 337).

Marx (2004) examined the personal beliefs and teaching actions of nine White PSTs in a field service experience. Students were placed in classrooms where they tutored English-language learners of Mexican origin. Using a theoretical framework of critical whiteness studies and critical race theory, Marx "wanted to learn more about their beliefs, the ways that their own racial backgrounds affected their beliefs, and how tenacious these beliefs would be if challenged" (p. 34). She found that while her students professed to being antiracist, their positive intentions were often overshadowed by whiteness and racism.

In the initial phase of the study, Marx (2004) found that participants' words or actions reflected a vision of whiteness as normal or neutral and color as a marked difference from that neutrality. She also found that the participants' personal beliefs showed an association of color with deficits. Throughout the study, students professed to seeing themselves as tolerant and open-minded and, in their writing, "maintained an abhorrence of racism" (p. 36). Marx noticed, however, that the students' visions' of racism only included overtly racist actions and did not include personally held racist beliefs and ideologies, thus releasing students from responsibility for their personal beliefs. In order to challenge their beliefs, Marx showed participants transcripts of their interviews, thus "objectifying" their words. She noted three steps for her methodology of intervention, including encouraging honest words and feelings, drawing attention to overtly racist comments, and challenging easy solutions. Concluding, Marx discussed the necessity of seeing examination of beliefs about race as an ongoing and continuous process. She challenged the narrative of "goodness" in the profession of teaching and stated that all educators must examine their personal beliefs about race.

Pennington (2007) used an autoethnographic method as pedagogy in working with PSTs. For the study, Pennington employed four aspects of autoethnographic method: narrative storytelling, autobiographical sharing, counter-narrative bridging, and reflexive engagement. She notes that these methods are "culled from previous conceptions of autoethnography and fashioned into pedagogical tools for [Pennington] to use with PSTs toward the recognition of whiteness in teaching contexts" (p. 97). Participants were PSTs in a field study placement, and data collected derives from university class-based discussions, as well as teaching observations at the school placement. Pennington sought to find out how White PSTs felt about teaching at a school where they were in the minority.

Through narrative storytelling, Pennington (2007) found that participants' narratives reflected either a White teacher savior mentality, a critique of saving, or what she describes as conquering (or assimilating) via saving. She also discusses the necessity of autobiographical sharing, in which she shared many of her own personal thoughts about teaching. Her analysis reveals that students were more willing to interrogate their own positions, having heard her frank narrative about her own experience. Through counter-narrative bridging, the participants in this study were able to challenge their perceptions of what it meant to be White in a setting where White norms and practices were not centered by members of the community at the school placement. Pennington also describes encouraging reflexive work with her students, making a space to transform the notion of saving, and creating a space to talk.

Picower (2009) asked, "How do White PSTs conceptualize race and difference and what role do these conceptualizations play in maintaining hierarchies?" (p. 197). In studying eight White PSTs in their 20s, as part of a multicultural education course, Picower found that the participants use various "tools of Whiteness" to protect their own White privilege and understanding of race. For this study, the author interviewed the participants, reviewed transcripts of class sessions, and analyzed written assignments. Picower examined how life experiences and identities shaped beliefs about race and difference. Specifically, participants' beliefs on these topics centered around their religious and White ethnic identities, experience with hierarchical relationships and people of color, and hegemonic understandings that promote fear and deficit views of color, while portraying Whites as victims.

When Picower (2009) challenged these beliefs and understandings, she found that students relied on various "tools of Whiteness" that "maintain[ed] and support[ed] hegemonic stories and dominant ideologies of race" which effectively upheld White supremacy (pp. 204–205). Picower divided these tools of whiteness into three categories: emotional, ideological, and performative. Emotional tools of whiteness stem from participants' feelings and are described as "emotional responses serving to obfuscate the concepts being introduced [in the class]" (p. 205). Examples of these tools include appeals such as: "I never owned a slave" and "Stop trying to make me feel guilty." Ideological tools were described as "raising dominant claims about the state of race relations" as a way of avoiding topics presented in class (p. 206). Two such examples are statements such as "Now that things are equal . . ." and "I don't even see color." Lastly, Picower describes performative tools of whiteness as "the behaviors in which participants engaged to protect their beliefs based on their ideological tools or hegemonic understandings" (p. 209). One of these performative tools, "I just want to help them" reflects a White teacher savior mentality.

Terwilliger (2010) raised the possibility that an active multicultural pedagogy based in self-study can support PSTs in detouring around whiteness in society. Traditional approaches involve immersing PSTs in field experiences where they encounter diverse learners, but these approaches often do not demand that PSTs situate and unpack their own racial identities. As a theoretical foundation, the study used Butler's (1999) poststructural work that defended identity as emerging from discourses and performed in constructive processes. In this perspective, identity is constructed in dialogue between societal discourses and lived experiences. Identity then is not culturally determined or an act of human free will. Instead, "the subject is formed by going through the process of assuming identities through available discourses" (p. 18).

The study focused on 13 White PSTs in a primarily White university in Pennsylvania. Surveys, class discussion transcripts, and tutoring field notes were used with an emphasis placed on journaling to discern the evolving experiences of these PSTs in their work with the migrant students. Terwilliger (2010) demonstrated how the identities of these PSTs had been constructed around myths of White superiority. Field experiences without guided reflection often reinforce these myths and allow PSTs to maintain a dichotomy of us/them or otherness with diverse learners. But detours from these discursive myths and resultant practices of othering can be found by critical self-reflection. Dominant discourses are naturally resistant to challenge and change. But discursive identity work with PSTs supports their efforts to make sense of their identities and pedagogical decisions with the hopeful result of resisting perceptions that other their students.

DEFENDING WHITE PRIVILEGE

Each of the articles selected for this analysis reveal how White PSTs react when asked to examine their White racial identity and the associated privileges and power. Authors described participants as becoming defensive, resistant, and paralyzed by guilt. Additionally, they described how students used a variety of tools and strategies to maintain and protect the privileges gained by dominant race membership. For the purposes of this analysis, it is of most interest to think about *why* and *how* White students, specifically PSTs, react to discussions about White racial identity and White privilege in ways that reinscribe hegemonic racial structures. Additionally, it is necessary to examine how White PSTs often deny discourses, emotions, and ideologies as having the potential for being racist. According to Marx (2004), students often equate racism with overt acts of hate and thus balk at attempts to point out racism in their own language. Through our analysis, we note that White PSTs often find discussions of White racism to be entirely dissonant with the "goodness" they associate with the teaching profession (Pennington, 2007). Students in courses or field placements that address these issues perceive that they are being accused or threatened with claims that contradict their chosen benevolent identities. The next section translates and synthesizes the strategies and tools the authors describe as responses to this feeling of identity dissonance. We argue that students often use "identity plays" to obstruct discourse and, either consciously or unconsciously, employ tools and strategies to maintain their dominant race privilege.

Playbook of Protective Strategies—Guarding Against the Threat

Each of the selected articles uses different terminology to describe defensive schemes (performances or discourses) that serve to protect White privilege. We liken these schemes to a playbook of defensive game strategies. Playbooks can exist for a wide range of game play, including athletic competition, board games (i.e., chess), and so on. For chess and football alike, defensive strategy has one objective—to prevent the other player(s) from advancing. In the selected articles, we found that many of the authors describe a reciprocal set of these defensive strategies wherein White PSTs resisted the destabilization of White privilege and even sought to protect it. Hytten and Warren (2003) use the term "appeals" to describe the discourses used by participants to resist and reinscribe their dominant status. The four categories of appeals—to self, to progress, to authority, and to extremes—are each divided into three types of discourses. The first category, "appeals to self," bears a strong resemblance to the "emotional tools of whiteness" described by Picower (2009). For Hytten and Warren (2003), these types of appeals revolved around discourses of "connections," "self-absorption," and "friends and family." Just as students who used a discourse about the racism of friends and family to separate themselves from blame or guilt, participants in Picower's study used the statement "I never owned a slave" for the same purpose. Similarly, the discourse of "self-absorption" (Hytten & Warren, 2003) can be correlated with the emotional tool, "Stop trying to make me feel guilty" (Picower, 2009).

Picower (2009) also describes a set of "ideological tools" that are used to preserve and protect whiteness. One of the ideological tools employed by PSTs in that study was the statement or perspective, "Now that things are equal." This tool, similar to Hytten and Warren's (2003) "appeals to progress," focuses on the progress that has already been made in working toward racial equality. These tools, including the discourse of "mark-it" (Hytten & Warren, 2003) are disabling because they allow for disengagement, claiming that much of the work has already been done. Another related metaphor, described by Pennington (2007), involves personalizing and exaggerating this sense of progress in the form of "war stories" that valorize the PST in field experiences in the so-called "trenches." This phenomenon of self-valorization is also referred to in many of the studies, identified by various terms including "a messianic complex" (Titone, as cited by Hytten & Warren, 2003), "savior" (Pennington, 2007), and "missionary" (Warren & Hytten, 2004). Many of the descriptions centered on this White savior perspective hinge on the idea that PSTs see themselves as "doing good" (Pennington, 2007) or "helping." In a "performative tool" described by Picower, students were quoted as saying "I just want to help them." This is similar to statements such as "I'm a big healer" and "You help anybody who needs help" (Pennington, 2007).

As PSTs take up this sort of "helping" attitude, race becomes a complicating factor. Because whiteness was described in most of the selected studies as "normal, neutral, or non-ethnic," color is cited as the mark of racial difference (Marx, 2004). According to Terwilliger (2010), all students in that study believed the "goal of multicultural curricula was to achieve colorblindness" (p. 19). Indeed, PSTs noted that a good teacher means "treating your students as if they are one" and "the color of one's skin should not make any difference." For Bollin and Finkel (2006), this narrative was apparent in the words of one participant who stated, "separating cultures will only create distress in the classroom." Showing that these discourses become enacted in the classroom, one student referred to the students she was tutoring, "I never thought about their color or ethnic group" (Bollin & Finkel, 2006).

Also stemming from a vision of color as a marker of difference, White PSTs expressed deficit views of people of color (Marx, 2004; Pennington, 2007). Though claiming themselves to be "open-minded, tolerant, and without prejudice," the words of the teachers in Marx's study showed they believed that there are "deficits in language" (for those who speak languages other than English), "deficits in families" (in terms of caring and love), as well as "deficits in intelligence and esteem." These deficits are also reflected in Pennington's study, where participants' writing reflected "deficit views of neighborhoods" and "parents and older siblings." Notably, the participants in both studies separate their students from their families in discourse and writing. One PST in Pennington's study stated, "I don't think she sees the value of being kind," implying that the student's parents were not capable of teaching the student kindness.

As we have discussed so far, PSTs who are encouraged to consider the effect of whiteness on their lives and their teaching often react with defensive or resistant mechanisms. Another common reaction is that of extreme guilt, exemplified in the torpefied face described by Warren and Hytten (2004). Though not resistant, this performance or position is ultimately disabling because the teachers are paralyzed and unable to move forward to a more thoughtful and reflective stance, like that of the critical democrat. Similar to the torpefied is the "discourse of real versus ideal." In this "appeal to extremes" (Hytten & Warren, 2003), the participants believe that there is validation in what they are learning about White privilege and oppression, but when faced with the "real-world" challenges of teaching, they will abandon this "ideal" way of thinking. Some PSTs also believe that racial inequality is "out of [their] control" (Picower, 2009). This also has some elements of the cynic face described by Warren and Hytten (2004). It is of note that the cynic and the torpefied faces overlap slightly when translated into metaphors used by other authors. This follows the matrix and description provided by Warren and Hytten (2004), in which "location" of performance is not fixed but is always in flux and "tension."

In another example of this tension, some strategies that are described have both enabling and disabling potential. Using "appeals to authenticity," participants would seek the "discourses of others" (Hytten & Warren, 2003). This could be enabling when students would seek to read and reflect upon works by authors of color but is disabling when students look to students of color in their classes to "speak for their race." Describing this phenomena, notably from the same data, in a performative light, Warren and Hytten (2004) name this "the intellectualizer."

Ultimately, the message that we obtain from each of the articles is that whiteness (actions, ideologies, and discourses) are so normalized in the lives of White PSTs that whiteness and White racial identity are ideologically invisible. Most PSTs suppose that their career choice indicates that they are caring, "helping," and "good." When this is challenged, White PSTs perceive a threat to their very identity. In the following section, we explore what we call "identity plays" that must happen in order for students to enact the strategies and tools discussed earlier.

IDENTITY PLAY: HOW WHITENESS AND IDENTITY PLAY WITH EACH OTHER

We began this chapter with the common schoolhouse dictum, "play well with each other." Our premise for the meta-ethnography is that whiteness, as the practice of a dominant hegemony in the classroom, has a unique and consistent relationship with identities. The harmony of this consistent relationship is that identity performances expressed as highly similar strategies were demonstrated in the seven articles of this study to obscure whiteness and White privilege. In this manner, our seven studies, to this point, have made a highly *reciprocal argument*.

In the methodology of meta-ethnography, a reciprocal argument simply means that the content of each article translates comfortably into the others because they are making a similar point with varying perspectives and metaphorical language (Noblit & Hare, 1988). To demonstrate this reciprocity, we constructed the sports analogy of defensive schemes.

In this section we want to begin to make visible that which desires to stay unseen, the identity plays that provoke the various strategies of defending or performances of obscuring whiteness. To begin this process, we want to examine identity theories used by the authors in our seven articles. This theoretical work in some articles is highly explicit and in others primarily implied. Some wrote directly about identity theory (Bollin & Finkel, 2006; Terwilliger, 2010), and others used critical race theories as platforms to address identity. But when we put the theorization of identity of our seven articles together in a comparative process, we find a *line-of-argument* relationship. In meta-ethnography, a line of argument involves qualitative studies that focus on portions of a whole, but, when put together, a larger reality beyond the scope of each study becomes more visible (Noblit & Hare, 1988). To accomplish this, we move from our previous analogy of coordinated athletic play to that of another analogy, school play at recess.

Our analogy focuses on the iconic school playground at recess. Whether it is the asphalt of a stereotypical city school or the open grass of a rural school, there are many enduring images of school play at recess. Recalling our theoretical frame on social practice theories of identity, the playground itself is a metaphorical representation of local spaces such as the classroom environment where PSTs are trained to become educators and where the variable figured worlds of whiteness are invoked. As we progressively construct this metaphoric, figured playground of whiteness, the diverse locations and functions of identity become more apparent, offering a more complete scaffolding of identity that produces the very reciprocal defensive practices and attitudes described in the previous section.

Advantages and Disadvantages

We think most would agree that playgrounds are often places of hierarchies and inequalities often oriented around popularity, friendship groups, physical strength, and attractiveness. The three kids who are little league all-star pitchers somehow always end up on the same dodgeball team, to the terror of the rest of the class. Popular children or groups of tightly aligned friends inevitably get longer times on the swing sets. The playground is one more space, like the classroom, where students see and experience the relational and social hierarchies of schooling. In terms of identity, several of the articles in this project relied heavily or primarily on critical race theory and critical whiteness theory (Marx, 2004; Pennington, 2007; Picower, 2009) with the result of demonstrating vividly the systemic inequalities of the playground. In these studies, one sees identity being constructed and hardened around the assumptions of inequalities and deficits.

In Marx (2004), the White PSTs were prone to consider people of color as lacking expected characteristics or disadvantaged using what Valencia (1997) terms "deficit thinking." As a result, they considered the "cultures, home languages, families, intelligence, and self-esteem of the children they tutored and the other people of color they discussed as sadly inhibited by extraordinary deficits" (p. 35). To demonstrate an example of this deficit thinking, Marx offered Michelle's perception of her tutoring site:

> Michelle described the predominantly African American school where she tutored the semester before this study, and its students, as "trashy." She was dismayed that the kids looked like "they just rolled out of bed" each time she saw them, but happy that the Latina/o children she now tutored were "cleaner" and, she felt, more concerned with their appearance. When I asked her how these schools compared to those she attended as a youth, she took a deep breath and exclaimed, "Gosh, I went to a private Jewish day school!" And left it at that." (pp. 35–36)

In Picower's (2009) use of theory, she cited Leonardo (2004) who complicated the idea of privilege as handed to Whites as in the "invisible knapsack" metaphor (McIntosh, 1990). This metaphor obscures active oppression perpetrated as those privileges are deployed. Again invoking theory from Leonardo, Picower noted that Whites set up a system that benefits themselves and "when interrogated about it, [they] stifle the discussion with inane comments about the 'reality' of the charges being made" (p. 198). In other words, when one challenges the three kids who are all-star pitchers as to why they are always on the same dodgeball team, they are likely to decry the injustice of being singled out rather than the inequality of the system where they always get to win and the rest of the kids all get bruised for good measure.

One of Picower's (2009) participants used her identity as a religious minority to "stifle" an accusation of her being in a dominant White group. Another PST was even more vivid in her deflection, focusing on her identity in an immigrant family who made it in the American meritocracy. On these identity grounds, she literally shouted,

> This is where I am feeling a little bit nervous. Like maybe I'm almost being a little bit racist because you just want to say sometimes [shouting]: "Get over it! Like get over it! It's 2005, get over it! You know, move on!" So what you're Black, so what I'm White—if I get better grades in school—maybe I worked harder. You know, if I get a job, maybe I deserved it! Why does it always have to be like, [whiny voice]: "Well, they're the minority, let's give it to them." I'm done with that, it's time to start a new life." (Picower, 2009, p. 201)

Pennington (2007), using critical race theory, cited Scheurich (2002) to frame the systemic social advantages of the playground for Whites:

> White racism is not primarily individual acts or beliefs; those are only social effects. White racism is the Onto-Logical; it is built into the very nature of the social reality. It is Epistemological; it is built into the very nature of accepted and legitimized assumptions. (p. 96)

One participant in Pennington's study demonstrated deficit thinking toward non-White families (and an implied comparison with her own superior White identity) when describing one of her elementary students:

> I see [one of my students] . . . how she was born—how she's been passed from mom to grandma to aunt how she was retained [in Grade 2]. How she uses her little body in a sexual manner already. That's what she values. She values her sexuality at such a young age. I had such trouble with that. I don't think she sees in her home the value of being kind, knowing how to read very well. (p. 99)

In each of these articles, critical race theory and critical whiteness theory demonstrated identities being developed among White PSTs that assumed the superiority of their whiteness that remained an invisible, unspoken, but very real condition in their thinking and practice as teachers. The figured world of whiteness, for many of these PSTs, is highly reminiscent of the playground environment where hierarchies and inequalities are resistant to critique when even noticed.

How the Games Are Played

When one thinks of playgrounds, one thinks of games—formal games like freeze-tag, organized sports like kickball, or simply improvised episodes of play like a moment of chase or a contest to see who can jump the highest and longest off the swing set. All of these examples of play or games are performances. These performances all, in a sense, stand on top the advantages and disadvantages of the playground. This means, regardless of whichever team one is on—the one with the stacked roster or the disadvantaged team—one still plays the game per force or by choice.

In this developing line of argument, three of the articles in this study focused on White identity as performances or discourses (Hytten & Warren, 2003; Terwilliger, 2010; Warren & Hytten, 2004). These studies have relied heavily on the theoretical work of Judith Butler and her "assertion that identities are constituted through repetitive exposure to mainstream discourses" (Terwilliger, 2010, p. 15). In other words, mainstream discourses and narratives construct how games are played on our metaphoric playground. Hence the team with the advantage always skews the fairness of the game, perhaps inviolate from any challenge. In Butler's (1999) poststructuralist approach, this is how identities are often formed, being constructed in specific contexts based on the available discourses. We saw these articles as demonstrating "games" being played or performed according to the stylized discourses sitting on top of the inherent advantages of whiteness.

In Terwilliger (2010), one PST used discourses of the concepts of "American" and "equality" to resist teaching African American literature:

> If a book is written by an African American and it is based on a piece of history that has taken place in America, why do we call it African American literature and not call it American literature? . . . I feel like we should be trying to breakdown racial barriers not using terms to segregate. (p. 21)

As previously noted, in Warren and Hytten (2004), White PSTs often performed "faces," which are masks or situational performances that are highly equipped to deflect inquiry about the inequalities of the classroom or, in our metaphor, the playground. Hytten and Warren (2003) organized White deflection and justification around a series of appeals that once again leave the discourses of the playground unchallenged and defended in a "this is the way it is" normal.

Looking to the Perimeter

If the playground is structured where some are systemically advantaged and others disadvantaged and if the games that are played are identity performances that are resultant of and reproductive of these advantages and disadvantages, one might ask if there are spaces where the discourses and inequalities are resisted or at least minimized. This takes us to the perimeter of the playground. All of these studies have implicated the typically White teacher who might have playground duty that day as passively complicit in the systemic inequalities and the performances of those inequalities. But that does not mean this adult is not busy on the playground. Judicious decisions are made, disputes are resolved, and occasionally punishments are meted out. In all of this activity, there are "quiet" spaces on the perimeter that demand less attention. The kids in these spaces may have figured out if they dress differently, talk quietly, and do not need intervention, then they will be left alone.

Pennington (2007) addresses this perimeter space and uses an appropriate metaphor of whispering. The title of the autoethnography is quite descriptive of the difference between the center space, where there was silence in the classroom regarding race, and the periphery (in this case the halls), which were sites of whispering and resistance. The teachers used tactics such as hyperpoliteness to silence racial conversation. But the halls were different. One PST stated, "There were a lot of people speaking Spanish a lot of times when I was sitting around and so I felt very out of place." Pennington shared her own experiences:

> I explained how my sixth grade students had called me "White Bread" under their breath as they exited the classroom one day. Their disruption of our

saving stance as teachers was painful and we preferred teaching the younger
students for that very reason. (p. 106)

The perimeter of the playground becomes the location where the systemic advantages are named and resisted. The discourses, like in the previous example of
White teachers as saviors, that shape the games are rejected. The game might be
rigged every day according to the common assumptions, but for some, its rejection becomes one more act of identity play in the constellation of the playground.

Grade Level Play

The games on the playground often become more sophisticated as children age.
Ring around the rosie and freeze-tag yield to organized sports and conversations
that reflect social hierarchies. Even at times, maturation creeps into the picture.
As the students age, they *can possibly* become more sensitive to exclusions or
appreciative of those who do not follow the primary discourses. Even the teachers, as they become more experienced, can wise up to the inequities, dominant
discourses, and what is really happening on the periphery. All of the articles in
this meta-ethnography showed some possibilities for challenging the hegemony
of whiteness.

In our meta-ethnography, two of the studies (Bollin & Finkel, 2006; Marx,
2004) introduced another important trajectory of identity theory that relates possibilities of growth and maturation from the performances of White supremacy.
Bollin and Finkel offered examples of White PSTs moving through Helm's (1990)
stages, including an example of a teacher reflectively reaching the latter stages:

I did not expect the children of PAL to have stable and loving relationships
with their parents. I know that sounds really uneducated but for reasons
I do not truly understand myself, I thought the students were going to be
unkempt and unloved. I was absolutely wrong. . . . This experience as a whole
has taught me that as much as I thought I was open-minded and culturally
aware I still carry with me a lot of biases. I always considered myself not to
hold any prejudices but I learned that as unconscious as it may be, I still have
a lot of work. (p. 29)

At least one of the included studies questioned the value of stage theories and
named Helms specifically (Warren & Hytten, 2004). Their concern was that
this conception of linear stages conflicts with the performances (in that case,
"faces") that are central to Butler's (1999) discursive and performance identity
theory. This surface refutation reveals some of the descriptive strengths of meta-
ethnographies, particularly when the studies craft a line of argument as has been
the case in the identity theorizing in our studies. Here one can see the possibility
that Butler and Helms (1990) are simply describing two different aspects of our
metaphoric playground.

Conclusion in 2013

In the 2013 meta-ethnography, we sought to illustrate the relationship between protection of White privilege and identity. When we examined this relationship from the perspective of defending White privilege, we found a highly reciprocal argument. There were very common and vivid descriptions of ways that White PSTs protect their privilege. Considering tools and strategies, it was easy to translate metaphors present in one article to those in other articles. To use our first translational metaphor, the playbook of defensive strategies was readily evident in each of the studies. This continuity was a significant finding in and of itself. Harkening back to Holland and colleagues' (1998) contribution to social practice theories of identity, the figured world of whiteness was readily invoked by PSTs in a variety of settings and through a variety of strategies. The power and durability of historically developed imaginaries in racial identity formation, whether liberative or in this case repressive, was affirmed in the meta-analysis. In the case of these studies, these imaginaries were dynamically essential to the construction and performance of defensive discourses and actions protecting whiteness.

Subsequent examination, using methods of authorial dialogue and reflexive member-checking, expanded the assertions we would make about identity and identity theory. Continued examination of the studies and our own dialogue about their differences yielded a second line-of-argument metaphor—the school playground. This was prompted by a comparative and inductive quandary, specifically due to the varying ways that the authors invoked identity theory. Various deployments of critical race theory, staged racial identity theories, and discursive/performative theories of identity situated these studies in rich but different spaces of assertion regarding White privilege. Ultimately, we realized the importance of geography in beginning to map distinct locations, imagined or otherwise, where whiteness was vigorously defended, and thus a spatial metaphor seemed powerfully appropriate. Further, Holland and Lave (2001) asserted that identities are forged in local spaces, where powerful imaginaries are invoked, contested, and deployed toward the formation of intimate identities, which only enhanced our interpretative move. The significance of local spaces and cultural worlds are seminal contributions of the study of identity. And, in our case, the overarching claims of social practice theory functioned to situate the multiple evocations of racial identity theory in a complex geographic metaphor. Mapping the field of practice of racial identity for White PSTs—using a social practice theory of identity—highlights the necessity of maintaining a complex theoretical picture that invites entry through multiple theoretical pathways. This not only exposes a new line of argument, but it provokes a meta-theoretical realization: Whiteness and White identity are complex ideological imaginaries with very real effects, and social practice theory allows us to invoke multiple theoretical stances in attempting to understand these imaginaries in more detail. In other words, we can use contested theoretical spaces as productive sites for understanding the practice of White racial formation.

META-ETHNOGRAPHIC ANTICIPATIONS

As we described earlier, the findings of meta-ethnographic analyses are necessarily tied to the time they were completed. These analyses represent a snapshot of the scholarly conversation at the time and, in this case, the practice of the educators involved in working with White PSTs.

We acknowledge that many other studies have been published over the course of the past three years that could inform this work. We take the cue of Jupp and Lensmire (2016) and use the recent special issue publication of the *International Journal of Qualitative Studies in Education* to illustrate how researchers employing meta-ethnographic methodology might "test" evolving theory and practice. In this meta-ethnographic test, we first provide a very brief summary of second-wave White teacher identities studies. Then we use two published studies from the special issue to demonstrate how we might test our prior analysis in light of more recent studies. Lastly, we provide a short discussion about the possibilities for engaging meta-ethnography over time and across both theoretical and practical shifts.

Second-Wave White Teacher Identity Studies

According to Jupp and Lensmire (2016), second-wave White teacher identity studies (SWWTIS),

1. Pa[y] careful attention to the nuances and complexities of white race-visible identities, and;
2. Provide detailed accounts of the actual pedagogies and curricula that form the complex contexts of white teachers' identities. (p. 986)

Taking a step back, SWWTIS evolved from a critique of White teacher identity studies that focused primarily on identifying White privilege. As we found in the reciprocal argument of our 2013 analysis, this pedagogical approach in teacher education classrooms, and the resulting defense of privilege, resulted in both practical and theoretical sticking points. These findings, and the assumptions surrounding them, presented a stagnant picture of White PSTs that had the effect of presenting their journeys toward racial consciousness as both failed and contained within a 16-week teacher education course (Mason, 2016). Another major concern of this approach was that focusing on these types of discursive defense moves promoted engagement at the expense of PSTs who identify as people of color.

The field of SWWTIS is sensitive to context and prioritizes process (Crowley, 2016; Jupp & Lensmire, 2016) and becoming (Mason, 2016) that extends into each PST's larger social world. While acknowledging that the recognition of privilege and oppression is a necessary step in developing racial consciousness, SWWTIS prioritize "new rhetorical structures to do so" (Mason, 2016, p. 1047). In this regard, these studies find possibility in a project of praxis, wherein PSTs examine their own racial identity, at the same time locating that identity with the complex and hegemonic racial structure of White supremacy. Additionally, SWWTIS embrace the complexity of theoretical interdisciplinarity.

Incorporating New Findings

We examined two articles situated in SWWTIS for this meta-ethnographic test (Crowley, 2016; Mason, 2016). We have provided a summary of those two studies in the same format as our analytic chart for the original analysis (Figure 8.2). We did not see the same easily translatable metaphors of tools and strategies but rather theoretical engagements that served to maintain or extend complexity. Thus we opted to call the findings of these newer studies "interpretations." In these studies, we noted that identity is significantly theorized. By claiming interdisciplinarity as vital, theory from fields such as feminist studies, anthropology, linguistics, and psychology becomes foundational to the emerging theoretical framework of the field of SWWTIS. As in our 2013 study, this centers contested spaces as productive sites for understanding White racial formation. Whereas these theoretical locations seemed disjunct in 2013, inviting complexity and interdisciplinarity serves to contextualize their multiple evocations, as well as further our line of argument that these diverse theories map onto a larger field of social practice.

We note that at the time of our original analysis, theory regarding White teacher identity studies was already shifting significantly (Applebaum, 2010; Leonardo, 2004, 2009). However, the available body of qualitative studies in this field had not yet coalesced around the theoretical shift. Much of the conceptual dialogue around White teacher identities at the time also noted undertheorization in empirical research, which contributed to an oversimplification of White racial identity as only White privilege examination. The authors in both Crowley (2016) and Mason (2016) provided significant theoretical framing for their research, one of the criteria we had included in selection of our original set of seven articles. This is encouraging and suggests that the number of qualifying studies for a similar meta-ethnographic analysis in 2016 would be larger.

A particularly interesting commonality between our findings and the field of SWWTIS is the emphasis on the complexity of racial hegemony within a White supremacist system. Each of the descriptions of SWWTIS that we reviewed (Crowley, 2016; Jupp & Lensmire, 2016; Mason, 2016) evoked a geographical metaphor of locations in that system corresponding highly to our impulse to describe our interpretation as a *field of practice* using a metaphor of physical place. Mason describes dialogic locations, framed with the linguistic theory of Gee (2005). Near the end of her piece, she also invokes figured worlds in describing the frames of meaning present in fields of practice (Holland et al., 1998). The impetus to "situate" or "locate" oneself within a negotiated space of White racial knowledge (Crowley, 2016) necessarily evokes geographical thinking. In our 2013 analysis, it was a feeling of the absence of this overlying and interwoven geography of contested spaces that pushed us to move beyond a reciprocal argument about White PSTs defense of White privilege.

	Mason (2016)	Crowley (2016)
Intent:	"challenge scholars and practitioners of teacher education to consider ways that our courses do and do not engage white teacher candidates to take on racially conscious orientations." (p. 1045)	"Explore experiences of White pre-service teachers as they discussed race, racism, and White-ness during the first semester of an urban teaching preparation program." (p. 1016)
Setting:	Regional comprehensive university in the Midwest U.S. – 35 miles from a major metropolitan area, classified as rural	Large research university in the U.S. Southwest.
Participants:	Larger study: Teacher education students (mostly female, 95% White) Selected Participants: -Sabrina – White female -Sam – White female -Jen – White female	6 White Pre-service teachers (2 male, 4 female).
Methods:	*Collected coursework artifacts in form of "writing portfolio" -Completed graphic organizers from class - 8 journal entries - 2 from self-study essays - other in-class assignments *Ethnographic observations in class *Interviews	Critical Case Study • Multicultural education course observations • written reflections • semi-structured interviews on racial biographies and a member-check.
Theory Used:	Britzman (200) Complicated conversations -Pinar (2011) Gee (2005)	Critical White Studies (Mills, 1997) White racial knowledge/Racial world view (Leonardo, 2009)
Theoretical Findings:	*Complicated conversation *Breaking through diversity discourse *Value of extension of time for continued development of race-consciousness *Value of multi-site engagement with PSTs regarding developing racial consciousness	*Transgressive White racial knowledge - "Combatting deficit discourses about students of color" (p. 1019) - "The normal-ness of being White" (p. 1020) *Negotiated White racial knowledge - "A safe space for talking about race" (p. 1022) -"Downplaying the salience of race" (p. 1024)

Figure 8.2 Additional Studies on Whiteness and Pre-service Teachers—2016.

Implications for Meta-Ethnographic Methodological Testing Over Time

The elaboration of SWWTIS offered an opportunity for us to test the findings from our 2013 meta-ethnography. This test showed the degree to which our synthesis anticipated where the field is currently and where it is going. We see this as promising and note that this type of methodological test can help fields predict and account for change in theory and practice over extended periods of time. In the case of our original analysis, we found the new literature on SWWTIS to test and confirm the theoretical position we derived from our original study. Our meta-ethnography was not available to the new authors and thus did not cause the outcome. That said, our original analysis anticipated an ongoing theoretical shift in the study of White PST identities, which was confirmed by the authors in this special issue. We see this confirmatory re-engagement with meta-ethnographic findings over time as a test for the robustness of the methodology. Meta-ethnographies are likely to accomplish a mix of confirmation, extension, and/or critique; these three outcomes, combined, encapsulate the evolving nature of any field of study and create new space for interpretive scholarly engagement. Our anticipation was not completely accurate: according to Jupp and Lensmire (2016), the shift toward SWWTIS was already happening, in a theoretical sense, about a decade before our 2013 meta-ethnography began. However, our findings did highlight the persistence of first-wave White teacher identity studies in *practice*, despite the shifting theoretical dialogue. We were effectively able to take the "temperature" of the existing qualitative studies, generate a critique from our findings, and anticipate a shift that is now apparent in emerging theoretical and practice-based work.

NOTE

1. Selected articles include Bollin and Finkel (2006), Hytten and Warren (2003), Marx (2004), Pennington (2007), Picower (2009), Terwilliger (2010), and Warren and Hytten (2004).

REFERENCES

Applebaum, B. (2010). *Being White, being good: White complicity, White moral responsibility, and social justice pedagogy*. Lanham, MD: Lexington.

Bollin, G. G., & Finkel, J. (2006). White racial identity as a barrier to understanding diversity: A study of PSTs. *Equity and Excellence in Education, 28*(1), 25–30.

Bourdieu, P. (1977). *Outline of a theory of practice*. New York: Cambridge University Press.

Butler, J. (1999). *Gender trouble: Feminism and the subversion of identity*. New York: Routledge.

Butler, J. (1990). Performative acts and gender constitution: An essay in phenomenology and feminist theory. In S. E. Case (Ed.), *Performing feminisms: Feminist critical theory and theatre* (pp. 270–282). Baltimore: Johns Hopkins University Press.

Conquergood, D. (1985). Performing as a moral act: Ethical dimensions of the ethnography of performance. *Literature in Performance, 5*(2), 1–13.

Crowley, R. M. (2016). Transgressive and negotiated White racial knowledge. *International Journal of Qualitative Studies in Education, 29*(8), 1016–1029.

De Certeau, M. (1984). *The practice of everyday life*. Berkeley: University of California Press.

Doyle, L. H. (2003). Synthesis through meta-ethnography: Paradoxes, enhancements, and possibilities. *Qualitative Research*, *3*(3), 321–344.

France, E. F., Ring, N., Thomas, R., Noyes, J., Maxwell, M., & Jepson, R. (2014). A methodological systematic review of what's wrong with meta-ethnography reporting. *BMC Medical Research Methodology*, *14*(1), 1.

Gee, J. P. (2005). *An introduction to discourse analysis: Theory and method* (2nd ed.). New York: Routledge.

Helms, J. E. (1990). *Black and White racial identity: Theory, research, and practice*. Westport, CT: Praeger.

Holland, D., Lachicotte, W., Skinner, D., & Cain, C. (1998). *Identity and agency in cultural worlds*. Cambridge, MA: Harvard University Press.

Holland, D., & Lave, J. (2001). *History in person: Enduring struggles, contentious practice, intimate identities*. Santa Fe, NM: School of American Research Press.

Hytten, K., & Warren, J. (2003). Engaging whiteness: How racial power gets reified in education. *Qualitative Studies in Education*, *16*(1), 65–89.

Jupp, J. C., & Lensmire, T. J. (2016). Second-wave White teacher identity studies: Toward complexity and reflexivity in the racial conscientization of White teachers. *International Journal of Qualitative Studies in Education*, *29*(8), 985–988.

Leonardo, Z. (2004). The color of supremacy: Beyond the discourse of "White privilege." *Educational Philosophy and Theory*, *36*(2), 137–152.

Leonardo, Z. (2009). *Race, whiteness, and education*. New York: Routledge.

Marx, S. (2004). Regarding whiteness: Exploring and intervening in the effects of White racism in teacher education. *Equity and Excellence in Education*, *37*(1), 31–43.

Mason, A. M. (2016). Taking time, breaking codes: Moments in White teacher candidates' exploration of racism and teacher identity. *International Journal of Qualitative Studies in Education*, *29*(8), 1045–1058.

McIntosh, P. (1990). White privilege: Unpacking the invisible knapsack. *Independent School*, *49*, 31–36.

Noblit, G. W., & Hare, R. D. (1988). *Meta-ethnography: Synthesizing qualitative studies*. Newbury Park, CA: SAGE.

Pennington, J. L. (2007). Silence in the classroom/whispers in the halls: Autoethnography as pedagogy in White PST education. *Race Ethnicity and Education*, *10*(1), 93–113.

Picower, B. (2009). The unexamined power of whiteness of teaching: How White teachers maintain and enact dominant racial ideologies. *Race Ethnicity and Education*, *12*(2), 197–215.

Scheurich, J. J. (2002). *Anti-racist scholarship: An advocacy*. New York: State University of New York Press.

Shenton, A.K. (2004). Strategies for ensuring trustworthiness in qualitative research projects. *Education for Information*, *22*(2), 63–75.

Terwilliger, C. (2010). Mapping stories: Taking detours to challenge whiteness. *Making connections: Interdisciplinary approaches to cultural diversity*, *11*, 14–25.

Valencia, R. R. (Ed.). (1997). *The evolution of deficit thinking: Educational thought and practice*. Washington, DC: Falmer.

Warren, J., & Hytten, K. (2004). The faces of whiteness: Pitfalls and the critical democrat. *Communication Education*, *53*(4), 321–339.

9

Native Youth Navigating Identity Through Colonization, Culture, and Community

A Meta-Ethnography

KARLA MARTIN AND LESLIE LOCKLEAR ■

INTRODUCTION

Currently, there are approximately 5.4 million Native American/Alaskan Native people in the United States with youth under the age of 25, making up 41% of the total population. (Center for Native American Youth, 2016). Native youth are working together to address important issues facing them and their communities: suicide, access to health care, investigating missing and murdered Indigenous women, promoting healthy lifestyles, ending domestic violence and sexual assault among Native women, gaining access to and increasing technology, protecting the environment, and fighting for the protection of tribal lands, sacred sites, and waterways (Center for Native American Youth, 2016). Native youth draw strength from their cultures and elders as they continue to fight some of the same fights that generations before them have fought—as well as addressing many different issues (Center for Native American Youth, 2016). These resilient Native youth represent a huge percentage of the overall Native population, showing us a bright future for Indian Country, Tribal Nations, and Tribal leaders.

More often than not, society labels Native youth by the problems they face. The dominant narrative tells us that Native American youth in the United States have fallen far below the bar when compared to their white counterparts. With the highest dropout rates and the lowest rates in terms of higher education access and enrollment (National Indian Education Association, n.d), it is evident that our current educational system is failing our Native youth. Through this chapter we aim to increase the understanding of Native American youth within today's society, particularly today's educational setting.

We conducted a meta-ethnography to analyze qualitative research conducted on or with Native American youth. In an effort to counter the colonial narratives that are prevalent in today's society, we sought out studies that gave way to Native youth voice and agency. This meta-ethnography examines qualitative research done on or with Native American youth of high school age. This research helps everyone to learn more about Native American youth identity and centers Native youth's voices to help us understand their experiences and ways we can support them. Our objectives with this particular focus were twofold. Though we sought to allow the voices of youth to speak loudly and clearly, we also used this opportunity to counter the often negative, racialized, and deficit studies and stories that plague Native American youth. We know the value of Native youth's voices, and we look to them to help us tell this story.

Karla. I come to this research as a Poarch Creek woman that has been raised in my tribal community almost all of my life, except when I left to pursue higher education and ultimately a PhD in education. I taught at a university before returning to my Tribe to work. I have served on our Tribe's Education Advisory Committee for nine years, served as cultural director for two years, and currently hold the position as Community Services Division Director. My focus in research and all aspects of life has always been on Native education and Indigenous issues. Therefore, I approach this research from my lived experience as a Poarch Creek woman and educator that works with my Tribal community and our Native youth.

Leslie. As a Native woman from the Lumbee and Waccamaw Siouan Tribes of North Carolina, I come to this research as an active member within my tribal community as well as an active member of various national Native American youth organizations. My work and research thus far has centered on Native youth and their success within the educational arena. My own voice, experiences, passions, and tribal culture have led me to not only seek to impart the history of Native Americans within today's current educational research but to do so by shining a light on the positive aspects of our culture and heritage.

CHAPTER FRAMEWORK

The remainder of this chapter is divided into six main sections: methods; article summaries; identity, culture; and relationships; synthesis; summary; and conclusion. The methods section includes a discussion of our purposeful focus on positive articles on Native youth identity. We then discuss our article search process, how we came to the selection of five articles focusing on Native American high school age youth identity, coding, trustworthiness, gaps in the research, and geographical limitations. Next is a summary of each of the articles in both text and a table. We identify the themes that emerged in the articles: language, ways of being, identity formation, cultural markers of identity, relationships, school climate, school policies, ideas for schooling and teaching, and colonization. We discuss how all of these articles together form a line of argument in the meta-ethnography process. We then provide a discussion of the most prominent themes throughout the five articles: language, culture, and relationships. We provide a synthesis of the themes and share what the articles identify as three key aspects that are essential to the identity development of Native youth: language, Indigenous knowledge systems, and social identity. We end the article with a summary and conclusion.

METHODS

The work presented through our critical approach to searching for studies and this meta-ethnography process seeks to reveal how Native youth identity is constructed in educational settings. This work brings forth the barriers that impede positive identity development and in turn brings to light factors that positively facilitate the development of cultural identity among Native youth. Through this meta-ethnography, we seek to better understand (a) Native youth identity, (b) factors that affect Native youth identity, (c) Native youth's experience in school, and (d) ways schools both colonize and support Native youth identity.

Text selection. Our text selection began with a broad search of all databases on the Illinois State University library system to draw from a wide range of disciplines. In our first search, we used the terms Native American, youth, qualitative, and identity, which resulted in 8,353 articles. After this initial search, we chose to only use refereed articles in our meta-ethnography. In our second search, we used all of those terms but replaced "Native American" with "American Indian," which resulted in a total of 5,697 articles. Therefore, we used the term "Native American" for all remaining searches because it always yielded more articles. In the third search, we added cultural to identity, making the search term "cultural identity," which resulted in a total of 1,178 articles. For the fourth search, we completed the first two searches again but changed "identity" to "identity theory," which resulted in 170 and 102 articles, respectively, most of which were the same as articles in previous searches. In all searches only about half of the articles had anything to do with Native Americans/American Indians.

Through these searches, we found that there were many studies on Native American youth where the age of youth was defined as adolescents, high school, and college age—a wide range of ages. After going through all of these articles' abstracts and skimming them for further details, we narrowed the age range for this meta-ethnography of "youth" to focus on high school students.

As we expected, many articles were focused on specific Indigenous groups/Tribes, colleges, and cities/states/locations throughout the United States and world. We found that there were not a wide range of Tribes represented in these articles, but instead there were many articles focused on southwestern Tribes/Native people. We chose then to narrow this meta-ethnography to focus on Native Americans in the United States, as the nation-state has dramatic effects on the situation of Indigenous peoples. We are fully aware that each Tribe has its own history, language, and culture and that Tribes and Native peoples differ by region, reservation, urban area, and so on. However, we searched articles across Tribal affiliation, location, language, culture, and history in recognition of the power of the United States as a nation in determining the situation of the Tribes. The goal of this meta-ethnography, then, is to provide a larger picture of the literature on Native youth identity instead of the specifics on one group or Tribe.

The most disheartening discovery in our search was that out of the 8,353 articles we reviewed, many studies done in the disciplines of health, psychology, social work, and counseling focused on negative concepts, issues, or problems with Native American youth. For example, many articles talked about the high drug use rate, dropout rate, and obesity rates among Native youth. The authors spoke from deficit voices and continued to talk about how they can "help" Native youth with their issues. It is interesting to us that so many people have opinions about how they think they can help youth with the issues they have identified but have rarely asked Native nations or Native youth what they want or need. The problem we have with this mode of research is that more often than not culturally appropriate methods were not used, Native people or Tribes had no input into the research or solutions, and the only discussion regarding Native youth was so negative that it was as if Native youth had nothing to contribute to society or to their own lives or community. Sadly, our search has shown that colonization is still prevalent and dominating qualitative research on Native people and Native youth.

What is lacking from many of these studies is a discussion about what Native youth add to their communities or nations. This interests us personally because not only were we both once Native youth but we work closely with many Native youth from whom we learn much. They are the leaders of their generation as well as leaders of our future nations. There are so many things that we can learn from Native youth that can help us learn about their generation and planning for future generations. Yet the qualitative research reflects little of this.

After reading these articles, we decided that there was enough written about the negative aspects of Native youth that we refused to continue such a discussion— purposely choosing to focus this chapter on the positive aspects of Native youth identity. We chose to center Native youth and their voices so that we can hear from Native youth and learn about their needs, experiences, and wishes. While there were some quantitative and mixed-methods research that fit all of these criteria, only two qualitative articles in our search met all of these criteria. Therefore, we continued our search for positive qualitative studies on Native youth identity. We asked scholars, read bibliographies, and purposely searched for the missing positive Native youth voices. We were able to find three more articles to add to this meta-ethnography.

This meta-ethnography, then, focuses on five qualitative studies on Native American youth identity. These five qualitative studies are based in the south-western United States. Therefore, our meta-ethnography is region based, covering youth from different Tribes, cultures, languages, and histories. From our knowledge and experiences as Native people and researchers, we know Native youth across the United States have very similar experiences as well as very different experiences. While we hope that the insights from the southwestern region can give insight into other Native youth experiences, we cannot extrapolate these findings to other Tribes or Native youth.

Coding and themes. After selecting the five articles, Karla worked to create a table of information from all of the articles. Leslie went back through and coded the articles. Together we discussed the articles and coding for the articles. After many revisions, coding, and recoding, we decided on final codes for the articles and used those codes to analyze the information (see Table 9.1).

Trustworthiness. Throughout our search process we continuously looked at how the research was conducted and written about. For us, these were the most important factors in determining our trust in the research and researcher. From the beginning we looked at the relationship between the researcher and participants, the researcher's stated involvement in the community, the researcher's engagement and relationships with the participants, who was telling the story, and how it was being told. As Native women who are very grounded in our communities, we know that the process of trust is earned and that our involvement, dedication to, and participation in our communities is in itself a validation of trustworthiness. From our understanding of and experiences with storytelling and oral histories, we know that the sharing of stories takes place within a relationship of trust. Our understanding of trustworthiness in qualitative research is a bit different from many white researchers. The traditional definition tends to assure that outsiders can have faith in the account. Our approach was to create a meta-ethnography that speaks to those of us who are inside Indian Country. We are less concerned if other readers find this meta-ethnography trustworthy because the vast majority of researchers studying Native Americans enact deficit accounts that document colonization. The studies we chose and the meta-ethnography we conducted speak against the

Table 9.1 Themes in the Studies

Theme	Lee & Quijada Cerecer (2010)	McCarty, Romero, & Zepeda (2006)	Nicholas (2009)	Quijada Cerecer (2011)	Quijada Cerecer (2013)
Language	X	X	X		
Ways of Being/ Living			X		
Identity Formation			X		
Cultural Markers of Identity			X		
Relationships	X	X		X	
School Climate	X			X	X
School Policies	X				X
Ideas for Schooling and Teaching	X			X	X
Colonization	X	X		X	X

common definition of trustworthiness—it presumes that we are to satisfy other researchers' concerns when in fact other researchers have proven to not be trustworthy to Native Americans repeatedly in the literature we have reviewed.

The five studies focus on many aspects of Native youth identity; the most prominent themes are language, culture, and relationships. These studies will help us to understand a much larger picture of what Native high school age youth add to their communities as well as issues they may be facing and ways we can support them. We summarize them next.

ARTICLE SUMMARIES

Lee and Quijada Cerecer (2010)

Lee and Quijada Cerecer (2010) center Navajo and Pueblo youth's voices to reflect on their experiences in socioculturally responsive Native language courses. The youth share their expectations and ideas for creating socioculturally (SCR) responsive teachers, schools, and classrooms.

The data for this article comes from two qualitative studies on Native youth's engagement with schools. The first study was based in New Mexico and conducted from January 2008 to March 2009. Focus groups and/or interviews were done in 13 schools—seven schools were on a reservation, four schools were in towns bordering reservation communities, and one school was in a city. The study was conducted with groups of mainly Navajo and Pueblo students ages 12 to 19, teachers, and community members. The second study was an ethnographic study where semi-structured interviews, focus groups, participant observations, and field notes were completed for six months with self-identified Pueblo youth who attended a public high school in New Mexico. All students lived on one of the reservations near the public high school.

The authors in this article analyze the data from their two studies using a counter-storytelling methodology and grounded theory approach to identify themes that challenge the majoritarian story that is told of youth of color. The authors deliberately tell a story that centers on these Navajo and Pueblo youth's voices and experiences. Through storytelling, these youth were able to reflect on their schooling experiences. Although there were five years between these two studies, "the concerns of Native youth and their relationships to schools and teachers remain constant, underlining the urgency to listen to the youth and their educational experiences" (Lee & Cerecer, 2010, p. 201).

There is so much to learn from these students about many aspects of their school experience, such as the school climate, curriculum, and teachers. There were many misperceptions and much intolerance, devaluing, stereotyping, and hostility that students felt in their schools from other students, staff, and teachers toward them and their cultural heritage, traditions, customs, knowledge, and language. All of these things directly affected students' motivation to succeed in school and their relationships with those at school.

Native students discussed how SCR courses, no matter what the subject, provided a safe and nurturing space for Indigenous knowledge, cultures, and histories to be centered and valued. These courses supported Native identity and ways of being, valuing their culture, strengthening their cultural identity, and allowing them to connect to what they were learning. For example, Native youth shared that the SCR language courses were always filled to capacity. Students discussed the importance of language to their heritage and in communicating with their families and elders in the community. The language courses offered by the school validated Indigenous students' cultures, traditions, customs, and languages, and students want to see more of these courses taught in their schools.

McCarty, Romero, and Zepeda (2006)

McCarty et al. (2006) look at the impact of Native language loss on Native communities and youth's lives as well as their Indigenous identity. This research is a part of a larger research study done at five school-community sites in the Southwest with a group of 144 adults and 46 youth in grades 4 through 12. This study used ethnographic interviews from a select group of Navajo youth from a single site in the interior of the Navajo Nation as counter-narratives to the dominant deficit narrative we noted earlier.

This article shows the complexity of Navajo language and the role of language in youth's lives and cultural identity. In all of the Navajo youth's stories about identity and language, we hear words of both shame and pride. Three themes emerged from their stories: "the politics of shame and caring in school, the hegemony of English, the iconic bonding of English with whiteness" (McCarty et al., 2006, p. 37). Students shared stories of how they saw power working in larger Native society and how that affects their perception of their cultural identity. Some examples given were about not seeing themselves on television, dressing or having a physical appearance different from those in mainstream pop culture, people in power being white, and being told by others that Navajo culture and language is inferior. At the same time, the youth find pride in their language and culture, making their thoughts and identities very complex for even them to completely understand.

This article highlights the challenges that Indigenous communities face in revitalizing and maintaining their languages, as well as the intricate role that language plays in the identity development of Indigenous youth. The importance of language and the critical role it plays in the identity of Indigenous people rings through clearly as Indigenous participants discuss the meaning of their language. Deemed by one participant as the essence of their being, the role that language played was made poignant by others who discussed its ability to help them understand their relation to other people as well as their relation to the natural world and also its role in their own uniqueness and its defining nature in making them who they are (McCarty et al., 2006, p. 28). The power of Indigenous language within Tribal communities is much more than a tool for communication; it is a connection, a way of knowing, a way of being, and a way of existing as Indigenous people. Thus this article presents the power of language and its revitalization as not only a gift but a necessary factor in the reassertion of self-determination and identity among the Indigenous population (McCarty et al., 2006, p. 44).

Nicholas (2009)

Nicholas (2009) presents ethnographic portraits of three Hopi youth who recently graduated from high school. All of these youth were "born into Hopi culture, raised on the Hopi reservation in northern Arizona, and participated in cultural traditions from early childhood, and expressed a strong affinity for their heritage culture" (p. 322). As Hopi people, "By birthright, these youth acquired 'cultural markers of identity'—maternal clan identity, maternal village affiliation, birth and ceremonial names—and the privileges of participation in Hopi society" (p. 322).

This research is part of a larger study of multiple, intergenerational case studies across three generations of households. The author discusses her culturally appropriate collection of oral stories and participant observations in cultural, ceremonial, and everyday activities when visiting families. This article discusses the process of Hopi identity formation, situating it in Hopi culture, history, rituals, and ways of life.

All three of the youth discuss what it means to "live Hopi" and how the Hopi language is the central part of "living Hopi." While all three youth vary greatly in linguistic ability, all three discussed the importance of the Hopi language in their culture. One main reason is because everything is passed down orally. They discuss the importance of

> active participation in Hopi religion, customs, and traditions as leading to the acquisition and demonstration of appropriate cultural standards of conduct and attitude in everyday life, while moving toward a deeper understanding of the purpose and meaning of cultural traditions in the Hopi way of life. (p. 322)

Therefore, even without linguistic fluency, by "living Hopi" Hopi youth are learning Hopi culture and ways of being.

The youth and author of this article discuss how language is important in Hopi learning of cultural knowledge, thinking, and understandings of the world that have sustained the lives of Hopi people for many generations. In this context, the expression of "living Hopi" was presented as more than just simply speaking the language; however, the integral part that the language played in this cultural aspect could not be ignored. Understanding that the most fully and complete way to live Hopi and understand the Hopi way of life was to do so through the expression of the Hopi language, one of the youth claimed, "I don't think it's fully complete without that missing piece of language, the tongue, the speaking" (Nicholas, 2009,

p. 333). The ritual songs and other cultural activities that involve the Hopi language can only be fully understood and embraced by those who understand the language. Thus the language shift to English leaves much to be lost in the way of Hopi traditions and way of life. In doing so, youth become disconnected from their elders, their traditions, their communities, and themselves as Hopi tribal members.

Quijada Cerecer (2011)

Quijada Cerecer (2011) explores adult–youth relationships in schools and looks at how Indigenous knowledge, culture, and power are the basis in these relationships.

Data were collected through ethnographic interviews and participant observations with 21 youth (11 female and 10 male) who (a) self-identified as American Indian, (b) lived on one of the nearby reservations, and (c) attended a particular high school. The high school was a small, rural public high school in the southwestern part of the United States with an enrollment of 190 students (66% American Indian, 21% Latino, and 13% White). The majority of these students' parents graduated from this high school and were very involved in school activities.

While most institutions purposefully position youth against adults, these Native students found it important to their development and identity to build community through reciprocal relationships with the adults they were learning with and from. Students shared examples of the school, teachers, and administrators being positioned against students. Students wanted the adults that work with them to form communities with authentic, committed, reciprocal relationships that legitimize and validate students.

Native youth wanted their educators to understand the importance of family and community to their learning and success. Students wanted schools to have activities that included their families and community. For example, the school changed the end of the year awards ceremony to be during the day when most parents could not attend. Students also wanted learning to be hands-on/participatory and student-centered, incorporating their experiences into their pedagogy, valuing Indigenous epistemologies, and creating reciprocal learning relationships with them. Students sought to be active in creating and learning the curriculum. In conclusion, the author spoke about the importance of valuing the Native youth voice within the educational setting and then using their experiences to find solutions.

Quijada Cerecer (2013)

Quijada Cerecer (2013) explored how a high school restricts, regulates, and controls Pueblo youth through their teaching methods, curriculum, and policies that are not supportive of Native youth and ways of knowing. Through storytelling, youth reflected on their schooling experiences and relationships and shared their ideas for changing the academic system.

The data for this article came from a five-year qualitative study. The qualitative methods used were participant observations, interviews, and focus groups done with 21 Native students who (a) self-identified as Pueblo youth, (b) attended a public high school in New Mexico, and (c) were either living (at the time of the study) or had lived on the reservation most of their lives.

Students discussed how their Indigenous identity directly affected how they were negatively treated as students in their school. Students felt restricted, regulated, and controlled by many things including the school and teacher's expectations for them to assimilate, not including Native history in school curriculum, banning of Native books, stereotyping students, and the school's assimilationist rules, procedures, and policies. These youth discussed how all of these things distanced them from learning and graduating and how that affected their futures.

More specifically students discussed how the school implemented policies that made all students conform to fit the dominant society's idea of how Native students should behave in school, which "challenged and marginalized their cultural knowledge, values, and agency as Indigenous youth" (Quijada Cerecer, 2013, p. 607). They also saw that the school's prejudiced policies marginalized them, depicting them and treating them as violent youth and in turn the school implemented "surveillance measures to closely monitor their bodies and their minds" (p. 607).

The author and youth from this article suggested that Indigenous knowledge systems be valued and included in educational institutions so that students and their histories, knowledge, and identities were integrated into school and they could become "active change agents" (Quijada Cerecer, 2013, p. 595). The article ended with implications for research, school administrators, and teachers.

The five qualitative articles discussed and summarized here provide insight into the identity development of Native American youth. Despite the vast amount of information these articles provided, readers, educators, and researchers are still left with a very prominent gap in the literature. All studies were conducted with southwestern tribal nations and Native peoples thus limiting the ways in which we can understand Native youth identity. The lack of qualitative studies that focus on the positive aspects of the identity development of Native youth in other regions of the United States limits the understanding of Native youth in other regions as well as the ways in which they can benefit within the educational setting. This gap begs for researchers who are willing to work with tribal communities that are often rendered invisible in this realm of research.

Despite the geographical limitations, the findings presented here give insight into Native youth identity. The themes that emerged in the articles include language, ways of being, identity formation, cultural markers of identity, relationships, school climate, school policies, ideas for schooling and teaching, and colonization. Together these five studies form a line of argument (Noblit & Hare, 1988, p. 62), each article contributing something to the larger understanding of Native youth identity and no one article looking at only one aspect of Native youth identity. These articles do a great job of looking at the positives of Native youth identity and call us all to look deeper into what our youth are telling us.

IDENTITY: LANGUAGE, CULTURE, RELATIONSHIPS

The five articles that are a part of this meta-ethnography took very different views on the development of Native American youth identity. In translating these articles into one another, we can see that Native youth discussed the following as being vital parts of their identity: language, culture, and adult-youth relationships. While these were the main themes, there were many other themes throughout these articles that are embedded into these three categories.

One of the first and most prominent parts of Native youth identity that youth discussed is language. Three Hopi youth drew strong links between their cultural identities and the Hopi language. The Hopi language was woven into culture in a way that language was viewed as "a cultural practice" (Nicholas, 2009, p. 330). The role of the language was more than communication for these youth. Dorian stated, "If you don't know it [the Hopi language], you don't really understand [Hopi culture]" (Nicholas, 2009, p. 326). For Navajo community members and youth, the language was also integral with one elder proclaiming that language held fundamental lessons that guided their daily lives as Navajo people: "We cannot leave behind the essence of our being" (McCarty et al., 2006, p. 28). Samuel, a participant in the McCarty et al. (2006) study, viewed language as a means for success (p. 35). Jonathan used Navajo as a way to "not get too far in, not to lose the identity of who I am, of where I come from" (p. 35). Not only vital to his identity, Jonathan also viewed his language as a way to "bring about positive change 'in this colonial world'" (McCarty et al., 2006, p. 36). Native youth within the Lee and Quijada Cerecer (2010) article also spoke passionately about learning and maintaining their traditional language as a link to their heritage but also as a means to preserve communication between themselves and elders within their communities (p. 202).

Though for some Native youth their language was a strong link to identity, for others the link was often marred by the dominance of English and the lack of language appreciation. Navajo youth often felt pressured to learn English in order to "make it in the Whiteman's world" (McCarty et al., 2006, p. 39). This left one student "confused" and questioning, "Where was I in the world" (McCarty et al., 2006, p. 39). The negativity of others with the students' language use left them wondering about the role of language in their world. Navajo students stated that "they're judged by it by other people that speak English more clear than they do and they just kind of feel dirty about the whole thing . . . and try to make it sound like they speak more English than they do Navajo" (McCarty et al., 2006, p. 38).

Another prominent theme throughout the articles was the role that culture played in the lives of Native youth—and their identity development. Though Dorian stated that her lack of fluency in the Hopi language "expressed a significant void in her cultural experiences" (Nicholas, 2009, p. 326), she proudly asserted that "I live Hopi, I just don't speak it" (p. 321). Dorian like many of the other Native youth were active participants in their traditional cultural activities and stated the importance of these activities on their identity as members within their community and as individuals. Justin, a Native youth within the Hopi community, connected the value of his cultural practices to his identity and being when he spoke about how he was grappling with the idea of moving away for college, "leaving this place and my farming, [and involvement in] the culture [activities], that just got to me" (Nicholas, 2009, p. 331). Hopi youth are immersed in the Hopi way of life from birth. Their involvement in ceremonial naming, ritual planting of corn by hand, and various song and dance ceremonies are considered key "cultural identity markers" (Nicholas, 2009, p. 328) that the youth avidly participated in.

Though Native youth were involved and connected within their communities, many of them wanted more of their culture and heritage within the classroom. They wanted to bring their identity: lives, lived experiences, cultures, histories, languages, families, Tribes, and so on into their learning. Brandon stated, "I'd like to walk in here and I'd like to see more Natives teaching Natives. I'd like to see information about our past and just things like that" (Lee & Quijada Cerecer, 2010, p. 202). The cultural teachings within one school in the Lee and Quijada Cerecer article allowed for the "strengthening cultural identity and self-confidence" (p. 203) among Native youth.

The last theme that we found throughout the articles was the role that adult–youth relationships played in the identity of Native youth. Within the Hopi community, the integral role that kinship values played ensured that "each of these youth had been encouraged and guided by a significant kin in conducting themselves according to Hopi standards" (Nicholas, 2009, p. 330). The adults and community members in the Hopi community were pivotal in the Native youth identity development. In the other four articles, it is this adult–youth relationship that students were longing for. Whether in the community or in the educational system, students spoke candidly about the role that these relationships played in their identity development as Native youth as well as their identity as students. "I don't know, it just seems like there are all these boundaries between students and teachers, teachers and administration . . . I think if we all worked together it would be better" (Lee & Quijada Cerecer, 2010, p. 203). William, a Navajo student, was very aware of the barriers between students and teachers. Erin wanted a much deeper connection with her teachers. "I wish we could get to know teachers, you know where they are from . . . things about how they grew up . . . why they are here teaching us. I want to learn from them but I also want to know them" (Quijada Cerecer, 2011, p. 175). The call of students for stronger relationships superseded the bounds of adult–youth relationships and called for cross-generational relationships that were resplendent and founded upon similarities, shared values, and reciprocity of understanding and respect. As was presented by the various Native youth, these reciprocal relationships were central to their development as youth and their own identity development (Quijada Cerecer, 2011, p. 178).

SYNTHESIS

All of these themes are connected within and across articles but most importantly are woven into one another. This makes it difficult to analyze these themes and connections separately. Instead, as the Native youth in these articles explain, it is the combination of all of these things that are important to their identity and learning. In our analysis we look more specifically at how language, culture, and relationships merge to create an environment that is either beneficial or toxic to the identity development of Native youth. We analyze that the conditions and assumptions that Native youth shared served as barriers or gateways to their identity.

As evident in Table 9.1, many of these articles have common themes, yet they are all different pieces to help us understand the larger state of Native youth identity and how Native youth experience the institution of schooling. In Noblit and Hare's (1987) terminology, they constitute a line of argument and taken together speak about more than any single article does. The first two articles talk about the impact of language on Native youth's identity. The first and fourth article talk about the impact of relationships on Native youth's identities. The third article focuses on cultural markers of identity, ways of being/living, and identity formation of Native youth. Together these articles share different perspectives of Native youth identity and the many Indigenous ways of being as well as the knowledge systems that Native youth value, are raised in, and live by daily. These articles show that when Native youth are connected to their cultures, histories, communities, languages, ways of being, and families, they have a stronger sense of self and who they are as Indigenous peoples and can act as advocates and change agents for their communities and Indigenous peoples worldwide.

Native youth enter into institutions of schooling where many of them are faced with expectations, policies, teaching styles, curriculums, and many other factors that do not match the ways of being, values, and cultural norms that they have been raised with. Therefore, their schooling experiences clash with their Native experiences and identities. Throughout these articles, Native youth reflect on their positive and negative experiences with being Native in school.

The first, fourth, and fifth articles discuss school climate and ideas for schooling and teaching. The first and fifth discuss school policies. All of the articles except for the third discuss the colonization that still exists in schools and the world. Native youth are constantly negotiating their identities in relation to dominant others. However, these articles do reveal what Native youth want their schooling experiences to be like so that they feel safe and supported—and so they can continue to grow and prosper. They want teachers, curriculum, schools, peers, institutions, classes, and other aspects to support their ways of knowing and what they bring with them, while learning more about their nations, languages, and cultures.

We identified three key aspects that are essential to the identity development of Native youth. In the next section we seek to synthesize the voices of the Native youth to delve deeper into the aspects of their identity while also showing the ways in which they are intricately woven together.

The "Missing Piece": Language

It is no secret that the atrocious historical events of assimilation and colonization have led to the near extinction of Native languages across the United States with many Tribes, in fact, completely losing their Native languages. The persistence of Native language is slowly waning, with few young people learning the language fluently. Within the articles presented by Nicholas (2009, p. 322) and McCarty et al. (2006), language and the role it plays within the identity development of Native American youth was the central focus.

Both articles presented the traditional Native language of the Navajo and the Hopi people as not only powerful in their impact on identity development but as a necessity for those identities. Previously used as a way to "identify the people—who we are, where we came from, and where we are going" (McCarty et al., 2006, p. 28), community members placed strong ties between the language and identity development. As stated by a Navajo elder, "If a child learns only English, you have lost your child" (McCarty et al., 2006, p. 29). Community members view language as a clear link to who they are as Native people. The Navajo youth saw their language as central to their identities (McCarty et al., 2006, p. 43) and also vital to understanding their way of life within the tribal community. This resonated also with the Hopi.

The impact of language on the identity development of Native youth, however, is being renegotiated by today's generation. Within both articles, elders and community members perceived the loss of language as the definitive loss of culture, summarized by the statement, "Once we've lost that, we have lost everything" (McCarty et al., 2006, p. 29) and by another Hopi grandparent who wanted to "confront youth with the questions, "Um himu? Um hintoqoovi qa Hopiituqayta?" ("What are you [a non-Hopi]? Why haven't you learned to speak Hopi?"; Nicholas, 2009, p. 324). Perceived as "tsaatsayom, children who, despite their chronological age, have not yet learned the precepts that guide one to think maturely and behave in a distinctively Hopi manner" (Nicholas, 2009, p. 324), Native youth who have yet to grasp the language of their tribal communities are often fighting an identity battle with both their communities and themselves. Defined as "the development of an emotional commitment to Hopi ideals—cultivated through the myriad practices that comprise the Hopi oral tradition" (Nicholas, 2009, p. 321), affective enculturation has assisted Native youth in their identity development despite the lack of their traditional language. Though plagued by the domination of the English language within today's modern society, Native youth, despite lacking a perceived essential part of their Native identity, their language, have nevertheless found ways to build their identity within their communities. Native youth within Nicholas's (2009) study had been encapsulated into the Hopi culture since birth. Through various cultural markers, such as "maternal clan identity, maternal village affiliation, birth and ceremonial names, ascribed roles established through the clan-kinship system" (p. 328), their identity begins taking shape the day they are born—even if they do not become fluent in the language.

Fighting the "White Man's Education": Indigenous Knowledge Systems

As is seen in the fight for language revitalization, modern society does not value traditional Native American language or ways of knowing. Today's educational system typically omits Indigenous knowledge systems from the curriculum

(Quijada Cerecer, 2011, p. 171). Thus youth are entering a classroom setting that is foreign from their home and community culture: "The Indigenous knowledge that youth bring to school each day remains invisible in curricula, textbooks, and policies" (Quijada Cerecer, 2013, p. 596). Within all of the studies, students were very aware of the hierarchy of knowledge systems within today's classroom.

"We should learn about our history and people. We never get to learn about this. If we aren't taught about our history at home, we don't even learn anything" (Quijada Cerecer, 2013, p. 602). These powerful words bring awareness to the lack of value and representation that is placed on Indigenous people and knowledge. "Why do we have to learn the White man's way? Why can't we learn our way?" (Quijada Cerecer, 2013, p. 602). This question is more than just a request. This desire to be affirmed as a Native resonated across the spectrum of youth in this meta-ethnography. The privileging and promotion of dominant bodies of knowledge renders invisible Native youth, their identities, their culture, and their voice.

The valuing of English within the classroom is also contributing to the loss of Native languages. The valuing of English within today's society is encouraging many adults to force Native youth to learn English as a means of survival (McCarty et al., 2006, p. 39). The struggle to assimilate to the dominant and expected culture coupled with the will to maintain their traditional language and culture plays a powerful role in Native youth identity development.

As mentioned, the current educational and community environment in which Native youth are growing up oftentimes suffocates their identity as Native people and stifles their ability to express themselves in a way that they feel inherently comfortable. Students voices were powerful when expressing the changes they wished to see in their schools and communities.

The suggestions from the Native youth were clear. "Students desired and advocated that schools place more emphasis on learning their Native language and history" (Lee & Quijada Cerecer, 2010, p. 202). The call for a culturally responsive educational setting would not only provide youth with the opportunity to learn about their culture within the classroom but would also seek to affirm and help the process of positive identity development as Native youth. Viewed as the merging of a student's home culture with their academic culture, culturally responsive schooling seeks to break down the hierarchy of knowledge systems by equally valuing all knowledge within the classroom.

The youth clearly understood the dire need to revitalize their language and its relevance to their identity as Navajo youth but needed "authentic caring—reciprocal, trusting, and respectful relations between youth and adults" (McCarty et al., 2006, p. 42). This need was magnified when one youth stated, "Elders say we're lost youth. No. We're only lost because [adults] won't take the time . . . to try to encourage us. . . . There's always hope" (McCarty et al., 2006, p. 42).

Students saw that teachers "don't want to take on that excess burden" (McCarty et al., 2006, p. 39). Samuel, a Navajo student, recognized that "administrators and teachers really don't have a one-on-one personal relationship with students" (p. 39) thus students were not encouraged to build relationships or to speak their traditional language, and they were not asked about their culture.

Students suggested building stronger relationships with adults with whom they interacted. This would give youth and adults the ability to not only understand each other but also to break the racialized identities that have long plagued the youth. Students sought out a community within their schools in order to build respectful and trusting reciprocal relationships (McCarty et al., 2006, p. 204). One youth stated, "I wish we could get to know teachers, you know where they are from . . . things about how they grew up . . . why they are here teaching us. I want to learn from them but I always want to know them" (Quijada Cerecer, 2011, p. 175).

An additional central part to engaged pedagogy and culturally responsive schooling within the classroom is a strong, trusting relationship between the adult and the youth. Not only prevalent throughout each article but extremely powerful as it relates to the development of Native American youth identity was adult–youth relationships. Presented in two different contexts, the discussion of adult–youth relationships in one article was discussed in relation to community members, family members, and elders (McCarty et al., 2006; Nicholas, 2009) and in relation to teachers, educators, and administrators (Quijada Cerecer, 2011, 2013; Lee & Quijada Cerecer, 2010).

Within the educational system, Native youth were avidly seeking adult–youth relationships and connections in order to not only help develop their identity but affirm their Native identity within the classroom. The discussion of teaching and relationships in Lee and Quijada Cerecer (2010) spoke loudly to the fact that the Native youth were "interested in establishing relationships that were reciprocal rather than one-sided" (p. 203). The development of trusting relationships within the educational system can allow educators to not only learn about the Native student as an individual but can help shape the work within the classroom to ensure that it is culturally relevant and conducive to the life and culture of the student.

The building of relationships between Native youth and adults not only creates a more positive environment within the school but also helps to reconfirm "the importance of understanding and valuing of Indigenous epistemologies" (Quijada Cerecer, 2011, p. 173). Through these relationships, Native youth and adults can work toward "culturally inclusive high school environments that diminish structural racism and produce socially conscious and productive citizens" (Quijada Cerecer, 2013, p. 609). Yet again, meeting the suggestion of the integration of culture within education as posed by the Native youth. Martha, a Navajo student, liked the "idea of coming into the school and seeing a lot of things that have to do with who I am" (Lee & Quijada Cerecer, 2010, p. 202).

Though yearning for trusting adult relationships and an engaging culturally relevant curriculum within their classrooms, Native youth met barriers to this goal in the form of racism, discrimination, and colonization.

The Scars of Racism, Discrimination, and Colonization: Social Identity

Within the classroom, students are fighting for much more than their opportunity to be represented in the curricula and textbooks. They are also fighting for much more than the ability to form trusting relationships with their educators. They are fighting a much deeper, long-standing battle. These youth are fighting the war against racism, discrimination, and colonization.

In order to better understand the context of the Native youth and the implications of language, culture, and adult–youth relationships on their identity, Quijada Cerecer (2013) posits that we must understand "the foundational cultural identities in the specific worlds they navigate (Holland et al., 1998) is essential to understanding their student identities and school-based experiences and recognizes how their identities have been constructed by and positioned against white middle-class values and culture" (p. 598). Thus far we have discussed how Native youth spoke about their language, culture, and adult relationships as being essential to their identity development in various, interwoven ways. We have also shown how, in various contexts, these essential parts of identity development for Native youth have been withheld from them. Quijada Cerecer states that the youths' experiences as they have been shared "illustrate how campus climates and instructional policies restrict and control Native students" (p. 601). The lack of culturally responsive schooling with these educational settings is prohibiting youth from connecting positively to their identity as Native youth and from sharing and learning their language and culture within the classroom; this leads to barriers within their adult–youth relationships that are based on preconceived racialized stereotypes of Native youth.

Students easily recognized that their Indigenous knowledge systems are not present or welcome within the classroom. The educational environment thus expects "Native youth to assimilate" to the dominant white middle-class culture (Quijada Cerecer, 2013, p. 602). Preconceived notions perpetuated by educators paint Native youth as uninterested and insufficient students. This dominant discourse within the school manifests itself by not integrating Indigenous knowledge into the curriculum, not valuing Indigenous languages, and building invisible barriers between students and their teachers. This discourse was also present within the communities in which elders and other adults saw an inherent value in the English language and sought instead to ensure that youth could "make it in the Whiteman's world" (McCarty et al., 2006, p. 39).

SUMMARY

Our goal in writing this chapter was to increase the understanding of Native American youth within today's society, particularly today's educational settings. We hoped to learn more about Native youth identity and factors that affect Native youth identity as described and defined by different youth from various Tribes. We know from experience that Native youth have a lot of amazing things to offer the current Native population, the world, and the future. We sought studies that shared positive research on/with Native youth identity.

Meta-ethnography provided us with a process to compare and contrast qualitative research. This process gave us the tools to look at the relationships between different qualitative research studies to find out what story was being told across the United States about Native youth. It also allowed us to identify studies that are not tainted by the dominant deficit narrative of Native American youth.

This meta-ethnography is a compilation of stories from five studies on or with Native youth that helps us to better understand their identity, factors that affect their identity, their experiences in school, and ways schools both colonize and support them and their identities. Through these articles, we have shown that Native youth are doing great things in their communities, have a deep understanding about their world, and are very clear about their needs. They make suggestions for how society, Tribes, youth and adults, and schools can better support and teach Native students.

Together these five articles form a line of argument. What we have learned from Native youth is that language, culture, and relationships are extremely important in Native youth identity and Native youth success. Native youth want schools to at the least be supportive of them and their knowledge. They want classes, curriculum, policies, teaching, and adult relationships in their schools that support their cultures, languages, histories, knowledges, and ways of being. These articles show that when Native youth are connected to their cultures, histories, communities, languages, ways of being, families, and so on they have a strong sense of self and who they are as Indigenous peoples and can act as advocates and change agents for their communities and Indigenous peoples worldwide.

Native youth's stories in all of these articles are best understood as the theories by which they live their lives. In these articles, the authors let the stories speak for themselves, allowing the youth to represent their Native youth identity and their experiences. The themes that emerged from the articles are language, ways of being, identity formation, cultural markers of identity, relationships, school climate, school policies, ideas for schooling and teaching, and colonization. Native youth (and the authors) articulated these into three key elements of their identity: language, Indigenous knowledge systems, and social identity.

CONCLUSION

To date, there are 567 federally recognized Tribes and many state-recognized Native American Tribes in the United States, each with their own distinctive culture and traditions. Thus we find it critical for the authors to explain the geographical as well as tribal context of the research participants. Though many aspects of this study can be shared across tribal lines, as Native and non-Natives the context of these studies is important. In doing so, researchers do not posit their findings and implications to be suitable for all Native youth and instead implicate that their research is contextualized by geographical location and Tribe. As is representative in most Native American research, the work in these five articles takes place in the southwestern United States and consequently is specific to the Navajo and Hopi Tribes of that area. We encourage Tribes and researchers to continue to look to all Native youth in all parts of the world to better understand who they are and what they are doing and saying.

For years, we have worked with Native youth within our own community as well as on a national level and are embracing the value in Native youth's voice. As southeastern Native women, it is very important for us to ensure that the voices of the Native youth have been and still are the primary focus and guide throughout our work. Indigenous people have long been spoken for, and we feel like it is time that we speak for ourselves. By listening to the voice of Native youth, we can ensure that their voices are expressed clearly and accurately.

All too often society, the media, researchers, teachers, and many others label Native youth by the challenges they are facing, the situations they are born into or living in, stereotypes of Native people, and many other negative factors. We know the value of Native youth's voice and we ask that readers listen to the voices of Native youth and look at them in a positive lens. They are the leaders of today and of our future.

REFERENCES

Center for Native American Youth. (2016, December). *Drawing strength from our cultures: The state of Native youth 2016.* State of Native Youth Report. Washington, DC: Center for Native American Youth at The Aspen Institute.

Holland D., Lachicotte W., Skinner D., & Cain C. (1998). *Identity and agency in cultural worlds.* Cambridge, MA: Harvard University Press.

Lee, T., & Cerecer, P. (2010). (RE) Claiming Native youth knowledge: Engaging in socio-culturally responsive teaching and relationships. *Multicultural Perspectives, 12*(4), 199–205.

McCarty, T. L., Romero, M. E., & Zepeda, O. (2006). Reclaiming the gift: Indigenous youth counter-narratives on Native language loss and revitalization. *The American Indian Quarterly, 30*(1), 28–48.

National Congress of American Indians. (n.d.). Tribal nations and the United States: An introduction. Retrieved from www.ncai.org retrieved

National Indian Education Association. (n.d.). Statistics on Native students. Retrieved from http://www.niea.org/Research/Statistics.aspx

Nicholas, S. E. (2009). "I live Hopi, I just don't speak it"—The critical intersection of language, culture, and identity in the lives of contemporary Hopi youth. *Journal of Language, Identity, and Education, 8*(5), 321–334.

Noblit, G. W., & Hare, R. D. (1988). *Meta-ethnography: Synthesizing qualitative studies.* Newbury Park, CA: SAGE.

Quijada Cerecer, P. D. (2011). Power in community building: Learning from indigenous youth how to strengthen adult-youth relationships in school settings. In A. Ball & C. Tyson (Eds.), *Studying diversity in teacher education* (pp. 171–182). Lanham, MD: American Educational Research Association.

Quijada Cerecer, P. D. (2013). The policing of native bodies and minds: Perspectives on schooling from American Indian youth. *American Journal of Education, 119*(4), 591–616.

10

The Denial of Competence

Race, Class, and Gender in the Construction of Smartness and Identity

BETH HATT ■

INTRODUCTION

Holland, Skinner, Lachicotte, and Cain (1998) define identity as "People tell others who they are, but even more important, they tell themselves and then try to act as though they are who they say they are" (p. 3). Our multiple identities can include being a mother, an athlete, a teacher, or a *smart* student. The interests of this chapter are focused on the latter and predicated upon the premise that the identities students adopt or reject around notions of ability powerfully shape and influence student experiences in schools.

Historically, ideas about intelligence or smartness have largely been framed by the field of psychology and connected to notions of biology and genetics (Gould, 1996). More recently, questions have been raised about the reification of smartness as something "real" and "objective" to instead claims of smartness being culturally shaped and produced. Within this cultural framing of smartness, a new area of research looking at the linkages between smartness and identity in schooling has emerged. Within this chapter, this new field of research is examined utilizing meta-ethnography as a method.

Meta-ethnography involves a synthesis of qualitative studies on a certain topic chosen by the researcher. Using an interpretive lens, meta-ethnography goes well beyond traditional notions of literature reviews that attempt to report "what is" to a reconceptualization of the studies as "data" to be analyzed (Doyle, 2003). Researchers examine the articles for the major metaphors utilized, taken-for-granted assumptions, key questions left unasked, and theoretical gaps in understanding to name a few of the possibilities. Keeping with the traditions of qualitative inquiry, my positionality and its connections to this research are discussed first. Second, the methodological process of conducting the meta-ethnography is discussed, followed by the key themes that arose from a synthesis of the articles including a reconceptualization of identity. Finally, the claims to a line of argument synthesis are provided.

Positionality

Meta-ethnography, like all research, involves layers of interpretation. Noblit and Hare (1988) state, "A meta-ethnography based in notions of translating studies into one another will inevitably be partially a product of the synthesizer" (p. 25) Who I am as the researcher shapes the interpretations found within this chapter. Rather than something to be avoided as within the positivist paradigm, interpretivism is less concerned with escaping bias and more concerned with the importance of being transparent about our biases (Fine, 1994; Peshkin, 1988). To be transparent, I attempt to provide a description of my identities in relation to this project.

Noblit (2004) states that "[M]ethods are ideas and theories in themselves. They have histories, are best understood as tentative, and are not separate from the theories they are used to test or explore" (p. 183). This meta-ethnography is no different; my methodology and paradigmatic framework intricately connect. I conducted my work utilizing a postcritical ethnographic/theoretical framework or approach. By postcritical, I mean a research epistemology that critiques dominant ideology and structures of power while simultaneously acknowledging that my critique is socially situated and constructed as well (Noblit, Flores, & Murillo, 2004). I have a critical framework in that I purposively wanted to conduct this meta-ethnography to expose "power" within perceptions of smartness. I want my research to work against oppressive ideologies such as notions of "intelligence" or "smartness" while also aiming to create change by making the hidden explicit and encouraging self-reflection in how we think about "being smart."

My positionality arises out of being female, cisgender, and heterosexual and growing up White, rural, and working class. Growing up, I desperately wanted to be smart—perhaps as a way to work against the shame I felt in knowing my family was working class. Although never identified as "gifted" in elementary school, I placed into honors courses throughout middle and high school, which gave me affirmation that I was "smart." I greatly benefitted from this affirmation, which helped me to believe that I was capable of being the first person in my family to go to college. I never once questioned the fairness of my placement. Sadly, the majority of working-class or first-generation college students do not receive affirmation that they are "smart" while in school.

In college, I struggled with how to negotiate my identities of being working-class and a college student. I continued with honors programming while in college and quickly realized I was like a fish out of water. To be perceived as "smart," I felt I had to change my styles of dress and ways of speaking valued in my rural home community. I tried to hide where I was from and would even go so far as to lie to cover it up.

It was not until graduate school that I began to shift from seeing my working-class background as a deficit to instead being a strength. Within this shift, I began to question normative notions of smartness. I began to challenge the idea that smartness only comes through schooling rather than personal experience. The ways elitism in the academy and schools frames valuable knowledge as academic rather than experiential is personal to me because within this framework my parents and grandparents are not framed as smart. My identities, as with most researchers, firmly frame what I believe is worth researching and how to conduct research. I have made the study of smartness one of my key research programs. As I study smartness and identity, my identities and lived experiences are lenses for my questioning and analysis.

Method: Meta-Ethnography

According to Noblit and Hare (1988), meta-ethnography involves seven phases. *Phase 1* includes identifying an intellectual interest. The intellectual interest determined for this chapter was to better understand the connections between identity, constructions of smartness, and K-12 schooling.

During *phase 2* the parameters are determined for how qualitative studies will be selected. Overall, the following terms were used to search for the articles: youth, identity, smart*, ethnograph*, qual*, and intelligence*. The terms were initially searched over five databases: ERIC, Sociological Abstracts, Abstracts in Anthropology, PsychINFO, and Academic Search Premier. Peer-reviewed articles that were grounded in ethnographies and centered identity and smartness, ability, and/or intelligence for their analyses were selected. The initial search revealed only five articles that met the criteria. Knowing of other articles that met the criteria but did not arise in the initial searches, an additional search was conducted with Google Scholar. A total of eight articles met the criteria and were included in the analysis. All of the articles were published in education journals except for two published in the field of communication. Six of the articles were based on research with middle and high school students while two of them focused on elementary school settings.

During *phase 3*, the studies were read carefully with particular attention to the ways identity and smartness were described and analyzed. *Phase 4* (i.e., determining how the studies are related) and *phase 5* (i.e., translating the studies into one another) involved approaching the synthesis more like an interpretive ethnography (Savin-Baden & Major, 2007), and thus the articles were analyzed according to Wolcott's (1994) approach to data analysis and interpretation.

Wolcott's (1994) first step is "description" and asking the question, "What is going on here?" In this step, a summary was written for each of the articles, and then they were coded to look for metaphors related to "identity" and "smartness." Focusing on language singularly through metaphors did not seem sufficient, so this piece of the analysis was expanded to include the language the articles used when referring to identity and ability as well. Additionally, key quotes from the articles highlighting the theorizing of identity and ability were included. The second step, analysis, asks the question, "How do things work?" (Wolcott, 1994). The findings across each of the articles were displayed using tables based on metaphors and additional language referring to identity and ability, the theorizing of identity, the theorizing of ability, and recommendations for practice. Then analytic memos were written for each of the tables focusing on the central questions of "What is going on?" and "How do things work?"

The third and final step of analysis involves interpretation of the data and asks the question, "What is to be made of it all?" (Wolcott, 1994). It was within this step that *phase 6* (i.e., synthesizing translations) was addressed. The tables and analytic memos were thoroughly reviewed, and numerous notes were written up regarding the various interpretations plausible when synthesizing the studies. In this phase, I determined that a refutational translation was not appropriate as the articles built upon one another and did not counter key findings within them.

In *phase 7* (i.e., expressing the synthesis), I discussed the analysis with one of the book editors, and a line-of-argument (Noblit & Hare, 1988) approach to the interpretation was determined to be the best approach because the ethnographies were all undertaken to "say something" about the constructions of identity and ability in schools. The line of argument offers a culminating synthesis of what the articles "say" about identity and ability holistically.

The Meta-Ethnographic Turn

Noblit and Hare (1988) state that meta-ethnography provides an opportunity "to talk to each other about our studies; to communicate to policy makers, concerned citizens, and scholars what interpretive research reveals; and to reflect on our collective craft and the place of our own studies within it" (p. 14). These points explain what I refer to as *the meta-ethnographic turn*. Qualitative research in the past three decades has been characterized as experiencing a paradigmatic shift known as the "interpretivist turn" where notions of objectivity are replaced with an emphasis on co-constructions of meaning and reflexivity in the research process (Mottier, 2005). Meta-ethnography, I believe, offers a similar turn in how qualitative researchers think about and process interpretivist qualitative scholarship.

We are typically trained as academic writers and researchers to conduct literature reviews and to examine our fields of study as postpositive interpretations. We often do a Malinowski-like reading of the literature and our fields of study that includes simply reporting and synthesizing an external reality or object. Meta-ethnography, however, asks us to look through an interpretivist lens, where our fields of study are co-constructions of meaning and self-reflexivity in our interpretations of the literature is essential. Typically, we think of qualitative research as having three layers of co-constructed meaning: participants, researchers, and readers. The meta-ethnographic turn adds a fourth layer of meaning by the meta-ethnographer but not of an individual study but a *field* of study. The fourth layer of meanings allows for a unique interpretivist reconceptualization of the taken for granted within a field, a broader interpretivist questioning of the area of study, and a deeper probe into the holes and assumptions that lie within.

The meta-ethnographic turn includes a shift in the audience as well. Noblit and Hare (1988) make it clear that meta-ethnography is primarily for interpretivists with no apologies. It is a purposeful turn away from the postpositivist practice of trying to make qualitative research more "scientific." Noblit and Hare go to great lengths to explain how meta-ethnography is conceptually similar but paradigmatically very different than postpositivist meta-analyses of quantitative research. For these reasons, the term "analysis" is replaced with the term "translation." I find "translation" to be an appropriate metaphor for meta-ethnography because the process involves a "translation" of discourse and language used within a field of study to conceptualize or frame particular concepts and understandings. "Translation" requires an unpacking of the co-construction of meaning that is personal whereas "analysis" implies the image of a removed investigator of a reality that is stable and fixed.

Finally, meta-ethnography as an interpretivist endeavor must be personal and reflexive. The most challenging aspect of meta-ethnography for me has been trying to work against myself as I work through the fourth layer of meaning making regarding a field of study (i.e., smartness) that I am embedded within and includes my own scholarship. I am one of the few chapter authors that attempted to do meta-ethnography on my own, despite contrary advice from Drs. Noblit and Urrieta. I have learned through this process that conducting a meta-ethnography does not lend itself to single authorship. Closely tied to the shift in the audience is a change of authorship. The interpretive nature of the work and construction of the fourth layer of meaning becomes much richer when one adds additional voices and subjectivities. Sole authorship does not truly allow for the complexity of meaning that meta-ethnography aims to achieve. The meta-ethnographic turn requires shared authorship and collaboration in ways that other forms of qualitative research do not.

Overview of Articles

Some interesting patterns emerged from the article search. First, all of the articles were published in the past 13 years, with over half published just within the past five years. Date of publication was not included as a limiting factor because purposeful attention was heeded to look at the development of ideas around identity and smartness over time. The recent dates and lack of research on this topic before 2003 suggest it is a developing, newer line of research.

A significant subset of articles also arose that focused on notions of "acting White" and academic achievement by students of color, Black students in particular. These articles spanned a greater time frame and are critical for understanding the ways race, identity, and academic achievement intersect. A decision was made not to include this subset of articles in the analysis because, although important, they did not center the concept of smartness or constructions of students' perceived abilities within their analyses. They should, of course, be candidates for a later synthesis effort.

Finally, the selected articles cut across different content areas in schools including science, math, language arts, and vocational education, suggesting identity and smartness play out across subject areas in schools. Participants crossed a broad range of demographics including age, race, and gender. Overall, the relationship between identity and smartness is undertheorized and understudied. This meta-ethnography provides a solid foundation for future research on the topic.

It is important to note that two of the articles were my own. My approach to this was to treat them in the same way as the other articles and not to privilege them in the synthesis. As with my positionality, I do not claim that I was objective about this—only careful—in the best sense of this word.

SYNTHESIS OF THE ARTICLES

Table 10.1 was created to look across the articles for the main metaphors or concepts used in relation to identity and smartness. Core metaphors and concepts related to smartness across the articles included street smarts versus book smarts, practical versus theoretical knowledge, smartness as a game, discursive constructions of stigma, smartness as a tool for social positioning and control of students, definitions of knowledgeable versus struggling students, and good students as producing answers versus asking more questions. Looking across these metaphors, I was able to determine connections between smartness and how the social construction of both knowledge and ability are intricately related.

As a result, I named two key themes through the synthesis: *epistemologies of schooling* and *teacher power* in shaping student identities. Epistemologies of schooling refer to the ways valuable knowledge and ways of knowing were defined as typically linked to whether students were perceived as "smart" or "dumb." Examples of this through the articles is explored in more depth later in this section. Second, perceptions of knowledge and students' abilities were often directed by teachers. Teachers have the power to influence what counts as valuable knowledge in their classrooms and to shape how students are positioned as smart or dumb. It was a common thread through all of the articles although it was not always explicitly named and resulted in the theme of teacher power.

Key metaphors for identity were identified as well and included such concepts as intellectual border crossers, intellectually weak versus strong students, schooled versus unschooled identities, mathematically dumb versus mathematically smart, and smart science student. Almost every metaphor related perceptions of ability to students' identities, which I labeled as the theme *learning as identity production*. Race, class, and gender were central to the ways ability, identity, and achievement interacted to shape students' understanding of such concepts such as "smart," "dumb," "failure," and "good student," which are interwoven among the discussion of the key themes.

Table 10.1 OVERVIEW OF ARTICLES

Authors	Title	Journal	Participants
Godley (2003)	Literacy learning as gendered identity work	*Communication Education*	High school English class
Harter et al. (2005)	The structuring of invisibility among the hidden homeless: The politics of space, stigma, and identity construction	*Journal of Applied Communication Research*	High school homeless youth
Hatt (2007)	Street smarts vs. book smarts: The figured world of smartness in the lives of marginalized, urban youth	*The Urban Review*	GED program— young adults
Korp (2011)	What counts as being smart around here? The performance of smartness and masculinity in vocational upper secondary education	*Education, Citizenship, and Social Justice*	High school vocational education
Carlone et al. (2011)	Assessing equity beyond knowledge and skills-based outcomes: A comparative ethnography of two fourth-grade reform-based science classrooms	*Journal of Research in Science Teaching*	Two fourth-grade classrooms
Bishop (2012)	"She's always been the smart one. I've always been the dumb one": Identities in the mathematics classroom	*Journal for Research in Mathematics Education*	Two female middle school students
Hatt (2012)	Smartness as a cultural practice in schools	*American Education Research Journal*	Kindergarten classroom
Carrillo (2013)	I always knew I was gifted: Latino males and the Mestiz@ Theory of Intelligences (MTI)	*Berkeley Review of Education*	Eight high-achieving Latino males—young adults

Epistemologies of Schooling

Epistemology relates to how we come to understand the world and seek to know the world through our developed worldviews and lived experiences (Ladson-Billings, 2000). Within schools, decisions are made about what epistemologies are valuable and worthy of affirmation (Bernal, 2002). Four out of the six articles directly addressed the ways traditional epistemologies in schools are used to frame smartness in a way that can leave low-income students and students of color feeling devalued and denied the identity of being a "smart" student.

In three of the articles (Harter et al., 2005; Hatt, 2007; Korp, 2011), the authors specifically addressed the ways "street smarts" are often devalued in school settings. Korp's article examined the ways notions of intelligence and smartness were culturally produced in a Swedish vocational, secondary education program. According to the author, many of the White, working-class youth before entering the program had been framed as "weak learners," and this influenced their identities as learners negatively. The vocational secondary school provided students an opportunity to rebuild their damaged confidence as learners. The authors discovered that smartness in the vocational school was framed as differing from traditional notions that connect smartness to academic knowledge. This alternative definition included power of action, independence, and a certain linguistic habitus. Some of the alternative valued skills included creative problem-solving, effective communication skills, a sense of humor related to working-class lived experience, and being able to complete their work and solve problems independently.

The students also tended to dichotomize knowledge in terms of being practical versus theoretical. Many of the students claimed to be smart with "practical things" or "with their hands" but not smart when it came to academic subjects or theoretical knowledge. This dichotomization led many students not to consider furthering their education, as they associated the university with theoretical knowledge.

Harter et al. (2005) conducted ethnographic research regarding youth homelessness and identity construction. Through the interviews with the youth, the authors identified numerous characteristics of being street smart. These included reliance on instincts to read a situation, preparedness, adaptability, heightened awareness of surroundings, and the ability to blend into one's surroundings. Many of the youth expressed pride in the street smarts they had developed through their difficult life circumstances. For example, one teen told the researchers, "You couldn't survive for a day in our world on your book smarts" (p. 321).

An important implication for practice that arose from this article was that not a single educator interviewed ever acknowledged street smarts as a valuable resource for the youth. In fact, the teachers focused on the importance for the homeless youth to master reading, writing, and arithmetic, what the youth referred to as book smarts, but never acknowledged street smarts as a valuable way of operating in the world and as a source of knowledge. The authors stated, "The rules and resources of mainstream education too often fall short of recognizing street smarts as an authentic form of knowledge" (Harter et al., 2005, p. 321). In doing so, the educators alienated the youth and were not successful in building relationships with them based on trust and mutual respect.

Hatt's (2007) ethnography of a GED program explored notions of smartness by the students. All of the participants in the study were from working-class backgrounds, and the majority of participants were Black. The author states, "Every student that is a part of the institution of schooling develops an academic identity that helps to shape who we think we are, who others think we are, and who we think we should become" (p. 146). Through the interviews with the youth, Hatt identified artifacts that the youth associated with being "smart" in school. The artifacts included grades, diplomas, labels (i.e., gifted or honors), standardized test scores, books, extensive vocabulary, and participation in college-prep courses. According to the article, these artifacts operate as semiotic mediators and "are what make smartness appear real and as something tangible or biologically based rather than as something socio-culturally produced" (p. 151).

The author analyzed how the youth responded to the dominant discourse around smartness in schools that operated to frame the youth as not smart. The youth made clear distinctions between being street smart versus book smart. The youth defined street smarts as being able to maneuver structures in their lives such as poverty, the police, street culture, and abusive people. Furthermore, street smarts were based upon valuing knowledge gained through personal experience rather than being based on a book or curriculum.

Racialized Lived Experience as Intelligence

In addition to highlighting the importance of valuing student knowledge gained through experience related to street smarts, an additional article (Carrillo, 2013) highlighted the ways racial, class, and gendered identities are connected to ways of knowing. Specifically, the article emphasizes how low-income, Latino male students are not allowed "smart" identities because their dominant ways of knowing and lived experiences are typically not included within notions of being smart or competent students in schools.

Arising from a larger ethnographic study, this article focuses on three case studies of Latino scholarship boys. The author proposes a new form of intelligence called the Mestiz@ Theory of Intelligences, which the author claims arise from the ways "Oppression, poverty, and segregated lives serve as a laboratory for the development of gifted identities" (Carrillo, 2013, p. 89). Specifically, the author claims these forms of intelligence arise out of personal experiences in relation to being Latino, working class, and male growing up in the United States. They are born out of hybridity, cultural trespassing, and efforts to not "sell out" by allowing one's mind to be colonized. The author critiques Howard Gardener's (2011) multiple intelligences framework for the ways it does not center or even consider issues of identity. In particular, the author claims Gardener's multiple intelligences are framed within Western, Cartesian ideologies and ways of knowing. Carrillo states that "Current ways of defining smart students has disenfranchised many Latin@s whose intelligence includes navigating through the educational system while seeking power and dignity in spaces outside of subtractive schooling environments" (p. 91).

Each of the articles demonstrates the ways students are devalued and left feeling incompetent and marginalized when teachers do not perceive all students as knowledge holders. When teachers do not recognize students' lived experiences outside of the classrooms as forms of knowledge and understanding to tap into and, instead, as being less important than "book" smarts, they miss the opportunity to allow working-class students and students of color in their classrooms to perform as smart or competent. By marginalizing the knowledges and ways of understanding students develop outside of the classroom, teachers denigrate who students are (i.e., their identities) and participate in the racialization of youth.

Learning as Production of Identity

A second key theme highlighted not just that learning and identity are connected but that there was an even stronger connection where learning could be defined as the production of identity—learning and identity production as synonymous. As identities are developed through our daily practices (Holland et al., 1998), so are our identities in classrooms. As teachers structure activities and practices in classrooms for learning, they are, in essence, structuring practices that shape identity. In the practices of learning, students are developing identities in relationship to those practices. As patterns occur within those practices, different identities "thicken" for students over time. Our identities are core to how we make meaning in the world, and learning is the making of meaning. As a result, learning does not occur outside of the shaping of identity.

Carlone, Haun-Frank, and Webb (2011) discovered in their work that identity was at the center of elementary students' learning during science class. The authors asked readers to reconceptualize equity away from "knowledge and skills outcomes" and instead "to center questions about culture and identity" (p. 460) as result of their research. The authors' conducted ethnographies in two fourth-grade, reform-based science classrooms to study the culturally produced meanings of "science" and "science person." The authors also situated identity specifically within science classrooms and defined it as "culturally produced meanings of 'science person' and the accessibility of those meanings" (p. 460).

Carlone et al. (2011) discovered that despite both teachers using a reform-based approach to science, the culturally produced meaning of a "smart science student" varied widely between both classrooms. Additionally, students who performed well on assessments did not necessarily identify themselves as a "smart science student," which was especially true for students of color in one class in particular. Carlone et al. claim close attention should be paid to "the cultural production of science student. Instead of asking, 'Who's smart,' we ask, 'Who's being given opportunities to perform themselves as smart? Who takes up opportunities to perform as smart? Who gets recognized as smart and why?'" (p. 483). They discovered that how the teachers structured learning practices and smartness in the classroom directly influenced the engagement and identities of students of color. Despite both teachers using a reform-based science approach, the production of students' identities around science and being smart were powerful influences on student engagement and achievement. These findings suggest that the classroom practices enacted by both teachers around science were more important than the assessments and actual achievement outcomes in students developing their identities as "smart science people." A more thorough discussion of the differences in practice is provided in the next section.

Hatt's (2012) article builds upon Carlone et al.'s (2011) in that the research examined notions of identity in relation to classroom management at the elementary level. In Hatt's article, the cultural construction of smartness in a kindergarten classroom was examined based on a one-year classroom ethnography. Hatt studied implicit theories of intelligence—everyday, informal perceptions of someone's intelligence. The author framed smartness as operating like a verb, rather than a noun, as "something *done* to others as social positioning" (p. 2).

Within the classroom, Hatt (2012) studied important artifacts representing smartness that developed powerful meaning for students. The two most powerful artifacts were the stoplight, used for classroom management, and the shoe-tyers club, with membership being a reward for students who could independently tie their shoes. The stoplight provided a constant visual reminder in the classroom of who was smart and who was not. Students who were able to keep their "cars" on green were framed as smart by children and the teacher while children who had to move their cars regularly (and all of the children could identify who those students were) were believed not to be as smart as the other kids.

As for the shoe-tyers club, membership in the club was framed as a "big" deal but how to tie one's shoes was never taught within the class. For this reason, whether students could be a part of the club was largely determined by home circumstances. "The concept of 'smartness' makes one's ability to tie shoes seem based upon one's innate 'smartness' rather than familial circumstances and teacher implementation" (Hatt, 2012, p. 15). The artifacts demonstrate how smartness operated as a "tool of social positioning" to assign social status to children. Hatt's article highlights that the ways teachers' frame classroom management and classroom practices are a vital part of learning and identity in the classroom. Through making the behavioral mishaps and lack of shoe-tying skills public and a regular practice in the classroom, the teachers were constructing students' identities as "failures" or "dumb" not just to be internalized by individual students but internalized by all members of the classroom community toward individual students. The students who were regularly framed as "failures" began to resist school by not wanting to attend or acting out further in the classroom. Finally, students of color and working-class students were more likely to be framed as "failures" within this classroom because these students were more likely to be a "fish out of water" regarding the White middle-class norms for student behavior in the classroom. Additionally, because the teacher did not always value the ways of being students brought into the classroom by students of color and working-class White students, these students were more likely to be framed in a deficit mindset with lower expectations (Valencia, 2012).

Bishop (2012), based on a larger qualitative study, builds upon Hatt (2012) and Carlone et al. (2011) by highlighting the importance of identity, smartness, and mathematical-learning classroom practices. Bishop's research focused on discourse analysis of two female middle school students in math class. Bishop claims learning is directly connected to how students develop identities across different subject areas. She states, "Learning goes beyond constructing new and flexible understanding and entails becoming a different person in relation to the norms, practices, and modes of interaction than the disciplines of mathematics, reading, history, and science" (p. 36). Bishop defines what she refers to as a *mathematics identity*, related to "the ideas, often tacit, one has about who he or she is with respect to the subject of mathematics and its corresponding activities" (p. 39). This is an interesting concept in that it implies students develop specific, multiple identities in relation to different subject areas in school. As a result, Carlone et al.'s study can be framed in a new light because it reinforces Bishop's claim that students develop multiple identities around ability toward different content areas. Both studies suggest that students' overarching identities around smartness are thickened or countered based on their experiences in different classes and content areas.

Bishop (2012) also draws interesting connections between notions of ability or smartness and mathematics identity. The author states, regarding one of her participants,

> Teri enacted her identity of the mathematically "smart one" by leveraging subtle discursive moves and positioning herself as mathematically knowledgeable . . . Bonnie enacted her identity as the mathematically "dumb one" through the familiar actions of waiting for more knowledgeable others to act and make decisions, participating primarily in low-level ways, frequently surrendering her freedom to direct mathematical action, and having her ideas ignored. (p. 66).

Within these discursive moves, students came to see themselves as either mathematically "smart" or "dumb" or began to resist these classifications.

Like Bishop, Godley (2003) explored through discourse analysis how high school students enrolled in an 11th-grade honors English class negotiated gendered identities within classroom literacy practices. The idea of "positions" was used to highlight "the sense that how we are seen and how we present ourselves are determined by social context and the people around us" (p. 275). A key position students used to describe either themselves or other students was "smart student" (p. 276).

Godley's (2003) research highlighted the ways students were able to position themselves and be positioned by others as "smart" students. In the high school, students who were White and male and who came from affluent backgrounds were more likely to be positioned by students and teachers as "smart," especially if they participated in whole-group discussions. One student, Steve, a football player, took up the position of "smart student" "through consistent bidding for turns at talk during whole-class discussion and volunteering to answer teacher questions" (p. 278). This was especially true if Steve answered whole-group questions by the teacher when other students were hesitant to do so. During small-group discussions, Steve positioned himself as "smart" by taking a leadership role in setting topics, making decisions for the group, and recognizing other students'

speaking rights. However, this was harder for Steve to do in the small-group settings because many of his friends were "more academically successful than he and
known as skilled debaters" (p. 279). Interestingly, this resulted in Steve talking
more about football during small-group discussions as it allowed him to claim
"power and superiority over other males . . . in the face of being denied . . . that of
smart student" (p. 280).

Another student in the same class, Eun-Jin, who was an adopted daughter of a
teacher in the school, struggled to position herself as a good debater or "smart"
in the class as it was strongly associated with masculinity—being competitive and
individualistic. Within the class, female students, who made up the majority of
the students, contributed less than 50% of student turns at talking during whole-
class discussions. In the end, despite having strong debate skills and being a part
of the debate team, Eun-Jin often excluded herself from this social category.

Each of the articles discussed in this section cut across elementary, middle, and
high school levels with all of them demonstrating the interrelatedness of identity
and learning. More specifically, an identity of being smart or competent in classrooms is a prerequisite for student engagement and a positive sense of belonging in school. Students regularly position themselves and others in the academic
environment as "competent" or "incompetent," often framed within the classic
binary of smart/dumb. In classrooms where teachers do not purposefully set up a
classroom culture and classroom activities where all students feel competent and
position each other as competent, inequities related to class, race, and gender are
produced such as those described in these articles. By not centering identity and
recognizing it as key to learning, teachers inhibit learning, especially for students
who are often decentered in the classroom and curriculum such as students of
color and women.

Teacher Power in Shaping Student Identities

Each of the articles revealed the connections between teacher practice and the
identities students developed. The practices the teachers implemented represent a
complex mixture regarding beliefs about knowledge, student behavior, learning,
and relationships with students.

Bishop's (2012) research revealed that the overall pedagogical practices of the
teacher and the ways being "smart" at math were defined in the classroom helped
to shape the discursive moves students made. These practices and constructions
included whether needing help, making mistakes, and asking questions were consistent or inconsistent with the notion of being smart or competent at math. In the
classroom studied, they were not. As a result, students, when seeing themselves as
"dumb" or "not good" at math, were more likely to avoid difficult tasks, to abstain
from seeking help, and to disengage within math class.

Godley (2003) states in her article based on a high school English class,
"Teachers need to be aware of the subject positions that students hold outside of
the classroom for these come to shape students' classroom discourse, their literacy

learning, and their sense of themselves as students" (p. 284). In the classroom Godley studied, the teacher did not monitor whole-class and small-group discussions to ensure all students were given equitable chances to respond and that a culture of respect was established within the conversations. As a result, female students and students who struggled with debate-style discourse, "contributed far less and became more withdrawn and resentful as the semester progressed" (p. 284).

Hatt (2012) examined smartness as a particular discourse within a kindergarten classroom and discovered the discourse of smartness operated as a "tool of social control" through the teachers framing "smart" students as those who obeyed authority (i.e., teachers), which was connected to maintaining a docile body and, if modeled appropriately, then "smart" kids could become authority figures in the classroom and be asked to take on special roles of leadership. Additionally, smartness related to a student's prior knowledge of taught material. Students who were already able to demonstrate mastery of kindergarten learning standards *before* being taught were announced publicly to be "geniuses" and "so smart."

Within the kindergarten classroom, smartness was used by the teachers to assign social power across students and to maintain authoritative control. An essential part of maintaining control involved displaying student performance publicly through a stoplight on the wall to remind everyone who misbehaved and a list of students who were in the shoe-tyers club. Students were framed as "smart" directly connected to race and class, with the students who had the most similar backgrounds and cultural capital as of the teacher were framed as the "smartest." As a result, White middle-class female students were more likely to be framed as "smart." Within the kindergarten classroom, students learned what it meant to be "smart" and whether they were smart themselves, as determined by the teacher and the culture she, along with the students, created in the classroom.

Carlone et al. (2011) studied fourth-grade science classrooms and discovered fundamental differences between the classes including an individualistic versus communal approach to learning science. The classroom where students of color were least likely to identify as a "smart science person" despite high academic achievement, constructed the meaning that science people "figure things out themselves and do not necessarily get ideas from others or productively share ideas with others" (p. 469).

The authors observed two African American female students offering to help other groups, but, most often, their efforts were rebuked and by the end of the unit these two girls' interest in finding quick solutions and sharing them had faded. Alternatively, Doug, a White male student from a wealthy background, who perceived himself as a "smart" science person, told the researchers that "scientific investigation is conducted in the service of discovering and constructing knowledge on one's own, holding those discoveries and knowledge private until the whole group debriefs, and then displaying the knowledge for the teacher" (Carlone et al., 2011, p. 469). Alternatively, in the other classroom, the teacher expected the students to "not to take turns with the tools" but instead to conduct the experiments as a collective group, with each person taking on different roles. Students in her class regularly used the pronoun "we" to describe what they learned rather than "I." In this teacher's classroom, students were "held accountable for critically listening to and jointly constructing knowledge with their partners in small groups and whole groups" (p. 471). Students of color, including English-language learners, were more likely to be engaged and to see themselves as "scientists."

Additionally, the two classrooms held very different cultural constructions around the purpose of sharing scientific ideas. In the classroom where students of color struggled, the primary goals were "to get to 'the' right answer; and to prove *to the teacher* that you were thinking, but more importantly, knew the answer" (Carlone et al., 2011, p. 474). In this teacher's class, the purpose of scientific investigation was to come up with the "right" answer. "Students with the 'right' answer, phrased in the 'right' way received the highest validation" (p. 476). In this way, sharing was not necessarily a safe endeavor with the teacher's role as that of validating the "right" ideas. As a result, some children were legitimized more often than others. The result was that "a scientific person, therefore, was the one who most often produced the answers. Our interpretations here are supported by students' descriptions of 'smart science people'. . . as those who held the most knowledge and most often produced the right answers" (p. 476).

In the more equitable classroom, the purpose of the scientific investigation was not to necessarily find the "right" answer but to ask more questions. In this classroom, scientific investigation "did not always have an endpoint; it opened up opportunities for more questions and investigation" (Carlone et al., 2011, p. 478). Additionally, the teacher framed scientific knowledge as "generative" and "social" while purposefully contesting "know-it-all" attitudes. As a result, students defined a "science person" more broadly as "someone who makes careful, insightful observations, and asks good questions" (p. 478).

These studies reveal that when learning and smartness are defined as getting the right answer to be determined by the teacher or knowing the content before it is taught, inequities around race, class, and gender are created by the privileging of knowledge embedded in whiteness and class privilege. Through these practices, teachers are structuring the identities available to students via race, class, and gender. Additionally, classrooms where teachers do not purposefully work against a competitive atmosphere between students around notions of smartness and/or ability, inequities of race, class, and gender are created through the structuring of identity. When teachers center their identities and frame themselves as *the* holder of knowledge while encouraging teacher-pleasing behavior, racial, class, and gender inequities are created. Finally, when teachers publicly shame students for misbehavior or for struggling academically, these students are framed as incompetent to everyone present in the room and, as a result, this shapes the identities of students as "trouble makers." Classroom teachers who purposefully and regularly counter these practices are more likely to have equitable classrooms where students of color, girls, and low-income students are more engaged and given the opportunity to perform as competent or smart within the classroom.

Reconceptualizing Identity

When looking across the articles studied, a fundamental weakness was a lack of precise framing and theorizing regarding identity. A few of the articles never defined identity or named a clear theoretical framework for how identity was being conceptualized. Within the articles that did have clear theoretical frames, there was rarely a critique offered of the theoretical frames or an expansion upon the ways identity might be theorized or understood differently.

Overwhelmingly identity within all of the articles was mostly framed within notions of multiplicity, but notions of "thickening" or more stable identities versus shifting identities were largely undertheorized. Holland et al. (1998) frame these differences in identity as positional versus figurative. Positional identities are associated with social categories (i.e., race, class, gender, and sexual orientation) connected to power and often cut across cultural worlds. On the other hand, figurative identities are unique to particular cultural worlds and are more likely to shift across cultural worlds. For example, the positional identity of being a Black woman in the United States would probably be more stable across multiple spaces and cultural worlds versus the figurative identity of being "smart," which could easily shift from a schooling context to a more local context in the community. For example, an African American male student may not be perceived as smart in school but is viewed as knowledgeable and quick-witted in his local community, which represents shifting figurative identities. However, it is unlikely the student would change his positional identities of being African American and male across contexts.

I argue that positional identities should be considered "anchor" identities that then heavily *determine* what figurative or, what I refer to as "localized," identities are available within different cultural worlds. Anchor identities are more static and less fluid across institutions and cultural worlds. Our anchor identities actively determine what possible identities are available to us within institutions and cultural worlds. Holland and Lave (2001) claim that some identities are more stable across time and place, "not because individual persons have essential or primal identities but because the multiple contexts in which dialogical, intimate identities make sense and give meaning are re-created in contentious local practice (which is in part shaped and reshaped by enduring struggles) (pp. 29–30). It is through these enduring conflicts related to political domination and power across institutions and cultural worlds that our anchor identities are sedimented or thickened. How these two types of identities interact within cultural worlds is key. For example, it is important to ask how anchor identities of being a White boy or a girl of color would influence the possibility of being identified with localized identities such as "smart" within schools. The studies within this meta-ethnography reveal that anchor identities related to class, race, and gender directly shape the access students have to the localized identity of being smart or competent within schools.

Furthermore, largely ignored within the articles was an examination of the *enduring struggle* or resistance students displayed when realizing that their anchor identities were being used to position them in a "less than" status within class-rooms or schools. The articles named how race, class, or gender related to the cultural production of who was competent or smart in the classrooms, yet the articles rarely described the ways students resisted or struggled against their positioning as *not* smart or competent. What we do not understand and know are the ways localized identities become sedimented at the end of K-12 schooling as a result of struggling against or even accepting the ways students have been positioned, at times even contradictory, based on different teachers and classrooms, primarily as *not* smart in interaction with their anchor identities.

Finally, teachers' identities in relation to the cultural worlds of smartness they created within their classrooms were also understudied across the articles. How do teachers respond when students resist? How do teachers understand students' identities in their classrooms and the ways they influence motivation and learning? How do teachers make sense of notions of ability and students' anchor and secondary identities? Because teachers are the authoritative positions of power within classrooms, understanding the ways they have the power to shape anchor and localized identities of students provides an excellent context for understanding how power plays out in local practices within cultural worlds (i.e., classrooms). Once we better understand how student and teacher identities interact and are shaped within the cultural worlds of classrooms, we can begin to determine practices that better allow all students to believe they are competent and smart and that the teacher sees them as such.

LINE OF ARGUMENT: ABILITY, IDENTITY, AND SCHOOLING

That the legacy of the social constructions of race, gender, and class is closely tied to the social construction of smartness in the United States is apparent in schools today. According to Cross and Donovan (2002), Black students are two times more likely than White students to be labeled as having an intellectual disability, and Native American students are 24% more likely to be labeled as learning disabled. The overrepresentation of Black, Native American, and Latino students is especially high in the categories relying on clinical judgment rather than verifiable biological data (Harry & Klingner, 2014). Furthermore, research has shown that these clinical decisions are likely biased against Black, Latino, and Native American children (Harry & Klingner, 2014).

On the flip side of the inequities in special education is the *underrepresentation* of students of color in gifted programs with White students being overrepresented (Sapon-Shevin, 1994; Staiger, 2004). In addition to being underrepresented in gifted courses, students of color are typically underrepresented in college preparatory courses as well (Delpit, 2012; Solorzano & Ornelas, 2002). Identification of students as "gifted" is also largely based on clinical judgment through teacher referral. This form of within-school segregation increases as the percentage of

Black students increase, with schools that are 30% to 60% Black showing the highest rate of segregation (Clotfelter, Vigdor, & Ladd, 2004).

Despite all of the examples of institutional discrimination mentioned here, identity and perceptions of ability are typically an afterthought or an add-on when curriculum, assessment, classroom management, and pedagogy are discussed within schools and teacher education. Additionally, when the opportunity gap (i.e., achievement gap) or educational debt (Ladson-Billings, 2006) is discussed within education, the intersection of identity and ability is rarely addressed beyond the vaguely stated need for teachers to have high expectations for all students.

The findings of this meta-ethnography demonstrate that identity must be centered and used as the foundation from which the design of curriculum, assessment, classroom management, and pedagogy is built upon. The line of argument that runs through this set of ethnographies is that how we understand learning needs to shift in definition to defining *learning as identity production*. This means that identity development occurs within the practices of learning. Furthermore, a critical aspect of identity in relation to schooling is ability—where students feel competent and capable within classrooms. If students do not feel this way, then the opportunities for learning are thwarted.

On the flip side of student learning, we need to understand that teaching includes the production of identities in the classroom. Teachers are never only teaching content. How teachers decide to structure their classrooms and curriculum influences the identities available to students and how students come to understand themselves in relation to each other, the curriculum, schooling, and the greater society around them. A key factor in how racial, class, and gender inequities are produced in classrooms relates to how teachers perceive student abilities. Furthermore, how teachers perceive their identities, valuable knowledge, and their role as teachers plays a foundational role in their perceptions of students' abilities and identities.

In summary, this meta-ethnography has demonstrated that notions of ability and identity influence student achievement and engagement across all grade levels and content areas. Furthermore, racial, class and gender inequities structure notions of ability within schools. As Carlone et al. (2011) claim, an essential part of teaching is "recreating worlds" (p. 481). With the worlds they create in their classrooms, teachers need to purposefully be asking if or how they are allowing all students to perform as competent academically. It is only then that they can begin to structure identities in ways that work against gender, race, and class inequities. Classrooms that provide narrow definitions of smartness that are centered on teacher pleasing and those that are highly competitive actively produce gender, class, and race inequities. As a newer line of research, there is much to be done to further identify the everyday practices and lasting consequences of the identities students develop within school. This meta-ethnography along with the others in this book clearly demonstrate we must center identity to understand teaching and learning.

REFERENCES

Bernal, D. D. (2002). Critical race theory, Latino critical theory, and critical raced-gendered epistemologies: Recognizing students of color as holders and creators of knowledge. *Qualitative Inquiry*, 8(1), 105–126.

Bishop, J. P. (2012). "She's always been the smart one. I've always been the dumb one": Identities in the mathematics classroom. *Journal for Research in Mathematics Education*, 43(1), 34–74.

Carlone, H. B., Haun-Frank, J., & Webb, A. (2011). Assessing equity beyond knowledge- and skills-based outcomes: A comparative ethnography of two fourth-grade reform-based science classrooms. *Journal of Research in Science Teaching*, 48(5), 459–485.

Carrillo, J. F. (2013). I always knew I was gifted: Latino males and the Mestiz@ Theory of Intelligences (MTI). *Berkeley Review of Education*, 4(1), 69–95.

Clotfelter, C. T., Vigdor, J. L., & Ladd, H. F. (2006). Federal oversight, local control, and the specter of "resegregation" in southern schools. *American Law and Economics Review*, 8(2), 347–389.

Cross, C. T., & Donovan, M. S. (Eds.). (2002). *Minority students in special and gifted education*. Washington, DC: National Academies Press.

Delpit, Lisa D. (2012). *"Multiplication is for White people": Raising expectations for other people's children*. New York: New Press.

Doyle, L. H. (2003). Synthesis through meta-ethnography: paradoxes, enhancements, and possibilities. *Qualitative Research*, 3(3), 321–344.

Fine, M. (1994). Dis-stance and other stances: Negotiations of power inside feminist research. In A. Gitlin (Ed.), *Power and method: Political activism and educational research* (pp. 13–35). New York: Routledge.

Gardner, H. (2011). *Frames of mind: The theory of multiple intelligences*. New York: Basic Books.

Godley, A. J. (2003). Literacy learning as gendered identity work. *Communication Education*, 52(3–4), 273–285.

Gould, S. J. (1996). *The mismeasure of man*. New York: W. W. Norton.

Harry, B., & Klingner, J. (2014). *Why are so many minority students in special education?* New York: Teachers College Press.

Harter, L. M., Berquist, C., Scott Titsworth, B., Novak, D., & Brokaw, T. (2005). The structuring of invisibility among the hidden homeless: The politics of space, stigma, and identity construction. *Journal of Applied Communication Research*, 33(4), 305–327.

Hatt, B. (2007). Street smarts vs. book smarts: The figured world of smartness in the lives of marginalized, urban youth. *The Urban Review*, 39(2), 145–166.

Hatt, B. (2012). Smartness as a cultural practice in schools. *American Educational Research Journal*, 49(3), 438–460.

Holland, D., Lachicotte, W. Jr., Skinner, D., & Cain, C. (1998). *Identity and agency in cultural worlds*. Cambridge, MA: Harvard University Press.

Holland, D., & Lave, J. (2001). *History in person: Enduring struggles, contentious practice, intimate identities*. Santa Fe, NM: School of American Research Press.

Korp, H. (2011). What counts as being smart around here? The performance of smartness and masculinity in vocational upper secondary education. *Education, Citizenship and Social Justice*, 6(1), 21–37.

Ladson-Billings, G. (2000). Racialized discourses and ethnic epistemologies. *Handbook of Qualitative Research, 2*, 257–277.

Ladson-Billings, G. (2006). From the achievement gap to the education debt: Understanding achievement in US schools. *Educational Researcher, 35*(7), 3–12.

Mottier, V. (2005). The interpretive turn: History, memory, and storage in qualitative research. In *Forum Qualitative Sozialforschung/Forum: Qualitative Social Research, 6*(2) Art. 33. http://nbn-resolving.de/urn:nbn:de:0114-fqs0502330.

Noblit, G. W., Flores, S. Y., & Murillo, E. G. (2004). *Postcritical ethnography: Reinscribing critique.* Cresskill, NJ: Hampton Press.

Noblit, G. W., & Hare, R. D. (1988). *Meta-ethnography: Synthesizing qualitative studies,* Vol. 11. Thousand Oaks, CA: SAGE.

Peshkin, A. (1988). In search of subjectivity—one's own. *Educational Researcher, 17*(7), 17–21.

Savin-Baden, M., & Major, C. H. (2007). Using interpretative meta-ethnography to explore the relationship between innovative approaches to learning and their influence on faculty understanding of teaching. *Higher Education, 54*(6), 833–852.

Sapon-Shevin, M. (1994). *Playing favorites: Gifted education and the disruption of community.* Albany, NY: SUNY Press.

Solorzano, D., & Ornelas, A. (2002). A critical race analysis of advanced placement classes: A case of educational inequality. *Journal of Latinos and Education, 1*(4), 215–229.

Staiger, A. (2004). Whiteness as giftedness: Racial formation at an urban high school. *Social Problems, 51*, 161–181.

Valencia, R. R. (Ed.). (2012). *The evolution of deficit thinking: Educational thought and practice.* New York: Routledge.

Wolcott, H. F. (1994). *Transforming qualitative data: Description, analysis, and interpretation.* Thousand Oaks, CA: SAGE.

11

Theorizing Identity from Qualitative Synthesis

Implications and Conclusions

LUIS URRIETA, JR. AND GEORGE W. NOBLIT ■

There are two primary audiences for this book. One is those interested in identity theory and the other is those interested in meta-ethnography. Clearly, the two are linked in this book, and what we say about one is bound up in the other. However, given the differences in these audiences, we organized this final chapter as "two takes" on what has been revealed so far. One take examines the lessons of the book for identity theory. The other take examines the lessons of the book for meta-ethnography (and incidentally for primary qualitative research studies on identity as well). We recommend, however, that both audiences read the full chapter, because what is frontloaded in either section is conditioned by the arguments in the other section.

IDENTITY THEORY

The first section of this chapter discusses and analyzes the major contributions of the identity meta-ethnography chapters in this book. We argue that the range of the chapters presented is important to the project of speaking to identity theory by focusing on how meta-ethnography can be a vehicle for data analysis and synthesis that can inform theory. In this book we address the cultural construction of identities in education in particular, with emphasis on race and ethnicity and their intersections with gender, class, and sexual orientation. Using cultural identity theory as an example, this final chapter highlights the contributions that can be drawn from these specific syntheses of studies to identity work, identification, and identity theory. As noted, this also has implications for what we argue in the section on future directions for qualitative synthesis. Together the chapters in this book contribute to identity studies and address cultural identity theory collectively, making this book itself a "synthesis" useful to identity studies scholars as well as qualitative research methodologists.

This first take is organized into three parts: theorizing identity, lessons from theorizing, and the contributions to identity theory. The first part of this section focuses on the processes the chapter authors used to make their synthesis speak to theory, the second addresses the substantive results of such theorizing, and the third identifies the theoretical value of our effort.

Theorizing Identity

We found that the contributors to this volume theorized with meta-ethnography in and through their studies. Guided by Lemert's (2016) perspective on theory, as "figuring out what other creatures of the same sort are doing with, to, or around them" (p. 2), we specifically did not limit the definition of theory nor did we impose a form from which to theorize for our chapter contributors. The democratization of theory allowed the sets of primary studies that each chapter represents to collectively demonstrate that the separation between synthesis and theorizing is a false separation. We contend, like Lemert, that theory has many forms and acknowledge peoples' skills in "figuring out" what is going on in their surroundings (cultural, social, political, etc., or "figured" worlds [Holland, Lachicotte, Skinner, & Cain, 1998]). Synthesis in meta-ethnography is no different. Meta-ethnography enabled the researchers to theorize with and through the synthesis process by "figuring out" what the individual studies collectively revealed about identity theory through their explicit claims, refutations, and/or omissions. In part, this was due to the more accessible and interdisciplinary theoretical frameworks that were used but also due to the more democratic understanding of theory being deployed.

Theory in meta-ethnography was seen as interpretive, critical, and inductive—an explanatory synthesis. As "explanatory," the goal of theory in the synthesis process was then to, in part, "figure out" or theorize for understanding what the studies collectively revealed about the study of identity. Further, in line with meta-ethnography's interpretivist and critical paradigms, theory was understood as translations rather than generalizations across the ethnographic studies selected around particular themes, topics, or issues studied but within larger nuanced, complex contexts. This book and meta-ethnography therefore challenges two big deceptions of the Western academy. One is that theory has a particular abstracted form and is the domain of an elite few. The second is that synthesis is about truth and power. Against both deceptions, the meta-ethnographers in this book press for theory and synthesis that advance the "figuring out" (understanding) of particular domains and about promoting democratic forms of knowledge and practice. The critical lenses used in these chapters see theory less as universalizing and more as strategic in promoting equitable relations. These same critical lenses demand meta-ethnography be a tool of "figuring out" (understanding) within projects that promote more democratic participation in theory and in society.

The contributors to this volume used identity theory as a way to understand, illuminate, and critique a set of studies and in turn to critique forces that affect the identity construction, most notably deficit perspectives, prejudiced understanding, and social structures that delimit identities. In the process these chapters helped us to better understand (figure and refigure) the relation between synthesis and social and cultural theory as one that is inseparable. Western thinking tends to divide and separate the epistemological, ontological, and axiological domains of research, but these meta-ethnographies show that theory, methodology, and researcher positionality are intimately interconnected and cannot be and should not be ignored. We therefore begin addressing the collective findings of this book by focusing attention on the relevance and importance of positionality as an embodiment of identity and disrupt the false separation between positionality and theory and between theory and method.

Theory and positionality. The chapters in this book have followed other meta-ethnographers in acknowledging the positionality of the researchers and have taken it a few steps further. Acknowledging such is common in primary qualitative research studies, and this volume asserts that researcher positionality is an essential part of the practice in meta-ethnographies as well. There are good reasons for many qualitative studies to include positionality as part of the methodology of the study, including the history of seeing the *researcher as the instrument*. Here the analogy is to the data collection devices of quantitative research, and this history probably explains positionality as being a part of qualitative methodology. Based on the contributing chapters in this book, we question the "instrument" metaphor on two grounds.

First, methods are arguably theories in themselves about "what is" and how "what is" can be understood and captured (Noblit, Flores, & Murrillo, 2004). The analogy of researcher-as-instrument, though, accepts a theory–method distinction that is problematic for all research but especially qualitative research. It understates the role of the researcher and contributes to what we see as a theory-light execution of qualitative research and meta-ethnography. By theory-light we mean that the researcher's positionality (including values, beliefs, worldviews, and theoretical lenses) is not deeply engaged, and therefore there can only be a superficial engagement of theory, which continues to encourage a false separation between theory and methods.

Second, positionality-as-method also replicates the idea of detached scholarship—the idea that we stand apart from what we study. For some, this is a desired objectivity, but our experiences in qualitative research (and in the meta-ethnographies contained in this book) are that qualitative research, like identity, is embodied. Identity is filtered through positionality. We do our research because it matters to us and to the world in which we live. We choose what to study for personal reasons and then get involved in it in order to understand or "figure it out." In this, positionality is essential because it is about the perspectives—experiential, theoretical, moral, ethical, political—that we invest in our work. Qualitative research is value explicit and engaged, not detached or objective. The authors in this volume see positionality not just as method but as an embodiment of their values and beliefs and embodiment of identity.

Positionality then is highly theoretical. When our authors say they are using a critical approach—they are not saying they simply *chose* a theory to use. They are saying that they *are* critical theorists. Positionality includes their theoretical perspective, and they drive themselves and their perspectives through their methodologies. This cannot be understated and is a major contribution of this book. The meta-ethnographies in this book confirm previous studies that emphasize that positionality is important in meta-ethnography (cf. Beach, Bagley, Eriksson, & Player-Koro, 2014; Doyle, 2003; Savin-Baden, McFarland, & Savin-Baden, 2008) and add that theory and positionality are linked.

Positionality itself does not signal a particular theoretical approach. Many descriptive studies that eschew even grounded theory have a statement about the researcher-as-instrument. However, it seems that the more interpretive and critical theory approaches are, the more adamant researchers are about positionality statements. This is because both approaches are quite aware of the responsibility of the authors for the interpretations and critiques offered. As Geertz (1973) explained for interpretive studies, the goal is to add an additional layer of interpretation over the interpretations that thick description yields—to say what meaning can be made of the webs of meaning of the participants. For critical theories, the explicit emphasis on power and ideology drives the studies. In both cases, it helps the reader to know what the researchers bring to the study in order for the reader to sort out what is more the product of the authors and what is more the product of the lived experience studied. The reader is invited into the acts of interpretation and critique, rather than being simply the recipient of those of the authors. This is equally true in meta-ethnography and ethnography. A deeper engagement with positionality (beyond superficial categories as descriptors of identity) allows the reader to be better informed about the theories driving the methodology while also being able to sort through the analysis and findings with more active criteria for assessing the contributions of the study. But let us be clear that we are not arguing for any particular form for discussing positionality. There are many ways to communicate what authors bring in way of identity and perspective to a study. What we are arguing for, as supported by the studies in this volume, is being as qualitative as possible when doing research synthesis and for understanding positionality as an embodiment of identity and as theory as much as method.

Lessons from Theorizing

One of our main concerns in this book was the question: What do these studies contribute collectively to identity studies? In other words, how do these meta-ethnographies speak to cultural identity theory collectively? What did we learn about how identity is studied in education? What are the problems with how it is studied? How do we come to understand identity differently? What did we learn from studying identity from different topics?

The meta-ethnographies collectively reveal that identity was often not defined clearly or engaged theoretically in the original studies. Searches led by the term "identity" generated an abundance of studies, but, upon closer examination, identity was too frequently separated from theory and only defined in basic terms, often as just a category most often equated with race or ethnicity. This made us wonder if the researchers in the original studies started out with an identity theory framework for their studies, or whether they came to an identity focus incidentally. We then wondered why scholars were not taking the time to historicize and situate identity in their studies in more engaged ways. Perhaps, in an era where the pressure to publish has increased exponentially and where the rapid turnover (expiration date) of research has accelerated, the hastiness of much of the identity research screened out from inclusion in the meta-ethnographies is telling.

Chapter 1 of this volume explored a selective genealogy of the origins of the concept of identity that exposed the rich and varied theoretical histories of this concept. From the time and energy that generations of scholars, including women and scholars of color, have devoted to the topic, we hope that studies that purport to study identity seriously engage and honor the theories and histories of this concept. We therefore exhort that researchers studying identity in education explore, situate, and contribute to these complex layering(s) of identity theories. Any serious engagement of identity must include clearly defining and situating the concept, as well as pointing out the theoretical contributions of its study. This is not to say that we are privileging any particular form of theory or that it is the domain of a few but rather that it is the "figuring out of what is going on" that is so important to the democratization of theory and the pursuit of social justice agendas.

Overall we found that the contributors' meta-ethnographies pointed their findings toward the study of cultural identities as inevitably (a) intersectional; (b) fluid, dynamic, and in process; (c) agentic and transgressive; (d) located in contextual specificity; and (e) situated within a backdrop of whiteness and White supremacy. We explore each of these five aspects of the findings related to identity in further detail as "lessons of identity theory" learned from the meta-ethnographies in this book. These findings confirm much of the existing literature on identity but also extend it in important ways while raising valuable unanticipated critiques.

INTERSECTIONALITY

Looking across a field of studies allows us to see the ways that intersectionality has not been addressed within some fields of study on identity and also to see the ways intersectionality and identity play out across types of identities. Different identities do different things and have different functions. Some identities are experienced in more durable ways than others, but no single identity exists in isolation of others that intersect in peoples' lives. Each of the chapters in this volume addresses various intersections of identity (gender, class, sexuality, age, im/migration, etc.) in relation to race and ethnicity in their findings. While the studies synthesized may not initially have addressed intersectionality, our contributors highlight the intersectional aspects of their analyses quite explicitly. It is important to remember that with meta-ethnographies the authors are limited by the design of the original studies and, while intersectionality (Crenshaw, 1991), simultaneity (Nash, 2008), or assemblages (Puar, 2007) are clearly theoretical concerns of great importance, they were less present in the original studies than the theory would warrant. In such cases the overall meta-synthesis, or line of argument, revealed the need for intersectional analyses when studying identity, especially racial and/ or ethnic identities. This was especially the case for several chapters that did not set out an intersectionality "criteria" for inclusion of their initial studies or for those initial studies in which the researchers failed to examine their own position-ality in more nuanced ways—beyond race and ethnicity.

In chapter 3, for example, Price and Burton's synthesis of dissertation stud-ies using Black racial identity theory (BRIT) finds that race, gender, educational outcomes, and age simultaneously played roles in how race as a category becomes race as identity. In particular, several studies included in their meta-ethnography highlighted the need for intersectional frameworks that address race and gender to study the experiences of African American women. In chapter 4, Bettez, Chang, and Edwards' meta-ethnography, one of their major findings as a line of argument was the lack of attention paid to intersectionality in their study of Multiracial identity, both in the studies themselves and by the authors of the studies in their positionality statements. Kolano, Childers-McKee, and King's study of Southeast Asian youth in chapter 6 similarly highlights the importance of intersectional-ity that includes race, gender, social class, immigration, culture, and "colorism" within specific sociopolitical, historical contexts of the Asian diaspora. Martin and Locklear in chapter 9 too argue that Native American (ethnoracial) youth identities cannot be studied without attention to the role that language, culture, knowledge systems, and relationships play into the construction of Native youth's social and cultural identities. In all of these studies racial, ethnic, or ethnora-cial identities could not be studied in nuanced ways without paying attention to intersectionality.

Other meta-ethnographies in this volume set out more deliberately to address intersectionality in their studies. Ender and Rodriguez in chapter 5, for exam-ple, challenge monolithic views of Latinx communities through their study of Latin@ communities in North Carolina. They purposefully disrupt perceptions of Latin@s as "new" and as "victims." Ender and Rodriguez highlight and work against a singular view of race and ethnicity for Latin@s. Parkhouse and Pennell, in chapter 7, start out with an intersectional set of criteria for including stud-ies in their meta-ethnography such as ethnicity, gender, and sexual orientation, revealing important intra- and intergroup differences in the lives of Latina youth. Their study concludes that expanding studies to address more than one category of analysis, or addressing more than race, can lead to more complex questions and further understanding of youths' nuanced experiences. Concluding that iden-tity must be centered when studying hierarchical constructions of knowledge and ability, Hatt, in chapter 10, also addresses intersectionality by focusing on how smartness is deployed according to race, class, and gender. Hatt finds that learning *is* identity and that teacher power is important in determining (according to race, class, and gender) who gets to be "smart" in schools and, as a result, in shaping students' identities in the classrooms.

When the authors of meta-ethnographies speak from their positionalities, they articulate another intersection—that of the person trying to "figure things out" (understand). With explicit positionality statements, the authors in this book show that identity is never a "done deal." It is perceived, asserted, rejected, and lived in the context of many others. Identity as theorized here is always in motion.

Identities as fluid, dynamic, and in process. Meta-ethnography functions to examine "fields of study," and even though scholars have increasingly acknowledged the fluidity of identity, the meta-ethnographies in this book revealed that fluidity in ways that looking at single studies can hide. By looking at the fields of study identified, the fluidity of identity and the ways it operates was made clearer along with the idiosyncratic ways associated with each topic (i.e., being Native American, Multiracial, or smart, etc.). Looking across studies allows us to see how fluidities play out in these unique, complex ways across the field of study.

The meta-ethnographies in this book further challenge conceptions of identities as static and completed processes and instead emphasize that identities are fluid, dynamic, and in process. Martin and Locklear specifically do this by focusing their meta-ethnography on Native American youth by synthesizing the only five studies they could find that centered youth voices in a positive light. They found that although the Hopi, Navajo, and Pueblo youth in their studies expressed, like their elders, that Indigenous languages are fundamental to Native American identity, the youth also challenged static notions that directly correlate native language fluency with "authentic" Native identities. One participant is cited as saying, "I live Hopi, I just don't speak it," highlighting dynamic generational differences. Martin and Locklear conclude that "even without language, Native youth have found ways to build their identities within their communities." Similarly, Kolano, Childers-McKee, and King point to "hybridization" in the identities of the Southeast Asian youth in their meta-ethnography to signal the fluid space of the youths' identity-making between the false dichotomy of "model minority and failure." They add, "Understanding hybridization acknowledges the fluidity of identity and the ways in which identity formation is influenced by societal structures within the context of current and past histories," thus pointing to the spaces and borders between cultures in the lives of the youth. Price and Burton also highlight the shortcoming of many quantitative approaches to studying racial identity development using BRITs by addressing the intergroup differences and fluidity of the Black (African American) community on the basis of gender and also in terms of what they refer to as "intrablack" discrimination. They state, "Black people may talk about themselves and each other in monolithic ways while simultaneously holding multifaceted views of blackness that do not rest easily with the rhetoric." Bettez, Chang, and Edwards also highlight the fluidity of identity by asserting that there is no way to essentialize Multiracial identities and that these identities challenge monoracialism and unidirectional models of identity development. For Ender and Rodríguez, North Carolina Latin@ identities are "in flux," highlighting the intersectional and "borderlands" aspect of navigating between cultures, contexts, and institutions in the Latinx diaspora. Drawing from Machado-Casas (2012), this was especially true for North Carolina Latin@s of Indigenous backgrounds who thrived in their *camaleonidad*, their chameleon-like "abilities to weave in and out of Indigenous communities, broader Latin@ spaces, and White-dominated spaces in North Carolina." LaGarry and Conder's study of White preservice teachers (PSTs) also highlights a version of *camaleonidad* in which "location" of PSTs performance of whiteness is not fixed but is always in flux and in "tension" in their defense of White privilege. In this case by neutralizing and "invisiblizing" White racial identity, these preservice teachers have to constantly work to "shore up" their White identities and whiteness as a social institution. Finally, Parkhouse and Pennell especially highlight Latina identities as "fluid" and "shifting" in regard to space, performance, and agency. They add that Latinas' complex and layered social worlds *call* for multiple and shifting identities.

In all this, identity is more a verb or gerund than a noun. Moreover, it is precisely this fluidity and motion that allows identity to be more than a deterministic force. Identity involves a host of players (selves and others), a host of negotiations, and a host of opportunities and demands. There is room to move, to make something amidst the processes, institutions, and structures. While many forces may work to make a particular identity a deficit, the fluidity of identity allows it also to be a resource and tool. It allows, within limits, self-authoring and the development of individual and collective strategies to be, as youth of color often say today, "more than a statistic."

Identities as Agentic and Transgressive

Holland and Lave (2001) assert that local contentious practice and enduring struggles are important in the creation of intimate identities, especially in response to oppressive practices or structures. Identities are thus built through struggle and in resistance develop counteridentities and agency. The studies in this book highlight that identities often function as agentic and transgressive, meaning that identities regularly, as Holland et al. (1998) assert, serve as semiotic mediators for agency and transgress boundaries. Anzaldúa (1987) also highlights "borderlands" (*nepantla*) as in-between spaces of transgression for new *mestiza* subject formation.

Both Holland et al. (1998) and Anzaldua (1987) influenced Parkhouse and Pennell's meta-ethnography of Latinas and sexuality where "in-betweenness" was a prominent line of argument that revealed how shifting and fluid identities for Latinas were also "tools for navigation" and "strategies of resistance." Latinas' use of space, agency, and performance served to "navigate between worlds" individually (personal agency) and collectively (group resistance). Similarly, Kolano, Childers-McKee, and King indicate that the identity-building spaces between cultures provided the Southeast Asian youth active contexts to navigate and "push back" against the stereotypes of "homogenized Asianness." The youth therefore disrupted "fixed, static, binary concepts of identity in favor of more fluid constructions." Bettez, Chang, and Edwards, also drawing from Anzaldua, show that fluidity functions as a space of agency and transgression for Multiracial peoples, who Chang refers to as *atravesado/as* (the crossed). The transgression is primarily because Multiracial identities and experiences in and of themselves challenge monoracial storylines and also because multiracialism creates a space of liminality (in-betweenness) for agency where Multiracial students often maneuver in and out of different racial/ethnic positionings. Ender and Rodriguez specifically highlight identity as agency and resistance by pointing to Latin@s' strength, *fuerza*, in the face of ethno-racial discrimination and adversity. Drawing from Trinidad Galvan (2011), Ender and Rodriguez identify *supervivencia* as North Carolina Latin@s' living beyond survival with dignity; thus they move North Carolina Latin@s beyond the idea of being "new" and "victims" and toward a forging of new ways and forms of being Latin@s in the New South.

In Martin and Locklear's study, Native youth asserted their agency in transgressive ways by being reflexive and by expressing their needs to educators and researchers. In a complex way, Native youth knew that language maintenance and revitalization was an important "missing piece," and simultaneously they did not see lack of Native language fluency as a complete impediment to being Native. Native youth wanted to be recognized by adults and to have personal relationships with them. They expressed this by stating that educators and administrators do not have "one-on-one personal relationships with students" and that many adults "don't want to take on that excess burden." Martin and Locklear also point out that Native youth lament not seeing their experiences reflected in the school curricula and were aware that "they were fighting a much deeper, long-standing battle," a "war against racism, discrimination, and colonization." Price and Burton point out their use of the capitalized signifier "Black" to make a political statement and to signal that it is a real experience; thus they challenge the elusive and evasive dismissal of colorblind approaches to race. BRITs have been particularly empowering for African Americans as a way to challenge the multidamaging effects of racism but also to struggle against racism in and of itself by defining it as an "underdeveloped" state of being. Finally, juxtaposing Hatt's synthesis with that of LaGarry and Conder, it is evident that Whites also are agentic in maintaining their privilege. They resist challenges to whiteness and deploy smartness to protect their status as those who can define who deserves privilege.

Identities as Located in Context Specificity

Context matters in the construction of identities, especially since geographic, social, cultural, economic, and political external forces influence the internal processes of identities and vice versa. Institutions such as schools as "contexts," for example, especially play an important role in shaping and creating localities for the construction of identities. The meta-ethnographies in this book point to the need to situate identities within the particular local context specificities in which they are formed and exist.

For instance, Price and Burton point out that BRITs have largely focused on studying racial identity development in the United States and with male college students, and that the application of BRITs in majority-Black contexts and with more gender diversity would invoke different needs and might generate other results. Ender and Rodriguez also highlight the context specificity of the New Latino diaspora (Hamann, Wortham, & Murillo, 2015) in their meta-ethnography of North Carolina Latin@s. Their study reveals that North Carolina Latin@ communities, as opposed to the historic presence of Latinxs in other parts of the country like the Southwest, adds to the diversity of Latinx experiences in the United States through their inter- and intragroup differences and specifically as "North Carolina Latin@s." Parkhouse and Pennell add to Latina inter- and intra-diversity by also pointing to context specificity. Not only did they address issues of space and place in their study, but in particular they state that "Participants assimilated or resisted depending upon the community and school contexts, as well as the gendered identities that formed within these contexts and in the context of ethnic traditions." Likewise Parkhouse and Pennell conclude that context specificity played a prominent role in participants' "having varying degrees of agency as well as varying commitments to collective, transformative resistance." Bettez, Chang, and Edwards similarly highlight context by suggesting that "Multiracial identity is contextually influenced by social, political, cultural, physical, and formal factors" in which multiracials may adopt a plurality of Multiracial identities. They call this intersection of "race" and context a third space of liminality. Through a Multiracial cultural intuition, they claim multiracials can "read" the racial spaces they occupy and respond accordingly. Martin and Locklear also highlight the importance of context in regard to Native American youth identities by exhorting that it is critical for researchers to explain the geographical as well as Tribal context of their studies. They attest that, while many aspects of their own meta-ethnography may be shared across Tribal lines, context matters, and researchers should not posit that their findings and implications are suitable for all Native youth but "instead implicate that their research is contextualized by geographical location and Tribe." Kolano, Childers-McKee, and King also point to school contexts as vitally important to the development of Southeast Asian youth identities advocating "for a stronger structural critique of school institutions that pull from racist, classist, and nativist narratives and 'box' students into narrowly prescribed racial/cultural roles."

The chapters by Hatt, Martin and Locklear, and LaGarry and Conder reveal the ability of Whites to enforce a context. For Hatt, a key context are that "traditional epistemologies in schools are used to frame smartness in a way that can leave low-income students and students of color feeling devalued and denied the identity of being a 'smart' student." Whites have agency obviously, but what Hatt is emphasizing here is that schools are instruments of agency for Whites. Interestingly, Martin and Locklear, in noting the overwhelming number of deficit studies of Native American youth, point to academic research as another instrument of

Whites to maintain their privilege. LaGarry and Conder reveal that "the various strategies and tools could be assigned to particular locations with a field of practice." Notably, PSTs "in courses or field placements that address these issues (of whiteness) perceive that they are being accused or threatened with claims that contradict their chosen benevolent identities." Context, then, is key to the identity construction of Whites as it is to other racialized groups, but what is notable is the power and the social institutions that invigorate their agency to maintain dominance. In all cases, the stakes around identity constructions are high and the contexts in which those identities are created, enforced, or denied matters.

Whiteblindness—The power of not naming. It is important to address that nearly all of the meta-ethnographies point out the largely ignored absence of a critique of whiteness, or what Bettez, Chang, and Edwards (in this book) coined a "whiteblindness," in the original studies. This point of critique is especially important since we began this volume with the traditional identity premise that *one is what the other is not*. Recall that the construction of difference was borne out of Euro-Whites' efforts to distinguish themselves in superior ways to non-Whites through the colonial and globalist enterprise. The construction of ethnic and racial identities for Whites and for minoritized groups therefore exists within a backdrop of whiteness and White supremacy that is difficult to "unhook from" (Mazurett-Boyle & Antrop-Gonzalez, 2013). As stated by cultural studies theorist Stuart Hall (1991): "When you know what everybody else is, then you are what they are not. Identity is always in that sense, structured representation which only achieves its positives through the narrow eye of the negative" (p. 21). We are not arguing that being of any ethnic or racial group is inherently negative or bad in and of itself. We are saying that ignoring a critique of whiteness and White supremacy when studying racial or ethnic identities is faulty because, as stated in chapter 1, ethnic and racial Others were constructed as the antithesis of Whites through colonialist and imperialist enterprises and their enduring discourses and practices.

Price and Burton begin their study by stating, for instance, that BRIT "implicates White racism and White cultural hegemony in the various expressions of Black identity." They proceed to assert that BRIT emerged as a response to scholarship by Whites that assumed Blacks were plagued with pathological tendencies and that models of identity and behavior based on Whites were universal. Martin and Locklear similarly begin their meta-ethnography by stating that Native American youth, like other youth of color, are held to academic standards and metrics in which White middle-class students are used to set the bar by which all other students are measured. They argue that Native youth are aware of this deficit positioning and challenge the "White man's education" by expressing that "they want teachers, curriculum, schools, peers, institutions, classes, and other aspects to support their ways of knowing and what they bring with them, while learning more about their nations, languages, and cultures." Implicit in this statement is that Native youths' ways of knowing and being are held against the backdrop of the whitestream, in which White middle-class ways of knowing and being are upheld as neutral, invisible, and as the standard "mainstream" (Urrieta, 2009).

Parkhouse and Pennell also point out that generally the studies included in their meta-ethnography of Latina youth defined academic success as associated with (whitestream) assimilation. However, their synthesis revealed that the Latina youth inevitably negotiated and disrupted this assimilation/resistance binary. They state, "gender and ethnicity are always at play in academic assimilation or resistance, but when we examine individual cases, self-authorship and the power of agency become more apparent." Kolano, Childers-McKee, and King also found that the Southeast Asian youth in their study disrupted a "traditional/Americanized" binary where Americanized was often associated with being "white-washed" and with "honorary whiteness." Moreover, academic success was associated with a "good" pan-Asianness (model minority), while specific Southeast Asian identities such as Cambodian, Lao, or Vietnamese were juxtaposed against a "good" versus "bad" Asian dichotomy that implicitly backdrops whiteness as normative.

LaGarry and Conder, further, come to a meta-theoretical realization in their study: whiteness and White identity are complex ideological imaginaries with very real effects, and social practice theory allowed them to invoke multiple theoretical stances in attempting to understand these imaginaries in more detail. Overall, their use of contested theoretical spaces as well as a time lapse in their syntheses afforded them productive sites for understanding the practice of White racial formation. Bettez, Chang, and Edwards's meta-ethnography is particularly revealing because they claim that their realization that an analysis of whiteness was missing was actually a "surprise." They write:

> The "surprise" in our meta-ethnography revolved around all of the voices—authors' and participants'—apparent whiteblindness. Collectively, we seemed to run in circles around the centrality of Whiteness within the discourses of multiraciality, either avoiding it, misrepresenting it, or being engulfed within it like fish in water.

Bettez, Chang, and Edwards come to the conclusion through their conception of *whiteblindness* that "all notions of racial identity and contentions around racialization are filtered through and permeated with White supremacist ideology." They further state that the struggle for social justice cannot operate from whiteblindness by failing to acknowledge the impact of whiteness and White supremacy on race and ethnic identity and the racialization of people of color. For Ender and Rodriguez, the original studies point to Whites, White institutions, and whiteness as the source of discrimination and oppression that the North Carolina Latin@s navigate and surpass with the agency and resistance of "creative imagination of possibility and hope"; this despite Villenas' overshadowing assertion that even today "Whites continue to occupy congressional, senatorial, and state governmental positions" that deny North Carolina Latin@s access to political and representational power.

Whiteblindness then stands as a critique of identity studies that in an effort to validate the lived experiences of oppressed and minoritized peoples focus narrowed only on the lived experience. We argue for identity studies in education that are more historically contextualized within sociopolitical landscapes of power than the ones that were available for synthesis to researchers in this volume. This also suggests that meta-ethnography itself may need to consider how to make research synthesis more historically, culturally, and sociopolitically contextual.

Contributions to Identity Theory

In chapter 1, we defined identities as self-understandings, especially those with strong emotional resonance that we come to embody in our daily lives. Identity, we said, is often constituted by historically produced socially and culturally constructed signifying "labels" that often help us identify certain people in relation to others. These labeled positionings change from being categories to become identities in our lives through the processes of identification. Identification is the work of belonging, or the processes of articulation, continuous classifying acts that enable us to acquire identities. Together identity and identification help us to form senses of individual and collective selves that help to shape our personhood or our status of "being" a person and being recognized as such by others, especially as mature functioning social actors in a culture and society.

Our main arguments about identity in chapter 1 were that identity is about subject formation and about power. By that we meant that identities are categories of belonging that determine who can and cannot belong to an identity. Who has the power to exclude from membership? Or, who has the power to impose identities on others? We also argued that identity has empowering political dimensions for people of color, especially for identity politics, activism, and social movements by minoritized and oppressed peoples. For those reasons, we determined that there is a lot at stake in the study of identity and that what is at stake changes depending on the time period and locations of those identities' embodiment.

We next address the overall contributions to identity theory from this book. The meta-ethnographies remind us that identity is indeed a Western concept that is set up as a binary (often referred to as relational) because it is based on the oppositional premise identified earlier: *one is what the other is not.* Our close readings of the chapters and the aspects of identity that emerged from them make us feel confident to assert and confirm that this identity binary set-up is about (a) power and (b) whiteness. Moreover, we affirm that fluidity of identity is a response to technologies of the state that attempt to manage difference. Fluid, dynamic, and process-oriented identities are flexible "adjustments" to the regulatory structures of power and whiteness. Identities in flux serve the purpose of adjusting the possibility for agency and set the stage for transgression in the local contextual specificities of identity constructions. Finally, we find that, despite the binding problematic of identity, it remains a powerful concept for people of color and must remain an important basis for organizing, lobbying, and collective action.

First, the distinction of difference that results in the creation of cultural identity binaries or dichotomies is based on power. The contributors to this volume identified explicit and implied binaries such as White/Black, smart/dumb, new/old, good Asian/bad Asian, real Native/non-Native or almost-real Native, Multiracial/monoracial, and so on in their meta-ethnographies. They show that these identity binaries are situated within larger historically produced sociopolitical genealogies of power that reveal how oppression works against certain groups and to the benefit of others. This includes through the creation and sustenance of categories of race and ethnicity, such as Asian (model minority), Latino, Indian (Native American), Black, or people of color (and the simultaneous avoidance of taking up and owning a racial category such as the case for Whites). For example, while the identifier "Latin@" may serve many political purposes such as that of enabling organizational, advocacy, policy, and political mobilization according to Ender and Rodriguez—Latino, like the Other(ed) groupings, also serves as a regulatory category. As regulatory categories these collective signifiers position and label these groupings into the landscape of the whitestream imaginary. In this imaginary the collective groupings are homogenized, often stereotypically, into categorical difference despite their intergroup diversities. It becomes a norming difference, "racial projects" of structured representation to fit into the White supremacist vertical racial order and matrix of domination on which this country is founded (Hill-Collins, 2002). Such dualistic and dichotomous racial/ethnic identity framings tend to be high-stakes us/them, we/they conceptions invested in power.

The meta-ethnographies, in contrast, show that in order to disrupt the power of an oppositional analysis (i.e., White/Black, model minority/bad minority, etc.) and the simplicity of a dualistic analytic framing, a multiplex intersectional analysis is key. To complicate the binaries all of the researchers concluded that to arrive at more nuanced and complex understandings of cultural identity, they could not study race and ethnicity alone. They argue that cultural identity has to be more than race or ethnicity to encompass also issues such as language, gender, sexuality, age, knowledge systems, and other ways of knowing and being. Pennell and Parkhouse, for example, suggest that the more variables of identity added, the more directions and more complex the avenues of identity revealed. Price and Burton add that BRITs scholars cannot afford to continue to only study race from surveys and quantitative methods that support unidirectional models of identity development but should use "experience-near" qualitative methods to better understand the intersectional lives of Blacks. We concur that in order to better "figure out" race or ethnicity, intersectionality must be addressed within the landscapes of racial formations in order to maintain and extend the complexities of identities. The more intersections of identity that are explored, the clearer become the intricate workings of power. In these chapters, binaries yield to multiplicities of intersections.

Second, the meta-ethnographies revealed that the race/ethnicity binaries exist also within a largely unnamed backdrop of whiteness and White supremacy. It was interesting but not surprising given their critical perspectives that nearly all of the researchers in this book addressed this largely ignored critique of whiteness in the original studies they included in their meta-ethnographies. Whiteness, as *whiteblindness*, was the unnamed elephant in the room in most of the original studies synthesized. The meta-ethnographies in this volume further the critique that an exclusive focus on race or ethnicity most closely helps to sustain identity power binaries and the racial regulatory projects of White supremacy. These binaries lock the dichotomies within cultural or identity boundaries and divisions (including intergroup oppressions such as "colorism" and hierarchies such as US-born Latino vs. immigrant Latino) and into oppositional power stances that ultimately uphold the various manifestations of US White, heteronormative patriarchy. This is so because whiteness, whitestream, and White supremacy, even if made invisible and unnamed through whiteblindness, remain in the backdrop of power hierarchies precisely because they are unnamed. This evasiveness to name and critique whiteness is clearly a strategy to protect White privilege as is the case in LaGarry and Conder's study of White PSTs.

The construction of identity as "always premised on what one is not" is therefore a Euro-Western set-up, a trap of sorts, for the maintenance of power hierarchies and the preservation of whiteness as normative. Intersectional analyses of identity reveal more of the power hierarchies and name the whiteness in the backdrop in an effort to unbind the trap. Naming the whiteness does not recenter it as normative but further exposes and disrupts the privilege of being invisible. Naming the whiteness also locates it within the local contexts of specificity that are so important for cultural identity constructions and for locating power. Making whiteness visible enables it to be explored and undercut.

The meta-ethnographies also collectively support previous identity work that signals that identities are fluid and dynamic; however, they extend this claim by adding that the fluidity and dynamism of identities is a response to the structures of power that attempt to regulate them in the local contexts where identification occurs and where identities are constructed. In local contexts, fluidity of identity adjusts the possibility for agency and sets the stage for transgression in response to the structures by providing tools and resources to adjust and evade the technologies of the state and the management of difference. These structures include institutions such as schools that are set up as technologies of the state to assimilate and incorporate children and youth into social and political landscapes of power and structured representation (identity), according to Hall (1991). These landscapes of power in their most intimate forms are the context specificity identified as an aspect of identity in the meta-ethnographies in this book. Clearly context specificity matters, as evident in Hatt's meta-ethnography, where smartness is deployed according to race, class, and gender in the intimacy of the classroom on a daily basis. The specificity of context is therefore not static and should not just become a separate "section" in a publication but must be engaged to trace processes of interaction and be actively incorporated into the analysis of power. The meta-ethnographies show that through localized context specificity, power now has locations. One could even argue that context is everything, but we do not go that far. We do, however, support that process-oriented identities are in flux in response to the management and regulation of difference in local contexts, not necessarily because they are ephemeral but because alterity is fundamental to the dignity of their existences.

The youth in the meta-ethnographies actively challenged the regulating structures of power and whiteness by rejecting "either/or" identity trap positions in favor of "both/and" identity possibilities. Nearly all of the meta-ethnographies invoke hybridization, liminality, in-betweenness (*nepantla*), space of authoring, and simultaneity (not either/or but both/and) as the sites and spaces where identity becomes a resource and tool for youth to contest, navigate, adjust, evade, and subvert power and whiteness. This was clearly evident in the Southeast Asian youths' rejection of the model minority stereotypes and Native youths' challenge to the myth of the disappearing Indian associated with Native-language fluency. The alterity revealed in fluidity and dynamism of identity is evident in the refusal to be pinned down into the "boxes" that the youth referred to in Kolano, Childers-McKee, and King's study. Further, identities framed and lived as fluid and dynamic function under a different set of rules that step outside of the Western conception of identity as stable and enduring not because they are not enduring or stable but because they stand in opposition to the forces of stratification and assimilation that stabilize White supremacy.

Finally, even while identity is a Western concept at the core and while a racial/ethnic binary is problematic because of its implications with power and whiteness, oppressed and minoritized communities cannot afford to completely eschew it. Identity, especially cultural identity, has served powerful and important purposes for identity politics and collective action, especially as collective movements have diachronically transgressed the initial single-axis, oppositional identity stances of their origins. Because identity was such a powerful concept for people of color, it was quickly politicized by some White elites who recognized it as a threat to the norming technologies of the state. They have since assailed strong critiques of identity politics as "political correctness," as "divisive" interest groups, and have ultimately locked identity politics (both the academic enterprise of ethnic studies and local grassroots collective movements) into a homogenized, confrontational, and indecorous imagined collective. The meta-ethnographies in this book, as identity "projects" in and of themselves, however, show the unfolding ways in which oppressed and minoritized communities creatively and dynamically have moved beyond the traps of historical and sociopolitical "either/or" identity ploys to unbind and free up the intersectional, fluid, agentic, transgressive, and context specific possibilities of their self-creations (identities). This is precisely why multiplex "both/and" intersectional analyses of identity (and identity politics) are so important, especially because they are better equipped to maintain and extend the complexities of identities beyond a single-axis oppositional analysis and stance. Further, multiplex identity coalitions have the potential to form powerful grassroots movements, if, and only if, we can move beyond the identity *one is what the other is not* en-"trap"-ment.

We therefore conclude that identity theory must move beyond the binary en-"trap"-ments in order to seriously engage and challenge the power hierarchies and whiteness that these identity dichotomies were meant to uphold. Identity scholars must move identity (concept, theory, and practice) beyond the "trappings" of its Western foundations. Breaking the "either/or," "us/them," "we/they" dichotomies is essential in order to more fully understand the more nuanced, more profound, and experience-near conceptions that will enable us to figure out what is going on in the spectrums of human experiences. Clearly we are not referring to humanist approaches to "human experience" that are embedded in whiteness as normative. Our collective contribution to theorizing (figuring out) human experiences through identity theory, especially in education, is tied to the struggle against vertical hierarchies of power and the norming of whiteness precisely by naming, locating, and untangling these "trappings" in our everyday lives, including for Whites. The meta-ethnographies in this book indicate that cultural identity theory can help us accomplish this by pushing beyond single-axis analyses of identity in order to scale up but especially to scale down to the local contextual specificities of identification where the daily work of constructing identities takes place.

META-ETHNOGRAPHY

In this final section, we shift the lens on the previous discussion. Our goal in this section is to reveal what is gained when we examine what we learned about theory from the perspective of meta-ethnography—and learn more about this method and its implications. The authors in this book remind us that research, and identity studies in particular, are political. This begs the question of whether the use of meta-ethnography for practical (best practices) and policy purposes has been ameliorative rather than transformative. In the ameliorative approach issues are addressed as "problems" to be solved, especially through empiricism, rationality, and objectivity. We admit that meta-ethnography has been used most commonly to approach issues from an ameliorative approach. Yet we would argue that the ameliorative approach has done little to reconceptualize the social world, let alone change it in any fundamental ways. Clearly, we hope research will lead to improvements in the human condition, but limiting research synthesis and theorizing to practical interests engenders a problematic reductionism. Further, using meta-ethnography to inform theory can be reductionist as well. Yet we have seen in this volume that a critical perspective can be at least a partial antidote to this. In each meta-ethnography, the authors pushed beyond the synthesis to new theorization. This was largely due to the authors' critical lenses. Where synthesis attempts such as meta-ethnography all too easily stay close to the primary studies and add little to knowledge, a critical perspective helped these meta-ethnographies achieve more robust and provocative interpretations—and reveal more than was at first evident in the initial or primary studies—and, in turn, engender a critique based on this revelation.

To better understand what a critical approach brings to meta-ethnography, it is important to draw out a key distinction between interpretive and critical approaches—and point out what they do differently. Luttrell (2010), reflecting an interpretivist perspective, argues for making explicit the implicit in a scene. Here she is focused on the primary interpretive purpose of revealing taken-for-granted assumptions. Such assumptions structure social life in a scene but, as reified beliefs, are not readily evident to those in the scene or to the casual observer. When interpretation reveals these reifications, participants and readers see the scene in new ways. The lesson for meta-ethnography is that interpretive syntheses should push the synthesis effort beyond what is similar and different about the set of primary studies and use the translation to reveal the assumptions evident in the studies being synthesized, individually and collectively. These assumptions can then be reconsidered as the synthesis proceeds and as the meta-ethnographers argue for that which future research should be concerned.

We do not wish to undervalue interpretive approaches. Revealing reified beliefs can be dangerous. Making explicit the implicit can threaten people and their interests. It can reveal, for example, that the intention to "do good" for others can also be based in essentialism and deficit conceptions. This can be too close for comfort for scholars and policymakers alike. Further, revealing the implicit can also show that some people are disproportionately benefitting from the existing set of assumptions, and those benefitting may attempt to suppress the research and intimidate the researchers as well as those directly studied. The interpretive goal of making the implicit explicit can have real effects in the world and should not be taken lightly. Savin-Baden et al. (2008) in their interpretive meta-ethnography found "overarching themes and hidden subtexts" that were "sometimes ignored, marginalized or dislocated from central arguments about teaching and learning" (p. 225). Some things are too disquieting to acknowledge about teaching and learning. We encourage interpretive meta-ethnographies precisely because they have the power to challenge everyday ways of understanding and acting and lead to rethinking how we understand and act.

Critical approaches to qualitative research are after assumptions as well but want more. Critical studies are particularly focused on how power and ideology work to suppress and oppress. Critical approaches remind us that identity is about positioning and power. Carspecken (1996) argued critical ethnography is a form of cultural and social criticism that is used to reveal, challenge, and change oppressive relations such as inequality. While somewhat different chapter by chapter, this is the approach used in this book. These meta-ethnographies were trying to understand how identity is situated by power and ideology as well as how identity is used as a form of agency in response to oppression. The identity theories, sometimes used in the primary studies and used in all of the meta-ethnographies, are critical theories that explain how people create selves and social collectives in struggles with oppressive forces that seek to deny the validity of those identities. Identity in this way stands in opposition to forces of stratification and assimilation, to the forces of White supremacy. As noted in the first section of this chapter, theory is not a neutral, objective rendition of reality but rather a strategy for understanding how oneself and one's group is positioned—and using that understanding as a source of strength, opposition, and action. In the language of critical race theory, identity theory can be seen as a counternarrative to the majoritarian story. Meta-ethnography as used in these chapters then sharpens our understanding of both narratives and, in addition, articulates a fuller and richer account of the counternarratives.

Meta-ethnography, used in a critical approach, speaks across qualitative studies of identity and offers second- and third-order interpretations/critiques that enable new understandings of identity and identity theory. At a minimum, the result is a better understanding of how oppression works against specific groups and how identity works as a form of agency as well as a product of domination. Hytten (2004), working from a postcritical approach (which requires that the critic also be subject to critique), elaborates what could be possible with critical meta-ethnography. She argues for three goals--to be educative, emancipatory, and empowering. Such goals push meta-ethnography to consider who the audiences are for a synthesis (beyond an academic audience), who is to be emancipated, and how a synthesis could be empowering. Meta-ethnography and theory need to fully develop these capabilities.

What was learned about identity theory through these meta-ethnographies has implications for the qualitative methods used in the primary studies as well. First, there is the issue of how researchers do the primary qualitative studies. As noted earlier, these in many ways limit the possibilities of synthesis and theorizing. For example, the studies in this volume (and we would argue most qualitative studies in general) use *themes* as the usual conceptual unit that emerges. However, there are many other conceptual units that could be used. We would think that studies of identity *construction* would want to "uncover mechanisms" (Small, 2009, p. 22) and trace processes. Themes can be all too static, but processes are more diachronic. A subtle shift from process to *mechanism* could be productive as well. Focusing on the mechanisms that link elements of a scene in the unfolding of the future elements allows us to see how something becomes something else. This is a productive definition of causation, for example, suggesting that a focus on mechanism could offer an alternative to simplistic correspondence notions of causation used in many quantitative studies. The meta-ethnographies that could result from studies focused on mechanism would lead to quite different syntheses than were possible in this book and, put all too simplistically, could render an identity theory in motion.

Similarly, context in many qualitative studies is pulled out of the data analysis as a stand-alone section and presented more as an introduction to the scene that is being analyzed. This strips context of its ability to explain and truncates an understanding of how context works in everyday life. Yet in the first section of this chapter, we noted the specificity of context revealed by the meta-ethnographies. The meta-ethnographies helped reveal these in ways missing in the primary studies. Whiteblindness, for example, in the Bettez, Chang, and Edwards' chapter is revealed as hidden but active in the structuring of what can be known about mixed race identity. Conceptions of whiteness and whitestream social institutions emerge from the syntheses even when they were muted in the primary studies. This new theoretical understanding then demands that qualitative studies of identity pay much more attention to context and how it is implicated in identity construction than currently is the case.

This also suggests a different way for meta-ethnographers to think about selecting studies for inclusion. Instead of searching for studies that all address the same topic (the usual process for meta-ethnography), we could adapt the extended case study method (Small, 2009) and select studies that iteratively examine the various contexts to a phenomenon of interest. Put simply, the extended case method (cf. Burawoy, 1998; Mitchell, 1983) does not work across studies limited to the phenomenon of interest but works from a case to its contexts "which examines how the social situation is shaped by external forces" (Burawoy, 1998, p. 6). As Small puts it: "It tells us about society as a whole rather than about a populations of similar cases" (p. 20). Consistent with the argument of this book, such an approach "refines or reconstructs a theory rather than identifying an empirical fact" (Small, 2009, p. 21).

Adapting the extended case study approach for meta-ethnography could allow scholars to interrogate the studies (one or more) of a phenomenon of interest for what contexts are implicated in those studies. Then they would seek studies of those contexts, and do this repeatedly until they have exhausted all contexts possible. Thus the meta-ethnography would reveal all the contexts and the relations between the contexts for a case. This then would enable a fuller theoretical explanation of the case. Further, the meta-ethnographer could employ time as a context and sequence studies along some time order—such as shifts in policy (cf. Beach et al., 2014) or critical events. As mentioned, this approach would allow an interpretation and/or critique to speak broadly across, say, scene to society (or globe), from first social and cultural form to later or last social and cultural form, and potentially both at the same time. Theory would be fully engaged in such meta-ethnographies and could be interrogated for how well it "figures out" what is going on.

The lessons of this book for meta-ethnography are many. First, meta-ethnographers need to push their work to be interpretive *and* critical. Synthesis is a theoretical effort—not just a methodological approach. Second, meta-ethnographies must speak back to the qualitative methods used in any field of study. Synthesis reveals new understandings of a phenomena of interest but also reveals the limitation of the theories and methods seen as usual in the primary research studies. Third, meta-ethnography itself needs to be reconsidered. Our exploration of identity theory here suggests that we could select studies differently, moving from the phenomenon of interest out through a host of salient contexts that would link a local scene to the wider society, for example. This could feed even broader theorization than was possible here. By linking theory, and especially critical theories, with qualitative research synthesis, our intellectual discourse concerning social and cultural phenomena and the methods we use to advance such understanding are enriched. These efforts can be used strategically to address, and alter, the injustices of our world.

CONCLUSION

This book has been an exploration of theory and how meta-ethnography can address theory, using identity theory as the case in point. To do this, we commissioned a set of meta-ethnographies from critical scholars who were both knowledgeable of identity theory and who had some interest and/or background with meta-ethnography. These scholars chose an arena of identity studies that interested them and collected studies related to their chosen arena. They then conducted synthesis efforts using the meta-ethnographic approach. The meta-ethnographies examined the use of identity theory in a set of qualitative studies, critiqued what the studies had to offer as well as the state of theory related to the specific arena, and offered new theoretical understandings that can inform future research on identity. We have summarized these in this chapter as identity being intersectional; fluid, dynamic, and in process; agentic and transgressive; located in contextual specificity; and within a backdrop of whiteness. We confidently asserted and confirmed that the Western identity binary is a set-up that (a) upholds power hierarchies and (b) protects whiteness. We concluded that fluid, dynamic, and process-oriented identities are flexible "adjustments" to the regulatory structures of power and whiteness and that despite the binding en-"trap"-ment of identity, it remains a powerful concept for people of color that must continue to a basis for organizing, lobbying, and collective action. This project also has pushed a different way of thinking about meta-ethnography. To date, its primary application has been in the realm of evidence-based practice. Meta-ethnography in this book has been about advancing scholarship through seeing synthesis as related to theory and especially critical theories.

We see this volume as setting the stage for much more work on both theory and alternative approaches to meta-ethnography. Identity theory is but one case of theory. Other theories should be investigated to ascertain what synthesis can contribute to a wider range of theories and what lessons these investigations offer for qualitative research synthesis. Meta-ethnography is but one form of qualitative research synthesis as well. Other qualitative synthesis approaches should be employed to address theory. It may be that the specific synthesis approach makes a difference in what synthesis can contribute to theory. The work has simply been started with this volume, and we invite others to join in these efforts.

REFERENCES

Anzaldúa, G. (1987). *Borderlands/la frontera: The new mestiza* (4th ed.). San Francisco, CA: Aunt Lute.

Beach, D., Bagley, C., Eriksson, A., & Player-Koro, C. (2014). Changing teacher education in Sweden: Using meta-ethnographic analysis to understand and describe policy making and educational changes. *Teaching and Teacher Education, 44*, 160–167.

Burawoy, M. (1998). The extended case study method. *Sociological Inquiry, 16*(1), 4–33.

Carspecken, P. (1996). *Critical ethnography in educational research.* New York: Routledge.

Collins, P. H. (2002). *Black feminist thought: Knowledge, consciousness, and the politics of empowerment.* London: Routledge

Crenshaw, K. (1991). Mapping the margins: Intersectionality, identity politics, and violence against women of color. *Stanford Law Review, 43*(6), 1241–1299.

Doyle, L. H. (2003). Synthesis through meta-ethnography: Paradoxes, enhancements, and possibilities. *Review of Qualitative Research, 3*(3), 321–344.

Geertz, C. (1973). *The interpretation of cultures.* New York: Basic Books.

Hamann, E., Wortham, S., & Murillo, E. G. Jr. (2015). *Revisiting education in the new Latino diaspora* (Education Policy in Practice: Critical Cultural Studies). Charlotte, NC: Information Age Publishing.

Hall, S. (1991). The local and the global: Globalization and ethnicity. In A. D. King (Ed.), *Culture globalization and the world-system* (pp. 19–40). London: Macmillan.

Holland, D. C., & Lave, J. (2001) *History-in-person: Enduring struggles, contentious practice, intimate identities.* Santa Fe, NM: School of American Research.

Holland, D., Lachicotte, W. Jr., Skinner, D., & Cain, C. (1998). *Identity and agency in cultural worlds.* Cambridge, MA: Harvard University Press.

Hytten, K. (2004). Post-critical ethnography: Research as a pedagogical encounter. In G. Noblit, S. Flores, & E. Murrillo (Eds.), *Post-critical ethnography: Reinscribing critique* (pp. 95–105). Cresskill, NJ: Hampton Press.

Lemert, C. (2016). *Social theory: The multicultural, global, and classic readings* (6th ed.). Boulder, CO: Westview Press.

Luttrell, W. (2010). Introduction: The promise of qualitative research in education. In W. Luttrell (Ed.), *Qualitative educational research* (pp. 1–17). New York: Routledge.

Mazurett-Boyle, R., & Antrop-Gonzalez, R. (2013). Our journeys as Latin@ educators and the perpetual struggle to unhook from whiteness. In C. Hayes & N. D. Hartlep (Eds.), *Unhooking from whiteness: The key to dismantling racism in the United States* (pp. 103–121). Rotterdam: Sense Publishers.

Machado-Casas, M. (2012). Pedagogias del camaleon/Pedagogies of the chameleon: Identity and strategies of survival for transnational indigenous Latino immigrants in the U.S. South. *The Urban Review, 44*(5), 534–550.

Mitchell, J. C. (1983). Case and situation analysis. *Sociological Review, 31*(2), 187–211.

Nash, J.C. (2008). Re-thinking intersectionality. *Feminist Review*, 89(1), 1–15.

Noblit, G., Flores, S., & Murrillo, E. (Eds.). (2004). *Post-critical ethnography: Reinscribing critique.* Cresskill, NJ: Hampton Press.

Puar, J. K. (2007). *Terrorist assemblages: Homonationalism in queer times.* Durham, NC: Duke University Press.

Savin-Baden, M., McFarland, L., & Savin-Baden, J. (2008). Learning spaces, agency and notions of improvement: What influences thinking and practices about teaching and learning in higher education? An interpretive meta-ethnography. *London Review of Education, 6*(3), 211–227.

Small, M. (2009). How many cases do I need? On science and the logic of case selection in field-based research. *Ethnography, 10*(1), 5–38.

Trinidad Galvan, R. (2011). Chicana transborder vivencias and autoherteorias: Reflections from the field. *Qualitative Inquiry, 17*(6), 552–557.

Urrieta, L. Jr. (2009). *Working from within: Chicana and Chicano activist educators in whitestream schools.* Tucson: University of Arizona Press.

Tables and figures are indicated by an italic *t* and *f* following the page/paragraph number.

CPSIA information can be obtained
at www.ICGtesting.com
Printed in the USA
BVHW080108310119
539089BV00002B/57/P